D0708756

About Island Press

Since 1984, the nonprofit Island Press has been stimulating, shaping, and communicating the ideas that are essential for solving environmental problems worldwide. With more than 800 titles in print and some 40 new releases each year, we are the nation's leading publisher on environmental issues. We identify innovative thinkers and emerging trends in the environmental field. We work with world-renowned experts and authors to develop cross-disciplinary solutions to environmental challenges.

Island Press designs and implements coordinated book publication campaigns in order to communicate our critical messages, in print, in person, and online using the latest technologies, programs, and the media. Our goal: to reach targeted audiences—scientists, policymakers, environmental advocates, the media, and concerned citizens—who can and will take action to protect the plants and animals that enrich our world, the ecosystems we need to survive, the water we drink, and the air we breathe.

Island Press gratefully acknowledges the support of its work by the Agua Fund, Inc., Annenberg Foundation, The Christensen Fund, The Nathan Cummings Foundation, The Geraldine R. Dodge Foundation, Doris Duke Charitable Foundation, The Educational Foundation of America, Betsy and Jesse Fink Foundation, The William and Flora Hewlett Foundation, The Kendeda Fund, The Forrest and Frances Lattner Foundation, The Andrew W. Mellon Foundation, The Curtis and Edith Munson Foundation, Oak Foundation, The Overbrook Foundation, the David and Lucile Packard Foundation, The Summit Fund of Washington, Trust for Architectural Easements, Wallace Global Fund, The Winslow Foundation, and other generous donors.

The opinions expressed in this book are those of the author(s) and do not necessarily reflect the views of our donors.

Poisoned for Pennies

Poisoned for Pennies

The Economics of Toxics and Precaution

By Frank Ackerman

ISLAND PRESS
Washington • Covelo • London

ISLAND PRESS is a trademark of the Center for Resource Economics.

Ackerman, Frank.
Poisoned for pennies : the economics of toxics and precaution / by Frank Ackerman.
    p.   cm.
   Includes bibliographical references.
   ISBN-13: 978-1-59726-400-6 (cloth : alk. paper)
   ISBN-10: 1-59726-400-8 (cloth : alk. paper)
   ISBN-13: 978-1-59726-401-3 (pbk. : alk. paper)
   ISBN-10: 1-59726-401-6 (pbk. : alk. paper)
   1. Environmental policy—Cost effectiveness. 2. Environmental health—Government policy—Cost effectiveness. 3. Medical policy—Cost effectiveness. I. Title.
   HC79.E5A268 2008
   363.738′4—dc22   2007040654

Printed on recycled, acid-free paper ♲

Manufactured in the United States of America
10 9 8 7 6 5 4 3 2 1

Keywords: cost-benefit analysis, precautionary principle, pollution, regulation, EPA, REACH, holistic evaluation, benzene, atrazine, bovine spongiform encephalopathy, PVC, MTBE

Contents

Contents

Acknowledgments

I did not do the work described in this book alone. Six of the twelve chapters have been published as coauthored articles, and appear here only lightly edited into book chapter format. Three other chapters, written by me in their current form, are based on joint work done at the Global Development and Environment Institute (GDAE) at Tufts University. (The authorship and publication histories of individual chapters are listed below.)

I owe the greatest debt to Rachel Massey, who was at GDAE and worked closely with me throughout most of the period when the research for this book was done. Although she is literally a coauthor of only four chapters, she participated in the work reflected in three others as well. Chapter 9, in particular, is based on a massive study that Rachel and I wrote together. Rachel's extensive scientific knowledge, tireless dedication to the research effort, and experience as a writer made an indispensable contribution to the agenda and the reports on which this book is built. Without her, this would have been a different, and thinner, book.

Elizabeth Stanton, an economist who has joined GDAE more recently, is a coauthor of the last two chapters. Her unusual combination of facility with both data and prose helped to ensure the success of these chapters and the underlying reports. Lisa Heinzerling, my coauthor on *Priceless: On Knowing the Price of Everything and the Value of Nothing*, is also a coauthor of the first two chapters of this book, and in general a co-conspirator in the development of the framework presented here.

Thanks also to the three other coauthors of individual chapters. Wendy Johnecke's knowledge of food policy and risk analysis helped to set the context for the analysis of BSE modeling in chapter 7. Brian Roach, an economist at GDAE, plumbed the depths of the data problems of chapter 11. Anne-Sofie Andersson, at the International Chemical Secretariat in Sweden, provided in-depth knowledge of REACH, and also coordinated the project with the European Parliament for the study described in chapter 11.

Activists and experts who have contributed to my understanding of the issues addressed here include Gary Cohen, Shelley Davis, Robert

Donkers, Tyrone Hayes, Lee Kettlesen, Per Rosander, Jennifer Sass, and Joel Tickner, among others. The Center for Progressive Reform (CPR) has provided a stimulating and supportive network of scholars addressing related issues. Rena Steinzor and others at CPR encouraged and supported the writing of chapter 2; a conversation with Tom McGarity at a CPR meeting led to the analysis in chapter 7.

Thanks to Megan Amundsen, Sam Bell, Chelsea Feerer, Regina Flores, Gabrielle Herman, Courtney Lane, Jennifer Lappin, Jessica Katz, Susan Powers, Tara Santimauro, and Raya Widenoja for research assistance. Thanks to Todd Baldwin at Island Press for his help throughout the project of turning this all into a book.

Financial support for the research in this book came from the Bauman Foundation, the John Merck Fund, the New York Community Trust, the V. Kann Rasmussen Foundation, the Center for Progressive Reform, the Alliance for a Healthy Tomorrow, the Mitchell Kapor Foundation, and the Farmworker Justice Fund.

Detailed comments on the manuscript were provided by Todd Baldwin, Cornelia Herzfeld, Rachel Massey, and Alejandro Reuss. Cornelia also took on the challenge of herding all the stray aspects of the manuscript into a single, more booklike entity. If there are any remaining errors of grammar, usage, or citation, it is undoubtedly because I did not always follow her advice.

Publication History

Authorship is identified for joint-authored chapters; others are by me alone.

Chapter 1, by Frank Ackerman and Lisa Heinzerling, first appeared as the 2002 report "Pricing the Priceless: Cost-Benefit Analysis of Environmental Protection," published by the Georgetown Environmental Law and Policy Institute. A revised version, with the same title, appeared in the *University of Pennsylvania Law Review* in 2002 and was reprinted as one of the ten best land use and environmental law review articles of 2002 in *Land Use and Environmental Law Review*, 2003.

Chapter 2, by Frank Ackerman, Lisa Heinzerling, and Rachel Massey, was originally a 2004 report funded and published by the Center for Progressive Reform, "Applying Cost-Benefit Analysis to Past Decisions: Was Environmental Protection *Ever* a Good Idea?" A revised version was published in the *Administrative Law Review* in 2005 and was reprinted as one of the ten best land use and environmental law review articles of 2005 in *Land Use and Environmental Law Review*, 2006. A slightly different version appeared as "Wrong in Retrospect: Cost-Benefit Analysis of Past Successes," in Jon D. Erickson and John M. Gowdy, editors, *Frontiers in Ecological Economic Theory and Application* (Northampton, MA: Edward Elgar, 2007).

Chapter 3 was published in the *Fordham Urban Law Journal* in 2006.

Chapter 4 is a greatly expanded and revised version of my short paper, "The Outer Bounds of the Possible: Economic Theory, Precaution, and Dioxin," which was presented at the "Dioxin 2003" conference (formally speaking, the International Symposium on Halogenated Environmental Organic Pollutants and Persistent Organic Pollutants) and published in the conference journal, *Organohalogen Compounds*, in 2003.

Chapter 5 was published in the *International Journal of Occupational and Environmental Health* in 2007.

Chapter 6 draws on my testimony in 2005 and 2006 on behalf of the United Farm Workers and other groups, which was supported in part by the Farmworker Justice Fund. Rachel Massey helped in the research for that testimony.

Chapter 7, by Frank Ackerman and Wendy Johnecke, was published in *New Solutions* in 2008, with the title "Modeling Uncertainty: The U.S. Response to BSE." My critique of the Harvard Center for Risk Analysis BSE model first appeared in Tom McGarity with Frank Ackerman, "Flimsy Firewalls: The Continuing Triumph of Efficiency over Safety in Regulating Mad Cow Risks" (Center for Progressive Reform, 2004).

Chapter 8, by Rachel Massey and Frank Ackerman, is based on a 2003 GDAE report, "Costs of Preventable Childhood Illness: The Price We Pay for Pollution," written for the Alliance for a Healthy Tomorrow, a Massachusetts anti-toxics coalition. The report is also by Rachel Massey and Frank Ackerman.

Chapter 9 is based on a 2003 GDAE report, "The Economics of Phasing Out PVC," by Frank Ackerman and Rachel Massey.

Chapter 10, by Frank Ackerman and Rachel Massey, is based on a

2004 report for the Nordic Council of Ministers, "The True Costs of REACH," which is also by Frank Ackerman and Rachel Massey.

Chapter 11, by Frank Ackerman, Elizabeth Stanton, Brian Roach, and Anne-Sofie Andersson, was published in *European Environment* in 2008. It is based on a 2006 report to the European Parliament, Directorate-General for External Relations, "Implications of REACH for the Developing Countries," for which Frank Ackerman was the principal investigator and Anne-Sofie Andersson was the project coordinator. Authors of the report included Frank Ackerman, Rachel Massey, Brian Roach, Elizabeth Stanton, and Raya Widenoja at GDAE; Julien Milanesi, William Parienté, and Bernard Contamin at the Research Center on East African Countries, Université de Pau et des Pays de l'Adour, Pau, France; Patrick Bond and Euripides Euripidou at the University of KwaZulu-Natal School of Development Studies, Durban, South Africa; and Anne-Sofie Andersson and Per Rosander at the International Chemical Secretariat in Gothenburg, Sweden.

Chapter 12, by Frank Ackerman, Elizabeth Stanton, and Rachel Massey, was published in *Renewable Resources Journal* in 2007.

Introduction

Once upon a time, protection of human health and the natural environment did not seem to require economic analysis. Throughout its first two decades, in the 1970s and 1980s, the modern environmental movement relied on impassioned public opinion combined with scientific and legal expertise; little or no formal economics was involved. It should be humbling, at least for economists, to recall how much was accomplished in this "pre-economic" era: the Clean Air Act, the Clean Water Act, and other protective measures made our air and water much cleaner, and made us all much healthier—at entirely affordable costs.

For better or worse, the pre-economic phase of environmentalism came to an end during the 1990s. Legal and scientific knowledge alone did not prepare environmental advocates for the new economic debates. Policy problems were increasingly recast as economic questions: if there are too many environmental problems to do something about them all, how should society set priorities? A common answer was, think like a business, rely on cost-benefit analysis, and enact only the policies that are "profitable."

Specifically, the cost-benefit framework, which is now widely accepted, involves three steps for deciding about a new policy:

1. Calculate the monetary value of the expected benefits of the policy.
2. Calculate the monetary value of the expected costs of the policy.
3. The policy should not be adopted unless the expected benefits exceed the expected costs.

There is a common-sense ring, a superficial plausibility, to this three-step process. Everyone makes decisions by weighing costs and benefits, on some level, in numerous areas of life. But in practice, the formal process of cost-benefit analysis frequently concludes that seemingly attractive environmental initiatives are not justified, since their costs exceed the estimated value of their benefits. There are problems with all three steps in the cost-benefit methodology: the benefits that matter most are subject to uncertainty and impossible to price; the costs are often exaggerated; and the "bottom line" comparison of the two is, in practice, an obscurely technical process that can easily conceal a partisan agenda. As demonstrated in the following chapters, remarkably small economic costs to business have been found to outweigh major health and environmental risks. Under the cover of economic logic, we are being poisoned for pennies.

The arguments for cost-benefit analysis of health and environmental policies were tolerated under the Clinton administration in the 1990s, and then passionately embraced by the Bush administration starting in 2001. The new administration's enthusiasm for cost-benefit techniques was matched by its obvious disdain for protecting the environment. This only raised the suspicion that the methodology is the message, that sparing polluters from clean-up costs loomed larger than protecting the rest of us from pollution.

I stumbled into this arena in 2000–2001, initially responding to a request from the Natural Resources Defense Council for an evaluation of EPA's cost-benefit analysis of standards for arsenic in drinking water. I got hooked on deciphering and rebutting the bizarre hypotheses that often pass for the state of the art in environmental economics, and on working to create a more sensible alternative—and I've been at it ever since. This is the second book to emerge from my work on the economics of environmental policy; it can either be read alone, or interpreted as a sequel to the first one.

In *Priceless: On Knowing the Price of Everything and the Value of Nothing,* Lisa Heinzerling and I critiqued the process of cost-benefit analysis and monetary valuation of health and environmental protection. There are no meaningful prices attached to protection of human life, health, nature, and the well-being of future generations, and no end of nonsense has resulted from the attempt to invent surrogate prices for them. The absence of prices is fatal to the cost-benefit project, but it is not the case that unpriced benefits are worthless: what is the cash value of your oldest friendship, your relationship with your children, or your right to vote and participate in a democratically governed country? As the German philosopher Immanuel Kant put it, some things have a price, or relative worth, while other things have a dignity, or inner worth. The failure of cost-benefit analysis, in Kantian terms, stems from the attempt to weigh costs, which usually have a price, against benefits, which often have a dignity.

Introduction

This book builds on and goes beyond the analysis of priceless benefits. The most important benefits are not only priceless, but often uncertain as well. Uncertainty may exist because the experts still disagree about the extent of hazards, or it may reflect the complexity of the natural systems that are involved. Thus there is a need for precautionary decision making—taking action before complete certainty is reached. A theory of decision making under uncertainty, described in chapter 4, suggests a focus on the most extreme credible outcomes, rather than an attempt to compromise or reach consensus. This does not eliminate consideration of economic costs, but reframes it as part of a deliberative process.

The argument for precautionary policies is a strong one, in part because the economic costs of health and environmental protection repeatedly turn out to be very small. The much-feared ruinous cost of regulations, the dilemma that cost-benefit analysis is conventionally supposed to resolve, vanishes on closer inspection, as seen in chapter 3 and throughout. Complex economic calculations, based on the inaccurate assumption of a problem of enormous costs, all too often serve as a technical-sounding excuse for inaction. Although the information presented in a cost-benefit analysis can often be used for other purposes, the cost-benefit conceptual framework is directly at odds with a precautionary approach.

Along the way to writing *Priceless*, Heinzerling and I wrote a summary of our analysis, "Pricing the Priceless," which was widely circulated as a pamphlet and was published in the *University of Pennsylvania Law Review*. It is included as the first chapter of this book; among its other merits, it may serve as a synopsis of what happened in the previous volume, for those who are joining the story at this point.

The other chapters in this book are based on work done at the Global Development and Environment Institute, a research institute at Tufts University, during 2003–2007. We launched a program called "Economics for Health and the Environment," setting out to develop a precautionary economic analysis that supports active efforts to protect human health and the natural environment. ("We," here and throughout, includes several colleagues and coauthors, as explained in the acknowledgments.) The result was a long series of reports, articles, and testimony, many of them focused on issues of toxic chemicals policy.

The twelve chapters included here, although written separately over a period of several years, fall naturally into three groups. The first group, on theory and methods, extends the critique of cost-benefit analysis, demonstrates how low the costs of regulation are in general, and sketches an alternative, precautionary approach to decision making. The second group presents U.S. case studies that apply these methods, calculating the vanishingly low economic gains from the use of potentially harmful pesticides; debunking the misleading arguments used to "prove" that the United States does not need to match international standards for bovine spongiform encephalopathy (BSE, or "mad cow disease") testing; estimating the monetary costs of childhood illnesses attributable to environmental factors; and examining the economics of replacing polyvinyl chloride (PVC) with less toxic materials.

The final group of chapters turns to one of the most ambitious environmental policies of recent years, REACH (Regulation, Evaluation, and Authorization of CHemicals), the European Union's new chemicals policy. In a series of studies, we found that the costs of REACH will cause only an insignificant change in the price of chemicals sold in Europe; that REACH will not place developing country exporters at a competitive disadvantage; and that compliance with REACH is far more profitable than defiance for U.S. exporters. One implication for U.S. policy is that the much more modest proposals now under consideration here are far too small to harm the economy; indeed, there is room to think more expansively, to consider policies as innovative as REACH, without causing noticeable economic losses.

A publication history for each chapter is included with the acknowledgments; the chapters are based on articles and reports that appeared in different venues over a period of years. As a result, they refer to monetary amounts in different years' dollars. During the period in question, inflation averaged about 3 percent per year, so that $1.00 in 2001 had the same purchasing power as $1.18 in 2007. For comparisons between chapters, therefore, monetary amounts of different vintages should be adjusted up or down by about 3 percent per year, to express them in the same year's dollars.

A description of the contents of each chapter follows in the next three sections.

Limitations of Cost-Benefit Analysis and the Need for Precaution

The first four chapters flesh out the critique of cost-benefit analysis, exploring its limits and suggesting the need for an alternative, precautionary approach to policy decisions. Chapter 1 summarizes the limitations of cost-benefit methods, as described above. The most important benefits of health and environmental protection have no meaningful monetary prices; the attempts to invent prices for priceless benefits are incoherent in theory, and often laughable in practice. The common practice of discounting the future trivializes our ethical beliefs about and social responsibility to our descendants. As a result of these and other limitations, cost-benefit analysis as a decision-making process is neither objective nor transparent; it does not offer a reasonable solution to any important problem in the realm of public health and environmental policy.

Chapter 2 responds to a claim often made by defenders of cost-benefit analysis: perhaps detailed economic calculations were not needed to take the obvious first steps toward environmental protection, but have become more essential now that all the easy decisions have been made. When the Cuyahoga River was catching fire, as it memorably did in 1969, one might not have needed an economic analysis to realize that water pollution had to be controlled. But after a few decades of putting out fires and picking low-hanging fruit, might cost-benefit analysis have become important in answering the more difficult questions about where regulation should go next?

If this were true, then past environmental policy decisions should easily pass a modern cost-benefit test. Yet in the three retrospective case studies examined in chapter 2, contemporary cost-benefit techniques could have produced the wrong answer every time. The elimination of leaded gasoline in the 1970s and 1980s was a lengthy process in which cost-benefit analysis played a valuable supporting role in the final stages; but in the decisive first round of the debate, cost-benefit calculations were not used and could not have been used to endorse the removal of lead. The 1960s decision *not* to build hydroelectric dams encroaching on the Grand Canyon was in fact supported by a cost-benefit analysis—but only because that analysis was spectacularly wrong in hindsight. The strict 1974 standard for workplace exposure to vinyl chloride was not and could not have been supported by cost-benefit analysis at the time; yet the decision proved to be prescient, as subsequent research has continued to discover new health hazards resulting from exposure to vinyl chloride.

The critique of traditional "command and control" policies and the call for cost-benefit analysis of new proposals rest on a crucial assumption: regulation is thought to be expensive, imposing a trade-off between environmental protection and economic growth. However, as chapter 3 demonstrates, several types of evidence confirm that regulatory costs are typically too small to harm economic growth. The argument is not about the theory; it would logically be possible to spend so much on environmental protection that it would compete with basic economic needs. But has this ever actually occurred?

By way of analogy, one could claim that automobile designers need to account for the effects of relativity on the weight of a car as it accelerates. After all, the theory of relativity and its predictions about the effects of approaching the speed of light are much more widely accepted than any economic theory. All that is missing is the empirical fact that automobiles travel at less than one-millionth of the speed of light, making relativistic effects infinitesimally, undetectably small. In practice, the only sensible approach is to ignore the effects of relativity on automobile transportation as it exists today.

The same is true for the economic burden of most environmental regulations. The problem with the presumed trade-off is not only that the actual costs of regulation are small. In addition, reductions in regulatory costs might not lead to the expected economic improvement. U.S. economic growth is limited in the short run by the Federal Reserve's anti-inflationary policies, not by environmental regulations or by a scarcity of resources. Finally, regulatory critics have taken to claiming that we would all be wealthier, and therefore healthier, without regulations; on the assumption that greater wealth would reduce death rates, regulations that are thought to be costly have been branded "statistical murder." This overwrought rhetoric is refuted by public health research showing that overall death rates are lower when more people are out of work.

Yet another obstacle to precise economic calculation is the uncertainty about many health and environmental risks. Chapter 4 looks at the effects of uncertainty and the resulting arguments for precaution, in the context of the controversy over dioxin. As with many potential hazards, there is a sharp division of opinion about the dangers of dioxin. Most researchers have concluded that dioxin causes cancer at extraordinarily low levels of exposure; a minority continues to argue that the evidence is inconclusive, and that the harm caused by dioxin has been greatly exaggerated.

Which view should be used in making policy toward dioxin? There is no objective way to assign numerical probabilities, or weights, to the two opposing views of dioxin; as a result, there is no meaningful average, or expected value. Splitting the difference (i.e., taking an unweighted average, in effect assigning equal weights to each extreme) does not seem like a useful approach. Ignoring problems such as this until science reaches a complete consensus would give a veto over public policy to intransigent minorities. The much discussed precautionary principle calls for taking action on the basis of serious warnings of harm, before scientific certainty is reached; but how should decisions be made about precautionary policy proposals?

There is a little-known, formal economic theory of decision making under uncertainty, coauthored by Nobel laureates Kenneth Arrow and Leonid Hurwicz; that theory suggests a methodology for approaching precautionary policies. Under conditions of extreme uncertainty, it turns out that evaluation of a policy depends only on the best and worst possible outcomes. When, as usual, people are risk-averse, then only the worst case matters. That is, under the assumptions of extreme uncertainty and risk aversion, policies can be judged solely on their credible worst case results—a reasonable interpretation of the precautionary principle. (The application of these principles to dioxin in chapter 4 incorporates a number of admittedly arbitrary simplifications; the estimate developed in that chapter is meant as a numerical sketch of the precautionary methodology, not as a precise or definitive calculation of dioxin impacts.)

Decision making based on worst-case possibilities is common enough in other areas of life, from insurance purchases to airport security screening; extension of this way of thinking to health and environmental risks could be interpreted as collective insurance, or screening for environmental security. Indeed, REACH could be described quite literally as screening potential chemical risks, as seen in chapter 10.

The Real Economics of Environmental Protection: Five Case Studies

The next section of the book includes five case studies, applying the principles developed in chapters 1–4 to issues and controversies in U.S. environmental policy. The first two involve the risks of pesticide use.

Atrazine, a powerful herbicide used on most of the corn grown in the United States, is a much debated potential health hazard. There is mounting, though still contested, evidence of effects on human health, and stronger evidence of endocrine disruption and other effects in amphibians and other species. Thus atrazine is a candidate for the precautionary approach discussed in chapter 4. One extreme, the worst case for a continued policy of inaction, is well explored in the scientific literature on health effects. Chapter 5 explores the other extreme, the worst case for a policy of banning atrazine: how large is the economic loss that would result from a ban, if it later turned out to be unnecessary? The question turns primarily on the effect of atrazine on corn yields. Major studies that have supported the need for atrazine have assumed that it adds about 6 percent to corn yields. An industry-sponsored database suggests 2 to 4 percent; other research suggests 1 percent, or even zero effect on corn yields. Two corn-producing countries, Italy and Germany, both banned atrazine in 1991 without any loss in corn yields. Ironically, the same company that makes atrazine also produces one of the best candidates for a replacement, and has sponsored research showing how well the replacement works. A ban on atrazine could mean simply that corn growers would pay slightly more to the same chemical company for an alternative herbicide that is equally effective in killing weeds, but so far does not appear to have serious health effects.

Chapter 6 presents an example of what can go wrong with cost-benefit analysis in practice, in the evaluation of two organophosphate pesticides that are harmful to the health of farmworkers. The discussion in chapters 1 and 2 deals largely with the theory of cost-benefit analysis, assuming it is applied in a fair and unbiased manner. Yet as chapter 6 shows, the densely technical nature of the analysis can conceal a blatantly one-sided treatment of the issues: EPA appeared to have decided in advance that the value of the pesticides to growers outweighed any harm to farmworkers, their families and communities, and the ecosystems of the affected region. Reliance on EPA's economic studies in this case led to the exact opposite of an objective, transparent decision-making process; rather, the opacity of the details hid the lack of objectivity from public view.

In my testimony on behalf of the United Farm Workers and other groups, which forms the basis for chapter 6, I reviewed two rounds of EPA's economic analysis. The agency's first study exaggerated the economic value of pesticides to growers, while minimizing or overlooking health and environmental impacts on farmworkers, communities, and ecosystems. After receiving public comment on this study, EPA then produced a very different analysis. The agency's second look at the issue concluded that the pesticides had almost no economic value to growers, but suggested that EPA's own data on farmworker health hazards should not be taken seriously, and introduced an inaccurate, unsupported claim that rapid phase-out of a harmful pesticide would hurt U.S. exports.

Another potential hazard, BSE, involves a deeper form of uncertainty: the extent of the problem is unknown in advance because the disease, which is fatal and incurable, cannot be definitively diagnosed until an autopsy is performed. Yet unlike many countries, the United States tests only a tiny fraction of all slaughtered cattle for BSE. As chapter 7 shows, seemingly objective economic and statistical analysis again obscures the biases that are built into U.S. policy. While the general result parallels that of chapter 6—dense technical arguments create an unfounded suggestion that the problem is not particularly severe—the economic models and techniques are very different. Elaborate computer models project that BSE is quite rare in the United States, and that if it were present at a low level, it would naturally die out rather than spread. These models reach their reassuring conclusions only by relying on optimistic assumptions and taking for granted that the most disturbing scenarios they have identified are not worth investigating. The U.S. Department of Agriculture has nonetheless relied on these models and rejected the much higher rates of BSE testing that are standard in Europe and Japan, even though international levels of testing would add only a few pennies per pound to the price of beef.

A common theme of the last few chapters is that the costs of precautionary policies, taking protective action against potential hazards, would be extremely small. Matching international standards for BSE testing, or substituting safer pesticides for potentially dangerous ones that are now in widespread use, would have only minimal economic costs. As argued in chapter 3, health and environmental regulations in general have low costs and have not caused noticeable economic harm. Chapter 8 turns to the other side of the coin: the costs of *inaction,* of tolerating current levels of exposure to chemical hazards, can be substantial.

Specifically, the costs of four childhood illnesses attributable to environmental factors range well into the tens of billions of dollars per year on a nationwide basis, and are more than $1 billion annually for a state the size of Massachusetts. Even larger numbers would result if we included estimates of the monetary value of pain and suffering, or a valuation of the deaths that result from these diseases. But for the reasons explained in chapter 1, these additional categories of costs are not meaningfully defined in monetary terms. The calculations of the costs of childhood illnesses in chapter 8 consist exclusively of things with well-defined price tags, such as medical expenditures, remedial education, and losses of future productivity that may result from childhood diseases.

Other illnesses affecting children, including birth defects, may also result from environmental factors; if data were available for other diseases, the totals would be even larger. Although the problems are national in scope, chapter 8 calculates the impact on the state level at the request of environmental advocates interested in using these numbers. The apparent paralysis of environmental decision making at the national level and ongoing devolution of policy to the states imply that nationwide policy questions will often require state-by-state analysis.

In another study requested by environmental advocates, chapter 9 considers a case in which a precautionary policy would have sweeping economic effects. Rather than examining a single regulation or single-use chemical, this chapter explores the costs and feasibility of phasing out PVC, a ubiquitous plastic that is associated with numerous hazards throughout its life cycle. The good news is that there are nontoxic alternatives to PVC in every major product line where it is currently used. The latest comprehensive economic analysis, dating from the 1990s, implies that replacing PVC with alternatives would impose an average annual cost increase of $25 per capita—not an impossible burden, but more than the costs encountered in other chapters.

There are reasons, however, why the true cost could be lower, and could be expected to decline over time. Looking beyond purchase prices to life-cycle costs, including maintenance and replacement schedules, may make other, more durable materials more attractive relative to PVC. Economies of scale and the benefits of "learning by doing" have reduced the cost of PVC in the past, and could do the same for alternatives in the future. Health hazards experienced during use and disposal of PVC make it less of a bargain than it appears to be. Introduction of alternatives would require the transformation of some thousands of jobs, from making PVC to making replacement materials; there is no reason to think that total industrial employment would decline. Health hazards associated with PVC are often felt most severely by workers in the industry; an economy as large and powerful as ours simply must be able to provide those workers with sustainable, nontoxic livelihoods. Ideally, they should be employed making the safer alternatives to PVC.

The complete replacement of PVC, the most expensive initiative analyzed here, is not currently on the policy agenda, in the United States or elsewhere. Indeed, recent U.S. initiatives have been generally timid, as environmental advocates have been forced to concentrate on defensive battles against proposed rollbacks in existing regulations. Might the finding of low costs of regulation simply reflect the fact that not much regulation is currently being considered? To examine more demanding regulatory measures, one has to look outside the United States. The final group of three chapters analyzes one of the biggest and boldest regulatory initiatives of recent years—REACH, the EU's chemicals policy—and finds that even in that case, costs are low and precautionary policies will not cause economic harm.

European Chemicals: Guilty until Proven Innocent?

Adopted in 2006, REACH requires manufacturers and importers of chemicals sold in the EU to register those chemicals, and to test them on a range of chemical properties (or provide test results, if they are already available). In the past, manufacturers were free to sell chemicals with minimal regulation, unless they were found to be hazardous; the burden of proof was on government agencies or nongovernmental organizations to demonstrate that a chemical was harmful. REACH reverses the burden of proof, requiring evidence that a chemical meets a prescribed set of health and environmental standards in order for it to be sold in Europe. This is a fundamental change in regulatory philosophy, shifting the traditional balance of power in the marketplace. It is no wonder, then, that REACH provoked extensive and passionate debate from the day it was first proposed in 2001.

An initial round of business-sponsored critiques claimed that REACH would have astronomical costs, and would crush major European economies. Responses and rebuttals started to appear almost at once, and no one except for a few industry trade associations ever projected such enormous costs of REACH, but the damage was done: the early business critiques, despite being discredited in detail, created a vague, widespread belief that REACH could somehow turn out to be impossibly expensive. The issue addressed in chapter 3, the great fear of unbearable regulatory costs, lingered for several years in the REACH debate. Chapter 10 is based on a study for the Nordic Council of Ministers (representing the governments of the Scandinavian countries), in which we developed an independent estimate of the costs of REACH and provided a detailed rebuttal to the most influential of the business-sponsored studies.

We found that the costs of REACH would total a few billion euros, spread over the eleven-year phase-in period for registration of chemicals. Studies for the European Commission found broadly similar costs, as did other government and academic research. Our estimate, like other non-business estimates, implied a cost of less than one euro per person per year, or less than 0.1 percent of the value of chemicals sold in Europe, during those eleven years. The business studies did not so much disagree about the costs of registration and testing per se, but estimated that those would be the foundation for enormous pyramids of indirect costs. The most influential of the business studies, discussed in chapter 10 and dissected in more detail in appendix C, introduced imaginative new ways to use technical jargon and complex calculations to conceal biased assumptions. Its sixteen-equation model not only contained misunderstandings of elementary economics, but also assumed that business would universally adopt a brittle and uninspired strategy of cutting back production in response to regulations, rather than innovating and adapting in a more profitable manner.

As concerns about the aggregate costs of REACH receded, the later stages of the debate shifted to aspects of the proposed regulations that might be burdensome for some types of businesses. Concerns were repeatedly raised about potential effects on small businesses, or "small and medium enterprises" (SMEs), and REACH was amended in response to these concerns. For example, the testing requirements for low-volume chemicals were reduced, because these chemicals were more likely to be produced or used by smaller businesses. At the same time, industry lobbies exaggerated the role of SMEs, perhaps suspecting that hard-working individual entrepreneurs would win more public sympathy than giant multinational corporations. The overstatement of the role of SMEs is a theme in chapter 10, and forms the backdrop to chapter 11 as well.

One of the last major issues to be raised in the REACH debate was the potential impact on developing-country exporters. The European Parliament commissioned a study of that question; I directed the four-country research team that produced the study, under an extremely tight deadline. Chapter 11 summarizes our results, focusing on exports to the EU from the African, Caribbean, and Pacific Group of States (ACP), an organization of seventy-nine developing countries with long-standing ties to Europe. Both ACP as a whole and South Africa, its leading economy, suggested that REACH would become a barrier to developing country exporters, particularly small businesses.

We reviewed all of the exports from ACP countries to the EU that could be affected by REACH. We found, in brief, that two-thirds of ACP's exports subject to REACH came from South Africa alone, and that almost all of ACP's REACH-affected exports were metals and minerals, rather than chemical industry products. Large multinational mining companies, and South African companies that are virtually as large as multinationals, were the principal exporters. These companies are just as able to comply with REACH as European companies; in some cases, they *are* European companies. The image of the struggling small enterprise that might need assistance in complying with REACH applies to very little actual trade between ACP and the EU. We did identify one case, the essential oils industry, where the classic small-business image does fit the facts; in this small industry, local producers may need help in understanding and complying with European regulations. But this is the rare exception, not the rule. We did not encounter any evidence of SMEs exporting aluminum, platinum, gold, or other major metals and minerals, which constitute the bulk of ACP's exports subject to REACH.

In chapter 11, common stereotypes fail to fit the facts because the relevant developing-country exporters, on closer examination, look a lot like the big businesses of the industrial world. In chapter 12, the tables are turned as a leading industrial nation, the United States, finds itself in a position often associated with developing countries—namely, being forced to comply with stricter environmental standards set in its export markets. U.S. government and business opposition to REACH was expressed forcefully throughout the European debate, continuing long after Europe's own business lobbies had accepted the inevitability of the new regulations. Once REACH went into effect, U.S. companies had to decide whether to swallow their pride and comply with the new rules, or risk losing access to the European market.

In our study of the effects of REACH on the U.S. economy, described in chapter 12, we began by asking what it would cost the United States to comply with REACH, and how much would be lost by refusing to do so. U.S. chemical exports subject to REACH total about $14 billion annually. As explained in chapter 10, the cost of compliance with REACH will average about 0.1 percent of chemical industry sales over the eleven-year registration period, or $14 *million* for the affected U.S. exports. It should not be difficult to choose between spending $14 million a year on regulatory compliance costs and losing $14 billion a year of export markets. Some 54,000 U.S. jobs depend directly or indirectly on these exports; $14 million a year to protect that many jobs is a bargain, compared to many state job-creation programs.

Could the United States actually lose export markets by ignoring foreign environmental standards? Unfortunately that has already happened, more than once. In the controversy over BSE testing, described in chapter 7, the refusal by the U.S. Department of Agriculture to meet international testing standards (or even to let U.S. firms voluntarily meet those standards) resulted in losing at least $2 billion a year of beef exports for two years after the discovery of an American case of mad cow disease. Similarly, the U.S. adoption of genetically modified corn in the 1990s quickly led to the near-elimination of corn exports to the EU; as U.S. producers undoubtedly knew in advance, there is widespread resistance to genetically modified food in Europe. A happier ending, from the perspective of exporters, occurred in the market for wheat. Perhaps learning from the experience with genetically modified corn, U.S. and Canadian wheat growers successfully resisted the introduction of genetically modified wheat, on the grounds that their export markets were too important to lose.

A brief conclusion considers the relationship between economics and precautionary policies, suggesting ways to avoid the pitfalls seen in the critiques and case studies. In a world of priceless values and uncertain outcomes, a humbler and subtler use of economics is required to make a sensible contribution to the protection of human health and the natural environment.

Chapter 1

Pricing the Priceless

How strictly should we regulate arsenic in drinking water? Or carbon dioxide in the atmosphere? Or pesticides in our food? Or oil drilling in scenic places? The list of environmental harms and potential regulatory remedies often appears to be endless. Is there an objective way to decide how to proceed? Cost-benefit analysis promises to provide the solution. The sad fact is that cost-benefit analysis is fundamentally unable to fulfill this promise.

Many approaches to setting environmental standards require some consideration of costs and benefits. Even technology-based regulation, maligned by cost-benefit enthusiasts as the worst form of regulatory excess, typically entails consideration of economic costs. Cost-benefit analysis differs, however, from other analytical approaches by demanding that the advantages and disadvantages of a regulatory policy be reduced, as far as possible, to numbers, and then further reduced to dollars and cents. In this feature of cost-benefit analysis lies its doom. Indeed, looking closely at the products of this pricing scheme makes it seem not only a little cold, but a little crazy as well.

Consider the following examples, which we are not making up. They are not the work of a lunatic fringe; on the contrary, they reflect the work products of some of the most influential and reputable of today's cost-benefit practitioners. We are not sure whether to laugh or cry, but we find it impossible to treat these studies as serious contributions to a rational discussion.

Chapter 1 by Frank Ackerman and Lisa Heinzerling.

1

Several years ago, states were in the middle of their litigation against tobacco companies, seeking to recoup the medical expenditures they had incurred as a result of smoking. At that time, W. Kip Viscusi—for many years a professor of law and economics at Harvard—undertook research concluding that states, in fact, *saved* money as the result of smoking by their citizens. Why? Because they died early! They thus saved their states the trouble and expense of providing nursing home care and other services associated with an aging population.

Viscusi didn't stop there. So great, under Viscusi's assumptions, were the financial benefits to the states of their citizens' premature deaths that, he suggested, *"cigarette smoking should be subsidized rather than taxed."*[1]

Amazingly, this cynical conclusion has not been swept into the dustbin where it belongs, but instead has been revived: the tobacco company Philip Morris commissioned the well-known consulting group Arthur D. Little to examine the financial benefits to the Czech Republic of smoking among Czech citizens. Arthur D. Little found that smoking was a financial boon for the government—partly because, again, it caused citizens to die earlier and thus reduced government expenditure on pensions, housing, and health care.[2] This conclusion relies, so far as we can determine, on perfectly conventional cost-benefit analysis.

There is more. In recent years, much has been learned about the special risks children face from pesticides in their food, contaminants in their drinking water, ozone in the air, and so on. Because cost-benefit analysis has become much more prominent at the same time, there is now a budding industry in valuing children's health. Its products are often bizarre.

Take the problem of lead poisoning in children. One of the most serious and disturbing effects of lead is the neurological damage it can cause in young children, including permanently lowered mental ability. Putting a dollar value on the (avoidable, environmentally caused) intellectual impairment of children is a daunting task, but economic analysts have not been daunted.

Randall Lutter, who became a top official at the U.S. Food and Drug Administration in 2003, has been a long-time regulatory critic. In an earlier position at the AEI-Brookings Joint Center for Regulatory Studies, he argued that the way to value the damage lead causes in children is to look at how much parents of affected children spend on chelation therapy, a chemical treatment that is supposed to cause excretion of lead from the body. Parental spending on chelation supports an estimated valuation of only about $1,500 per IQ point lost due to lead poisoning. Previous economic analyses by the U.S. Environmental Protection Agency (EPA), based on the children's loss of expected future earnings, have estimated the value to be much higher—up to $9,000 per IQ point. Based on his lower figure, Lutter claimed to have discovered that too much effort is going into controlling lead: "Hazard standards that protect children far more than their parents think is appropriate may make little sense. The agencies should consider relaxing their lead standards."[3]

In fact, Lutter presented no evidence about what parents think, only about what they spend on one rare variety of private medical treatments (which, as it turns out, has not been proven medically effective for chronic, low-level lead poisoning). Why should environmental standards be based on what individuals are now spending on desperate personal efforts to overcome social problems?

For sheer analytical audacity, Lutter's study faces some stiff competition from another study concerning kids—this one concerning the value, not of children's health, but of their lives (more precisely, the researchers talk about the value of "statistical lives," a concept addressed later in this chapter). In this second study, researchers examined mothers' car-seat fastening practices.[4] They calculated the difference between the time required to fasten the seats correctly and the time mothers actually spent fastening their children into their seats. Then they assigned a monetary value to this interval of time based on the mothers' hourly wage rate (or, in the case of nonworking moms, based on a guess at the wages they might have earned). When mothers saved time—and, by hypothesis, money— by fastening their children's car seats incorrectly, they were, according to the researchers, implicitly placing a finite monetary value on the life-threatening risks to their children posed by car accidents.

Building on this calculation, the researchers were able to answer the vexing question of how much a statistical child's life is worth to its mother. (As the mother of a statistical child, she is naturally adept at complex calculations comparing the value of saving a few seconds versus the slightly increased risk to her child.) The answer parallels Lutter's finding that we are valuing our children too highly: in car-seat-land, a child's life is worth only $500,000.

The absurdity of these particular analyses, though striking, is not unique to them. Indeed, we will argue, cost-benefit analysis is so inherently flawed that if one scratches the apparently benign surface of any of its products, one finds the same kind of absurdity. But before launching into this critique, it will be useful first to establish exactly what cost-benefit analysis is, and why one might think it is a good idea.

Dollars and Discounting

Cost-benefit analysis tries to mimic a basic function of markets by setting an economic standard for measuring the success of the government's projects and programs. That is, cost-benefit analysis seeks to perform, for public policy, a calculation that happens routinely in the private sector. In evaluating a proposed new initiative, how do we know if it is worth doing or not? The answer is much simpler in business than in government.

Private businesses, striving to make money, only produce things that they believe someone is willing to pay for. That is, firms only produce things for which the benefits to consumers, measured by consumers' willingness to pay for them, are expected to be greater than the costs of production. It is technologically possible to produce men's business suits in brightly colored polka dots. Successful producers suspect that few people are willing to pay for such products, and usually stick to at most minor variations on suits in somber, traditional hues. If some firm *did* happen to produce a polka-dot business suit, no one would be forced to buy it; the producer would bear the entire loss resulting from the mistaken decision.

Government, in the view of many critics, is in constant danger of drifting toward producing polka-dot suits—and making people pay for them. Policies, regulations, and public spending do not face the test of the marketplace; there are no consumers who can withhold their dollars from the government until it produces the regulatory equivalent of navy blue and charcoal gray suits. There is no single quantitative objective for the public sector comparable to profit maximization for businesses. Even with the best of intentions, critics suggest, government programs can easily go astray for lack of an objective standard by which to judge whether or not they are meeting citizens' needs.

Cost-benefit analysis sets out to do for government what the market does for business: add up the benefits of a public policy and compare them to the costs. The two sides of the ledger raise very different issues.

Estimating Costs

The first step in a cost-benefit analysis is to calculate the costs of a public policy. For example, the government may require a certain kind of pollution control equipment, which businesses must pay for. Even if a regulation only sets a ceiling on emissions, it results in costs that can be at least roughly estimated through research into available technologies and business strategies for compliance.

The costs of protecting human health and the environment through the use of pollution control devices and other approaches are, by their very nature, measured in dollars. Thus, at least in theory, the cost side of cost-benefit analysis is relatively straightforward. (In practice, as we shall see, it is not quite that simple.)

The consideration of the costs of environmental protection is not unique to cost-benefit analysis. Development of environmental regulations has almost always involved consideration of economic costs, with or without formal cost-benefit techniques. What is unique to cost-benefit analysis, and far more problematic, is the other side of the balance, the monetary valuation of the benefits of life, health, and nature itself.

Monetizing Benefits

Since there are no natural prices for a healthy environment, cost-benefit analysis requires the creation of artificial ones. This is the hardest part of the process. Economists create artificial prices for health and environmental benefits by studying what people would be willing to pay for them. One popular method, called "contingent valuation," is essentially a form of opinion poll. Researchers ask a cross-section of the affected population how much they would be willing to pay to preserve or protect something that can't be bought in a store.

Many surveys of this sort have been done, producing prices for things that appear to be priceless. For example, the average American household is supposedly willing to pay $257 to prevent the extinction of bald eagles, $208 to protect humpback whales, and $80 to protect gray wolves.[5] These numbers are quite large: since there are more than 100 million households in the country, the nation's total willingness to pay for the preservation of bald eagles alone is ostensibly more than $25 billion.

An alternative method of attaching prices to unpriced things infers

5

what people are willing to pay from observation of their behavior in other markets. To assign a dollar value to risks to human life, for example, economists usually calculate the extra wage—or "wage premium"—that is paid to workers who accept more risky jobs. Suppose that two jobs are comparable, except that one is more dangerous and better paid. If workers understand the risk and voluntarily accept the more dangerous job, then they are implicitly setting a price on risk by accepting the increased risk of death in exchange for increased wages.

What does this indirect inference about wages say about the value of a life? A common estimate in cost-benefit analyses of the late 1990s was that avoiding a risk that would lead, on average, to one death is worth roughly $6.3 million.[6] This number is of great importance in cost-benefit analyses because avoided deaths are the most thoroughly studied benefits of environmental regulations.

Discounting the Future

One more step requires explanation to complete this quick sketch of cost-benefit analysis. Costs and benefits of a policy frequently occur at different times. Often, costs are incurred today, or in the near future, to prevent harm in the more remote future. When the analysis spans a number of years, future costs and benefits are *discounted,* or treated as equivalent to smaller amounts of money in today's dollars.

Discounting is a procedure developed by economists to evaluate investments that produce future income. The case for discounting begins with the observation that $100, say, received today is worth more than $100 received next year, even in the absence of inflation. For one thing, you could put your money in the bank today and earn a little interest by next year. Suppose that your bank account earns 3 percent interest. In that case, if you received the $100 today rather than next year, and immediately deposited it in the bank, you would earn $3 in interest, giving you a total of $103 next year. Likewise, to get $100 next year you need to deposit only $97 today. So, at a 3 percent *discount rate,* economists would say that $100 next year has a *present value* of $97 in today's dollars.

For longer periods of time, the effect is magnified: at a 3 percent discount rate, $100 twenty years from now has a present value of only $55. The larger the discount rate, the smaller the present value: at a 5 percent discount rate, for example, $100 twenty years from now has a present value of only $38.

Cost-benefit analysis routinely uses the present value of future benefits. That is, it compares current costs, not to the actual dollar value of future benefits, but to the smaller amount you would have to put into a hypothetical savings account today to obtain those benefits in the future. This application of discounting is essential, and indeed commonplace, for many practical financial decisions. If offered a choice of investment opportunities with payoffs at different times in the future, you can (and should) discount the future payoffs to the present to compare them to each other. The important issue for environmental policy, as we shall see, is whether this logic also applies to outcomes far in the future, and to opportunities, such as long life and good health, that are not naturally stated in dollar terms.

The Case for Cost-Benefit

Before describing the problems with cost-benefit analysis, it will be useful to set forth the arguments in favor of this type of analysis. Many different arguments for cost-benefit analysis have been offered over the years. Most of the arguments fall into one of two broad categories. First, there are economic assertions that better results can be achieved with cost-benefit analysis. Second, there are legal and political claims that a more objective and more open government process can emerge through this kind of analysis.

Better Results

Economics frequently focuses on increasing efficiency—on getting the most desirable results from the least resources. How do we know that greater regulatory efficiency is needed? For many economists, this is an article of faith: greater efficiency is always a top priority, in regulation or elsewhere. Cost-benefit analysis is thought by its supporters to further efficiency by ensuring that regulations are adopted only when benefits exceed costs, and by helping direct regulators' attention to those problems for which regulatory intervention will yield the greatest net benefits.

But many advocates also raise a more specific argument, imbued with a greater sense of urgency. The government, it is said, often issues rules that are insanely expensive, out of all proportion to their benefits—a problem that could be solved by the use of cost-benefit analysis to screen proposed regulations. Thus, much of the case *for* cost-benefit analysis depends on the case *against* current regulation.

Scarcely a congressional hearing on environmental policy occurs in which fantastic estimates of the costs of federal regulations do not figure prominently. Economists routinely cite such estimates as proof of the need for more economic analysis. Browse the Web sites of any of a variety of think tanks, and you will find numerous references to the extravagant costs of regulation.

The estimates typically bandied about are astonishingly high: according to several widely circulated studies, we are often spending hundreds of millions, and sometimes billions, of dollars for every single human life, or even year of life, we save through regulation.[7] One widely cited study claims that the cost of life-saving interventions reaches as high as *$99 billion for every life-year saved*.[8] Numbers like these would suggest that current regulatory costs are not only chaotically variable but also unacceptably high. They have even been interpreted to mean that the existing regulatory system actually *kills people* by imposing some very costly life-saving requirements while other, less expensive and more effective life-saving possibilities remain untouched. Indeed, one study concluded that we could save as many as 60,000 more lives every year with no increase in costs, if we simply spent our money on the least rather than most expensive opportunities for saving lives.[9] Relying on this research (of which he was a coauthor), John Graham, a top official in the U.S. Office of Management and Budget from 2001 to 2006 and a prominent proponent of cost-benefit analysis, has called the existing state of affairs "statistical murder."[10]

From this perspective, cost-benefit analysis emerges as both a money-saver *and* a life-saver. By subjecting regulations to a cost-benefit test, we would not only stop spending hundreds of millions or billions of dollars to save a single life, we could also take that money and spend it on saving even more lives through different life-saving measures.

That, at least, is the theory. We will argue in the following sections that there are good reasons to question both the theory and the facts it rests on. Nevertheless, the notion that the current system produces crazy, even deadly, rules, and that better economic analysis would avert this terrible result, remains one of the most persistent arguments offered on behalf of cost-benefit analysis.

Objectivity and Transparency

A second important set of arguments holds that cost-benefit analysis would produce a better regulatory process—more objective and more transparent, and thus more accountable to the public.

The holy grail of administrative law is agency decision making based on objective standards. The idea is to prevent an agency either from just doing anything it wants or, more invidiously, from benefiting politically favored groups through its decisions. Cost-benefit analysis has been offered as a means of constraining agency discretion in this way.

Another important goal said to be promoted by cost-benefit analysis is transparency of administrative procedures. Decisions about environmental protection are notoriously complex. They reflect the input of biologists, toxicologists, epidemiologists, economists, engineers, lawyers, and other experts whose work is complicated and arcane. The technical details of these decisions often conceal crucial judgments about how much scientific uncertainty is too much, which human populations should be protected from illness and even death, and how important the future is relative to the present.

For the public to be part of the process of decision making about the environment, these judgments must be offered and debated in language accessible to people who are not biologists, toxicologists, or other kinds of experts. Many advocates of cost-benefit analysis believe that their methodology provides such a language. They also assert that cost-benefit analysis renders decision making transparent insofar as it requires decision makers to reveal all of the assumptions and uncertainties reflected in their decisions.

Fundamental Flaws

As we have seen, cost-benefit analysis involves the creation of artificial markets for things, such as good health, long life, and clean air, that are not bought and sold. It also involves the devaluation of future events through discounting.

So described, the mind-set of the cost-benefit analyst is likely to seem quite foreign. The translation of all good things into dollars and the devaluation of the future are inconsistent with the way many people view the world. Most of us believe that money doesn't buy happiness. Most religions tell us that every human life is sacred; it is obviously illegal, as well as immoral, to buy and sell human lives. Most parents tell their children to eat their vegetables and do their homework, even though the rewards of these onerous activities lie far in the future. Monetizing human lives and discounting future benefits seem at odds with these common perspectives.

The cost-benefit approach also is inconsistent with the way many of us make daily decisions. Imagine performing a new cost-benefit analysis to decide whether to get up and go to work every morning, whether to exercise or eat right on any given day, whether to wash the dishes or leave them in the sink, and so on. Inaction would win far too often—and an absurd amount of effort would be spent on analysis. Most people have long-run goals, commitments, and habits that make such daily balancing exercises either redundant or counterproductive. The same might be true of society as a whole as it undertakes individual steps in the pursuit of any goal, set for the long haul, that cannot be reached overnight, including, for example, the achievement of a clean environment.

Moving beyond these intuitive responses, we offer in this section a detailed explanation of why cost-benefit analysis of environmental protection fails to live up to the hopes and claims of its advocates. There is no quick fix, because these failures are intrinsic to the methodology, appearing whenever it is applied to any complex environmental problem. In our view, cost-benefit analysis suffers from four fundamental flaws, addressed in the next four subsections:

1. The standard economic approaches to valuation are inaccurate and implausible.
2. The use of discounting improperly trivializes future harms and the irreversibility of some environmental problems.
3. The reliance on aggregate, monetized benefits excludes questions of fairness and morality.
4. The value-laden and complex cost-benefit process is neither objective nor transparent.

1. *Dollars without Sense*

Recall that cost-benefit analysis requires the creation of artificial prices for all relevant health and environmental impacts. To weigh the benefits of regulation against the costs, we need to know the monetary value of preventing the extinction of species, preserving many different ecosystems, avoiding all manner of serious health impacts, and even saving human lives. Without such numbers, cost-benefit analysis cannot be conducted.

Artificial prices have been estimated for many, though by no means all, benefits of regulation. As discussed, preventing the extinction of bald eagles reportedly goes for somewhat more than $250 per household. Preventing intellectual impairment caused by childhood lead poisoning comes in at about $9,000 per lost IQ point in the standard view, or a mere $1,500 per point in Lutter's alternative analysis. Saving a life is ostensibly worth $6.3 million.

This quantitative precision, achieved through a variety of indirect techniques for valuation, comes at the expense of accuracy and even common sense. Though problems arise in many areas of valuation, we will focus primarily on the efforts to attach a monetary value to human life, both because of its importance in cost-benefit analysis and because of its glaring contradictions.

There Are No "Statistical" People

What can it mean to say that saving one life is worth $6.3 million? Human life is the ultimate example of a value that is not a commodity, and does not have a price. You cannot buy the right to kill someone for $6.3 million, nor for any other price. Most systems of ethical and religious belief maintain that every life is sacred. If analysts calculated the value of life itself by asking people what it is worth to them (the most common method of valuation of other environmental benefits), the answer would be infinite, as "no finite amount of money could compensate a person for the loss of his life, simply because money is no good to him when he is dead."[11]

The standard response is that a value such as $6.3 million is not actually a price on an individual's life or death. Rather, it is a way of expressing the value of small risks of death; for example, it is one million times the value of a one in a million risk. If people are willing to pay $6.30 to avoid a one in a million increase in the risk of death, then the "value of a statistical life" is $6.3 million.

Unfortunately, this explanation fails to resolve the dilemma. It is true that risk (or "statistical life") and life itself are distinct concepts. In practice, however, analysts often ignore the distinction between valuing risk and valuing life.[12] Many regulations reduce risk for a large number of people, and avoid actual death for a much smaller number. A complete cost-benefit analysis should, therefore, include valuation of both of these benefits. However, the standard practice is to calculate a value only for "statistical" life and to ignore life itself.

The confusion between the valuation of risk and the valuation of life itself is embedded in current regulatory practice in another way as well. The U.S. Office of Management and Budget, which reviews cost-benefit analyses prepared by federal agencies pursuant to Executive Order, instructs agencies to discount the benefits of life-saving regulations from the moment of avoided death, rather than from the time when the *risk* of death is reduced.[13] This approach to discounting is plainly inconsistent with the claim that cost-benefit analysis seeks to evaluate risk. When a life-threatening disease, such as cancer, has a long latency period, many years may pass between the time when a risk is imposed and the time of death. If monetary valuations of statistical life represented risk, and not life, then the value of statistical life would be discounted from the date of a change in risk (typically, when a new regulation is enforced) rather than from the much later date of avoided actual death.[14]

In acknowledging the monetary value of reducing risk, economic analysts have contributed to our growing awareness that life-threatening risk itself—and not just the end result of such risk, death—is an injury. But they have blurred the line between risks and actual deaths by calculating the value of reduced risk while pretending that they have produced a valuation of life itself. The paradox of monetizing the infinite or immeasurable value of human life has not been resolved; it has only been glossed over.

People Care about Other People

Another large problem with the standard approach to valuation of life is that it asks individuals (either directly through surveys, or indirectly through observing wage and job choices) only about their attitudes toward risks to themselves.

A recurring theme in literature suggests that our deepest and noblest sentiments involve valuing someone else's life more highly than our own: think of parents' devotion to their children, soldiers' commitment to those whom they are protecting, lovers' concern for each other. Most spiritual beliefs call on us to value the lives of others—not only those closest to us, but also those whom we have never met.

This point echoes a procedure that has become familiar in other areas of environmental valuation. Economists often ask about existence values: how much is the existence of a wilderness area or an endangered species worth to you, even if you will never personally experience it? If this question makes sense for bald eagles and national parks, it must be at least as important when applied to safe drinking water and working conditions for people we don't know.

What is the existence value of a person you will never meet? How much is it worth to you to prevent a death far away? The answer cannot be deduced solely from your attitudes toward risks to yourself. We are not aware of any attempts to quantify the existence value of the life of a stranger, let alone a relative or a friend, but we are sure that most belief systems affirm that this value is substantial (assuming, of course, that the value of life is a number in the first place).

Voting Is Different from Buying

Cost-benefit analysis, which relies on estimates of individuals' preferences as consumers, also fails to address the collective choice presented to society by most public health and environmental problems.

Valuation of environmental benefits is based on individuals' private decisions as consumers or workers, not on their public values as citizens. However, policies that protect the environment are often public goods, and are not available for purchase in individual portions. In a classic example of this distinction, the philosopher Mark Sagoff found that his students, in their role as citizens, opposed commercial ski development in a nearby wilderness area, but, in their role as consumers, would plan to go skiing there if the development was built.[15] There is no contradiction between these two views: as individual consumers, the students would have no way to express their collective preference for wilderness preservation.

Their individual willingness to pay for skiing would send a misleading signal about their views as citizens.

It is often impossible to arrive at a meaningful social valuation by adding up the willingness to pay expressed by individuals. What could it mean to ask how much you personally are willing to pay to clean up a major oil spill? If no one else contributes, the cleanup won't happen regardless of your decision. As the Nobel Prize–winning economist Amartya Sen has pointed out, if your willingness to pay for a large-scale public initiative is independent of what others are paying, then you probably have not understood the nature of the problem.[16] Instead, a *collective* decision about collective resources is required.

In a similar vein, the philosopher Henry Richardson argued that reliance on the cost-benefit standard forecloses the process of democratic deliberation that is necessary for intelligent decision making. In his view, attempts to make decisions based on monetary valuation of benefits freeze preferences in advance, leaving no room for the changes in response to new information, rethinking of the issues, and negotiated compromises that lie at the heart of the deliberative process.[17]

Cost-benefit analysis turns public citizens into selfish consumers, and interconnected communities into atomized individuals. In this way, it distorts the question it sets out to answer: how much do we, *as a society,* value health and the environment?

Numbers Don't Tell Us Everything

A few simple examples illustrate that numerically equal risks are not always equally deserving of regulatory response. The death rate is roughly the same, somewhat less than one in a million, for a day of downhill skiing, for a day of working in the construction industry, or for drinking about twenty liters of water (about the amount that a typical adult drinks in two weeks)[18] containing fifty parts per billion of arsenic, the regulatory limit that was in effect until 2001.[19] This does not mean that society's responsibility to reduce risks is the same in each case.

Most people view risks imposed by others, without an individual's consent, as more worthy of government intervention than risks that an individual knowingly accepts. On that basis, the highest priority among our three examples is to reduce drinking water contamination, a hazard to which no one has consented. The acceptance of a risky occupation such as construction is at best quasi-voluntary—it involves somewhat more individual discretion than the "choice" of public drinking water supplies, but many people go to work under great economic pressure, and with little information about occupational hazards. In contrast, the choice of risky recreational pursuits such as skiing is entirely discretionary; obviously no one is forced to ski. Safety regulation in construction work is thus more urgent than regulation of skiing, despite the equality of numerical risk.

In short, even for ultimate values such as life and death, the social context is decisive in our evaluation of risks. Cost-benefit analysis assumes the existence of generic, acontextual risk, and thereby ignores the contextual information that determines how many people, in practice, think about real risks to real people.

Artificial Prices Are Expensive
Finally, the economic valuation called for by cost-benefit analysis is fundamentally flawed because it demands an enormous volume of consistently updated information, which is beyond the practical capacity of our society to generate.

All attempts at valuation of the environment begin with a problem: the goal is to assign monetary prices to things that have no prices, because they are not for sale. One of the great strengths of the market is that it provides so much information about real prices. For any commodity that is actually bought and sold, prices are communicated automatically, almost costlessly, and with constant updates as needed. To create artificial prices for environmental values, economists have to find some way to mimic the operation of the market. Unfortunately the process is far from automatic, it is certainly not costless, and it has to be repeated every time an updated price is needed.

As a result, there is constant pressure to use outdated or inappropriate valuations. Indeed, there are sound economic reasons for doing so: no one can afford constant updates, and significant savings can be achieved by using valuations created for other cases. In 2000, in EPA's cost-benefit analysis of standards for arsenic in drinking water, a valuation estimated for a case of chronic bronchitis, from a study performed more than ten years earlier, was used to represent the value of a nonfatal case of bladder cancer.

This is not, we hope and believe, because anyone thinks that bronchitis and bladder cancer are the same disease. The reason is more mundane: no one had performed an analysis of the cost of bladder cancer, and even the extensive analysis of arsenic regulations did not include enough time and money to do so. Therefore, the investigators used an estimated value for a very different disease. The only explanation offered for this procedure was that it had been done before, and the investigators thought nothing better was available.

Use of the bronchitis valuation to represent bladder cancer can charitably be described as grasping at straws. Lacking the time and money to fill in the blank carefully, the economists simply picked a number. This is not remotely close to the level of rigor that is seen throughout the natural science, engineering, and public health portions of EPA's arsenic analysis. Yet it will happen again, for exactly the same reason. It is not a failure of will or intellect, but rather the inescapable limitations of time and budget, that lead to reliance on dated, inappropriate, and incomplete information to fill in the gaps on the benefit side of a cost-benefit analysis.

Summing Up

There is, in short, a host of problems with the process of valuation. On a philosophical level, human life may belong in the category of things that are too valuable to buy and sell. Most ethical and religious beliefs place the protection of human life in the same category as love, family, religion, democracy, and other ultimate values, which are not and cannot be priced.

It is a biased and misleading premise to assume that individuals' willingness to pay to avoid certain risks can be aggregated to arrive at a figure for what society should pay to protect human life. Risk of death is not the same as death itself, and not all risks can reasonably be compared one to the other. Moreover, the value to society of protecting human life cannot be arrived at simply by toting up individual consumer preferences.

The same kinds of problems affect other valuation issues raised by cost-benefit analysis, such as estimating the value of clean water, biodiversity, or entire ecosystems. The upshot is that cost-benefit analysis is fundamentally incapable of delivering on its promise of more economically efficient decisions about protecting human life, health, and the environment. Absent a credible monetary metric for calculating the benefits of regulation, cost-benefit analysis is inherently unreliable.

2. *Trivializing the Future*

One of the great triumphs of environmental law is its focus on the future: it seeks to avert harms to people and to natural resources in the future, and not only within this generation, but within future generations as well. Indeed, one of the primary objectives of the National Environmental Policy Act, which has been called our basic charter of environmental protection, is to nudge the nation into "fulfill[ing] the responsibilities of each generation as trustee of the environment for succeeding generations."[20]

Protection of endangered species and ecosystems, reduction of pollution from persistent chemicals such as dioxin and DDT, prevention of long-latency diseases such as cancer, protection of the unborn against the health hazards from exposure to toxins in the womb—all of these protections are afforded by environmental law, and all of them look to the future as well as to the present. Environmental law seeks, moreover, to avoid the unpleasant surprises that come with discontinuities and irreversibility—the kinds of events that outstrip our powers of quantitative prediction. Here, too, environmental law tries to protect the future in addition to the present.

Cost-benefit analysis systematically downgrades the importance of the future in two ways: through the technique of discounting, and through predictive methodologies that take inadequate account of the possibility of catastrophic and irreversible events.

The most common, and commonsense, argument in favor of discounting future human lives saved, illnesses averted, and ecological disasters prevented, is that it is better to suffer a harm later rather than sooner. What's wrong with this argument? A lot, as it turns out.

Do Future Generations Count?
The first problem with the later-is-better argument for discounting is that it assumes that one person is deciding between dying or falling ill now, or dying or falling ill later. In that case, virtually everyone would prefer later. But many environmental programs protect the far future, beyond the lifetime of today's decision makers. The time periods involved span many decades for a wide range of programs, and even many centuries, in the case of climate change, radioactive waste, and other persistent toxins. With time spans this long, discounting at any positive rate will make even global

catastrophes seem trivial. At a discount rate of 5 percent, for example, the death of a billion people 500 years from now becomes less serious than the death of one person today. The choice implicit in discounting is between preventing harms to the current generation and preventing similar harms to future generations. Seen in this way, discounting looks like a fancy justification for foisting our problems off onto the people who come after us.

Does Haste Prevent Waste?

The justification of discounting often assumes that environmental problems won't get any worse if we wait to address them. In the market paradigm, buying environmental protection is just like buying any other commodity. You can buy a new computer now or later—and if you don't need it this year, you should probably wait. The technology will undoubtedly keep improving, so next year's models will do more yet cost less. An exactly parallel argument has been made about climate change (and other environmental problems) by some economists: if we wait for further technological progress, we will get more for our climate change mitigation dollars in the future.

If environmental protection was mass-produced by the computer industry, and if environmental problems would agree to stand still indefinitely and wait for us to respond, this might be a reasonable approach. In the real world, however, it is a ludicrous and dangerous strategy. Too many years of delay may mean that the polar ice caps melt, the spent uranium leaks out of the containment ponds, the hazardous waste seeps into groundwater and basements and backyards—at which point we can't put the genie back in the bottle at any reasonable cost (or perhaps not at all).

Environmentalists often talk of potential "crises," of threats that problems will become suddenly and irreversibly worse. In response to such threats, environmentalists and some governments advocate the so-called precautionary principle, which calls upon regulators to err on the side of caution and protection when risks are uncertain. Cost-benefit analysts, for the most part, do not assume the possibility of crisis. Their worldview assumes stable problems, with control costs that are stable or declining over time, and thus finds precautionary investment in environmental protection to be a needless expense. Discounting is part of this non-crisis perspective. By implying that the present cost of future environmental harms

18

declines, lockstep, with every year that we look ahead, discounting ignores the possibility of catastrophic and irreversible harms.

For this very reason, some prominent economists have rejected the discounting of intangibles. As William Baumol wrote in an important early article on discounting the benefits of public projects:

> There are important externalities and investments of the public goods variety which cry for special attention. Irreversibilities constitute a prime example. If we poison our soil so that never again will it be the same, if we destroy the Grand Canyon and turn it into a hydroelectric plant, we give up assets which like Goldsmith's bold peasantry, "their country's pride, when once destroy'd can never be supplied." All the wealth and resources of future generations will not suffice to restore them.[21]

Begging the Question

Extensive discounting of future environmental problems lies at the heart of many recent studies of regulatory costs and benefits that charge "statistical murder." When the costs and benefits of environmental protection are compared to those of safety rules (like requiring fire extinguishers for airplanes) or medical procedures (like vaccinating children against disease), environmental protection almost always comes out the loser. Why is this so?[22]

These studies all discount future environmental benefits by at least 5 percent per year. This has little effect on the evaluation of programs, like auto safety rules requiring seat belts and fire safety rules requiring smoke alarms, that could start saving lives right away. However, for environmental programs like hazardous waste cleanups and control of persistent toxins, that save lives in the future, discounting matters a great deal—especially because, as explained above, the benefits are assumed to occur in the future when deaths are avoided, rather than in the near term when risks are reduced.

By using discounting, analysts *assume* the answer to the question they purport to be addressing, which is which programs are most worthwhile. The researchers begin with premises that guarantee that programs designed for the long haul, such as environmental protection, are not as important as programs that look to the shorter term. When repeated without discounting (or with benefits assumed to occur when risks are reduced), these studies support many more environmental programs, and the cry of "statistical murder" rings hollow.

Citizens and Consumers—Reprise

The issue of discounting illustrates once again the failure of cost-benefit analysis to take into account the difference between citizens and consumers. Many people advocate discounting on the ground that it reflects people's preferences, as expressed in market decisions concerning risk. But again, this omits the possibility that people will have different preferences when they take on a different role. The future seems to matter much more to American citizens than to American consumers, even though they are of course the same people.

For example, Americans are notoriously bad at saving money on their own, apparently expressing a disinterest in the future. But Social Security is arguably the most popular entitlement program in the United States. The tension between Americans' personal saving habits and their enthusiasm for Social Security implies a sharp divergence between the temporal preferences of people as consumers and as citizens. Thus private preferences for current over future consumption should not be used to subvert public judgments that future harms are as important as immediate ones.

3. Exacerbating Inequality

The third fundamental defect of cost-benefit analysis is that it tends to ignore, and therefore to reinforce, patterns of economic and social inequality. Cost-benefit analysis consists of adding up all the costs of a policy, adding up all the benefits, and comparing the totals. Implicit in this innocuous-sounding procedure is the controversial assumption that it doesn't matter who gets the benefits and who pays the costs.

Yet in our society, concerns about equity frequently do and should enter into debates over public policy. There is an important difference between spending state tax revenues to improve the parks in rich communities, and spending the same revenues to clean up pollution in poor communities. The value of these two initiatives, measured using cost-benefit analysis, might be the same in both cases, but this does not mean that the two policies are equally urgent or desirable.

The problem of equity runs even deeper. Benefits are typically measured by willingness to pay for environmental improvement, and the rich are able and willing to pay for more than the poor. Imagine a cost-benefit analysis of siting an undesirable facility, such as a landfill or incinerator. Wealthy communities are willing to pay more for the benefit of not having the facility in their backyards; thus the net benefits to society as a whole will be maximized by putting the facility in a low-income area. (Note that wealthy communities do not actually have to pay for the benefit of avoiding the facility; the analysis depends only on the fact that they are *willing* to pay.)

This kind of logic was made (in)famous in a 1991 memo circulated by Lawrence Summers (who later served as Secretary of the Treasury and as President of Harvard University), when he was the chief economist at the World Bank. Discussing the migration of "dirty industries" to developing countries, Summers' memo explained:

> The measurements of the costs of health impairing pollution depend . . . on the foregone earnings from increased morbidity and mortality. From this point of view a given amount of health impairing pollution should be done in the country with the lowest cost, which will be the country with the lowest wages. I think the economic logic behind dumping a load of toxic waste in the lowest wage country is impeccable and we should face up to that.[23]

After this memo became public, Brazil's then-Secretary of the Environment José Lutzenberger wrote to Summers:

> Your reasoning is perfectly logical but totally insane. . . . Your thoughts [provide] a concrete example of the unbelievable alienation, reductionist thinking, social ruthlessness and the arrogant ignorance of many conventional 'economists' concerning the nature of the world we live in.[24]

If decisions are based strictly on cost-benefit analysis and willingness to pay, most environmental burdens will end up being imposed on the countries, communities, and individuals with the least resources. This theoretical pattern bears an uncomfortably close resemblance to reality. Cost-benefit methods should not be blamed for existing patterns of environmental injustice; we suspect that pollution is typically dumped on the poor without waiting for formal analysis. Still, cost-benefit analysis rationalizes and reinforces the problem, allowing environmental burdens to flow downhill along the income gradients of an unequal world. It is hard to see this as part of an economically optimal or politically objective method of decision making.

In short, equity is an important criterion for evaluation of public policy, but it does not fit into the cost-benefit framework. The same is true of questions of rights and morality, principles that are not reducible to monetary terms. Calculations that are acceptable, even common sense, for financial matters can prove absurd or objectionable when applied to moral issues, as shown by the following example.

A financial investment with benefits worth five times its costs would seem like an obviously attractive bargain. Compare this to the estimates that front airbags on the passenger side of automobiles may cause one death, usually of a child, for every five lives saved. If we really believed that lives—even statistical lives—were worth $6 million, or any other finite dollar amount, endorsing the airbags should be no more complicated than accepting the financial investment. However, many people do find the airbag trade-off troubling or unacceptable, implying that a different, nonquantitative value of a life is at stake here. If a public policy brought some people five dollars of benefits for every one dollar it cost to others, the winners could in theory compensate the losers. No such compensation is possible if winning and losing are measured in deaths rather than dollars.[25]

In comparing the deaths of adults prevented by airbags with the deaths of children caused by airbags, or in exploring countless other harms that might be mitigated through regulation, the real debate is not between rival cost-benefit analyses. Rather, it is between environmental advocates who frame the issue as a matter of rights and ethics, and others who see it as an acceptable area for economic calculation. That debate is inescapable, and is logically prior to the details of evaluating costs and benefits.

4. Less Objectivity and Transparency

A fourth fundamental flaw of cost-benefit analysis is that it is unable to deliver on the promise of more objective and more transparent decision making. In fact, in most cases, the use of cost-benefit analysis is likely to deliver less objectivity and less transparency.

For the reasons we have discussed, there is nothing objective about the basic premises of cost-benefit analysis. Treating individuals solely as consumers, rather than as citizens with a sense of moral responsibility to the larger society, represents a distinct and highly contestable worldview. Likewise, the use of discounting reflects judgments about the nature of environmental risks and citizens' responsibilities toward future generations which are, at a minimum, debatable. Because value-laden premises permeate cost-benefit analysis, the claim that cost-benefit analysis offers an "objective" way to make government decisions is simply bogus.

Furthermore, as we have seen, cost-benefit analysis relies on a byzantine array of approximations, simplifications, and counterfactual hypotheses. Thus, the actual use of cost-benefit analysis inevitably involves countless judgment calls. People with strong, and clashing, partisan positions will naturally advocate that discretion in the application of this methodology be exercised in favor of their positions, further undermining the claim that cost-benefit analysis is objective.

Perhaps the best way to illustrate how little economic analysis has to contribute, objectively, to the fundamental question of how clean and safe we want our environment to be is to refer again to the controversy over cost-benefit analysis of EPA's regulation of arsenic in drinking water. As Cass Sunstein has argued, the available information on the benefits of arsenic reduction supports estimates of net benefits from regulation ranging from less than zero, up to $560 million or more. The number of deaths avoided annually by regulation is, according to Sunstein, between 0 and 112.[26] A procedure that allows such an enormous range of different evaluations of a single rule is certainly not the objective, transparent decision rule that its advocates have advertised.

These uncertainties arise both from the limited knowledge of the epidemiology and toxicology of exposure to arsenic, and from the controversial series of assumptions required for the valuation and discounting of costs and (particularly) benefits. As Sunstein explained, a number of different positions, including most of those heard in the controversy over arsenic regulation, could be supported by one or another reading of the evidence.[27]

Some analysts might respond that this enormous range of outcomes is not possible if the proper economic assumptions are used; if, for example, human lives are valued at $6 million apiece and discounted at a 5 percent yearly rate (or, depending on the analyst, other favorite numbers). But these assumptions beg fundamental questions about ethics and equity, and one cannot decide whether to embrace them without thinking through the whole range of moral issues they raise. Yet once one has thought through these issues, there is no need then to collapse the complex moral inquiry into a series of numbers. Pricing the priceless merely translates our inquiry into a different, and foreign, language, one with a painfully impoverished vocabulary.

For many of the same reasons, cost-benefit analysis also generally fails to achieve the goal of transparency. Cost-benefit analysis is a complex, resource-intensive, and expert-driven process. It requires a great deal of time and effort to attempt to unpack even the simplest cost-benefit analysis. Few community groups, for example, have access to the kind of scientific and technical expertise that would allow them to evaluate whether, intentionally or unintentionally, the authors of a cost-benefit analysis have unfairly slighted the interests of the community or some of its members. Few members of the public can meaningfully participate in the debates about the use of particular regression analyses or discount rates that are central to the cost-benefit method.

The translation of lives, health, and nature into dollars also renders decision making about the underlying social values less rather than more transparent. As we have discussed, all of the various steps required to reduce a human life to a dollar value are open to debate and subject to uncertainty. However, the specific dollar values kicked out by cost-benefit analysis tend to obscure these underlying issues rather than encourage full public debate about them.

Practical Problems

The previous section showed that there are deep, inherent problems with the theory of cost-benefit analysis. In practice, these problems only get worse; leading examples of cost-benefit analysis fall far short of the theoretical ideal. The continuing existence of these practical problems further undercuts the utility and wisdom of using cost-benefit analysis to evaluate environmental policy.

The Limits of Quantification

Cost-benefit studies of regulations focus on quantified benefits of the proposed action and generally ignore other, nonquantified health and environmental benefits. This raises a serious problem because many benefits of environmental programs, including the prevention of many nonfatal diseases and harms to the ecosystem, either have not been quantified or are not quantifiable at this time. Indeed, for many environmental regulations, the only benefit that can be quantified is the prevention of cancer deaths. On the other hand, one can virtually always come up with *some* number for the costs of environmental regulations. Thus, in practice, cost-benefit analysis tends to skew decision making against protecting public health and the environment.

For example, regulation of workers' exposure to formaldehyde is often presented as the extreme of inefficiency, supposedly costing $72 billion per life saved. This figure is based on the finding that the regulation prevents cancers, which occur only in small numbers but which have been thoroughly evaluated in numerical terms. But the question is not just one of preventing cancer. Formaldehyde regulation also prevents many painful but nonfatal illnesses that are excluded from the $72 billion figure. If described solely as a means of reducing cancer, the regulation would indeed be very expensive. But if described as a means of reducing cancer *and* other diseases, the regulation makes a good deal of sense. Workplace regulation of formaldehyde is not a bad answer, but it does happen to be an answer to a different question.

The formaldehyde case is by no means unique: often the only regulatory benefit that can be quantified is the prevention of cancer. Yet cancer has a latency period of between five and forty years. When discounted at 5 percent, a cancer death forty years from now has a "present value" of only one-seventh of a death today. Thus, one of the benefits that can most often be quantified—allowing it to be folded into cost-benefit analysis—is also one that is heavily discounted, making the benefits of preventive regulation seem trivial.

Ignoring What Cannot Be Counted

Many advocates of cost-benefit analysis concede that the decision-making process must make some room for nonquantitative considerations. Some environmental benefits have never been subjected to rigorous economic evaluation. Other important considerations in environmental protection, such as the fairness of the distribution of environmental risks, cannot be quantified and priced.

In practice, however, this kind of judgment is often forgotten, or even denigrated, once all the numbers have been crunched. No matter how many times the EPA, for example, says that one of its rules will produce many benefits, such as the prevention of illness or the protection of ecosystems, that cannot be quantified, the nonquantitative aspects of its analyses are almost invariably ignored in public discussions of its policies.

When, for example, EPA proposed strengthening the standard for arsenic in drinking water, it cited many human illnesses that would be prevented by the new standard but that could not be expressed in numerical terms. Subsequent public discussion of EPA's cost-benefit analysis of this standard, however, inevitably referred only to the numerical analysis and forgot about the cases of avoided illness that could not be quantified.

Overstated Costs

There is also a tendency, as a matter of practice, to overestimate the costs of regulations in advance of their implementation. This happens in part because regulations often encourage new technologies and more efficient ways of doing business; these innovations reduce the cost of compliance. It is also important to keep in mind, when reviewing cost estimates, that they are usually provided by the regulated industry itself, which has an obvious incentive to offer high estimates of costs as a way of warding off new regulatory requirements.

One study found that costs estimated in advance of regulation were more than twice actual costs in eleven out of twelve cases.[28] Another study found that advance cost estimates were more than 25 percent higher than actual costs for fourteen out of twenty-eight regulations; advance estimates were more than 25 percent too low in only three of the twenty-eight cases.[29] Before the 1990 Clean Air Act Amendments took effect, industry anticipated that the cost of sulfur reduction under the amendments would be $1,500 per ton. In 2000, the actual cost was less than $150 per ton.

Of course, not all cost-benefit analyses overstate the actual costs of regulation. But given the technology-forcing character of environmental regulations, it is not surprising to find a marked propensity to overestimate the costs of such rules.

In a related vein, many companies have begun to discover that environmental protection can actually be *good* for business in some respects. Increased energy efficiency, profitable products made from waste, and decreased use of raw materials are just a few of the cost-saving or even profit-making results of turning more corporate attention to environmentally protective business practices. Cost-benefit analyses typically do not take such money-saving possibilities into account in evaluating the costs of regulation.

The Many Alternatives to Cost-Benefit Analysis

A common response to the criticisms of cost-benefit analysis is a simple question: what's the alternative? The implication is that despite its flaws, cost-benefit analysis is really the only tool we have for figuring out how much environmental protection to provide.

This is just not true. Indeed, for more than thirty years, the federal government has been protecting human health and the environment without relying on cost-benefit analysis. The menu of regulatory options that has emerged from this experience is large and varied. Choosing among these possibilities depends on a variety of case-specific circumstances, such as the nature of the pollution involved, the degree of scientific knowledge about it, and the conditions under which people are exposed to it. As the following brief sketch of alternatives reveals, cost-benefit analysis—a "one-size-fits-all" approach to regulation—cannot be squared with the multiplicity of circumstances surrounding different environmental problems.

For the most part, environmental programs rely on a form of "technology-based" regulation, the essence of which is to require the best available methods for controlling pollution. This avoids the massive research effort needed to quantify and monetize the precise harms caused by specific amounts of pollution, which is required by cost-benefit analysis. In contrast, the technology-based approach allows regulators to proceed directly to controlling emissions. Simply put, the idea is that we should do the best we can to mitigate pollution we believe to be harmful.

Over the years, EPA has learned that flexibility is a good idea when it comes to technology-based regulation, and thus has tended to avoid specifying particular technologies or processes for use by regulated firms; instead, the agency has increasingly relied on "performance-based" regulation, which tells firms to clean up to a certain, specified extent, but doesn't tell them precisely how to do it. Technology-based regulation generally takes costs into account in determining the required level of pollution control, but does not demand the kind of precisely quantified and monetized balancing process that is needed for cost-benefit analysis.

Another regulatory strategy that has gained a large following in recent years is the use of "pollution trading," as in the sulfur dioxide emissions trading program created for power plants under the 1990 Clean Air Act Amendments. That program grants firms a limited number of permits for pollution, but also allows them to buy and sell permits. Thus, firms with high pollution control costs can save money by buying permits, while those with low control costs can save money by controlling emissions and selling their permits.

The fixed supply of permits, created by law, sets the cap on total emissions; the trading process allows industry to decide where and how it is most economical to reduce emissions to fit under the cap. Trading programs have become an important part of the federal program for controlling pollution. These programs, too, have not used cost-benefit analysis in their implementation. Congress, EPA, or other officials set the emissions cap, and the market does the rest.

It is theoretically possible that cost-benefit analysis could be used to choose the overall limit on pollution that guides both performance-based and market-based regulatory programs. However, this has not been standard practice in the past; the limit on sulfur emissions in the 1990 Clean Air Act Amendments, for example, was set by a process of political compromise. Given the problems with cost-benefit analysis, political compromise cannot be viewed as an inferior way to set a cap on emissions. Many regulatory programs have been a terrific success without using cost-benefit analysis to set pollution limits.

One last example is informational regulation, which requires disclosures to the public and/or to consumers about risks they face from exposures to chemicals. These "right-to-know" regimes allow citizens and consumers not only to know about the risks they face, but also empower them to do something about those risks. The Toxics Release Inventory created by the Emergency Planning and Community Right-to-Know Act, the product warning labels required by California's Proposition 65, and the consumer notices now required regarding drinking water that contains hazardous chemicals, are all variants of this type of information-based regulation. Not one of these popular and effective programs relies on cost-benefit analysis.

The arguments for flexible, technology-based regulation and for incentive-based programs like pollution trading and disclosure requirements are sometimes confused with the arguments for cost-benefit analysis. But both technology-based and incentive-based regulation take their *goals* from elected representatives rather than from economic analysts, even though the *means* adopted by these regulatory strategies are strongly influenced by attention to costs. The current style of cost-benefit analysis, however, purports to set the *ends*, not just the means, of environmental policy, and that is where its aspirations amount to arrogance.

Economic analysis has had its successes and made its contributions; it has taught us a great deal over the years about how we can most efficiently and cheaply reach a given environmental goal. It has taught us relatively little, however, about what our environmental goals should be. Indeed, while economists have spent three decades wrangling about how much a human life, or a bald eagle, or a beautiful stretch of river is worth in dollars, ecologists, engineers, and other specialists have gone about the business of saving lives and eagles and rivers, without waiting for formal, quantitative analysis proving that saving these things is worthwhile.

Conclusion

Two features of cost-benefit analysis distinguish it from other approaches to evaluating the advantages and disadvantages of environmentally protective regulations: the translation of lives, health, and the natural environment into monetary terms, and the discounting of harms to human health and the environment that are expected to occur in the future. These features of cost-benefit analysis make it a terrible way to make decisions about environmental protection, for both intrinsic and practical reasons.

Nor is it useful to keep cost-benefit analysis around as a kind of regulatory tag-along, providing information that regulators may find "interesting" even if not decisive. Cost-benefit analysis is exceedingly time- and resource-intensive, and its flaws are so deep and so large that this time and these resources are wasted on it. Once a cost-benefit analysis is performed, its bottom-line number offers an irresistible sound bite that inevitably drowns out more reasoned deliberation. Moreover, given the intrinsic conflict between cost-benefit analysis and the principles of fairness that animate, or should animate, our national policy toward protecting people from being hurt by other people, the results of cost-benefit analysis cannot simply be "given some weight" along with other factors, without undermining the fundamental equality of all citizens—rich and poor, young and old, healthy and sick.

Cost-benefit analysis cannot overcome its fatal flaw: it is completely reliant on the impossible attempt to price the priceless values of life, health, nature, and the future. Better public policy decisions can be made without cost-benefit analysis by combining the successes of traditional regulation with the best of the innovative and flexible approaches that have gained ground in recent years.

Chapter 2

Was Environmental Protection *Ever* a Good Idea?

As discussed in the previous chapter, cost-benefit analysis of environmental protection involves adding up the costs—for example, for pollution control equipment—and comparing them to estimates of the monetary value of the resulting benefits—for example, the dollar value of the deaths and diseases avoided by reducing pollution. This effort routinely fails, primarily because the benefits of health and environmental protection are vitally important, but cannot be meaningfully expressed in monetary terms. In a word, the benefits are priceless. The attempt to assign monetary prices, although required for the cost-benefit calculation, ends up distorting, misrepresenting, and narrowing the priceless values of life, health, and nature, and belittling the widespread concern for the well-being of future generations. In practice, therefore, cost-benefit analysis is an opaque and technically intricate process accessible only to experts, and one that all too frequently recommends rejection of sensible policies on the grounds that their costs exceed economists' estimates of their benefits.

In this chapter, we examine an argument that proponents of cost-benefit analysis have offered as a linchpin of the case for cost-benefit: that this technique is neither anti- nor proregulatory, but is a neutral tool for evaluating public policy. In making this argument, these observers have

Chapter 2 by Frank Ackerman, Lisa Heinzerling, and Rachel Massey.

often invoked the use of cost-benefit analysis to support previous regulatory decisions (their favorite example involves the phase-down of lead in gasoline, which we shall shortly discuss) as a sign that this technique can be used to support as well as to undermine protective regulation. As we demonstrate, however, cost-benefit analysis would have stood as an obstacle to early regulatory successes.

Looking Backward

We are not the first to explore cost-benefit analyses of past regulatory decisions. Some retrospective cost-benefit studies have supported environmental protection; some commentators have suggested that such studies show that cost-benefit analysis contains no systematic bias against environmental regulation.[1] We believe that the wrong lesson has been drawn from these studies, exaggerating the prospects for cost-benefit analysis to support environmental protection in the future.

One widely cited retrospective study is a multiyear, peer-reviewed EPA study of the first twenty years of the Clean Air Act (1970–1990), published in 1997. This study found benefits from U.S. air pollution regulation equal to about forty times the costs.[2] More recently, annual analyses by Office of Information and Regulatory Affairs (OIRA), an agency within the federal Office of Management and Budget, have estimated, retrospectively, the monetized costs and benefits of major regulations of the recent past. The OIRA report for 2004 estimated that major EPA regulations adopted from 1993 to 2003 imposed $22–24 billion in costs, and yielded $38–132 billion in benefits.[3] OIRA cautioned against getting too excited about these upbeat numbers:

> The majority of the large estimated benefit of EPA rules is attributable to reduction in public exposure to a single air pollutant: fine particulate matter. Thus, the favorable benefit-cost results for EPA regulation should not be generalized to all types of EPA rules or to all types of clean-air rules.[4]

In general, as OIRA suggested, cost-benefit analysis tends to endorse efforts to reduce a handful of high-volume air pollutants. The huge estimated benefits of these measures account for EPA's favorable analysis of the Clean Air Act, as well as OIRA's numbers for EPA regulations as a whole. Look beyond the criteria air pollutants, and the evidence becomes quite sparse for cost-benefit analysis supporting environmental protection. Furthermore, John Graham, director of OIRA from 2001 to 2006, worked long and hard to reduce the apparent benefits of controlling even these widespread and harmful air pollutants.[5]

Moreover, EPA's positive cost-benefit analysis even here would not have been possible at the time the Clean Air Act protections were put in place. A huge proportion of the benefits found by EPA came from regulating emissions of fine particles in the air, but the full magnitude of the harm done by such particles was not known for many years after the Act was first implemented. If a favorable cost-benefit analysis of the Clean Air Act's regulation of fine particles had been required before adoption of the act, the result would have been the same as in the lead and vinyl chloride case studies we examine later in this chapter: the Act's requirements would have been rejected for lack of sufficiently definitive data.

In another frequently cited study, economist Richard Morgenstern assembled twelve case studies of regulations in which EPA's economic analyses played an important role.[6] His case studies, written by analysts who played a major role in the regulatory process, were chosen to highlight the positive contribution of EPA's economic analyses (through the first term of the Clinton administration).

Morgenstern's case studies divide naturally into three groups. In four cases, no monetization of benefits was attempted, so no formal quantitative comparison of costs and benefits was possible. In four cases, some benefits were monetized, but the regulatory decision was based on technology standards or other criteria, and did not maximize net benefits. In the remaining four cases, cost-benefit analysis appeared to endorse the final decision, weakly in one case and strongly in the other three. However, in two cases the cost-benefit analysis was not completed until after a decision had been made on other grounds, so it was not a factor in the regulatory process. The two cases in which cost-benefit analysis was a crucial input into decision making both involved lead pollution. The famous cost-benefit analysis of removing lead from gasoline is the subject of one of our case studies in this chapter. The regulation of lead in drinking water was almost a sequel to lead in gasoline, addressed by the same analysts using much of the same data, just a few years later.

Like Morgenstern, we find that cost-benefit analysis played little role in the regulatory processes we evaluate. Good thing, too, because we also find that requiring a positive cost-benefit analysis before adoption of regulations, as currently advocated, would have prevented some of the great policy successes of the past decades. Our first example involves getting the lead out of gasoline.

Lead in Gasoline

Whenever fans of cost-benefit analysis want to show how it can be used to protect the environment, they cite the example of EPA's phase-down of lead in gasoline in the 1980s. With this rule, EPA ordered a more than tenfold reduction of levels of lead in gasoline. EPA's decision was supported by an extensive cost-benefit analysis demonstrating that the benefits of the phase-down greatly outweighed the economic costs. Such notable regulatory scholars as John Graham,[7] Robert Hahn,[8] Richard Stewart,[9] Cass Sunstein,[10] and Jonathan Wiener[11] have pointed to the influence of cost-benefit analysis on the 1980s-era lead phase-down as evidence of the evenhandedness of this analytical framework.

However, that cost-benefit analysis appeared only in the last act of a long drama. To summarize the plot in brief: leaded gasoline, introduced in the 1920s despite clear early warnings of severe health hazards, dominated the market for fifty years.[12] Regulations removing most of the lead from gasoline were finally adopted in the 1970s, and upheld by the courts in a landmark legal decision. The 1970s regulation was adopted on a precautionary basis without reliance on cost-benefit analysis, under the Clean Air Act's provision giving the EPA the authority to "control or prohibit" fuel additives if they "will endanger the public health or welfare."[13] EPA's new rule was quickly effective in lowering blood lead levels. One convenient side effect was the creation of the data that then allowed a later cost-benefit analysis, in the 1980s, to confirm the wisdom of staying the course and going even further to remove the last bit of lead from our fuel. Thus, the cost-benefit analysis of the 1980s phase-down of lead in gasoline would not have been possible in the absence of the more important 1970s-era regulation, which was not itself based on cost-benefit analysis. Had we waited in the 1970s, as some argue we should do in policy disputes today, for cost-benefit analysis to show us the way, we might still be waiting now.

Lead Comes Knocking

Lead was introduced into gasoline in the 1920s, at a time of fierce competition in the growing market for automobiles. Then as now, two of the features that could set one car apart from another were power and speed. Increasing compression in the car engine increases power and speed, but it can also increase "knocking," or the loss of power accompanied by the familiar popping sound of very old cars.[14]

General Motors set out to find an antiknock compound that would allow its cars to increase their power and speed without increasing knocking. Thomas Midgley Jr., an engineer in a GM research lab, tested numerous substances for this purpose, including tetra ethyl lead (TEL). Pursuing the enticing possibility of a substance one could patent (and thus corner the market in), Midgley shunted to the side another potential antiknock compound, ethanol, in favor of TEL.[15] As Jamie Lincoln Kitman put it in his indispensable account of the development of TEL, "any idiot with a still" could make ethanol, which made it far less attractive as an antiknock compound to the profit-conscious GM.[16]

GM, at the time controlled by Pierre du Pont, eventually teamed with Standard Oil of New Jersey to form a new company—the Ethyl Corporation—to market TEL.[17] Even before this, plants in Ohio and New Jersey were busy making the chemical. The problems started immediately. Within the first month of producing TEL, a worker died at the Ohio plant.[18] Eventually fifteen workers died, and hundreds more fell ill.[19] Workers called one production facility in New Jersey the "House of Butterflies" because high lead exposure caused hallucinations that led workers to swat imaginary insects off of their bodies.[20]

The Surgeon General convened a panel of experts to study the potential health effects of TEL, but gave them only seven months in which to come to a conclusion. The Ethyl Corporation voluntarily suspended production of TEL while the Surgeon General's committee did its work.[21] The committee did find more lead in the blood of people occupationally exposed to lead, such as chauffeurs and garage men, but, within its tight timeline, it was unable to find health effects from these higher exposures. The committee ultimately found "no good grounds for prohibiting the use of ethyl gasoline . . . as a motor fuel, provided that its distribution and use are controlled by proper regulations."[22] (Those "proper regulations" did not appear until almost fifty years later.) The panel also issued the following cautionary note:

> It remains possible that, if the use of leaded gasolines becomes widespread, conditions may arise very different from those studied by us which would render its use more of a hazard than would appear to be the case from this investigation. Longer experience may show that even such slight storage of lead as was observed [among humans] in these [1925] studies may lead eventually to recognizable lead poisoning or to chronic degenerative diseases of a less obvious character. . . . The vast increase in the number of automobiles throughout the country makes the study of all such questions a matter of real importance from the standpoint of public health.[23]

It would be many years, however, before anyone took up the issue again. Within months of the committee's report, TEL was back on the market.

The "Kehoe Rule"

In a 1922 letter to his brother Irénée (the head of DuPont Chemical), GM chief Pierre du Pont described TEL as "a colorless liquid of sweetish odor, very poisonous if absorbed through the skin, resulting in lead poisoning almost immediately."[24] Yet for the next fifty years, the makers of leaded gasoline would deny this basic fact about lead: it is a poison. When faced with the warnings of public health authorities about the potentially dire effects of spewing lead into the atmosphere from millions of automobiles, the industry had a simple response: prove it.

The trouble was, it was hard to prove that the day-to-day, low-level exposures to lead caused by leaded gasoline hurt people. The kinds of health effects we now know come from lead—reduced learning capacity, neurological disorders, and high blood pressure—are quite common, and have several potential causes, so it is difficult to say which portion of these effects is due to lead. Thus, although the U.S. government had suspected the risks of adding lead to gasoline from the very beginning, it would not seriously try to regulate leaded gasoline until lead had been pouring from almost every automobile in the country for half a century.

The "prove it's dangerous" approach was dubbed by Jamie Kitman the "Kehoe Rule" after Robert Kehoe, the medical director for the Ethyl

Corporation, who pursued and perfected the approach during decades of asserting the safety of leaded gasoline. The Kehoe Rule was particularly effective in silencing dissent because most of the lead-related research conducted in the middle part of the twentieth century was funded by the interested industries themselves. Kehoe maintained that the blood lead levels of the people most exposed to lead—those who were exposed on the job—gave little cause for alarm because these levels were not a great deal higher than the blood lead levels of the presumably unexposed "control" population.[25]

The idea that high levels of lead in the blood were natural, normal, and benign got its comeuppance from an unlikely source: a geochemist studying the age of the Earth. Clair Patterson's research on this subject involved precise chemical analysis of ocean sediments and archaeological material, which incidentally established that the contemporary body burden of lead was far above preindustrial levels.[26] His findings directly refuted Kehoe and the lead industry's claim that the blood lead levels prevailing in the United States were natural.

Like many other scientists who dared challenge the lead industry's story line, Patterson found himself at the receiving end of the industry's wrath and was materially (and adversely) affected by it.[27] Nevertheless, scientific findings by Patterson and others had begun to chip away at the factual basis for the industry's longstanding denials of the potential dangers of leaded gasoline.

Congress Acts

With the passage of the federal Clean Air Act Amendments of 1970, the era of leaded gas finally began to draw to a close. The Act directed the brand new EPA to regulate fuel additives (of which lead was the most important) if either of two conditions was met: first, if the agency found that the additive "will endanger the public health or welfare,"[28] and second, if the additive would impair the performance of the pollution control devices that were also required by the amendments to the Act.

A review of the legislative history leading to these developments shows considerable concern in Congress about the potential dangers of airborne lead. It also reveals, however, how keenly aware Congress was of the scientific uncertainty that continued to surround this issue.[29] Perhaps it goes without saying that Congress performed no cost-benefit analysis of the consequences of its decision to require regulation of fuel additives; none would have been possible, given the lack of quantitative data on the health and welfare effects of leaded gasoline.

Within weeks of the adoption of the amendments,[30] EPA's first administrator, William Ruckelshaus, had declared that leaded gasoline endangered the public health and welfare and impaired the performance of catalytic converters, and had given public notice that he intended to issue a regulation reducing allowable levels of lead in gasoline.[31]

In 1972, EPA proposed a significant reduction in the allowable levels of lead in gasoline,[32] requiring removal of most of the lead within just a few years. EPA also proposed to require the availability of at least one grade of unleaded gasoline. The agency thought lead would damage the catalytic converters that were required on new cars to reduce other forms of harmful air pollution. In addition, the agency thought that lead itself was a threat to public health. Although EPA could not put exact numbers on the health effects caused by lead, it thought the existing scientific evidence was strong enough to justify strict limits on lead in gas. The agency stated that the then-existing levels of airborne lead were "associated with a sufficient risk of adverse physiologic effects to constitute endangerment of public health."[33] It concluded that its proposals to regulate lead would "provide for the protection of health in major urban areas within the shortest time reasonably possible."[34]

In 1973, EPA responded to the extensive public comments it had received on leaded gasoline by retreating somewhat from the 1972 proposal. The agency extended the deadline for the reduction of lead in gasoline and changed the calculations used to demonstrate refineries' compliance with the agency's requirements.[35] At the same time, EPA also softened its earlier claims about the link between airborne lead levels and public health. The agency admitted that scientific findings suggesting a correlation between air lead levels and blood lead levels could not "be taken as conclusive evidence that airborne lead by itself is a current public health problem."[36] Even so, EPA worried that airborne lead might be contributing to "excessive total lead exposures among the general urban population."[37]

As noted above, in order to regulate lead in gasoline for purposes of protecting public health, EPA was required by Congress to find only that lead "will endanger the public health." It was not required to perform a cost-benefit analysis of reducing lead in gasoline, and it did not do so. Indeed, in its 1973 proposal, EPA admitted that "the benefits associated with the accelerated lead reduction have not been quantified."[38]

In December 1973, EPA issued final regulations on the subject.[39] Large refineries were required to remove roughly 80 percent of the prevailing (early 1970s) level of lead from gasoline by 1979, and small refineries had to meet the same target by 1982.[40] The agency explained:

> [I]t is difficult, if not impossible, to establish a precise level of airborne lead as an acceptable basis for a control strategy. . . . [However,] [s]trong evidence existed which supported the view that through these routes [air and dust] airborne lead contributes to excessive lead exposure in urban adults and children. In light of this evidence of health risks, the Administrator concluded that it would be prudent to reduce preventable lead exposure.[41]

EPA explained that it had extended the deadline for lead reduction from four to five years to "moderate the economic and technological impacts of the regulations during the period over which the reduction would be accomplished." EPA continued: "[T]hough the benefits associated with the . . . lead reductions have not been quantified, the Administrator has concluded that this approach is not unreasonably costly and will prudently prevent unnecessary exposure to airborne lead."[42] Indeed, as a later analysis of this decision pointed out, "[c]osts . . . were projected to be less than 0.1 cent per gallon refined, adding only between $82 million and $133 million to the total of $1.5 billion the industry was to invest in refining capacity through the year 1980."[43]

In a hard-fought court battle, industry tried to resuscitate the Kehoe Rule, arguing that EPA should not be allowed to regulate unless it could prove leaded gasoline had actually harmed identifiable people in the past. Nonetheless, EPA's new restrictions on leaded gasoline were upheld.[44] The court's ultimate decision in the case is considered a landmark in U.S. environmental law because it established that EPA could act in a precautionary fashion, rather than waiting for scientific certainty about the harmfulness of a substance before acting. EPA set its standards for lead based on the goal of protecting virtually all children from lead exposures that would harm their health and cognitive development.

NHANES and Needleman

Around the same time that EPA's initial lead phase-down was taking effect, additional evidence of the wisdom of EPA's actions was accumulating.

The little-remarked National Health Survey Act of 1956 required periodic national surveys of the population's health.[45] This statute, also enacted without reliance on cost-benefit analysis, led to a national study in 1976–1980 of children's blood lead levels.[46] The National Health and Nutrition Examination Study—called NHANES II because it was the second of its kind—showed marked decreases in children's blood lead levels in the period examined. Because this period coincided with the implementation of EPA's reduction of lead in gasoline, it was possible to study the relationship between the reduced blood lead levels found in NHANES II and the reductions in leaded gasoline required by EPA. The relationship turned out to be remarkably consistent: children's blood lead levels declined in direct proportion with the reduction of lead in gasoline. This relationship became a cornerstone of EPA's 1980s-era economic analysis of requiring further reductions in the lead content of gasoline.

In the same period, Herbert Needleman published his path-breaking study demonstrating a link between children's blood lead levels and IQ.[47] The study answered the question that had dogged lead researchers for decades: even if blood lead levels were higher than they naturally would be, was this causing any harm? Needleman's answer was an emphatic yes. Needleman's study also made it possible to state, in quantitative terms, the effect of reducing blood lead levels on human health and well-being.

Unfortunately, Needleman suffered the same fate as other lead researchers before him who had dared take on the lead industry. Researchers funded by the lead industry challenged his work, going so far as to press a formal charge of scientific misconduct with the National Institutes of Health.[48] As Needleman put it in later years, after he had been completely exonerated, "If you ever want to be intensively peer-reviewed, just produce a study with billions of dollars of implications and you will be reviewed to death."[49]

Meanwhile, the lead industry was also active on another front: with President Ronald Reagan's election in 1980 after campaign promises to make government smaller, arguments in favor of relaxing the requirements for lead in gasoline suddenly gained a more sympathetic hearing. At this point, cost-benefit analysis did play a useful supporting role in helping Congress and sympathetic administrators to uphold the previous commitment to removal of lead from gasoline, despite the wavering of top Reagan appointees.

Gorsuch Winks

A month after taking office, President Reagan formed the Task Force on Regulatory Relief, headed by Vice President George H. W. Bush. The ostensible purpose of the task force was to coordinate actions among the various executive agencies and also to oversee compliance with Reagan's brand new Executive Order 12291, requiring agencies to conduct cost-benefit analyses for significant new regulatory initiatives.[50] The real aim of the task force was to reduce regulation in any way possible.[51]

One of the first actions to come within the sights of the task force was EPA's lead phase-down.[52] The phase-down was nearly, but not quite, complete: although EPA had required large refineries to meet its new limits by 1979, small refineries were given until 1982 to do so. In 1982, following a task force recommendation, EPA not only proposed to delay the requirement for small refineries,[53] but also invited public comment on whether to relax the requirements for large refineries as well.[54]

Reagan's EPA administrator at the time, Ann Gorsuch, appears to have been on the same page as the task force. During a meeting with Ethyl representatives, she was asked whether she would enforce the existing rules to phase down lead. Her reported response: she winked.[55]

Nevertheless, the public outcry over news that the phase-down might be weakened made EPA back off from its proposals. Eventually, the 1970s-era rules were tightened rather than relaxed,[56] and a federal court upheld the new rules almost in their entirety, even going so far as to opine that a complete ban on lead in gasoline would be justified.[57]

By March 1983, Gorsuch had resigned amidst a scandal arising out of the Superfund hazardous waste program. One EPA official was sent to jail for lying to Congress about the matter.[58] More than 1,000 EPA employees had lost their jobs early on in the Reagan administration,[59] and the remaining employees' morale had hit an all-time low. It was time to restore credibility to the embattled agency.

Ruckelshaus and Cost-Benefit to the Rescue

Just weeks after Gorsuch resigned, EPA's first administrator, William Ruckelshaus, returned to the agency in its time of need. One of his stated aims was to restore rigorous analysis and to displace the political forces that had recently dominated the agency's actions.[60] Alvin Alm, his deputy, later recalled that at the time the agency was "really in need of some help," and that the agency's new leaders needed to "creat[e] confidence that we were getting work done."[61]

It is only at this late date in the story that cost-benefit analysis made its famous, and helpful, appearance. Within six months of the regime change at the agency, Alm asked EPA's economics office (the Office of Policy, Planning, and Evaluation) to put together a preliminary cost-benefit analysis of further regulation of lead in gasoline, including an outright ban. As Albert Nichols, who became intimately involved with the eventual analysis, recalled, Alm became interested in reviving the lead issue both because of a remark by a lobbyist for the ethanol industry (ethanol was a potential substitute for lead)[62] and because "lead appeared to offer an opportunity to demonstrate that the risk management principles being promoted by Administrator William Ruckelshaus and Alm were not just a sophisticated way of saying 'no' to proposed regulations; they also could help identify cases in which additional regulation was justified."[63]

Although Albert Nichols' account of EPA's decision to do a cost-benefit analysis of further lead reductions stated that EPA "was *not* under significant pressure from . . . environmental groups to take additional action,"[64] Nichols also acknowledged, in a footnote, that "[o]ther prominent environmentalists—such as Ellen Silbergeld of the Environmental Defense Fund—had been active for many years in efforts to reduce lead."[65] Others recall a more prominent role for environmental groups, in particular the Environmental Defense Fund, in persuading EPA to take another look at lead. Robert Percival, now a professor of law at the University of Maryland but then a young attorney at the Environmental Defense Fund, suggested during a meeting with Alvin Alm in the fall of 1983 that EPA undertake a cost-benefit analysis of phasing out lead from gasoline.[66] Several years later, Alm wrote that one of EPA's most important achievements—the 1980s-era phase-down of lead in gasoline—had "come about through a chance encounter" with someone he did not know, who had suggested doing a cost-benefit analysis of further lead regulation.[67]

Whatever the origins of Alm's request, EPA's analysts complied, producing a cost-benefit analysis clearly demonstrating that additional regulation of leaded gasoline was amply justified in economic terms. Armed with this analysis, EPA not only upheld the original rule, but adopted a new rule in 1985 that went much further, requiring the removal by 1988 of about 90 percent of the lead that was still allowed in gasoline under the 1970s rule.[68] By this time, EPA felt confident enough to include in its final economic analysis enormous benefits from reducing blood pressure in men through phasing out lead in gasoline. These benefits alone, EPA predicted, would be about ten times higher than the total costs of the rule by the late 1980s.[69]

Crunching the Numbers

The second wave of reduction of lead in gasoline, required by EPA in the 1980s, is the example widely touted as evidence that cost-benefit analysis is a neutral decision-making tool, tilting in favor of neither regulation nor laissez faire.

However, the cost-benefit analysis performed by EPA in the 1980s could not have been performed if the regulation of the 1970s, the ensuing "first wave" removal of roughly 80 percent of the lead in gasoline, and the government-sponsored national survey of blood lead levels, had not already occurred. EPA's cost-benefit analysis depended crucially on evidence gained from the studies showing a strong relationship between reduction of lead in gasoline and reduction in blood lead levels in children. This evidence was available only because regulation had already achieved such a substantial reduction of lead in gasoline. It is indeed useful that the lead cost-benefit analysis helped to prevent backsliding in the early years of the Reagan administration, and even justified the rapid removal of most of the remaining lead from gasoline. But this is very different from doing the job alone, or even playing the leading role.

Moreover, the story of cost-benefit analysis in supporting lead regulation stands almost alone: it is so universally cited that a skeptical observer might ask, is there an additional example of cost-benefit methods being used to support environmental protection? According to researchers involved in the studies, the cost-benefit analysis of leaded gasoline and the subsequent study of lead in drinking water (done just a few years later by the same analysts, using much of the same data) were "anomalous" successes, drawing on unusually strong data sets and enjoying a clear mandate from above to support protective regulations.[70] Normally, of course, it is not possible to remove most of a pollutant from the environment to develop the data supporting the removal of the remainder. And the political and administrative support for regulation that existed when Ruckelshaus returned to the EPA in the mid-1980s has been sadly lacking in the opening years of the twenty-first century.

In different hands, with a different political agenda, the cost-benefit analysis of lead regulation could have looked quite different. In fact, one prominent regulatory analyst has shown how this might have happened. Randall Lutter's (later) study of the valuation of the benefits of lead reduction was introduced in chapter 1. Rather than valuing the immense health improvements and the gains in children's IQ that have been traced to lead reductions, as EPA has done, Lutter argued that society should not value lead removal any more highly than individuals do,[71] which, he suggested, could be determined from studying what parents spend on chelation therapy to lower their children's lead levels. Because chelation is proven to work only for very high levels of lead poisoning, there is unsurprisingly little evidence that people choose to spend money on it for more common, chronic low-level lead problems. Applying the chelation yardstick, Lutter found that EPA had overstated the benefits of lead reduction, perhaps by as much as eightfold. In Lutter's view, therefore, less protective expenditure would be warranted—and the historic role of cost-benefit analysis in supporting lead reduction could have been less important.

Thus, it is not only the strong data and robust empirical studies that allowed cost-benefit analysis to support environmental protection in this case. Also crucial was the political support for a methodology that valued benefits relatively expansively. A different methodology, like Lutter's, could point in the opposite direction. The use of cost-benefit analysis by an administration hostile to environmental protection will almost certainly not produce the equivalent of another lead phase-down.

Damming the Grand Canyon

> Leave it as it is. You cannot improve on it. The ages have been at work on it, and man can only mar it. . . . What you can do is to keep it for your children, your children's children, and for all who come after you, as one of the great sights which every American if he can travel at all should see.
>
> Theodore Roosevelt, on the Grand Canyon[72]

> What's so special about the Grand Canyon anyway?
>
> Ken Wilson, Western Area Power Administration[73]

The water wars of the arid American West have transformed the natural landscape. With the help of countless billions of public dollars, the region's meager supplies of water have been rerouted to allow agriculture, industry, and residential development to flourish on barren desert lands, as described by Marc Reisner in his classic account, *Cadillac Desert*.[74] At times, the "water wars" have almost ceased to be metaphorical: in 1934, Arizona mobilized its National Guard in an attempt to stop construction of a dam that would divert Colorado River water into California.[75]

In the 1960s, collateral damage in the water wars nearly claimed parts of the Grand Canyon, as huge dams were proposed on the Colorado River, just above and below the national park. The dams were defeated in part by the massive opposition organized by the Sierra Club and other environmentalists—and in part by an influential cost-benefit analysis performed by RAND Corporation economists, showing that the economic benefits of the dams were slightly less than the costs.

This could be considered a triumph for the environmentally benign use of cost-benefit analysis, except for one drawback: the RAND analysis is, in retrospect, absurd. The same methodology combined with better information, which became available just a few years later, would have led to the opposite conclusion and firmly endorsed the dams.

Raising Arizona

The Colorado River is one of the few major sources of water in Arizona, skirting the northern and western edges of the state. Most of the agriculture, industry, and people in Arizona are hundreds of miles away, many of them in and around Phoenix and Tucson—and separated from the river by mountains as well as desert. The proposed damming of the Grand Canyon arose as part of the Central Arizona Project, a colossal scheme to move water from the river to the people.

After decades of battles in the courts and in Congress (as well as the armed confrontation at the riverbank in 1934), Arizona finally won a legal entitlement to a significant share of the Colorado River's water in the early 1960s. This cleared the way for the Central Arizona Project, proposed years earlier, to proceed. However, the effort needed multibillion-dollar financing to build its enormous aqueducts, and huge amounts of energy to pump the water up over the mountains.

The Bureau of Reclamation, the federal agency that dammed so many western rivers, had been "solving" problems like this since the 1940s. Its preferred method was called "river-basin accounting," treating the development of a river and related waterworks as a single project. Profitable dams could be built on fast-flowing rivers, generating hydroelectric power that would finance money-losing irrigation and water diversion schemes, as well as powering the massive pumping stations required to move the water. If the projects in a river basin were unbundled, the logic of the market might dictate building the dams but skipping the irrigation and other unprofitable pieces of the picture. However, the federal government repeatedly bought the whole package deal, as the New Deal enthusiasm for big public construction projects meshed with the local interests of western politicians—many of them ideologically opposed to expensive public-sector initiatives that benefited anyone else.[76]

By the time the Central Arizona Project got underway, most of the best sites on the Colorado had been taken for earlier developments. The only remaining options for big, profitable "cash register dams" that would finance the project were the Marble Gorge (or Marble Canyon) Dam and the Bridge Canyon Dam, later renamed Hualapai Dam to "honor" a Native American community. Marble Gorge, just upstream from the Grand Canyon National Park, would have flooded the Inner Gorge, essentially the first forty miles of the river's course through the canyon. Hualapai, downstream from the national park, would have created a ninety-four-mile-long reservoir, entirely flooding the Grand Canyon National Monument and extending thirteen miles into the national park itself.

Both dams were included in the revised Central Arizona Project proposal, launched in 1963. In support of the proposal, the Bureau of Reclamation performed an economic analysis comparing the dams to thermal (fossil fuel) power plants; the result was that the dams were much cheaper, with benefit/cost ratios of 2.0 and 1.7. These numbers emerged from a variant of cost-benefit analysis that is common in evaluation of power plants. The analysis assumes that if the dams were not built, something else would have to be built to generate the same amount of electricity. The "benefit" of building the dams is that it would avoid the construction of the next best alternative, which was a thermal power plant, according to the Bureau of Reclamation. A benefit/cost ratio of 2.0 for a dam means that the "benefit," that is, the avoided cost of an equivalent power plant, is twice the cost of the dam.

In the bureau's analysis, almost nothing was said about recreational benefits, and no mention was made of the value of the existence of the Grand Canyon per se (what environmental economists now call "existence value" or other varieties of "non-use value"). The analysis simply compared the two methods of generating electricity. Although referred to at the time as a cost-benefit analysis, this might be better described as a cost-effectiveness analysis, seeking the minimum-cost way to meet the goal of generating a fixed amount of electricity.[77] The bureau's result, strongly favoring the dams, is not a surprising one. Hydroelectric facilities built at places where large rivers are flowing rapidly downhill—like the Marble Canyon and Bridge Canyon sites—are routinely among the lowest cost sources of electricity. If nothing of importance is lost by the creation of the reservoir or other changes in river flow, hydroelectric development on fast-flowing major rivers is frequently a profitable way to generate electric power.

Yet many people felt that something of great importance would be lost. The Sierra Club quickly organized widespread, vocal opposition to the dams, easily winning the war for public opinion. Defenders of the dams suggested that the elevated water level of the Hualapai reservoir would allow more visitors to see the canyon from tour boats; the Sierra Club asked if we should also flood the Sistine Chapel so that tourists could get closer to the ceiling. Soon thereafter, the Internal Revenue Service revoked the Sierra Club's tax-exempt status.[78]

Too Cheap to Meter

After four years of debate, the dams were defeated in 1967. Although love of nature in general and the Grand Canyon in particular played an essential role, the Sierra Club and other opponents of the dams did not win on environmental arguments alone. Also crucial to the outcome was a rival cost-benefit analysis by two RAND Corporation economists, Alan Carlin and William Hoehn. Their work was publicized by the Sierra Club and by congressional opponents of the dams; it was presented and debated at length in the congressional hearings on the issue. Using a methodology much like the Bureau of Reclamation analysis, Carlin and Hoehn compared the dams to the cheapest alternative source of electricity; they again included almost nothing for the value of recreation, environmental amenity, or the existence of the Grand Canyon. But Carlin and Hoehn used a different alternative source of power as their benchmark. They compared the dams to nuclear power plants, which they believed to be astonishingly cheap.

Although their predictions of nuclear costs turned out to be hopelessly below the mark, Carlin and Hoehn did no worse than most people writing about nuclear power in the mid-1960s. At the time, nuclear power was a relatively new idea, still on the verge of commercial application. The hazards of nuclear power were not yet well known; the escalating costs of nuclear plants were not yet in sight. Instead, industry and government boosters of the new technology promoted the notion that nuclear energy would soon be "too cheap to meter." A decade of intensive research and development in the 1950s, mostly government-sponsored, had led to the first orders for nuclear plants in the early 1960s—and to wild optimism about the future of the technology. Almost half of the plants ordered during 1964–1966, the years just before and during the Carlin-Hoehn analysis, were sold on fixed-price terms, with substantial subsidies from vendors seeking to increase their share of an exploding new market. The *average* plant being ordered in those years was more than three times the size of any that had yet been built, accompanied by exaggerated hopes about the declining costs that would come with growth.[79]

In 1967 the federal Atomic Energy Commission predicted that there would be 1,000 nuclear plants in operation by the year 2000, a prediction that turned out to be almost ten times too high. Although 196 nuclear plants were ordered by electric utilities between 1967 and 1974, many of the later orders were cancelled.[80] After 1974, the energy crisis and resulting price hikes brought an abrupt halt to the growth in demand for electricity, and hence diminished interest in building new plants. Meanwhile, the seemingly endless series of hazards, accidents, and near misses at nuclear plants led to one expensive requirement for redesign after another. Each safety problem appeared to be controllable, at an additional cost—with the result that costs were steadily driven upward.

A 1997 analysis of nuclear power offered a retrospective evaluation of early cost forecasts:

> The magnitude of nuclear cost forecasting errors [before 1970] was extraordinary. Nuclear plants persistently cost about twice the inflation adjusted price predicted when they were purchased. The last forty-three plants coming on line in the U.S. (1983–present) cost . . . more than six times the constant dollar sum projected in the mid-sixties, and generate electricity at . . . more than five times the average rate predicted from 1963–1972.[81]

What the RAND analysis of the Grand Canyon essentially did was to compare the proposed dams to new reactors at 1960s fantasy prices. The result was that the reactors were slightly—not enormously—cheaper, so the dams narrowly failed the cost-benefit test. In the first version of the Carlin-Hoehn analysis, the Marble Canyon dam had a benefit-cost ratio of 0.95 (that is, a reactor at fantasy prices was just 5 percent cheaper than the dam), while Hualapai had a ratio of 0.86 (a reactor beat this dam by 14 percent). Subsequent revisions lowered the ratios; in what appears to be the final version, published after the dams had been defeated, the ratios were 0.76 for Marble Canyon and 0.61 for Hualapai.[82]

Even the Sierra Club, an organization that is in general strongly opposed to nuclear power, was briefly disoriented by the mirage of the cheap nuclear alternative. As David Brower, the head of the Sierra Club at the time, said in an interview recalling the battle over the Grand Canyon, "Alan Carlin, who was of the Rand Corporation, an economist, began to feed numbers into the system that were devastating. The principal argument that Larry Moss [a nuclear engineer working for the Sierra Club] was coming up with was we could go to nuclear instead. I was trapped in that briefly, but got out of that trap."[83] At the height of the debate, in the

Sierra Club Bulletin of May 1966—described as the "Grand Canyon issue"—editor Hugh Nash wrote, in arguing against the dams, "Cheaper electricity is available from other sources. . . . A nuclear power plant in New Jersey will produce power for 4 mills (compared with the dam's 5.3 mills) by 1969. . . . Proponents of the dams try to make out that nuclear power is still pie in the sky. Not so. The TVA has contracted for a nuclear power plant which . . . will generate power for only 2.37 mills per kilowatt-hour."[84]

The RAND cost-benefit analysis involved many technical details; however, the decisive economic data were the capital costs of constructing the dams, on the one hand, and equivalent-sized nuclear plants, on the other. In each case the huge one-time costs were converted to annual charges, assuming that the construction costs would be paid back over the lifetime of the facility—just as a mortgage converts the one-time cost of buying a house to a series of payments over many years. In the RAND analysis, the "mortgage payments" on the construction cost amounted to two-thirds or more of the annual cost of owning and operating either the dams or the nuclear plants.

In the final revision of their analysis of the dams, Carlin and Hoehn estimated the capital cost of building the dams, in 2003 dollars, at a total of $4.27 billion, or $2,186 per kilowatt of electrical generating capacity.[85] The capital cost of equivalent nuclear power plants, they thought, would be less than a third as much: about $1.3 billion total, or a mere $665 per kilowatt of capacity.[86] The Carlin-Hoehn prediction of nuclear costs is very much in line with other forecasts from the mid-1960s, as seen in figure 2.1. Forecasts from that era averaged $657 per kilowatt, virtually identical to the Carlin-Hoehn guess.[87] That is to say, the RAND study appeared to rely on the "sound science" of its day, but failed to notice—along with most of its contemporaries—that that "science" was unusually reliant on wishful thinking rather than hard data.

The analysis of the Grand Canyon occurred just before the rapid escalation in the costs of nuclear power. By 1969–1972, forecasts of nuclear costs had risen more than 25 percent, to $838 per kilowatt; even this moderate increase would have eliminated most or all of the projected economic advantages of nuclear power over the dams. Two years later, in 1973–1974, forecasts of nuclear costs had jumped to $1,538 per kilowatt, more than double the mid-1960s level. Redoing the RAND analysis with

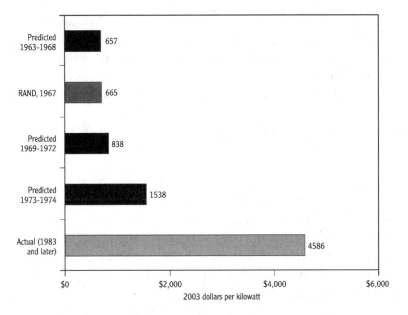

FIGURE 2.1   **Nuclear Plant Capital Costs: Predicted versus Actual. Source (except RAND): Cohn, *Too Cheap to Meter*, p. 105.**

this figure would clearly reverse the benefit/cost ratio. That is, using the cost estimates available six to eight years after the RAND study, the same methodology would end up agreeing with the Bureau of Reclamation (and common sense) that big dams are the cheapest way to generate electricity, if that is all that matters.

Furthermore, as figure 2.1 shows, nuclear costs continued to rise well beyond the level of the 1973–1974 forecasts. The last plants completed—those that came on line in 1983 or later—had average capital costs of $4,586 per kilowatt, almost seven times the RAND estimate. (All costs cited here have been converted to 2003 dollars, so these increases are not due to inflation.)

An Expensive Aqueduct Runs through It

The dams were defeated, but not the Central Arizona Project, which they were supposed to finance. Indeed, the Central Arizona Project was approved by Congress, without dams or other visible revenue sources, in 1968. The aqueduct is 336 miles long and 80 feet wide. Construction started in 1973 and finished in 1993 at cost of more than $4 billion, of which $1.6 billion will be paid back to the federal government by users over the first fifty years of operation.[88] Unless water levels are above average, the Colorado may not have enough water for all the commitments that have been made to Arizona, other states, and Mexico; the water that is supposed to flow through the expensive aqueduct may not always be there.[89]

As if taking the RAND analysis to heart, the huge Palo Verde nuclear plant was built in Arizona, not long after the defeat of the dams. Construction began in 1976 and finished in 1988. The cost, according to the plant's operators, was $2,608 per kilowatt in 2003 dollars, or almost four times the RAND projection.[90] At this price, needless to say, nuclear power was more expensive by far than the dams would have been, and also more expensive than the thermal power plants that the Bureau of Reclamation offered as the next best alternative to the dams.

In the end, the Grand Canyon was preserved for future generations to see, as Theodore Roosevelt urged. In the more prosaic present, however, there were large numbers of people who wanted water and electricity provided in an inhospitable environment. Damming the Grand Canyon was unmistakably the cheapest, but not the best, way to provide these services to central Arizona. (Important questions about the wisdom, and the sustainability, of urban development in the midst of a desert lie just beyond the scope of this discussion.)

The RAND analysis that was instrumental in saving the Grand Canyon was right for the wrong reasons, erring spectacularly in favor of one environmental objective only by drastically underestimating another environmental problem. A cost-benefit analysis of the Grand Canyon performed today would include new categories of non-use value: what is the mere existence of the Grand Canyon worth to people who may or may not use (i.e., visit) it? What is the value of the opportunity to pass it on to the next generation? Yet the calculation of huge existence values for unique natural wonders such as the Grand Canyon introduces a new set of problems into cost-benefit analysis. Estimates of these values differ widely, with similar survey questions about the dollar value of major national parks eliciting answers that differ by almost 100 to 1 between one academic study and the next.[91] Existence values are important, but they do not bear much resemblance to prices; they are real, but they are not really numbers.[92]

If you support the preservation of the Grand Canyon, how would you react to a study showing that the benefits of the Canyon, including its existence value to the American people, were twenty percent lower than the benefits of damming it for hydroelectric development? Would you accept this as scientific proof that the Grand Canyon should in fact be dammed, despite your personal preferences? Or would you insist that the value of its existence must have been underestimated, because you know that it is worth more than that? The former answer is difficult to imagine, but the latter implies that there is no empirical information conveyed by estimates of existence value. Rather, existence values offer only an awkward translation of independently established conclusions into the artificially constrained language of economics.

The cost-benefit analysts of the 1960s, of course, knew nothing about the theoretical dilemmas and measurement problems surrounding existences values. It is fortunate, in retrospect, that they knew equally little about the economics of nuclear power.

Vinyl Chloride in the Workplace

> There is little dispute that [vinyl chloride] is carcinogenic to man and we so conclude. However, the precise level of exposure which poses a hazard and the question of whether a 'safe' exposure level exists cannot be definitively answered on the record. Nor is it clear to what extent exposures can be feasibly reduced. We cannot wait until indisputable answers to these questions are available, because lives of employees are at stake.
>
> Occupational Safety and Health Administration, 1974[93]

> That some must die so that all can eat is one thing; that some must die so that all can have see-through food packaging is another.
>
> David D. Doniger[94]

Polyvinyl chloride, also known as vinyl or PVC, is a ubiquitous plastic, used in plumbing, siding, toys, car interiors, medical equipment, and countless other products. Vinyl chloride, the chemical building block from which PVC is made, is a known human carcinogen.[95] Because vinyl chloride can be emitted, either in plants where it is made or where it is used to make PVC, workers in those plants are at risk of hazardous exposures on the job.[96]

In 1974 the Occupational Safety and Health Administration (OSHA) adopted a strict new standard that sharply reduced allowable workplace exposure to vinyl chloride. Consistent with its governing statute, the agency did not justify the rule on the basis of a cost-benefit analysis. Rather, the strict exposure limit was based on the level OSHA determined industry could meet—or, in the words of the statute, the "feasible" limit.[97] The agency acted in response to a series of deaths attributable to vinyl chloride exposure, combined with disturbing new information on carcinogenicity of vinyl chloride in laboratory animals. OSHA acted on precautionary grounds, taking action when evidence of harm began to appear without waiting for precise, definitive quantification of the expected effects.

In the years since then, data have accumulated to confirm the toxicity of low doses of vinyl chloride, and on the range of organs affected by vinyl chloride exposures. These data have repeatedly confirmed the wisdom of OSHA's action. It is clear in retrospect that OSHA was right to regulate vinyl chloride exposure strictly. But what would have happened if OSHA had used cost-benefit analysis to make its decision, using the data that were available at that time? If performed in the manner favored today, such an analysis would have guided OSHA in the wrong direction, justifying little if any regulatory action.

Incriminating Evidence

Laboratory experiments documented the toxicity of vinyl chloride as early as 1925, and a range of adverse effects were documented in people in the 1930s and 1940s.[98] In the 1950s, Dow Chemical found that inhalation exposure to vinyl chloride damaged the liver and kidneys of laboratory animals; the company took steps to decrease employees' exposures, but did not inform them of the hazard. Two men died after acute inhalation exposure to vinyl chloride in 1960.[99] In the mid-1960s, industry researchers found that many vinyl chloride workers suffered from a disease they named acroosteolysis—a painful and disabling disease affecting bones and connective tissue, especially in the hands.[100] Industry worked actively to hide the link between vinyl chloride and acroosteolysis from the public.[101]

The industry had established its own standard for vinyl chloride exposure in 1954, limiting the "time-weighted average" over the course of a workday to 500 parts per million (ppm), but allowing short-term exposures above that limit.[102] In 1967, as evidence of the hazards of vinyl chloride continued to grow, industry lowered its standard to a 200 ppm time-weighted average and 500 ppm absolute exposure limit.[103] OSHA, which was founded in 1970, initially adopted the industry standard for vinyl chloride in 1971; the agency's first in-depth review of the issue came in 1974.[104]

Evidence about the effects of vinyl chloride on human health also continued to accumulate, in particular concerning one uncommon form of cancer, angiosarcoma of the liver. It is a rare disease; in the 1970s there were only twenty to thirty cases per year of angiosarcoma in the United States.[105] The disease is strongly associated with vinyl chloride exposure, occurring among PVC workers at 400–3,000 times the rate in the general population.[106] In January 1974, B.F. Goodrich announced the death of three PVC workers from angiosarcoma of the liver.[107] This disclosure tipped the balance, making it clear to regulators that workers were dying from vinyl chloride exposure.

At the same time, other serious evidence about the health effects of vinyl chloride was bursting into public view. Data linking vinyl chloride to cancers in laboratory animals were first presented at a conference in 1970.[108] An Italian scientist, Perluigi Viola, published data in 1971 showing that rats exposed to high doses of vinyl chloride developed a variety of tumors. Meanwhile, another Italian researcher, Cesare Maltoni, had been hired by the European chemical industry to conduct additional tests on vinyl chloride. In 1972 he found that kidney and liver cancers appeared in laboratory animals exposed to 250 ppm vinyl chloride—that is, at half the short-term exposure limit accepted at the time. The American and European industries entered a secrecy agreement to prevent public circulation of this new information.[109] But more damaging information continued to appear. By the time of a public hearing held by OSHA in 1974, Maltoni presented evidence of carcinogenicity in animals exposed to levels as low as 50 ppm of vinyl chloride.[110]

In response, OSHA issued an emergency standard in April 1974, requiring companies to keep vinyl chloride levels at or below 50 ppm. OSHA then held hearings to determine what the permanent standard for occupational vinyl chloride exposure should be. The agency initially proposed a standard of "no detectable level" of vinyl chloride in air; industry vigorously opposed this proposal, arguing it would force factories to shut down. Over the course of the hearings, thousands of pages of testimony were submitted from industry, unions, and occupational health experts. Industry representatives argued that low levels of vinyl chloride exposure had not been demonstrated to harm human health and that strict regulation of the carcinogen would put factories out of business. Labor and health advocates argued for stronger regulation. OSHA issued a permanent standard for occupational vinyl chloride exposure in October 1974, setting a maximum allowable exposure level of 1 ppm averaged over an eight-hour period. The standard was a slight retreat from the "no detectable level" proposal, in response to industry objections.[111] However, 1 ppm was the next strongest vinyl chloride standard considered by the agency, and a huge improvement over previous standards.

What OSHA Knew

At the time of OSHA's decision, substantial incriminating evidence was available on the carcinogenicity of vinyl chloride, but many questions remained unanswered. OSHA's success in regulating vinyl chloride depended on the agency's willingness to take precautionary action in the face of uncertainty. Had the agency attempted to estimate a monetary value for the likely benefits of reducing vinyl chloride exposure, it would have had difficulty making the case for the regulation. Much of the information required for the "benefits" side of the balance sheet was simply unknown at the time of OSHA's decision.

For example, OSHA had no firm estimate of how many people had been or would be killed by angiosarcoma of the liver resulting from vinyl chloride exposure. There was not enough information available, either from the Italian studies or from the U.S. fatalities, to draw a dose-response curve. OSHA was aware of carcinogenic hazards to other organs, including the lung, kidney, brain, and skin, as well as some noncancer effects,[112] but the agency possessed little epidemiological data on the relationship of these other disorders to vinyl chloride exposure in humans. The extent of OSHA's knowledge about the applicability of animal data to human health was also limited. It would not have been possible, in other words, to quantify the expected health impacts resulting from a given exposure level. Quantifying effects, however, is exactly what cost-benefit analysis requires. In the absence of hard estimates of the magnitudes involved, many benefits would typically be omitted from a cost-benefit analysis—in effect, valued at zero.

Although precise quantitative estimates of impacts were not available, important aspects of both laboratory (animal) and epidemiological (human) evidence were available to OSHA in 1974. Animal evidence available to OSHA at the time of the ruling included data from Cesare Maltoni and others showing high levels of cancer in laboratory animals exposed to concentrations as low as 50 ppm of vinyl chloride. In one set of experiments, 200 mice were exposed to 50 ppm of vinyl chloride in air for eleven months; half of them died.[113] In short, the allowable exposure level established by OSHA's emergency action in early 1974 was still high enough to kill laboratory animals within months.

On top of the laboratory evidence, OSHA also knew that vinyl chloride workers were dying. There were at least thirteen confirmed cases of angiosarcoma of the liver, which had led to deaths at B.F. Goodrich, Union Carbide, Firestone Plastics, and Goodyear Tire & Rubber.[114] In OSHA's view, the link between cancer and vinyl chloride was clear from these animal and human data.[115]

What OSHA did not have was any hard information on the effects of vinyl chloride exposure below 50 ppm. The industry presented arguments that an exposure threshold for tumor induction had been identified; OSHA discussed and rejected this view.[116] Instead, OSHA's final ruling cited the conclusion of the Surgeon General's ad hoc committee, which found that "safe exposure levels for carcinogenic substances cannot be scientifically determined," and noted that testimony provided by the National Institute for Occupational Safety and Health (NIOSH) also supported the view that no safe threshold could be defined.[117] Retreating under industry pressure from the "no detectable level" standard favored by NIOSH and others on scientific grounds, OSHA adopted the next best option.

Vinyl Chloride since 1974

In the years following OSHA's decision, scientists have continued to collect information on the health effects of vinyl chloride exposure, and have continued to document the growing numbers of people affected. For example, a 1976 article documented an increased likelihood of birth defects in populations living near vinyl chloride polymerization facilities.[118] A 1977 article presented evidence suggesting that non-occupational exposure routes, such as living near a polymerization or fabrication plant, might also play a role in causing angiosarcoma of the liver.[119] A 1980 review article found that research since the OSHA ruling had shown vinyl chloride to be carcinogenic to other organs, including the brain and lung.[120] A 1985 article supported a link between vinyl chloride exposure and testicular damage in laboratory animals.[121] An epidemiological study published in 1990 linked vinyl chloride exposure to human liver tumors other than angiosarcoma.[122]

In summary, since OSHA's 1974 ruling, the evidence on health hazards associated with vinyl chloride exposure has steadily mounted. In retrospect, we know that vinyl chloride exposure posed severe hazards to workers—and the communities around the manufacturing plants—even at low doses. OSHA acted decisively on the incriminating information that was already available at the time of the ruling; subsequent history has shown that the costs of inaction would have been even higher than OSHA knew at the time. With this history in mind, in the next section we look at what might have transpired if OSHA had relied on formal cost-benefit analysis to arrive at its decision.

Cost-Benefit Analysis

If OSHA had used cost-benefit analysis to evaluate its options in 1974, what would the result have been? For cost-benefit analysis, we need dollar values. On the cost side, OSHA had access to a variety of estimates. Industry representatives had put forward several estimates of what it would cost to reduce workplace vinyl chloride exposure. In addition, OSHA commissioned an independent study, by the consulting firm Foster D. Snell, to gauge the likely costs of several regulatory options.[123]

OSHA's consultant analyzed the costs of several regulatory options, but did not produce estimates for the cost of the 1 ppm standard that was ultimately adopted. For a somewhat looser standard, they estimated annual compliance costs of $109 million.[124] A widely cited account of the regulation, published in 1995 by the U.S. Office of Technology Assessment, says that the best information available to OSHA implied that the cost of the 1 ppm standard would be $1 billion.[125] It appears likely that this is a total cost for conversion, not an annual cost.[126] If so, it implies an annual compliance cost of roughly $200 million.[127] Had OSHA carried out a cost-benefit analysis, we assume it would have relied on a figure of about $200 million for annual costs.

At the time of the ruling, OSHA lacked much of the data on benefits that cost-benefit analysts would rely on today. The agency noted that about three-quarters of the employees with the highest vinyl chloride exposure had not been located; that the average latency period for development of liver cancers appeared to be twenty years; and that the dose-response relationship for angiosarcoma of the liver was not known. For all these reasons, there was no way to determine the total number of people who would ultimately be affected. Evidence on other cancers or non-cancer diseases caused by vinyl chloride was even less complete. In many cost-benefit analyses, benefits with such inadequate data are routinely ignored, on the grounds that they are impossible to quantify.

However, even in the absence of hard data on benefits, it is possible to do the calculation in reverse: what estimates would have been needed for the regulation to pass a cost-benefit test? The principal benefit is the reduction in deaths caused by vinyl chloride exposure; how many lives would OSHA have had to think it was saving to justify an annual cost of $200 million? That is, if human lives were expressed as dollar values and placed on one side of the scale, how many lives would it take to balance out $200 million in expenses for the industries using vinyl chloride?

The calculation can be done either with recent estimates of the dollar value of a life, or with the much lower estimates that were common back in 1974. The highest value of a life that has been widely employed for regulatory analysis is EPA's estimate of $4.8 million in 1990 dollars, which was used in a number of decisions in the late 1990s.[128] This value was based largely on statistical analysis of the wage differentials between slightly more and less dangerous jobs. Adjusted forward for ten years of inflation, $4.8 million in 1990 dollars is equivalent to $6.3 million in 2000 dollars, the value discussed in chapter 1. If similarly adjusted backward for inflation between 1974 and 1990, the same value of a human life would have equaled $1.81 million in 1974 dollars. Thus, to break even against a $200 million cost in 1974, OSHA's standard would have had to save about 110 human lives per year.

The revelations that spurred OSHA into action involved thirteen cases of vinyl chloride workers who died of angiosarcoma. In retrospect, this is not an unreasonable estimate for the annual death rate from angiosarcoma of the liver caused by vinyl chloride exposure.[129] It would have been impossible for OSHA to argue that more than 100 workers were dying of angiosarcoma each year; and data were not available on any other causes of death linked to vinyl chloride. Therefore, cost-benefit analysis would have supported the industry contention that the benefits of strict regulation of workplace exposure did not justify the expense.

The above calculation is only one version of what a cost-benefit analysis might have looked like. Another variant would have argued even more strongly against the regulation. The crucial estimate of $1.81 million per life is a modern figure transported back in time. At the time of the OSHA decision, in 1974, the wage-risk calculations used to value life in the 1990s were not yet widely accepted; much lower values of life were in use for cost-benefit calculations. In the infamous calculation in the Ford Pinto controversy,[130] which occurred at about the same time, Ford's economists cited government agency estimates of the value of a life of only $200,000, based largely on lost earnings.[131] If OSHA had actually tried to do a cost-benefit analysis in 1974, it might easily have ended up using the "Pinto value" of $200,000 per life. With this value per life, a regulation would need to save 1,000 human lives per year to break even against a $200 million cost.

A total of about 1,500 workers were employed in vinyl chloride production in 1974, and about another 5,600 worked in PVC resin production, for a total of just over 7,000 in the affected industries.[132] So to support OSHA's regulation with a cost-benefit analysis using the Pinto value, it would have been necessary to show that one of every seven workers in the industry would have died from vinyl chloride exposure each year in the absence of regulation.

If the agency had discounted future benefits, the number of deaths required to support the regulation would have been even larger. The average latency period for angiosarcoma cases is about twenty years. If the value of a human life is discounted at a 3 percent discount rate over the average twenty-year delay before the diagnosis of fatal cancer, then each life becomes worth only 55 percent as much:[133] the $1.81 million "modern value" drops to a present value of $1 million, while the $200,000 Pinto value shrinks to $110,000. At these rates, about 200 deaths per year in the former case, or around 2,000 in the latter, would have to be averted for the policy to be worth its billion-dollar price tag. A higher discount rate, which analysts commonly used at the time, would have reduced the present value of the fatalities even more, raising the number of averted deaths required to "justify" the regulation even further beyond the bounds of plausibility. At a 7 percent discount rate, the break-even number of avoided deaths is about 400 per year with the modern value of life, or 4,000 with the Pinto value. At a 10 percent discount rate, the break-even point jumps to roughly 700 with the modern value, or 7,000—the entire workforce of the industry—with the Pinto value. That is, using a 10 percent discount rate and the value of life estimated in the 1970s, it would be necessary to show that every worker in the industry, every year, would have died in the absence of the standard, to justify the regulation in cost-benefit terms.

The report by OSHA's consultants included estimated costs for more lenient standards, with ceilings of 10, 25, or 50 ppm of vinyl chloride in the air. These would have required smaller, but still substantial, numbers of avoidable deaths to justify their adoption in cost-benefit terms. With the number of known deaths in the low two figures, cost-benefit calculations would have indicated that even these standards were too expensive for the meager benefits that would be achieved.

An Unexpected Bargain

As it turned out, the advance estimate of the costs of reducing vinyl chloride exposure was just that: an estimate. Producers quickly adopted innovative technologies that made it much easier to limit vinyl chloride in air. A 1978 study estimated that the industry had spent only $20 million per year—a tenth of the predicted value—on compliance in the four years since the rule was passed.[134] A former economist at the U.S. Department of Labor concluded that the actual cost of complying with the standard was only 7 percent of the predicted cost.[135] According to a later retrospective overview by the Office of Technology Assessment, the total cost of compliance with the regulation was about a quarter of what had been estimated, and none of the producers were driven out of the industry by regulatory costs.[136] Whether the actual costs were 7 percent, a tenth, or a quarter of the original estimate, it is clear that compliance costs were a fraction of the best guess OSHA was able to come up with in advance. Meanwhile, our knowledge of the benefits continues to grow as the evidence accumulates on a wide variety of disorders associated with vinyl chloride exposure. OSHA did not know any of this at the time of the ruling; but its precautionary decision has been vindicated by the science, as well as the economic information, that has accumulated since 1974.

Cost-benefit analysis would have argued strongly against OSHA's prescient regulation; once again, it would have been wrong in retrospect.

Conclusion: Wrong Every Time

If EPA had been required to conduct a cost-benefit analysis before taking lead out of gasoline, the agency might never have acted. Ironically, that would have meant that the famous 1980s cost-benefit analysis of removing lead from gasoline would never have happened either, because there would have been no data on falling levels of lead in children's blood. Likewise, cost-benefit calculations with realistic nuclear costs would have led the RAND analysts to the obvious conclusion that they happily and mistakenly missed: big dams are a very cheap way to generate electricity, if that is all that matters. And cost-benefit analysis would have shown that vinyl chloride regulation was too expensive for the benefits it produced. It would seemingly have been optimal, in cost-benefit terms, to have allowed more workers to die of cancer every year in order to have cheaper vinyl siding on the market.

Our country has enacted many farsighted, protective laws and regulations governing public health and the environment. Economic analysis has sometimes played an important supporting role in improving these regulations. But economics has not been the gatekeeper, allowed to make the final decision on which regulations will take effect and which will not. A rigid insistence on making regulations pass cost-benefit tests would, in retrospect, have gotten the wrong answer time after time. There is no reason to expect the same narrow methods to perform any better today.

Chapter 3

The Unbearable Lightness of Regulatory Costs

Will unbearable regulatory costs ruin the U.S. economy? That threat is repeated, often enough, by critics of environmental protection. The supposed need for cost-benefit analysis, the problematic technique discussed in the previous two chapters, flows from the belief that numerous unaffordable proposals are high on the public agenda. On this view, hardheaded economic calculation is required to save us from naïve attempts to protect more of health and nature than we can pay for. Fears of the purported costs of regulation have been used to justify a sweeping reorganization of regulatory practice, in which the Office of Management and Budget (OMB) is empowered to, and often enough does, reject regulations from other agencies on the basis of intricate, conjectural economic calculations.

This chapter argues for a different perspective: what is remarkable about regulatory costs is not their heavy economic burden, but rather their lightness. There are two broad reasons to doubt that there is a significant trade-off between prosperity and regulation: first, regulatory costs are frequently too small to matter; and second, even if the costs were larger, reducing them would not always improve economic outcomes.

Two Arguments against the Trade-off

In theory, it would unquestionably be possible to spend so much on environmental protection that basic economic needs could not be met. At a sufficiently high level of regulatory expenditures, protecting nature and cleaning up the air and water *could* absorb enough of society's resources to compete with the provision of more fundamental goods, such as food and shelter. From this it is a short leap to the conclusion that the clash between economy and environment actually *is* an urgent problem, requiring detailed analysis of regulations to prevent worsening the terms of the trade-off. But the latter statement follows logically only if environmental policy is in fact consuming substantial resources that are transferable to other, more basic needs. That is, the assumed urgency of the trade-off rests on the implicit assumptions that the costs of environmental protection are both large and fungible. Either of these assumptions could fail in practice:

- The costs of environmental protection could be nonexistent, or too small to matter; or
- Reduction of regulatory costs might not produce the desired economic benefits.

Environmental Protection with Little or No Costs

Costless environmental improvement is frequently assumed to be impossible by definition. The hidden premise underlying this form of the trade-off argument is that the market economy is already performing as well as possible. From this perspective, any new expenditure on environmental protection necessarily represents a loss, because it diverts resources away from the things that consumers in their wisdom have chosen for themselves.

Reverence for market outcomes is at odds with the beliefs of many environmental practitioners, who assume that environmental improvements can bring economic benefits as well. The rhetoric of joint economic and environmental progress includes such overused imagery as "win-win solutions," the "double [or triple] bottom line," and opportunities to pick the "low-hanging fruit." The ubiquity of these phrases underscores the extent to which the market appears to be improvable—implying that it could not have already been at an optimum.

In a more academic vein, the Porter hypothesis maintains that carefully crafted, moderately demanding regulations can improve economic competitiveness and success in the marketplace.[1] Likewise, studies of energy conservation and greenhouse gas reduction frequently find opportunities for energy savings at zero or negative net cost, as in the "no regrets" options for climate change mitigation.[2] The critique of these opportunities is not that they are undesirable; who could argue with free environmental improvements? Rather, economists have argued that, in their own overused metaphors, there are no free lunches, nor $20 bills on the sidewalk. If lunch is expensive and the sidewalk is bare, then the Porter hypothesis must be impossible, and there must be hidden costs associated with energy conservation.

Without attempting a thorough review of this debate, it seems plausible that there are significant cases in which essentially costless energy savings and other environmental improvements are possible. In such cases, the fears of regulatory cost burdens and concerns about trade-offs are presumably easy to resolve; there should be a broad consensus supporting the adoption of costless improvements.

However, literally costless improvements are not the only ones to escape from the trade-off; economic constraints do not immediately become relevant to real decisions as soon as regulatory costs are greater than zero. Very small costs of regulation presumably have very small impacts on the economy. Regulations could easily have costs that are too small to matter—and the next few sections will suggest that this is the case in many important instances. The theoretical consensus that supports costless environmental improvement may vanish once costs become positive, however small; but practical concerns about economic impacts need not arise until costs become large in some meaningful sense.

The question naturally arises: what counts as large? Here it is important to resist the illusion of superficially big numbers. Quantities in the billions, which are commonplace in federal programs and nationwide impact assessments, are essentially impossible to understand in isolation. Some standard of comparison is needed to bring them down to a comprehensible scale. (A million seconds is about twelve days; a billion seconds is about thirty-two years.) Amounts in the billions of dollars are inevitably thought of as part of a ratio: if x billion dollars is the numerator, what is the appropriate denominator? When none is specified, the default denominator tends to be the listener's personal finances—in which case one or a few billion looks very large indeed.

In contrast, a penny per person per day sounds small. But for the United States, with its population of about 300 million, a penny per person per day and a total of $1 billion per year are roughly the same. Per capita impacts, as in this example, are sometimes appropriate, particularly when the costs in question are spread across the population as a whole. Comparison to the revenues of the affected industry is also a useful standard for evaluating regulatory impacts. For issues affecting the entire United States (or the European Union), or even a large industry, a few billion dollars (or euros) per year is not a large number.

Environmental Costs that Cannot Be Traded for Economic Gains

Even when environmental policies impose noticeable economic costs, it does not necessarily follow that these costs could be traded for greater private incomes and consumption, or for the benefits that are thought to accompany higher incomes. There are two strands to this unfamiliar argument, presented below, and briefly anticipated here.

First, deregulation might not produce increased economic growth. If a regulation or other environmental policy has measurable economic costs, it consumes resources such as labor and capital that could have been used elsewhere in the economy. The policy, then, can only be "traded" for whatever those resources could have produced elsewhere—in economic terms, the opportunity cost of those resources.

During a recession, labor and capital are typically less than fully employed. Supplying more of resources that are already in surplus may not produce anything more; the short run opportunity cost of additional resources could be zero. On the other hand, during expansions such as that of the late 1990s, the Federal Reserve carefully controls the level of employment and rate of growth; making more resources available for increased growth might just lead the Fed to step harder on the brakes to maintain the (unchanged) target pace of expansion. Again, the short-run opportunity cost of additional resources could be zero.

Second, economic growth may not produce the expected or desired benefits. An increasingly common style of analysis converts regulatory costs into health and mortality impacts, based on correlations between income and health. In the extreme, regulatory costs that are thought to lower market incomes have been labeled "statistical murder," because richer people live longer.

This line of argument is flawed in several respects. Perhaps the most dramatic response to the "statistical murder" story is the epidemiological evidence that mortality decreases in recessions. If deregulation leads to economic growth, which boosts employment, the expected result is paradoxically not a reduction in mortality.

In the long run, the availability of resources such as labor and capital must have something to do with growth rates, economic opportunities, and improvements in health and welfare. However, the relationship is a subtler and more tenuous one than is often recognized.

The Low Cost of Regulating Europe's Chemicals

Expensive regulations are less likely to be adopted in the United States at present, both because of exaggerated fears about regulatory costs and because of a commitment to hands-off, market-oriented policies. Examples of more expensive regulations may be easier to find elsewhere, such as in the European Union (EU). Regulation has a better name in the EU than in the U.S.; government-imposed constraints on private business that are taken for granted in Brussels would be immediately dismissed as beyond the pale in Washington.

REACH (Registration, Evaluation, and Authorization of CHemicals), Europe's new chemicals policy, is one of the EU's most ambitious and demanding environmental regulations; it is explored in greater detail in chapters 10–12. Adopted in 2006, REACH requires chemical manufacturers and importers to register and test their chemicals for safety. During the eleven-year phase-in period, some 30,000 chemicals will be registered and tested. Depending on the outcome of the tests, some chemicals (probably a very small minority) may be subject to partial or complete restrictions on their use in Europe. An appeals procedure allows economic and other arguments to be raised against restrictions on the use of a chemical.

As in the United States, industry groups have claimed that the costs of regulation will be prohibitive. A German industry federation commissioned a study that presented lengthy calculations purporting to show that REACH would devastate German industry as a whole.[3] A French industry group sponsored another study, released only in the form of PowerPoint slides, claiming that France, too, would be flattened by REACH.[4]

Studies done without industry funding have reached very different conclusions, as explained in chapter 10, finding that the costs of REACH would be much lower, and entirely manageable. The estimated costs of registration and testing total just a few billion euros, or less than one euro per person per year over the eleven-year phase-in of REACH. Perhaps a better standard of comparison is that the cost, if fully passed on to customers, would increase the average prices of the European chemical industry by less than 0.1 percent. This is, by any reasonable standard, a very small price change.

U.S. industry and government have been emphatic in their opposition to REACH, issuing alarmist predictions of its possible impact on the United States. (These, too, are greatly exaggerated; at worst, as discussed in chapter 12, U.S. companies exporting to Europe might face the same percentage cost increase as European companies. A small percentage is a small percentage, whether it is expressed in euros or in dollars.) It seems safe to say that no recent U.S. regulations have approached the ambition or scope of REACH. If one of Europe's most demanding regulations will increase prices by less than 0.1 percent, imagine how much less the costs will be for the timid proposals that still pass muster in Washington.

Pollution Havens: Theory versus Reality[5]

If regulatory costs imposed significant burdens on the economy, it should be easy to find their footprints. Because the costs are not uniformly distributed, there should be dramatic extremes where regulations have trod most heavily on the human landscape. Companies that have closed because of environmental costs, moving to other countries where the regulatory climate was more lenient; workers thrown out of jobs by rigid environmental strictures; formerly prosperous communities shut down by the economic burdens of command-and-control regulation—they should be all around us. If the fabled regulations of mass destruction exist, there is no way to hide them in a bunker; they should be visible for all to see. But the actual, identifiable examples of jobs lost to regulations rarely extend beyond a handful of stories about small numbers of workers in the most directly environmentally damaging, rural industries such as logging and coal mining.

The economic impacts of environmental regulations have been intensively studied for years. As Eban Goodstein has demonstrated, there is no evidence that significant numbers of jobs or businesses have ever been lost for environmental reasons.[6] Companies don't move, between states or between countries, to avoid expensive environmental standards, because environmental standards aren't that expensive. Environmental compliance costs are above 2 percent of industry revenues only in a handful of the most polluting industries; Goodstein cited a maximum of 7 percent for pulp mills. Among the reasons for major layoffs, as reported by the U.S. Bureau of Labor Statistics, environmental- and safety-related shutdowns are among the least common, accounting for about 0.1 percent of job losses.[7] Contrary to predictions, the Clean Air Act Amendments of 1990 did not destroy jobs; the same is true for the stringent local air quality regulations imposed by the South Coast Air Quality Management District in southern California. A study of the South Coast regulations concluded, "In contrast to the widespread belief that environmental regulation costs jobs, the most severe episode of air-quality regulation of industry in the [United States] probably created a few jobs."[8]

Economists have carried out extensive studies of the "pollution haven hypothesis," that is, the notion that polluting industries will flee to countries with lax environmental standards. The results have been almost entirely negative. A 1995 review of the literature on the subject concluded:

> Overall, there is relatively little evidence to support the hypothesis that environmental regulations have had a large adverse effect on competitiveness, however that elusive term is defined. . . . Studies attempting to measure the effect of environmental regulation on net exports, overall trade flows, and plant-location decisions have produced estimates that are either small, statistically insignificant, or not robust to tests of model specification.[9]

A more recent literature review reached similar conclusions.[10] Eric Neumayer demonstrated that neither the United States nor Germany has had unusually large net outflows of investment in dirty industries; a section of his chapter on the subject is subtitled, "Why is there so little evidence for pollution havens?"[11] Brian Copeland and Scott Taylor, in a very thorough theoretical and empirical analysis of trade and the environment, concluded that "the evidence does not support the notion that trade patterns are driven by pollution haven motives."[12] Kevin Gallagher showed that the dirtiest industries in the United States have not been migrating to Mexico, either before or after the North American Free Trade Agreement; although these industries have been declining in the United States, their share of manufacturing has been declining even faster in Mexico. Moreover, a handful of major industries—steel, aluminum, and cement—appear to be cleaner (i.e., emit smaller amounts of criteria air pollutants per dollar of sales) in Mexico than in the United States. A plausible explanation for this unexpected pattern is that the Mexican plants are newer than their U.S. counterparts, and incorporate newer, cleaner technology.[13]

The economics literature is nearly, but not quite, unanimous on this question. Two recent articles found modest empirical support for the pollution haven hypothesis. Matthew Kahn and Yutaka Yoshino used intricate and indirect methods of measuring the pollution intensity of trade inside and outside of regional trading blocs. They found that for trade outside of blocs, middle-income countries tend to expand dirty exports as they grow, while high-income countries expand cleaner exports. The effect is weaker inside regional trading blocs.[14]

Matthew Cole presented complex findings on trade between the United States and Mexico, some of which support the pollution haven hypothesis.[15] On the one hand, the trade flows in both directions are becoming cleaner, but Mexico's exports to the United States are becoming cleaner (declining in air pollution intensity) faster than U.S. exports to Mexico. Since 1988, Cole found, "The pollution embodied in U.S. imports from Mexico [has been] less than that embodied in exports to Mexico and, furthermore, this gap has been widening rather than narrowing."[16] On balance, it is Mexico rather than the United States that is escaping from trade-related air pollution on the other side of the Río Grande, seemingly contradicting the pollution haven hypothesis. On the other hand, Cole also found that U.S. imports, from Mexico and from the world, are growing faster (as a share of U.S. consumption) in industries that have higher pollution abatement costs, just as the pollution haven hypothesis would suggest.

Neither of these articles found a strong effect, and neither presented a clear, easily interpreted picture of the movement of industry in response to U.S. pollution control costs. Meanwhile, the bulk of the economics literature, as described earlier, continues to suggest that a good pollution haven is hard to find.

Advance Overestimates of Regulatory Costs

By now there is a substantial literature demonstrating that the best-known claims of extraordinary costs imposed by environmental policy do not stand up to careful examination. Tales of billions of dollars spent per life saved by esoteric regulations are based on errors and misrepresentation; they represent, as Lisa Heinzerling put it, "regulatory costs of mythic proportions."[17] No attempt will be made to summarize the full extent of that literature here.

However, one aspect of the issue is worth expanding upon, namely the biases in prospective estimates of regulatory costs. Prospective estimates are, of course, all that is available when a new policy is under discussion. And the evidence is clear: the costs of environmental protection are much more often overestimated, rather than underestimated, in advance.

A classic example is the 1974 Occupational Safety and Health Administration (OSHA) standard for workplace exposure to vinyl chloride, discussed in chapter 2. Consultants to OSHA estimated the costs of reducing vinyl chloride exposure at around $1 billion; industry estimates were even higher. Actual costs turned out to be at most a quarter of OSHA's estimate, because industry quickly developed new, cost-effective technologies to comply with the regulation.[18]

As noted in chapter 1, similar patterns have been found for many environmental standards. One study found that compliance costs for environmental regulations were overestimated in advance in eleven out of twelve cases.[19] Another study, conducted by Winston Harrington et al., found that advance cost estimates for environmental compliance turned out to be more than 25 percent too high in fourteen out of twenty-eight cases, while they were more than 25 percent too low in only three of the twenty-eight cases.[20] A study for Environment Canada and the Ontario Ministry of Energy, Science, and Technology, focusing specifically on the costs of controlling chlorinated substances, confirmed that overestimation of regulatory costs is more common than underestimation.[21]

An in-depth examination of prospective cost estimates for regulations by Thomas McGarity and Ruth Ruttenberg reviewed most of these as well as quite a few other examples, and identified a series of reasons why cost estimates are biased upward in advance:[22]

- Regulators rely on regulated industries for empirical data, and the industries have a clear interest in secrecy and/or inflated cost estimates, either of which will discourage strict regulation.
- The likelihood of court challenges to strict regulations pushes agencies toward making conservative assumptions, again tilting in favor of the regulated industries.
- For lack of information, agency analyses often compare the costs of a proposed regulation to a zero regulation baseline, rather than the appropriate measurement of the incremental costs relative to existing regulations.
- Companies' reported costs of regulatory compliance sometimes include costs of upgrading other equipment at the same time that environmental controls are installed.
- Regulatory analyses frequently take a static approach, ignoring the learning curve effects, economies of scale, and regulation-induced productivity increases that may result from new environmental standards.

On the other hand, McGarity and Ruttenberg noted that there are also downward biases in cost estimates:

- There is a tendency for cost estimates to ignore indirect social costs of regulation.
- Estimates often rely on data from vendors of control technologies, who are eager to win new markets.
- There is often a failure to take sufficient account of "Murphy's law" in projecting responses to regulatory requirements.

On balance, the factors producing upward bias appear more numerous and more powerful.

The OMB Response: 2004

However, the opposite perspective has been argued in the annual reports from OMB's Office of Information and Regulatory Affairs.[23] The 2004 report devoted three pages[24] to the discussion of ex ante versus ex post regulatory cost estimates, leading with the assertion that many commenters believe costs are underestimated in advance. OMB cited three studies in support of the view that regulatory costs are typically underestimated. Yet all three simply claim that costs are large, not that advance estimates are consistently low. The details of these claims are not impressive:

- Mark Crain and Thomas Hopkins, in a consultant report for the Small Business Administration, agonized at length over the plausible idea that there are economies of scale in regulatory compliance, so that smaller firms have a higher compliance cost per employee.[25] For its estimates of environmental regulatory costs, the study used the high end of the range published by OMB. So in citing this study, OMB was effectively citing itself, not a new source of information.
- Harvey James estimated the costs of compliance with twenty-five OSHA regulations as of 1993.[26] But he also observed that the cost per firm was 5.5 times higher in a 1974 study of OSHA compliance costs done by the National Association of Manufacturers. James then simply asserted that the costs per firm could not be lower today than in 1974. On that basis, he multiplied his 1993 numbers by 5.5, thereby eliminating all empirical content in his study of 1993 costs, and simply recycling a 1974 estimate by an antiregulatory industry group.[27]
- Finally, a detailed economic modeling exercise by Dale Jorgensen and Peter Wilcoxen estimated the impact of all major environmental regulations on U.S. economic growth.[28] They stated at the outset that they had not attempted to assess any of the benefits, to consumers or to producers, of a cleaner environment. As a result, they observed, "the conclusions of this study cannot be taken to imply that pollution control is too burdensome or, for that matter, insufficiently restrictive."[29]

  Modeling costs but not benefits, they found that the growth rate of the U.S. economy was reduced by 0.19 percent as a result of regulations during 1974–1983. They analyzed a scenario involving the complete absence of regulations, including removal of all limitations on the use of high sulfur coal and all motor vehicle pollution controls. Even if one were willing to contemplate such a wholehearted embrace of smog, acid rain, and toxicity, there are two reasons why the effect on the growth rate would be smaller today: the study was based on a period when the first and largest round of spending for compliance with the Clean Air Act and the Clean Water Act was underway; and it was also a period when the dirty industries that account for most pollution control spending represented a larger fraction of the U.S. economy than at present.

The OMB Response: 2005

In its 2005 report, OMB took a different tack. In a chapter entitled "Validation of benefit cost estimates made prior to regulation," the report reviewed "47 federal rules where pre-regulation estimates of benefits and costs were made by federal agencies and some post-regulation information is published by academics or government agencies."[30] The bottom-line judgment was that overestimates of benefit-cost ratios were more common than underestimates: eleven were declared accurate (meaning that advance estimates were within 25 percent of the retrospective judgments), twenty-two advance estimates were too high, and fourteen were too low.

OMB's report was not strictly comparable to other literature on advance cost estimates. It differs from other analyses in restricting its attention to estimates made by federal agencies; many of the most controversial and politically significant estimates are made by or sponsored by industry groups. Moreover, OMB examined both costs and benefits, and found advance estimates to be too high much more often for benefits than for costs. Evaluating OMB's judgments on benefits estimates would be a substantial task, which for the most part is not undertaken here.

Despite these differences in approach, OMB's discussion of the forty-seven rules appeared to be a response to the findings of advance overestimates of costs. Even on its own terms, accepting OMB's judgments on the individual rules, the report is fundamentally unpersuasive for two reasons. First, the report did not establish a reasonable basis for inferring that federal agencies tend to overestimate; its data did not contain a statistically significant bias toward overestimates. Second, the report's main finding was entirely a result of its treatment of OSHA estimates, which raise a number of unique issues unrelated to general biases in estimates.

The choice of rules was based solely on data availability, heavily skewed by a few sources that reviewed multiple rules. OMB referred to the rules as a "convenience sample" that is not necessarily representative of federal rules in general.[31] But let us suppose for the moment that they were a true random sample of federal rules and agency estimates, and see what the sample would imply about the overall tendency to overestimate.

(Warning: The next few paragraphs involve a bit of statistical reasoning; readers who are willing to accept my conclusion that the OMB analysis failed to make its case for overestimation of regulatory costs can skip ahead to the section called "Opportunity Costs and Growth-Growth Trade-Offs.")

With eleven advance estimates accurate, twenty-two over, and fourteen under, OMB's sample is not terribly far from finding the average estimate to be accurate. Change just four of the overestimates to under, and all trace of bias would disappear. How likely is it that the appearance of bias has occurred purely by chance? For the purpose of statistical analysis, OMB's judgments can be converted to numbers: 0 for accurate, -1 for underestimates, and $+1$ for overestimates. Then the sample mean is 0.17, and the standard error is 0.13. The null hypothesis that the true mean is zero, that is, no bias, cannot be rejected, with $p = 0.19$ (meaning that the probability of this result occurring by chance alone is 0.19). In other words, if there was no bias in reality and we drew a random sample of forty-seven cases, there is a 19 percent probability that it would look at least as biased as the OMB sample.

In contrast, the Harrington et al. study mentioned earlier,[32] which found three underestimates of costs, fourteen overestimates, and eleven accurate, passes the significance test with flying colors: using the same numerical scoring, the sample mean is 0.38, with a standard error of 0.13. The null hypothesis that the true mean is zero is clearly rejected, with $p = 0.005$; there is less than a 1 percent probability of getting the Harrington et al. results by chance if there is no real bias in advance cost estimates. (Note that Harrington et al. found a tendency to overestimate regulatory *costs,* while OMB alleged a tendency to overestimate *benefit-cost ratios:* "overestimate" has opposite implications in the two contexts.)

Not only does the slight appearance of bias in the OMB study turn out to be statistically insignificant, it is also entirely the result of OMB's treatment of the thirteen OSHA rules. As shown in table 3.1, all of the tilt toward overestimates comes from the OSHA rules, for which OMB believes that overestimates of benefit-cost ratios are essentially the norm. (OSHA's 1974 vinyl chloride rule, discussed above, a famous case in which advance estimates of costs were far too high, did not make it into OMB's "convenience sample.") Among the non-OSHA rules in OMB's sample, underestimates slightly outnumber overestimates, although with p > 0.5 (see table) it is completely clear that this pattern is not statistically significant.

As can be seen from a glance at the data, there is essentially no chance that the true mean, or bias, is the same for the OSHA and non-OSHA rules (statistically, the hypothesis that the two groups have equal means is rejected with p < 0.00001).

In the end, the scant evidence of overestimates provided by OMB comes down to their treatment of the thirteen OSHA rules. In six of the thirteen cases, OMB relied on a single source, an article by Si Kyung Seong and John Mendeloff.[33] That article discussed OSHA's tendency toward prospective overestimates of benefits, suggesting several explanations. Prospective estimates from regulatory agencies typically assume complete implementation of proposed rules, whereas retrospective evaluations reflect actual, potentially incomplete implementation. The availability of data on workplace fatalities improved significantly in 1992, allowing more accurate estimates of reduced mortality attributable to regulations; nine of the thirteen OSHA rules in the OMB study were adopted before 1992. Seong and Mendeloff also suggested that OSHA is more likely to be inaccurate in analyzing less expensive rules, which normally receive less analytical effort; and they concluded that OSHA systematically overestimates the benefits of training programs.

Thus, the allegation that OSHA overestimates benefits could simply reflect the agency's beleaguered status. Ever since the Reagan administration, OSHA has been particularly hard hit by industry and conservative attacks, budget cuts, and defeats in the courts. As a result, OSHA may be more constrained and powerless than other regulatory agencies. It is all too believable that OSHA is constantly planning on complete implementation of its rules but unable to achieve it, or that it has been forced to stick to small proposals, frequently involving nothing more than training programs. According to Seong and Mendeloff, the result would be a pattern of overestimation of benefits of OSHA regulations. This is an im-

TABLE 3.1   OMB analysis of advance benefit-cost estimates.

	Number of regulations		
	Total	OSHA	All other
Advance estimates of net benefits turned out to be:			
Accurate	11	2	9
Overestimate	22	11	11
Underestimate	14	0	14
p value for no bias	0.19	0.00	0.56

portant story, but it does not justify OMB's suggestion of a pattern of systematic overestimation of benefit-cost ratios by government agencies.

Opportunity Costs and Growth-Growth Trade-Offs

The previous sections have suggested several reasons to doubt that environmental regulations impose huge economic costs. This section turns to the economic context of the debate, arguing that even if regulatory costs look significant, deregulation might produce surprisingly little additional growth and personal consumption.

The costs of regulation, of course, do not consist of goods that would be of direct use to consumers; if regulations were rolled back, it would not be helpful to simply redistribute scrubbers, filters, catalytic converters, and the like to other uses. Rather, the trade-off hypothesis must be that regulation requires the use of productive resources, principally labor and capital; in the absence of regulation, these resources *could* be used to produce consumer goods (or other desirable products). A related assumption, normally taken for granted, is that expanding the available supplies of labor and capital *would* in fact increase the production of consumer goods.[34]

Yet the truth of that related assumption is less obvious than it might seem. Suppose that deregulation occurs during a recession. In that case, unemployed labor and capital are already available on the market; indeed, that is almost the definition of a recession. It is far from certain that increasing the surplus of idle labor and capital will produce any economic benefit in the short run.

Alternatively, suppose the deregulation occurs during an economic expansion. It is becoming increasingly standard practice for the Federal

Reserve to maintain tight control of the pace of expansion, effectively preventing an acceleration of growth above a target level. In the late 1990s, for instance, economic growth was limited by Federal Reserve intervention, not by regulations, or by the availability of labor or capital. Again, an increase in available productive resources might not have led to any additional output, income, or consumption in the short run. If deregulation had put more labor and capital on the market, the Fed might have simply clamped down harder to achieve its targets.[35]

In the long run, the availability of labor and capital must have something to do with the pace of economic growth. The manner in which that long-run effect occurs, however, depends on macroeconomic mechanisms about which there is no consensus. Would additional labor and capital somehow accelerate the recovery from recession, or make the next recession less deep? In an expansion, would the Fed quickly notice that increased output is now possible without risking inflation, or would it take years—perhaps even another business cycle—for the Fed's targets to adjust to the additional resources? Both theoretical and empirical macroeconomic analysis would be required to have confidence about the answers to these questions.

A common critique of risk-reducing regulation today is that it should examine "risk-risk" trade-offs, considering not only the risk directly addressed by regulation, but also the offsetting risks that might be indirectly created by the regulation. It is equally the case that calculations involving the costs of regulation should examine the "growth-growth" trade-offs, considering not only the resources used in regulatory compliance, but the actual benefits available from using those resources elsewhere. In the short run, there may be no foregone growth at all. If the claim is that deregulation would create additional growth only in the long run, via slow, complex pathways, then the usual arguments about the need to discount future benefits would apply to this economic gain. Not only the extent of growth, but also the timing, must be calculated to determine the real opportunity cost of the resources used to comply with regulations.

Is Employment Hazardous to Your Health?

A clever rhetorical strategy has appeared in recent economic arguments for deregulation. Rather than emphasizing the monetary costs of regulation per se, critics of regulation have converted these costs into numbers of deaths that supposedly result from the expenditures. Expensive regulations can thus be charged with "statistical murder." As Lisa Heinzerling and I have argued,[36] the statistical murder theory is doubly fallacious. The correlation between income and mortality is weak in developed countries, except at very low income levels; different variants of the statistical murder story have used widely differing prices per life saved, resting on different indirect inferences from very limited data. Moreover, regulation does not remove money from the economy, so much as cause it to be spent in different sectors. Incomes decrease for those who produce and sell polluting products, but increase for those who develop, install, and operate pollution controls, monitor compliance, and research and debate regulatory options. Whether or not one considers this reallocation to be desirable, it is primarily a change in the composition, not the aggregate level, of national income.

But an even more decisive rebuttal is available. Remarkably enough, the empirical evidence on public health shows that mortality decreases during recessions, and increases as employment rises. So even if the costs of regulation were large enough to matter (despite the evidence to the contrary presented earlier in this chapter), and even if deregulation boosted economic growth and employment in the short run (despite the arguments to the contrary in the previous section), the result might well be an increased death rate.

The evidence on mortality and business cycles was presented in a symposium in the December 2005 issue of the *International Journal of Epidemiology*. The lead article, by José Tapia Granados, presented and analyzed data for the United States throughout the twentieth century.[37] Age-adjusted mortality rates are significantly, negatively correlated with unemployment rates—meaning that death rates go up when unemployment goes down—for the population as a whole, and separately for men and women, and for whites and nonwhites. The relationship is strongest for the working-age population.

Looking at individual causes of death, in the late twentieth century (after 1970), deaths from traffic accidents, major cardiovascular diseases, and cirrhosis of the liver were all significantly, negatively related to the rate of unemployment. In earlier periods, there was also a strong relationship between employment and flu and pneumonia deaths, and a weaker but significant relationship with cancer deaths, in the same "perverse" direction.

Of the major causes of death examined in the article, only suicide showed the naïvely "expected" pattern of worsening when unemployment rose.

Another study, by Christopher Ruhm, similarly found that for 1972–1991, increased unemployment was associated with decreases in total mortality in eight of ten major causes of death.[38] The two exceptions were Ruhm's findings of no significant relationship between unemployment and cancer deaths, and, as in the Tapia study discussed above, more suicides at times of higher unemployment.

There are plausible explanations for these patterns. When more people are working, there is more traffic and therefore more traffic fatalities. There is also more stress at work and hence more cardiovascular disease. During economic upturns, alcohol and tobacco consumption increase, as does obesity; meanwhile, time spent on exercise, sleep, and social interactions decreases. In the past, workplace contagion may have caused deaths by spreading infectious diseases such as flu and pneumonia. Even though some underlying causes of mortality, such as stress, involve chronic, long-term conditions, the timing of deaths may reflect short-term triggers related to employment. Heart attacks among the working-age population are known to peak on Mondays.[39]

Although counterintuitive, the finding of an association between increased employment and increased mortality is not new. Peer-reviewed articles making this point date back to 1922, and have continued throughout the intervening years. Most have been in public health journals, although at least one has appeared in a leading economics journal.[40] U.S., Canadian, and British data all support the idea that recessions are somehow better for health. One epidemiologist, M. Harvey Brenner, has long challenged this finding,[41] but Tapia and Ruhm both provide effective critiques of Brenner's statistical methodology.[42] Tapia maintains that Brenner has used excessively complicated models with too little data to validate them, undermining the credibility of his time series results. Ruhm suggests that Brenner's earlier study of a forty-year span from the 1930s to the 1970s primarily reflects the decline in mortality that occurred as the United States emerged from the 1930s depression. This era witnessed important medical and nutritional advances, as well as rising incomes and declining unemployment.

Two other major objections should be noted. First, at an individual level, death rates are higher for the unemployed than for the employed.

This is not incompatible with the aggregate pattern. Although mortality is always higher for the unemployed than for the employed, it is also higher within each group during economic expansions than during recessions. As a result, overall mortality increases during expansions.[43]

Second, over the long run it is clear that rising incomes have been associated with falling death rates. However, the correlation is not perfect; the periods of fastest declines in death rates are not the times of fastest increases in incomes. The long-run decreases in mortality are caused by changes that are frequently only loosely correlated with income, such as improvements in sanitation, public health, and achievement of minimum nutritional standards. Over the long run, the decrease in mortality rates is one of the most important effects of economic development; but this does not imply any relationship to short-term economic fluctuations in an already developed country. Small gains in average income, hypothesized to occur as a result of deregulation, could be associated with no improvement, or even a decline, in public health and nutritional standards for the poor.

Needless to say, there is not much left of the antiregulatory "statistical murder" story once this perspective on unemployment and mortality is acknowledged.

Conclusion

This chapter has presented several pieces of the picture of regulatory costs; by way of conclusion, it may be helpful to summarize the argument as a whole.

Reports of the economic burden imposed by regulatory costs have been greatly exaggerated. The widely imagined trade-off between economic prosperity and environmental protection rests on two mistaken premises. First, many environmental policies impose little or no net costs on the economy. Second, even when regulatory costs appear to be substantial, this may not matter: there may be no short-run opportunity to exchange those costs for additional economic growth, and no guarantee that growth would lead to desired outcomes such as reduced mortality.

Regarding the first premise, even a policy as ambitious as REACH will lead to very small cost increases, raising the price of chemicals sold in Europe by less than 0.1 percent. Likewise, there is little evidence of jobs actually lost to regulations, outside of a few of the most environmentally damaging, extractive industries. The "pollution haven hypothesis," suggesting that companies move to regions or countries with more lenient environmental regulations, has been rejected by virtually all analysts who have studied the question. Several researchers have found that prospective estimates of the costs of regulation are more likely to be too high than too low. Attempted refutations by Bush administration officials were unpersuasive.

Regarding the second premise, even when regulations have significant costs, it is not necessarily the case that these costs could be converted to other uses. In a recession, idle economic resources are already available and are not creating short-run growth; in an expansion, the Federal Reserve may enforce predetermined limits on the pace of growth in order to prevent inflation. It is now common to discuss the need for a "risk-risk analysis," comparing old risks alleviated by policies to the new risks created by the same process. It is equally necessary to consider a "growth-growth analysis," comparing economic costs imposed by policies to the actual opportunity cost of the same resources used elsewhere. Finally, even if growth were to occur as a result of deregulation, it is not certain that it would lead to the anticipated beneficial consequences, such as reduced mortality. A remarkable line of empirical research demonstrates that in the United States and several other countries in the twentieth century, age-adjusted mortality rates increased during economic expansions and declined during recessions. The rhetorical equation of regulations with reduced growth and increased mortality, dubbed "statistical murder" by regulatory critics, turns out to be dead wrong.

The lightness of regulatory costs is thus matched by the vanishingly small benefits available from rolling back those rules. The imagined trade-off between environmental protection and economic prosperity remains only an abstract theory, refuted by the facts.

But if the trade-off is mythical, and cost-benefit analysis is biased and problematic, how should decisions about health and environmental policy be made? The next chapter sketches an alternative, precautionary approach to a complex case, the regulation of dioxin, developing the beginnings of a theory of decision making under extreme uncertainty.

Chapter 4

Precaution, Uncertainty, and Dioxin

How should we decide on public policy toward dioxin? It is a widely discussed and feared pollutant, implicated in public health tragedies including a major industrial accident at Seveso, Italy; the severe contamination and eventual evacuation of Times Beach, Missouri, and Love Canal, New York; the widespread spraying of the defoliant Agent Orange by the United States during the Vietnam War; and the dust and debris in Manhattan following the attacks of September 11, 2001.

Dioxin is also a subject of great uncertainty and ongoing debate. Although most scientists agree that it has extremely serious health effects, even in minute quantities, a minority continues to argue that the science is unsettled and the dangers of dioxin have been vastly overstated. It is a case in which the objective, logically structured approach of cost-benefit analysis would be particularly welcome, if only it worked as advertised. Yet the uncertainty and debate surrounding dioxin make cost-benefit analysis even less appropriate than in other cases, and call for a different method of decision making. This chapter uses the example of dioxin to spell out the beginnings of an alternative theory of precautionary decision making under conditions of uncertainty.

Exactly how bad is dioxin for human health? Dioxin has been implicated in a broad range of effects;[1] for example, high doses of dioxin cause chloracne, a severe form of acne and skin discoloration. Ukrainian President Victor Yushchenko suffered from a very visible case of chloracne in 2004, apparently as a result of an intentional poisoning with dioxin. But much of the debate concerns the connection between dioxin and cancer.

Decades of research have led to the conclusion that dioxin is one of the most potent carcinogens ever created—unless, of course, it does not cause cancer at all. On the one hand, in 1997 the widely respected International Agency for Research on Cancer (IARC, part of the World Health Organization) classified dioxin as a Class 1 carcinogen, meaning that it is known to cause cancer in humans. On the other hand, U.S. EPA's slow-moving reassessment of dioxin has been underway since 1985, and still has not reached a final decision. As recently as 2006, a National Academy of Sciences re-evaluation of EPA's reassessment process called for additional research on a number of outstanding questions.

Some specific information about the hazards of dioxin will appear in the pages that follow, but the primary purpose of this chapter is to explore the general options for deciding on public policy in cases where the experts disagree as drastically as they do over dioxin. Note that such unsettled clashes of opinion overwhelm any attempt at cost-benefit analysis: aside from all the other problems with monetary valuation of death and disease (see chapter 1), should the calculations include a huge monetary estimate for the damage done by dioxin, or none at all?

Precaution and the Costs of Controversy

For those of us watching the scientific debate from the sidelines, one obvious but difficult way to respond is to try to jump in and evaluate the two sides—in effect, to become an amateur dioxin expert. My own amateur opinion is that it reminds me of the state of the tobacco debate, perhaps ten years or less before it was unambiguously settled. The great majority of scientific opinion appears to be on the side of identifying dioxin as a major cancer risk; a review of evidence that has emerged since the IARC decision concludes that the indictment of dioxin has only become stronger since that time.[2] However, there is an opposing side in the academic literature, which is still raising complex technical critiques; at least some of its research is funded by the affected industry, the Chlorine Chemistry Council.[3]

But even if (as I suspect) the answer can be divined in this case, having everyone dive into the technical details is in general an unsatisfactory way to debate policies and make decisions. It is exhausting and impractical: in order to make intelligent public policy, must we all learn the aca-

demic literature on every scientific controversy? Since industries not surprisingly seek out, and provide funding to, scientists who find that their
products are harmless, there is likely to be a technical controversy surrounding every regulation of a major hazard. Most people will not have
the time, inclination, or ability to reach an informed judgment on the
merits of such debates.

Another alternative is to do nothing until the debate is over and science speaks with a single voice. But this is also unsatisfactory. Waiting until the scientists finish slugging it out is costly, in two respects.

First, the research process itself is expensive: there are so many chemicals to study, and so little research time and funding. Other urgent social
priorities—even other environmental health priorities—inevitably impose limits on the affordable extent of research and debate about each individual chemical hazard. Reaching consensus on the harmful effects of
tobacco was extraordinarily slow, expensive, and contentious, as was the
similar convergence of opinion on the effects of lead. Research on dioxin,
which has not yet entirely reached a consensus, has already been time-
consuming and expensive. There is a large annual conference of researchers studying dioxin and related chemicals; I presented an early version of part of this chapter at "Dioxin 2003." The world cannot afford a
tobacco-sized or dioxin-sized debate on every potential health hazard, or
an annual academic conference on every chemical; it is important to find
a decision-making process that can reach closure with much lower information costs. REACH, the new European policy (discussed in chapters
10–12), has made an important step in this direction by requiring standardized testing of industrial chemicals.

Second, the costs of waiting for scientific consensus include the harms
done by inaction during the long period of waiting and debating. Credible warnings of risk often appear decades before a consensus is reached.
The "precautionary principle," introduced in chapter 1, argues that action
should be based on those early warnings, to avoid additional harm. In its
2001 study, "Late Lessons from Early Warnings," the European Environment Agency presented more than a dozen case studies in which accurate
early warnings were ignored, including the dangers of asbestos, radiation,
mad cow disease, and other hazards that are now widely recognized.[4] In
each case, precautionary decisions based on the earliest credible warnings
would have avoided substantial human, environmental, and economic costs.

For example, estimates of the eventual number of cancer deaths that will be attributable to asbestos now range into the hundreds of thousands. (Because of the long latency period, many of those deaths have not yet occurred; indeed, many of the cancers have not yet been identified.)[5] Dozens of companies that produced or used asbestos were driven into bankruptcy, in a tidal wave of lawsuits that arose in the 1980s and continued into the twenty-first century; Lloyd's of London almost collapsed in the 1990s under the weight of asbestos liabilities. Yet the first medically accurate description of the harm done to the lungs by asbestos was published by a British factory inspector in 1898! By 1918, some insurance companies in the United States and Canada were already refusing to cover asbestos workers because of their occupational health risks. By the 1930s, articles in the medical literature in several countries linked asbestos to lung cancer, and a number of government officials urged regulation of asbestos. But the use of asbestos continued to rise rapidly during World War II and the early postwar years. Most of the exposures that caused hundreds of thousands of cancer deaths and massive corporate losses occurred decades after there were credible warnings of the dangers of asbestos.

As the "Late Lessons" study demonstrates, it is easy to find important cases of "false negatives"—situations where the precautionary principle was ignored, and policy decisions were based on the false belief that there was no risk. Conservative critics of environmentalism have raised the specter of making expensive mistakes in the opposite direction: a precautionary approach to potential risks could lead to "false positives," taking action that later proves unnecessary when the risk proves to be less serious than was initially believed. But it turns out to be hard to find "false positives"; in practice, it is surprisingly rare for policies to be based on false beliefs about the existence of risks. In a study of this question, Steffen Hansen examined eighty proposed "false positive" policy decisions that have been cited by critics and found that only four of them, all more than twenty years old, actually fit the definition.[6] (It is possible, however, that implementation of a more precautionary approach to public policy would create more false positives in the future, a point discussed below.)

Economists, in the words of an old joke, see something working in practice and ask whether it can work in theory. That is what I propose to do here with the precautionary principle. At the level of anecdote and case study, precaution is amply supported. Numerous early warnings of harm have turned out to be well worth paying attention to; the painfully obvious losses from moving too slowly in health and environmental policy appear to greatly outweigh the losses, if any, that have resulted from moving too quickly. But how does this work in theory? How does society decide what precautionary action to take, in advance of a scientific consensus? Remarkably enough, there is a formal economic theory that is directly applicable to this problem. It concerns optimal policy decisions under what might be called conditions of "pure uncertainty."

The Economics of Pure Uncertainty

A little known but important economic theorem, coauthored by Nobel laureates Kenneth Arrow and Leonid Hurwicz many years ago, demonstrates that in cases of great uncertainty, the most efficient approach to public policy is based solely on knowledge of the extremes of the range of possible outcomes. Nothing is added by attempts to find the midpoint, average, or best point estimate, if the uncertainty is sufficiently great.

In 1972 Arrow and Hurwicz presented an analysis of the problem of choice under what they called conditions of "ignorance." Perhaps "pure uncertainty" would be a better term; the key point is that absolutely no information is available about the probability of different possible outcomes.[7] Although Arrow and Hurwicz did not discuss the problem in terms of precaution, their analysis of pure uncertainty provides a useful framework for understanding and implementing the precautionary principle. Published in an obscure location and presented in dense technical terms, the Arrow-Hurwicz analysis was for many years discussed only in specialized analyses of economic philosophy. Its importance for environmental policy was first recognized in 1997 by Richard Woodward and Richard Bishop.[8]

Woodward and Bishop discussed a generalized case of pure uncertainty in public policy, which they call the "Expert Panel Problem." A panel of experts, all of whom have in-depth knowledge of an issue, disagree about the expected outcome of alternative policies. All of the expert forecasts are known to be plausible, but nothing is known about which forecast is more probable. In the absence of *any* information about probabilities, the standard models of economics and risk assessment cannot be used to make a decision. In particular, averaging the opinions of the experts is not a valid solution under these rules: using the average implicitly assumes that are all equally likely to be correct, which is not the same as knowing nothing about probabilities.

Formally speaking, Arrow and Hurwicz analyzed a set of actions that could be taken under conditions of pure uncertainty. They were interested in finding criteria for choosing the optimal actions, assuming that the criteria meet several straightforward conditions of logical consistency. The only one of their conditions that sounds at all controversial is the irrelevance of repetition: the desirability of an action does not depend on how many times it is duplicated, in the list of available choices. This is the assumption that embodies pure uncertainty. In the expert panel interpretation of the theory, the analogous result is that if nothing is known about the probability that any one expert's forecast is correct, then it doesn't matter how many members of the panel agree with a given position. The situation would be quite different if every expert were assumed equally likely to be correct; then repetitions of a view would be evidence in its favor, and would influence the panel's average forecast.

This does not, however, escape all scientific controversy; rather, it trades the impossible problem of identifying *the* best estimate for the difficult problem of identifying the outer bounds of possibility. Who is entitled to a seat on the expert panel? Is the view that dioxin does not cause cancer still part of the spectrum of informed scientific opinion? (In historical terms, at what point did the view that tobacco does not cause lung cancer lose its legitimacy as an expert opinion worth considering?) At the other end, which studies count as the most extreme credible estimates of risk? Should the upper end of the 95 percent confidence interval be used, or is it more appropriate to use the central estimate from the studies? The progress of scientific understanding could be seen as gradually narrowing the range of credible forecasts. Meanwhile, the range of forecasts as it exists at the moment, the expert panel with its current membership, provides a basis for policy analysis.

Arrow and Hurwicz found that any criterion consistent with their assumptions ranks actions, or policies, solely on the basis of their best and worst possible outcomes. Rational decision making under conditions of pure uncertainty, in other words, is based entirely on the outer bounds of the possible, not on midpoints, averages, or consensus forecasts of the most likely outcome. Appendix A summarizes the Arrow-Hurwicz proof in semi-technical terms.

Several different criteria are consistent with the Arrow-Hurwicz result: for instance, an optimist could form judgments based only on the best possible outcome for each policy, while a pessimist could rely only on the worst case. Subsequently, other analysts using similar assumptions have shown that if society is risk-averse, or prefers a diversity of options in the face of uncertainty, then the pessimist's decision rule is the only appropriate one to use.[9] That is, risk aversion or a desire for diversification should lead to choosing the policy option with the least harmful worst-case outcome—exactly as the precautionary principle would suggest.

Precautionary Dioxin Policy: A Numerical Sketch

The hypothesis of pure uncertainty and the framework of the expert panel problem seem plausible as approximate characterizations of the ongoing debates over policy on dioxin. There is a set of divergent expert estimates of the health impacts of dioxin, but there is nothing approaching agreement about the probabilities that should be attached to rival estimates. What would the Arrow-Hurwicz approach imply for how we should go about setting policies on dioxin?

The Arrow-Hurwicz approach calls for a focus on the extremes of the range of expert opinion. At one extreme, some participants in EPA Science Advisory Board reviews of the Draft Dioxin Reassessment have argued that there was no proof that dioxin is a human carcinogen.[10] At the other extreme, other participants in the EPA reassessment, and researchers publishing in the peer-reviewed literature, find that infinitesimal quantities of dioxin can cause cancer.[11]

In several recent studies of dioxin and cancer, the high (dangerous) end of the 95 percent confidence interval implies that lifetime exposure to as little as one picogram, per kilogram of body weight, per day (pg/kg/day), could lead to an increased cancer risk of about 1 percent.[12] (On the meaning of picograms and other such minute quantities, see box 4.1.) For the purposes of calculation, let's take that to represent the upper extreme of expert opinion on dioxin risks. And, to allow easy calculation, let's assume an answer to another ongoing controversy: the dose-response relationship is linear—twice as much dioxin, twice as much cancer—and there is no threshold below which dioxin exposure is safe.

The next few bits of arithmetic are designed to calculate first the number of cancers per gram of dioxin exposure, and second, the amount of dioxin absorbed by the U.S. population in a year. The product of these two numbers is an estimate of the annual number of cancers attributable to dioxin.

Cancers per gram of dioxin exposure: Assume that a typical person lives 75 years, with a lifetime average weight of 70 kg (154 pounds). Then a 1 percent increase in cancer risk for one person, caused by a lifetime exposure of 1 pg/kg/day, is associated with a total exposure of almost 2 micrograms (µg), or millionths of a gram, of dioxin:

1 pg/kg/day * 70 kg * 365 days/year * 75 years = 1.916 µg

One excess cancer would be expected, on average, from 100 times this quantity, or 191.6 µg. Equivalently, the number of excess cancers expected per gram of exposure would be:

1 cancer /.0001916 g = 5,220 cancers / g

Total U.S. dioxin exposure per year: The Draft Dioxin Reassessment estimated average exposure to dioxin of 41 pg/day for adults, and very similar amounts, 36–43 pg/day depending on age, for children and adolescents.[13] For the 285 million residents of the United States as of 2001, this implies a national total exposure of

$(41*10^{-12})$ g/person/day * $(285*10^6)$ people * 365 days/year = 4.27 grams/year

For the sake of comparison, note that this implies that human exposure amounted to 0.14 percent of the 3,125 g of dioxin emissions to air in 1995, as reported in the reassessment.

Number of cancers attributable to dioxin: Under the assumptions described above, a single year's exposure causes

5,220 cancers/g of exposure * 4.27 g = 22,300 cancers

We now have precise statements of the two extremes of the range of expert opinion, the alternate hypotheses (1) that dioxin at recent emission levels causes 22,300 cancers annually, and (2) that it does not cause cancer. Policies that call for action to control dioxin will look their best under hypothesis (1), and worst under (2); the reverse will be true for policies that do little or nothing about the threat of dioxin. There would be no meaning to considering an average of these two hypotheses, and no additional

BOX 4.1 How Big Is a Picogram?

Research on the harmful effects of dioxin often refers to amounts measured in picograms, which are almost unimaginably small quantities of matter. Even a gram itself is small by ordinary standards, filling about one-fifth of a teaspoon; there are 28 grams in an ounce. But the science of toxic chemicals frequently requires measurement of tiny fractions of a gram, and discussion of concentrations in parts per thousand, million, billion, or trillion.

Some important fractions of a gram are as follows:

- A milligram (mg) is one-thousandth (10^{-3}) of a gram.
- A microgram (µg) is one-millionth (10^{-6}) of a gram (its abbreviation starts with µ, the Greek letter "mu," to avoid confusion with "m" for milligram).
- A nanogram (ng) is one-billionth (10^{-9}) of a gram.
- A picogram (pg) is one-trillionth (10^{-12}) of a gram.

But how should one visualize those fractions? Most people have no real picture of what one in a billion, or one in a trillion, looks like. To put these tiny quantities in perspective, consider the corresponding fractions of the human race, which was estimated to number 6.6 billion people as of 2007:

- One-thousandth of the global population is 6.6 million people, which is close to the population of Massachusetts, El Salvador, or Switzerland.
- One-millionth of the human race is 6,600 people. If you have attended major concerts, sports events, or big-city holidays, parades, or demonstrations, then you have been in crowds consisting of more than one part per million of humanity.
- One-billionth of all the people alive today is six to seven people. Odds are that you have had one part per billion of the human race in your house on many occasions.
- If you have been eating more than usual lately, and have gained a pound, you have added at least one part per trillion to the total weight of the human race.*

Dioxin research, incredibly enough, involves laboratory detection of concentrations as low as a few parts per trillion—comparable to putting the whole human race on a scale in order to measure the last few pounds that one person gained.

* With a total population of 6.6 billion, if the average weight per person is 150 pounds or less, then the human race weighs less than one trillion pounds. Note that the average includes children of all ages as well as adults, making it essentially certain that the average person on earth weighs less than 150 pounds. Adults-only average weights are 177 pounds for the United States, and 165 pounds for the United Kingdom and Canada (Wikipedia, "human weight"). Many countries seem likely to have lower average weights than the United States, the United Kingdom, and Canada, even for adults.

information would be gained by evaluating policies under the assumption that the effects of dioxin fall somewhere in between. Rather, policies should be evaluated under the extreme cases of hypotheses (1) and (2).[14]

Should PVC Be Banned?

Dioxin is a chlorinated hydrocarbon, and can be created when organic matter is burned together with materials that contain chlorine. But not just any source of chlorine will do: in ordinary salt, the sodium and chlorine atoms are too tightly bonded to each other, so that very little chlorine escapes to take part in creating dioxin. For dioxin formation, a source of more loosely bonded chlorine is needed, such as polyvinyl chloride (PVC), the only common plastic that contains chlorine. Burning PVC waste, in combination with paper, wood, food waste, or other organic matter, as occurs in waste incinerators, is likely to create small quantities of dioxin.[15] But as shown above, only small quantities are needed to do great harm. (For more on PVC, see chapter 9.)

Consider two policies for dealing with dioxin emissions: (a) banning the use of PVC, and (b) doing nothing. How does this choice of policies relate to the range of expert opinion about the potential harms from dioxin? If, as seems likely, society is risk-averse in this area, it is appropriate to choose the policy with the least harmful worst case. That is, the costs of PVC elimination, if it turns out to be unnecessary, should be weighed against the cancers that could have been prevented, if dioxin turns out to be highly carcinogenic. One more heroic simplifying assumption is needed, to illustrate the process of policy analysis.

The production, use, and disposal of PVC accounts for many but not all sources of dioxin. Other processes such as chlorine bleaching in paper mills, or the production of other chlorinated chemicals, also have been found to create dioxin. Assume, therefore, that half of dioxin emissions are attributable to the PVC lifecycle, and could be prevented by phasing out the use of PVC. (Burning of PVC waste would continue for a while after production stopped, but would gradually taper off.) Then, under hypothesis (1), the elimination of PVC prevents half of 22,300, or 11,150 cancers annually. The policy of doing nothing fails to prevent those 11,150 cancers.

As explained in chapter 9, a comprehensive study of the cost of elimination of PVC, performed for Environment Canada, implies an average cost increase of U.S. $0.55 per pound (in 2002 dollars) for replacement of PVC by alternative products. Consumption of PVC in the United States and Canada amounted to 13.4 billion pounds in 2001.[16] If consumption is proportional to population, then U.S. consumption was 90 percent of that amount, or 12.1 billion pounds. The cost of replacing all PVC consumption in the U.S can thus be estimated at roughly 12.1 billion pounds * $0.55/pound = $6.7 billion.[17]

Conclusion: Numbers and Policies

Returning to the underlying question of policy evaluation, the precautionary principle calls for an evaluation of which worst case is least harmful. Rather than fighting over a single best estimate, it acknowledges and considers both ends of the spectrum.

With the multiple illustrative assumptions about dioxin used here, one worst case fails to prevent 11,150 cancers, while the other imposes needless costs of $6.7 billion. These impacts are logically incommensurable: there is no natural, meaningful way to assign dollar values to profound health impacts such as cancer. The application of cost-benefit analysis to health and environmental regulation is frequently stymied by exactly this obstacle, as seen in chapter 1. A value judgment is inescapably required at this point. Unlike the technical details of dioxin science, this is a judgment about which most people can form meaningful opinions.

It is no accident that the policy analysis ends up weighing monetary costs and priceless health benefits; this is the normal state of affairs when considering health hazards. The worst case for one policy option is that it allows preventable deaths and diseases to occur; the worst case for the other is that it spends money on precautionary alternatives that turn out to be unnecessary in retrospect. In this respect, there is a fundamental asymmetry between the costs of false negatives—acting too slowly in cases of real harm—and the costs of false positives—acting too quickly in cases where harms turn out to be limited or nonexistent. One is denominated in deaths, and the other in dollars. Mistakes measured in dollars can often be undone; avoidable deaths never can be.

Some might still object that the dollar costs of repeated precautionary policies might mount up to an unaffordable total. As shown in chapter 3, the costs of regulation have been very low; while health and environmental protection could in theory hamper economic growth, it doesn't come close to doing so in practice. Nonetheless, in the more modest spirit of cost-effectiveness analysis, it is easy to calculate the cost per avoided health outcome: in the dioxin example, the hypothesized prevention of 11,150 cancers for $6.7 billion amounts to $600,000 per prevented cancer. This is much lower than the costs of many environmental regulations that regulatory critics have complained about in recent years, as seen in chapter 1.

But calculation of the cost per unit of a single health outcome misses much of the story. In this case, elimination of PVC would have other health benefits—including prevention of cancers caused by other hazardous byproducts of the PVC lifecycle—beyond the dioxin-related benefits. Thus, under the assumptions used here, elimination of PVC would probably prevent cancers at a lower cost than $600,000 per case. And the benefits of reducing dioxin emissions are not confined to cancer prevention.

The focus on a number, such as $600,000 per avoided cancer, ignores all the reasons why one risk is different from another. Why should the same cost per avoided cancer be applied to well known, voluntarily accepted risks, and to hidden risks involuntarily imposed on innocent bystanders? The precautionary approach, as suggested by the Arrow-Hurwicz analysis and sketched here, focuses attention on the worst-case outcomes for rival policy options. Often, this means considering specific risks of economic loss on the one hand, and specific risks of death and disease on the other hand. Nothing forces us to collapse that consideration into an abstract formula that ignores everything else we know about the social context and meaning of a particular hazard. There is no mathematical algorithm that replicates the democratic deliberation upon which public policy should be based.

The applications of this precautionary approach are not limited to dioxin. The next chapter, the first in a series of case studies of U.S. policies (including somewhat more data and fewer assumptions than this sketch of dioxin), presents another case where scientists continue to disagree: it explores the implications of the same precautionary framework for policies toward atrazine, a leading pesticide.

Chapter 5

The Economics of Atrazine

In nearly 50 years of use, atrazine has proven cost effective, reliable, flexible and safe when used in accordance with federal label instructions. . . . If atrazine use was discontinued in Illinois, losers would include corn growers, Illinois' economy and the environment.

University of Chicago economist Don Coursey[1]

I'm not saying it's safe for humans. I'm not saying it's unsafe for humans. All I'm saying is that it makes hermaphrodites of frogs.

University of California biologist Tyrone Hayes[2]

Atrazine, one of the most widely used pesticides in the United States and the world, is an effective weed killer, applied to most of the U.S. corn crop each year. Without it, say its defenders, the economy of corn-growing states would be devastated. Recent estimates of the cost of an atrazine ban have ranged as high as one-sixth of gross receipts from the sale of corn, although, as shown below, these estimates are not universally accepted.

Atrazine is also the pesticide most frequently found in groundwater in the United States. It was often found in groundwater in Europe, in the years when it was used there. It is a possible cause of several types of cancer, and, according to many researchers, a proven endocrine disruptor with visible effects, such as hermaphrodism in frogs, even at extremely low levels of exposure. One study even suggested a correlation between exposure to atrazine and low sperm quality among men in an agricultural area of the United States.[3] The health and environmental evidence, however, continues to be debated, with U.S. EPA, among others, arguing that there are no proven harms if atrazine is used in accordance with regulations.

The dilemma posed by these contradictory aspects of atrazine applies to many other chemicals as well. Modern agriculture is extraordinarily dependent on pesticides. We enjoy vast quantities of food, at low prices, in part because crops are routinely sprayed with chemicals that control weeds and insects. But the harm that these pesticides sometimes do is not entirely accidental: designed to kill living organisms, they are often harmful to humans and other species, as well as the targeted pests.

How should public policy respond to the economic benefits versus health and environmental risks of a pesticide such as atrazine? Answers to this question have been widely varied. The EU has banned atrazine, on the basis of its persistent contamination of groundwater. Meanwhile, the United States has renewed the registration of atrazine, rejecting the claims that it has serious risks.

Evaluation of the rival perspectives on the subject might seem like an ideal application for cost-benefit analysis: how do the economic benefits of atrazine compare to the health and environmental damages? However, there are several categories of problems with cost-benefit analysis in this case, echoing the general limitations of cost-benefit analysis of health and environmental policy discussed in chapter 1.

First, it is difficult or impossible to put prices on the health effects of agricultural chemicals. It is also a challenge to price the multiple environmental implications of current agricultural practices. For example, the hidden costs of large-scale monoculture, and its implications for problems such as erosion and runoff, tend to be lost in such an analysis. Indeed, one might question the implicit goal of a cost-benefit study, namely the maximization of corn production: do we really need to produce more beef, and more high-fructose corn syrup? Is corn-based ethanol a sensible way to produce liquid fuels?

Even if all the other problems were somehow resolved, cost-benefit analysis would require a resolution to the ongoing debate about the probability of harm. With a significant but uncertain probability of serious damages, atrazine is instead a candidate for precautionary policy making, as described in chapter 4. Rather than trying to resolve the scientific debate about the effects of atrazine, it is more useful to focus on the risks associated with worst-case outcomes. For instance, how bad would it be if atrazine remained in use, while its critics ultimately prove to be right about its harmful effects? Conversely, how expensive would it be if atrazine were banned, and later turns out to be harmless?

The former question, on the potential health and environmental impacts of atrazine, has been extensively studied.[4] This chapter addresses the latter question, that is, the costs of banning atrazine. Those costs could be surprisingly small, according to several major studies of the topic. Moreover, there is a new alternative herbicide on the market, which, according to some industry-funded research, does about the same amount for corn yields as atrazine. In addition, it is worth considering the experience of Italy and Germany, two corn-producing countries that both banned atrazine in 1991, without visible harm to corn production.

Four Studies of Atrazine

Ideally, a study of the value of atrazine should compare the current economics of U.S. corn production, using atrazine, to the next best alternative available to corn growers if atrazine were banned. The difference between these two scenarios is the appropriate measure of the value of atrazine. Three of the four studies discussed here offer a quite incomplete economic picture; thus it may be useful to start by outlining the components of a complete analysis.

In the scenario without atrazine, several aspects of farm revenues could change, with contradictory effects on farmers' bottom lines:

1. Farmers will buy and apply other herbicides, potentially increasing costs per acre.
2. Yields per acre could decrease, if the other herbicides are less effective.
3. Acreage planted in corn could decrease, if corn production becomes less profitable.
4. The market price of corn could increase, if production decreases.
5. Acreage withdrawn from corn production could be used to grow other crops, generating additional revenue.

The first three effects represent losses for farmers, or decreases in net farm income. The last two, in contrast, represent increases in farm incomes. It is not clear, a priori, which effects will predominate: gains from the increased price of corn, plus revenues from expansion of other crops, might or might not outweigh the more obvious costs of doing without atrazine.

When growers receive the full market price, as they do at the relatively high corn prices resulting from the ethanol boom, all five of these factors affect farm income directly. That is, since late 2006, the price of corn has been above the former subsidized price of $2.60 per bushel, so that subsidies no longer have a direct effect on the price. The situation was slightly more complicated when market prices were lower and growers received a fixed, subsidized price that was well above the prevailing market price. Under those circumstances, a price increase was a benefit to the government's price support program, not to farmers: if the market price for corn increased from $2.00 to $2.10 a bushel while the government was guaranteeing growers $2.60, farmers' subsidized incomes would remain unchanged, while the cost to the government of the subsidy would shrink from $0.50 to $0.40 per bushel. However, in either era, the same five effects, as listed above, describe the impacts on suppliers as a whole, combining the effects on farmers and government support programs.

U.S. Department of Agriculture (USDA)

A relatively complete study of the economics of banning atrazine, estimating all five effects, was performed for a 1994 USDA report,[5] and was subsequently described in two academic articles.[6] Using 1991 data,[7] this study applied Iowa State University's CEEPES (Comprehensive Environmental Economic Policy Evaluation System) suite of models to simulate the effects of pesticide bans and other policies on a multistate growing area that includes more than 80 percent of U.S. corn acreage.

For the ban on atrazine, the study projected:

1. Increased herbicide costs of $1.08 per acre.
2. Yield losses of 1.19 percent, or 1.3 bushels per acre.
3. A decrease in corn acreage of 2.35 percent, or 1.7 million acres.
4. A 1.83 percent increase in the price of corn.
5. Increases of 1.5 million acres planted in soybeans and 0.1 million acres in wheat—almost exactly absorbing the reduction in corn acreage.

The net annual loss to farmers (of ten major crops, not just corn) of $269 million was outweighed by savings of $287 million for government support programs, since market price increases would reduce subsidy payments to farmers. The combined result was an $18 million gain to suppliers as a whole (farmers plus the government) from banning atrazine. Thus the fourth and fifth effects—the benefits of the price increase and the expansion of other crops—were slightly more valuable than the revenue lost to increased herbicide costs, yield losses, and decrease in corn acreage. The study estimated the loss to domestic and foreign consumers, who would face higher prices for corn-based products such as beef and corn syrup, at $258 million. The aggregate economic effect on society was therefore a loss of $240 million—equivalent to $355 million in 2006 dollars.[8]

Not all studies have been this complete. Three other, more recent studies, by EPA, Fawcett, and Coursey, consider only the first two of the five effects, the costs of alternative herbicides and the impact on yields.

EPA

EPA studied the costs of partial or complete restrictions on atrazine.[9] Published in 2002, the study used 2000 economic data. For the crucial question of the effects of atrazine on yields, EPA relied on a 1996 report from the Triazine Network, which was said to reflect studies of pesticide performance published between 1986 and 1995.[10] EPA estimated that

1. Substitute pesticides would cost an additional $5.43 per acre.
2. Yields would decrease by 8.8 bushels per acre, a 6.4 percent drop from the average yield of 137 bushels per acre. The yield decrease was priced at $2.60 per bushel, the (fixed) support price received by farmers; it therefore amounted to $22.88 per acre.

No change in corn acreage or price was included in the study, although a 6.4 percent change in supply would be expected to affect prices, and the change in profitability would be expected to affect corn acreage.[11] The combined effect of higher costs for substitute pesticides and lower farm revenues from diminished yields implied a loss of $28.31 per acre. This loss, applied to 55.8 million acres of corn treated with atrazine, amounted to a national total of almost $1.6 billion per year. Adjusted for inflation, this was equivalent to $1.8 billion in 2006 dollars, or five times the estimate from the USDA study.

Fawcett (Triazine Network)

A similar cost estimate can be found in a Triazine Network study of the effects of atrazine on corn yields.[12] The Triazine Network is a coalition founded by agricultural trade organizations in 1995, to bring farmers' views on the regulation of triazine herbicides to the attention of EPA.[13] (Atrazine is the most widely used, but not the only, triazine herbicide.)

The study, performed for the Triazine Network by Iowa consultant Richard Fawcett, was a review of other research. It listed 236 studies performed from 1986 through 2005, each of which contained evidence on corn yields with and without atrazine. Documentation and citation of the studies were incomplete, and the same investigators appeared repeatedly; see appendix B for discussion of the quality of Fawcett's data.

Fawcett estimated that:

1. Non-atrazine alternatives would increase herbicide costs by $10.07 per acre.
2. The average yield would decrease by 6.1 bushels per acre, according to the eleven studies he cites from 2005; at the $2.60 per bushel support price, this was worth $15.86 per acre. (For those eleven studies from 2005, the mean yield loss was 3.8 percent, and the median was 3.1 percent. Apparently 2005 was a typical year; Fawcett's database, as discussed in appendix B, implied that the twenty-year average loss estimates were quite similar to these figures.)

Fawcett's combined estimate for 2005 was therefore a loss of $25.93 per acre, or $1.45 billion nationwide for the 55.8 million acres of corn treated with atrazine.

Coursey (Syngenta)

Another recent study also restricted itself to the same two effects, but arrived, apparently mistakenly, at a much larger bottom-line impact. In 2007, Don Coursey completed a study, performed for Syngenta, the principal producer of atrazine, of the value of atrazine to the Illinois economy.

Coursey is an economist at the University of Chicago's Harris School of Public Policy; although his atrazine study described itself as a Harris School working paper, it was released and distributed by the Illinois Farm Bureau.[14]

In terms of the effects of an atrazine ban on farm revenues, Coursey projected that

1. Herbicide costs would increase by $4.86 per acre.
2. Yields would decrease by 4–7.6 percent, or 5.8–11 bushels per acre. The midpoint of Coursey's range was a yield loss of 5.8 percent, or 8.4 bushels per acre. At $1.95 per bushel, the price used in the study, the midpoint yield loss was worth $16.48 per acre.

Combining these two effects, Coursey's midpoint estimate was a cost of $21.34 per acre. As with the EPA and Fawcett studies, no estimate was included for reduction of corn acreage, price increases, or revenues from other crops that might replace some corn acreage. Most of the difference between Coursey's midpoint estimate and the EPA and Fawcett calculations was due to the use of different prices of corn. If Coursey had used the same corn price, $2.60 per bushel, his midpoint estimate (combining herbicide costs plus yield losses) would have been $26.70 per acre, compared to EPA's $28.31 and Fawcett's $25.93. It seems appropriate, therefore, to describe these studies as roughly agreeing on the costs of banning atrazine.

Coursey's strong point is his detailed, up-to-date data on the costs of alternative herbicides. He found that banning atrazine would increase herbicide costs by almost $5 per acre, or about $0.03 per bushel of corn at today's yields.

However, in his estimates, as in EPA's and Fawcett's, the bulk of the cost impact came from yield losses—an area where Coursey's work was less thorough. Although he mentioned the existence of sixteen studies of the effects of atrazine on corn yields, he included citations sufficient to locate his sources for only five of them.[15] Coursey commented that his estimates were also consistent with independent estimates of the value of atrazine, citing four estimates that range from $10 to $35 per acre. Of the four independent figures, one was the EPA estimate of roughly $28 per acre, discussed above; the other three were attributed only to his personal communication with other researchers.[16]

Then, in a final calculation, he added these independent estimates of the value of atrazine to his own estimates of yield loss without atrazine, as if they were separate impact categories.[17] This was certainly double-counting in the case of the EPA estimate, which consists primarily of the value of yield loss, as shown above. It may have been double-counting in the other cases as well.[18] This double-counting problem could explain how, with herbicide cost increases and yield decreases slightly smaller than EPA's, Coursey reached a bottom-line estimate of losses nearly double the EPA figure.

Newer Evidence on Atrazine and Yields

This review of rival studies highlights the critical question for economic analysis: by how much would an atrazine ban reduce corn yields?

Both the EPA estimate and Coursey's midpoint estimate, corrected for double-counting, assumed that a ban on atrazine would decrease corn yields by roughly 6 percent. The Fawcett study suggests a smaller effect: as discussed in appendix B, its mean yield decrease is 4.0 percent for all observations, or 3.2 percent if a few extreme outliers are excluded; its median is 2.4 percent for all observations, or 2.3 percent without the outliers. (Its higher costs for substitute herbicides bring it into approximate bottom-line agreement with EPA and the corrected Coursey figure for the total economic value of atrazine.) The USDA study estimated even smaller yield losses, of about 1 percent; this, together with a more complete economic analysis, implied small net gains for producers as a whole, but higher corn prices for consumers. An academic review of earlier studies discussed estimated yield losses of 1–3 percent from a number of studies, suggesting that the USDA researchers were not alone in finding such small effects.[19]

Yet even if one granted the EPA/Coursey assumption that earlier studies implied a 6 percent yield loss from an atrazine ban, would this estimate still apply today? If more effective alternative herbicides have been developed, the gain in corn yields due to atrazine may be correspondingly reduced, because the next best alternative would now look better.

In fact, a powerful new herbicide has appeared in recent years, thanks to the work of researchers at Syngenta. In addition to producing atrazine, Syngenta now also produces mesotrione, a triketone herbicide, under the trade name Callisto. The story began with a happy accident: a scientist, working at a chemical company that is now part of Syngenta, noticed that weeds did not grow around bottlebrush plants at his home in California. Research on this effect found that the bottlebrush or Callistemon tree produces leptospermone, which acts as a weak natural herbicide. Further research led to development of a closely related compound, mesotrione, which is a more powerful herbicide.

When registering mesotrione, EPA declared that it did not know of any toxic effects of the new herbicide.[20] As described by Syngenta, its proud corporate parent, Callisto (mesotrione) is what every corn grower needs:

> The combination of excellent crop tolerance and the wide application window gives the farmer a product that he can rely on to perform whenever he uses it. CALLISTO is quickly degraded by soil micro-organisms (ultimately to carbon dioxide and water) and is therefore non-persistent in the environment. When used as directed, it is safe to wildlife, aquatic organisms and relevant, beneficial insects in corn. CALLISTO is suitable for use in Integrated Pest Management (IPM) programs and is an attractive solution to farmers due to its timing and mixing flexibility. It can be used in a wide range of climates and on different soil types and no instances of resistance to CALLISTO have been recorded, even in artificial studies designed to provoke resistance development.[21]

In the less eloquent words of EPA's 2001 conditional registration of mesotrione,

> Callisto Herbicide is an effective [sic] in controlling broadleaf weeds in field corn. It will replace atrazine and isoxaflutole herbicides.[22]

Others have been more cautious: the Pesticide Action Network says that mesotrione is "not likely" to be a carcinogen, and is not a cholinesterase inhibitor, but finds insufficient evidence to judge four other categories of toxicity. In contrast, atrazine is known or suspected to be a problem in four of Pesticide Action Network's six categories, as shown in table 5.1.

At least one research study, funded by Syngenta, reported on the effects of mesotrione on corn yields.[23] The study mentioned the growing evidence of weeds that are resistant to atrazine, and suggested that

TABLE 5.1   Pesticide Action Network rankings of mesotrione and atrazine.

Hazard category	Mesotrione	Atrazine
Acute toxicity	Unknown	Slight
Carcinogen	Not likely	Highly toxic
Cholinesterase inhibitor	No	No
Groundwater contaminant	Unknown	Highly toxic
Developmental/reproductive toxin	Unknown	Unknown
Endocrine disruptor	Unknown	Suspected

Source: Pesticide Action Network (www.pesticideinfo.org), as of June 12, 2007.

"herbicides with other modes of action should be evaluated to reduce selection pressure on the weed community."[24]

In the study, conducted in Virginia, researchers tested the effects on weeds and corn yields of ten different mixtures of three leading herbicides: mesotrione, acetochlor, and atrazine. Four of the ten treatments included atrazine, and six did not. For the three years of the study, 1999–2001, the average corn yield per acre under the best non-atrazine treatment was 101.8 percent of the yield of the best treatment including atrazine.[25] That is, atrazine did almost 2 percent *worse* than the alternative! Atrazine's disadvantage, however, resulted entirely from the first year of the study, 1999, which had anomalously low yields for all treatments, perhaps reflecting start-up problems and low rainfall; the first-year problem was particularly pronounced for the best atrazine treatment. For the second and third years, 2000–2001, yields were much higher throughout the study—somewhat above the national average, rather than far below it. For those two years, corn yields in the best non-atrazine treatment averaged 99.8 percent of the yield in the best treatment with atrazine. If those years are more typical, then there is virtually no effect on yields of switching between atrazine and mesotrione.[26]

Other studies undertaken at about the same time, evaluating corn yields in Illinois and Arkansas, also reported finding no significant difference between mesotrione and atrazine treatments, but did not publish the supporting numerical results.[27] This research suggests that Syngenta's new product eliminates the benefit of using its older one; at least under the conditions of the Virginia study, and reportedly in the Illinois and Arkansas ones as well, atrazine does not increase yields relative to the best available alternative. Mesotrione remains somewhat more expensive than atrazine; one could still argue that atrazine produces the same weed-killing, yield-boosting benefit at lower cost than the alternatives. But this leaves atrazine with only a thin economic advantage: Coursey's calculation of the increased cost of herbicides needed to replace atrazine amounts to $0.03 per bushel of corn, less than 1 percent of the market price of corn in 2007.

Europe: Life after Atrazine

Regulation of pesticides has followed a different path in Europe than in the United States, with important implications for atrazine. The divergence dates back at least to the EU's 1980 Drinking Water Directive,[28] which specified 5 micrograms per liter (µg/L) as the maximum allowable level of any pesticide in drinking water. By 1998 the allowable limit was lowered to 0.1 µg/L of any one pesticide and no more than 0.5 µg/L of total pesticides.[29] Meanwhile, a 1991 EU directive on pesticides curtailed the use of products suspected of harming human health, groundwater, or the environment. It also established a twelve-year review period for products already on the market, such as atrazine, to determine their impact.[30]

Twelve years later, in 2003, the scientific committee reviewing atrazine concluded that it had the potential to contaminate groundwater at levels exceeding the allowed 0.1 µg/L, even when used appropriately.[31] This set in motion the process for a regulatory ban. In 2004 the European Commission announced a ban on atrazine applying to all EU member states, which went into effect in 2005; a handful of extensions for limited uses expired in 2007.[32] As a result, Europe is now launching a continent-wide experiment in agriculture without atrazine.

But this experiment was preceded by several individual European countries, which had moved to ban atrazine on their own, well before the EU decision. Sweden, Finland, and Denmark had all banned atrazine by 1994, but none of these countries is a significant corn producer. More remarkable, and more informative for economic analysis, is the fact that two countries that produce millions of tons of corn, Italy and Germany, both banned atrazine in 1991.

Italy adopted the EU's Drinking Water Directive in 1985, earlier than many EU nations. It soon became clear that the groundwater used for drinking in many areas exceeded allowable levels of pesticides. This was particularly true in the fertile Po River valley, where atrazine was commonly used on corn and rice.[33] Since more than 80 percent of farmers in northern Italy get their drinking water from groundwater, public concern about the safety of their water supplies may have been particularly strong.[34]

By 1987 the Italian government had to shut off drinking water to some parts of northern Italy to comply with the pesticide standards, resulting in public outrage.[35] Trying to lower pesticide concentrations, the government enacted several temporary bans on atrazine use, at first only in areas where the chemical was found in unacceptable concentrations. After a few years of temporary and/or local bans, the ban on selling atrazine became permanent, national policy in 1991.[36]

Germany, another corn-producing nation, also banned atrazine in 1991.[37] Germany's decision may have been influenced by two large-scale chemical accidents that polluted the Rhine River in 1986, killing vast numbers of fish and seeming to undermine the long-term efforts to clean up the Rhine. One of the two accidents involved a company that is now part of Syngenta, which dumped 400 liters of atrazine into the river.

These public policy decisions provide a natural experiment: while Italy and Germany both banned atrazine in 1991, the United States continued to allow its use. If atrazine is crucial to corn yield or profitability, then the data for Italy and Germany should look worse, relative to the United States, after 1991 than before. More specifically, if the ban on atrazine had a negative effect on corn producers, then either yields or harvested area, or both, should be depressed by the loss of that herbicide in Italy and Germany after 1991. Conversely, the United States, where atrazine remained available, should look relatively better on one or both of these measures after 1991.

As seen in figures 5.1 and 5.2, a comparison of international data provides no support for the hypothesis that banning atrazine in 1991 harmed corn production in either Italy or Germany. For yields, the trend was upward in all three countries, but with wide fluctuations around the trend.[38] To smooth out some of the year-to-year variability, figure 5.1 shows three-year moving averages of corn yields for 1981–2001.[39] To highlight the international comparison, the values for Italy and Germany for each year are expressed as a ratio to the U.S. value for the same year. Figure 5.1 shows

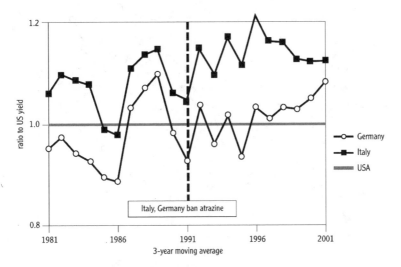

FIGURE 5.1.   Corn Yields, Relative to US

no sign of yields dropping in Germany or Italy after 1991, relative to the U.S. yield, as would be the case if atrazine were essential.

Figure 5.2 shows the change in harvested area. Because the areas involved were so different in the three countries—as of 1991, Italy had about 3 percent, and Germany about 1 percent, as much corn acreage as the United States—each country's data series is converted to an index number, with its own 1991 area set equal to 100. Far from showing any slowdown after 1991, both Italy and (especially) Germany showed faster growth in harvested area after banning atrazine than before. The United States, in contrast, showed no upward trend in the decade after 1991. This is just the opposite of the pattern that would be expected if atrazine made a major contribution to profitability in corn.

Of course, soil and climate conditions are different in the United States and Europe; the population of weeds may also differ in ways that are relevant to the efficacy of atrazine. It is logically possible that atrazine could be of little value in Europe, but more important for corn production under U.S. conditions But the total lack of response to the ban on atrazine in Italy and Germany, shown in both figures, at least suggests that atrazine is not a magical, one-size-fits-all solution to the problems of productivity in corn production.

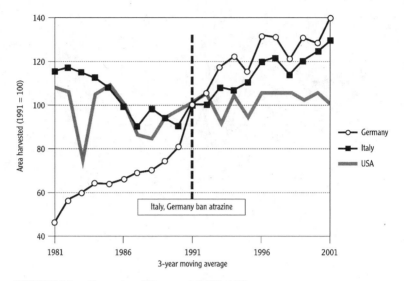

FIGURE 5.2.   Corn: Area Harvested (1991=100)

Conclusion

Policymaking for atrazine is inevitably a process of decision making under uncertainty. As pointed out in previous chapters, conventional cost-benefit analysis is inadequate to the task both because health and environmental harms do not always have meaningful monetary values, and because it is unrealistic to expect consensus on precise estimates of those harms. There is a growing, but still contested, body of research on those harms, enough to raise the question of the appropriate policy toward atrazine, but apparently not enough to settle the question. Indeed, the question has been answered in an opposite manner in the United States and the EU.

For the European approach to atrazine policy, the failure to meet minimum environmental standards is decisive. No calculation of economic benefits is involved. For the American approach, in contrast, economic analysis is central, since, presumably, no one would endorse the use of a potentially harmful substance unless it had economic benefits. Rather than attempting a precise cost-benefit analysis, it may be more helpful to compare the extremes of the debate, as suggested by the theory of precautionary policy making introduced in chapter 4. In those terms, one might ask, how serious are the damages in the worst-case outcomes for atrazine science and policy?

One of the extremes is, implicitly, evaluated in much of the scientific literature on the hazards of atrazine. If atrazine remains in use, and it turns out to be as bad as the leading scientific critics suggest, the result will be significant damages to human health and the natural environment, in exchange for the economic benefits of atrazine.

The other, less widely studied extreme is addressed in this chapter. If atrazine turns out to be harmless, but it is mistakenly banned, how much will be lost? Of the four studies discussed earlier, USDA estimated the ban would reduce corn yields by about 1 percent, and would result in a slight gain to producers, but a larger loss to consumers because of higher corn prices. The EPA study, and the more recent Syngenta-sponsored Coursey study, using a less extensive analytical framework than USDA, estimated 6 percent yield losses due to an atrazine ban, and costs to producers of about $28 (EPA) or $21 (Coursey midpoint estimate) per acre. Adjusted for the same price of corn, EPA and Coursey are in reasonably close agreement, representing a common, worst-case estimate for the economics of an atrazine ban. The Fawcett study, sponsored by the Triazine Network, had an intermediate estimate of yield loss (a mean estimate of 4.0 percent, or a median of 2.4 percent), but a higher estimate of the costs of substitute herbicides, again producing a similar cost per acre.

However, these estimates are deficient in at least two respects. EPA, Coursey, and Fawcett did not include the full range of economic impacts that were (appropriately) included in the USDA study, some of which represent increases in farm income, partially or wholly offsetting the losses. If, as EPA and Coursey predicted, an atrazine ban were to cause a roughly 6 percent decline in corn output, what would happen to corn prices as a result? The assumption of no change in prices, implicit in the studies other than USDA, is simply not credible. Opinions could differ on *how much* the price would increase, but a 6 percent cut in supply of a basic grain is not likely to leave the market price unchanged.

Second, the EPA and Coursey studies, despite 2002 and 2007 publication dates, rested on much older (and inadequately cited) data on corn yields. Since the time those data appeared, Syngenta has introduced an alternative herbicide, mesotrione, and sponsored research suggesting that mesotrione is fully as effective as Syngenta's older product, atrazine.

Fawcett's massive but incompletely documented tabulation of past studies did not appear to include any of the recent comparisons of atrazine versus mesotrione. Moreover, the experience of Italy and Germany, two countries that banned atrazine in 1991, does not support the hypothesis that atrazine is essential to corn yields or profitability. In the decade after banning atrazine, both countries matched or surpassed the U.S. performance, both in yields per acre and in the growth rate of planted area.

The most important single number in the economic analysis of atrazine is the effect on corn yields. If an atrazine ban reduced corn output by 6 percent, there would be visible economic consequences, although not as great as EPA and Coursey suggested, once the offsetting effects of increased prices were included. At a 6 percent yield loss, it still might be the case that the economic risks of banning atrazine look less serious than the health and environmental risks of continuing to use it. EPA's cost estimate for an atrazine ban, based on a 6 percent yield loss, was less than $2 billion for the United States as a whole; Fawcett's and Coursey's corrected midpoint estimate were somewhat lower than EPA's. An estimate corrected for the ensuing price increase would be smaller still.

If, on the other hand, the yield impact is on the order of 1 percent, as USDA estimated, or close to zero, as suggested by the newer evidence discussed here, then the economic consequences become minimal. The USDA study, with a 1 percent yield loss, found a slight net economic benefit to producers; the entire economic loss in that study came from the impact on consumers, due to the increase in corn prices of almost 2 percent. This would likely translate into a smaller percentage increase in the price of corn-based products such as beef, corn syrup, or now ethanol.[40] The newer evidence, both from the study of mesotrione and corn yields, and from the experience of Italy and Germany, suggests that there might be no effect on yields; the only economic impact would then be the increased price of herbicides, raising the price of corn by less than 1 percent.

Could the "need" to prevent such tiny price increases in corn-based products justify the continued use of a chemical about which such serious scientific doubts have been raised? The ethanol boom has already raised corn prices by a vastly greater amount, leading to rapid expansion of U.S. corn production. It is hard to believe that this suddenly booming industry could not withstand the remarkably small economic impacts of banning atrazine.

In this case, application of the precautionary framework, comparing the worst cases for each of the major policy options, is revealing: one option, doing nothing and continuing to trust in the safety of atrazine, faces a potential worst case of serious health and environmental impacts, above all to farmworkers and other residents of farm communities. The other option, replacing atrazine with the next best combinations of pesticides and farming practices, risks an unnecessary cost increase (if atrazine turned out to be harmless after all) of less than 1 percent of the price of corn. Ironically, this option apparently would involve buying at least as much herbicide from the company that now produces atrazine. Turning down this alternative on the grounds of its incremental costs would truly risk being poisoned for pennies.

Chapter 6

Ignoring the Benefits of Pesticides Regulation

While investigating a mysterious crime, Detective Olivia Benson became very sick and had to be rushed to a hospital. There the doctors discovered that she had dangerously low levels of cholinesterase, an enzyme that is essential to the human nervous system. Several types of neurotoxins are cholinesterase inhibitors, including some snake venoms, the nerve gases sarin and VX, and organophosphate pesticides. In Benson's case, the culprit turned out to be a pesticide.

Benson, as some readers will recognize, is a character on the television show *Law & Order: Special Victims Unit*. Her exposure to organophosphate pesticides occurred in a February 2007 episode; the specific pesticide in question was an imaginary one, invented by the script writers.[1] But in real life beyond the TV screen, real people are affected by real organophosphates, which do, in fact, interfere with the action of the crucial enzyme cholinesterase in the body. Although detectives and others can be exposed to excessive doses of pesticides, the worst effects are felt by the farmworkers who handle and apply pesticides, and work in pesticide-treated fields.

Detailed evaluation of pesticides will always be needed to ensure that they are selected and used in ways that do as little damage as possible to people and nature. As with atrazine in chapter 5, this seems like a question that cost-benefit analysis was designed to answer: do the benefits of a pesticide for growers outweigh the health and environmental costs for farmworkers and others who are harmed? Moreover, the applicable law encourages comparison of costs and benefits. Pesticides are regulated under the Federal Insecticide, Fungicide, and Rodenticide Act (FIFRA), and have to be registered with the federal government—a process that sets conditions and limits, where necessary, on the application of pesticides. In contrast to many environmental laws, FIFRA calls for examination of costs and benefits; specifically, EPA is obliged to consider costs and benefits when pesticides come up for registration or re-registration. A different law regulates the effects on consumers of pesticide residues in food; FIFRA evaluations often focus on health effects on farmworkers, who frequently have the highest and longest-lasting exposures to pesticides.

Unfortunately, there are a number of obstacles to cost-benefit analysis of pesticides. As explained in chapter 1, there is no way to assign meaningful monetary costs to many of the health and environmental impacts of pesticides. As seen in chapters 4 and 5, unresolved scientific debate can lead to uncertainty about the magnitude of the effects that should be included in the analysis; such uncertainty provides a strong argument for precautionary approaches to potential harm. Even a good-faith effort at objective cost-benefit analysis would be inherently flawed for these reasons.

This chapter illustrates another flaw of cost-benefit analysis in practice: contrary to claims that the methodology will bring objectivity and transparency to decision making, cost-benefit calculations are opaque to outsiders, allowing biases to enter behind a smokescreen of technical details. All too often, it has appeared that a prior decision has been made to minimize regulations, and economic calculations were an afterthought, a form of quantitative rhetoric tacked on to support a preferred policy. A careful listener can hear the hollowness in the official numbers.

A case in point is EPA's treatment of two common organophosphate pesticides, azinphos-methyl (AZM) and phosmet. In the hearings on these pesticides in 2005 and 2006, I submitted testimony on behalf of the Farmworker Justice Fund, the United Farm Workers, and other organizations representing workers who were potentially affected by the pesticides. I found that although EPA expressed deep concern about the negative effects on growers of a ban on AZM and phosmet, the agency's own numbers suggested that the economic value to growers of these pesticides is actually quite small. On the other side, some (not all) of the harmful impacts on farmworkers and their families, surrounding communities, and the natural environment were mentioned, but no attempt was made to decide whether these harms outweighed the modest financial gains for growers; the possibility never seemed to have occurred to EPA's analysts.

Sold under the names Guthion and Imidan, respectively, AZM and phosmet are used to kill insect pests on a wide variety of fruits, vegetables, and grains, and on cotton and ornamental plants; the largest users are apple orchards.[2] Both are organophosphates, a category of pesticides whose detrimental effects on the human nervous system are well established. When humans suffer a very high exposure to AZM or phosmet, the result can be respiratory failure and death.[3]

EPA made interim decisions in 2001 to continue to allow some uses of (i.e., "re-register") both AZM and phosmet. The United Farm Workers responded by filing suit to block the re-registration of both pesticides. In 2004, a settlement was reached with the United Farm Workers, giving EPA until 2006 to reevaluate its decision. New analyses of AZM and phosmet released in 2006 were subjected to a further round of public scrutiny, and EPA's final decisions were issued a few months later: all use of AZM will be phased out by 2012, but most uses of phosmet will be allowed to continue, in some cases with slightly improved safety measures. The decision to phase out AZM is a good one, but the long phase-out period allows for six more years of risking farmworkers' health, for no good reason.

Round One: Ignoring Workers and the Environment

How did EPA justify the conclusion that AZM was eligible for a leisurely phase-out, and phosmet was acceptable for continued use? There were two rounds to the process, the first accompanying the interim decision in 2001, and the second supporting the final decision in 2006. The agency's first round of economic analysis was biased in favor of continued pesticide use in three major ways, as seen, in particular, in the analysis for apple orchards.[4]

- EPA overlooked and/or underestimated the value of the leading alternatives.
- EPA failed to give adequate weight to the harm to farmworkers and their families caused by continued use of AZM and phosmet.

- EPA failed to assess harm to the natural environment, including harm to salmon, thus omitting a substantial part of the risk picture.

How Good Are the Alternatives?

Although EPA's analysts expressed sympathy for the plight of the apple growers and suggested that the economic benefits of the pesticides were substantial, the numbers they presented in 2001 were surprisingly small. (Note the reversal of the usual terminology: the analysis considered economic benefits of pesticide use for growers, versus health and environmental costs to workers and others.) Withdrawal of AZM alone would cause an estimated annual loss to apple growers of $67 million; withdrawal of phosmet alone would cause an $8 million loss; the withdrawal of both would be worth $114 million per year.[5] The comparable figure for pear growers, who are also important users of AZM and phosmet, was $100 million per year for the two pesticides combined.

A credible economic assessment of benefits must consider the full range of alternatives, including biological controls, alternative chemicals, integrated pest management, and organic approaches. However, EPA either overlooked entirely, or minimized the benefits of, several viable alternative technologies. In particular, EPA gave little or no attention to increased use of pheromone mating disruption, or protection of fruit with kaolin clay (a nontoxic film that can be sprayed on fruit, and easily washed off after harvesting). Nor did the agency consider the benefits of a switch to organic apple production, where higher prices might offset slightly lower yields. Instead, EPA's analysis of the withdrawal of AZM and/or phosmet relied primarily on increased use of other pesticides, with only a supporting role for pheromones.

Other analyses have found the benefits of pheromones to be substantial. A study conducted for the California Department of Pesticide Regulation evaluated pheromone dispensers referred to as "puffers" to control the codling moth in pear orchards. The researchers found that the puffers allowed good control of these pests, enabling growers to avoid organophosphate applications completely during the study season.[6] Another study in California, Oregon, and Washington found that large-scale mating disruption through introducing sterile moths or placing dispensers of synthetic pheromones throughout an orchard is effective.

Although mating disruption was initially more expensive than chemical controls, over time mating disruption became more cost-effective than the conventional approach, owing to its effects on secondary pests.[7] Likewise, trials of kaolin clay to control a major insect pest, the plum curculio, have found that treated fruit showed 1 percent damage or less, while untreated controls suffered 20 to 30 percent damage.[8]

Studies have also shown that a shift to organic production could be profitable for some growers. A comparison of conventional and organic production of Granny Smith apples in California found that organic production had significantly higher yields, while economic damage from pests did not differ significantly between the two systems. After the first year of the multiyear study, organic production yielded higher net profits because of the superior yield per acre as well as the premium on certified organic sales.[9] Another study, comparing organic and conventional apple orchards in Washington, likewise concluded that the organic system had the greatest economic as well as environmental sustainability; there were no major differences among the systems in pest or disease levels or in cumulative yields.[10]

By failing to analyze these available alternatives, EPA is likely to have overstated the benefits of AZM and phosmet to apple growers. A scenario based on increased use of pheromone mating disruption, kaolin clay, and conversion to organic apple production might outperform the mix of other pesticides that EPA assumed would be used to replace AZM and phosmet. If so, then the economic benefits of AZM and phosmet—that is, the effect on growers' net revenues that results from using these pesticides instead of the next best alternatives—would be even smaller than EPA's estimates of $114 million per year.

What Happens to Farmworkers and Their Families?

Human contact with pesticides is often measured by the "margin of exposure" (MOE), or the ratio of the maximum level that causes no effects in animals to the human exposure. For instance, an MOE of 10 means that the maximum safe level in animals is ten times the human exposure being measured—or in other words, the human exposure is one-tenth of the maximum safe level in animals. Because it is based on the inverse of the human exposure, a larger MOE means a lower, and safer, exposure. A widely used standard of safety requires an MOE of 100 or more, meaning that people should be exposed to 1 percent or less of the maximum no-effects level in animal studies. In numerous cases, EPA found that farmworkers applying AZM and phosmet, or working in areas where these pesticides have been sprayed, had MOEs lower than 100—in some cases, much lower—even when protective clothing and enclosed pesticide mixing, loading, and application systems were in use.[11]

The states with the best data on pesticide exposure incidents, such as California and Washington, provide additional confirmation that workers are being exposed to dangerous levels of pesticides.[12] Cholinesterase monitoring data from Washington State indicate that AZM is one of the leading causes of overexposure for farmworkers who mix, load, and apply organophosphates and related pesticides.[13] Similarly, a 1994 study of peach harvesters working in AZM-treated orchards in California found that workers who reentered the orchards thirty days after AZM had been applied suffered a median cholinesterase reduction of 19 percent.[14] (As noted above, cholinesterase is not a pollutant; rather, it is the essential enzyme that organophosphates inhibit.)

EPA, however, made no attempt to quantify the costs to farmworkers—or to their families and nearby communities—resulting from the use of AZM and phosmet. EPA's failure to consider the health costs of AZM and phosmet deviates from its practice in many other cases in which the agency has called for quantification and monetary valuation of costs to human health and the natural environment.

There is ample medical evidence of harm done to farmworkers and their families by organophosphate pesticides. For example, Parkinson's disease is more common among people who live in rural areas and work on farms.[15] People with Parkinson's disease are much more likely to have a prior exposure to insecticides.[16] Several studies have suggested a specific connection between organophosphates and Parkinson's disease.[17] Another potential result of organophosphate poisoning is "organophosphate-induced delayed polyneuropathy," characterized by burning, itching, and tingling of the limbs, muscle cramping, motor weakness, and in severe cases, paralysis.[18]

Acute organophosphate poisoning can have long-term neurological consequences, even when the victims appear to have completely recovered. One study, testing people nine years after they were poisoned by organophosphates, found that poisoned individuals scored significantly lower than control subjects on tests of intellectual functioning, academic skill, abstraction and flexibility of thinking, simple motor skills, and other functions. Twice as many of the poisoned participants as controls had scores consistent with brain damage or dysfunction.[19] In another study, two years after organophosphate poisoning, poisoned workers performed worse than controls on tests of motor skills, memory, language, and other abilities.[20]

The risks of pesticide use extend to the families of farmworkers. Infants and children are particularly susceptible to toxic exposures because their organ systems are developing rapidly. Because organophosphates are toxic to the developing nervous system, exposing infants and children to these pesticides can lead to learning disabilities and permanent neurological damage. (The costs of childhood illnesses are discussed in greater detail in chapter 8).

Children living in agricultural areas, especially the children of migrant workers, are exposed to higher pesticide levels than other children.[21] Children may be exposed to pesticides carried home on parents' clothing or skin; they may also receive exposures by eating food directly from sprayed areas, be exposed to pesticide drift from adjacent fields or orchards, and put pesticide-contaminated objects, soil, or dust in their mouths.

In addition, many children accompany their parents during agricultural work. Children as young as ten can legally work in agriculture with written parental consent.[22] In practice, children end up in the fields at even younger ages: the U.S. General Accounting Office has reported that seven percent of farmworkers with children five years of age or younger took their children with them, at least sometimes, when they worked.[23]

A study found AZM residues in the dust of 85 percent of farmworker homes and in 87 percent of workers' vehicles in eastern Washington in 2002.[24] In another study, researchers estimated the extent of AZM and phosmet exposure for farmworker children, based on urine samples. They found that 56 percent of the children had received AZM doses, over the spray season, that exceeded EPA's acceptable level for long-term exposure, and 35 percent had absorbed AZM doses that exceeded EPA's safe level for a single-day exposure. The corresponding percentages for phosmet were 9 percent and 6 percent.[25]

Do the economic benefits to growers outweigh the health and environmental costs of AZM and phosmet use? In recent cost-benefit analyses, avoided deaths have often been valued at several million dollars apiece, and avoided major illnesses have often been assigned values in the hundreds of thousands of dollars per case.[26] By that standard, a few dozen avoided deaths or a few hundred avoided major illnesses would offset the entire estimated benefit to apple growers of the two pesticides. EPA made no attempt to prove that the damages are smaller than this, as would be required in conventional cost-benefit calculations, to support the agency's conclusion that benefits outweigh the costs.

Effects on Salmon and Other Ecosystem Inhabitants

EPA also failed to account for the damage to the natural environment caused by AZM and phosmet. Many of the apple orchards of the Northwest are in the watersheds of rivers that are essential to economically important and endangered species such as salmon. Thus the impact of pesticide runoff on salmon and other species should be considered in any assessment of costs and benefits. As with health impacts, there are reasons for concern, but EPA did not provide any quantitative assessment of the potential damage to the natural environment.

EPA did note that AZM has been responsible for more "aquatic incidents in the Agency's ecological incident database than any other pesticide," and that AZM "is responsible for over 21 percent of all reported aquatic incidents." The magnitude of ecological damage caused by individual accidents involving AZM has also been unusually large compared with the effects of other pesticides. In ten AZM incidents, EPA recorded that 10,000 fish were killed.[27] At many sites where AZM was used, EPA found that "the aquatic levels of concern are exceeded for marine/estuarine and freshwater fish and aquatic invertebrates." The agency mentioned toxicity to a variety of fish, including salmon, but did not attempt to quantify these adverse effects.[28]

Meanwhile, the U.S. Geological Survey (USGS) has surveyed surface waters for pesticides through its National Water Quality Assessment Program. USGS detected AZM in 65 percent of the samples in the Yakima River basin, making it the most widely detected insecticide.[29] USGS found AZM at levels dangerous for aquatic life in its surveys in the Yakima, Willamette, and San Joaquin–Tulare basins.[30]

EPA's inaction on these issues has even led to legal proceedings. A lawsuit challenged EPA's failure to consult, as required, on the impacts of AZM and phosmet on salmon and steelhead that are protected under the Endangered Species Act.[31] In 2002, a federal district court ordered EPA to initiate such consultations. In 2004, the court imposed interim protections in the form of buffers to protect salmon and steelhead during the consultation process. As of 2006, the consultations on AZM and phosmet had not yet been completed, and EPA had yet to develop safeguards to protect salmon and steelhead from these pesticides.[32]

Valuation of endangered species, for the purposes of cost-benefit analyses, has found that people are willing to pay what would add up to enormous sums for the existence of these species. These estimates are largely based on the so-called passive use or non-use value attributed to the existence of the species, although they also include the commercial and recreational value of the fish that are caught.[33]

A 1991 study looked at valuation of salmon and steelhead habitat in the Pacific Northwest, asking households what they would be willing to pay to double the population of salmon in the Columbia River. Among people who never fish for salmon, the average answer was $27 per household per year; among those who currently fish for salmon, the average was $74 per household per year.[34]

Subsequent studies have confirmed the finding of widespread, large willingness to pay for protection of salmon and their habitat. Despite differences in detail among studies, numerous analysts agree that households in the Pacific Northwest, and in the nation, would be collectively willing to spend millions of dollars for the continued existence of salmon.[35]

With endangered species conventionally valued in the hundreds of millions of dollars at stake, and evidence that AZM has a damaging effect on the valuable species, it is impossible to assess the costs and benefits of pesticide use without considering this factor. How much damage is pesticide runoff causing to the salmon of the Northwest or other endangered species? EPA did not even attempt to answer this question.

Round One: Summary

According to EPA's 2001 estimate, the value of AZM and phosmet use to apple growers was $114 million or less per year—how much less is unknown because EPA did not perform an adequate analysis of some of the leading alternatives that might prove cost-effective. One side of the ledger contains the economic benefit of $114 million or less; the other side should contain an uncertain number of serious, often long-lasting health effects, plus an uncertain but possibly significant amount of damage to endangered species that are valued highly by the local and national population. EPA mentioned some of these harms, but did not monetize them; nor did it offer any other means of comparison between the economic benefits and noneconomic harms of AZM and phosmet use.

Thus in 2001, EPA completely failed to demonstrate that the economic benefits outweigh the risks and justify the continued use of AZM and phosmet. In the subsequent revisions, EPA went on to make its case even weaker.

Round Two: New Errors for Old

The United Farm Workers suit resulted in a 2004 settlement that gave EPA until 2006 to reevaluate its decision.[36] In 2006, EPA released its proposed decisions for AZM and phosmet, including an updated economic analysis of the benefits of these pesticides for apple and pear growers. The critique of the earlier cost-benefit analyses—that EPA had failed to show that the modest financial benefits of AZM and phosmet use outweigh the substantial health and environmental risks—was only reinforced by the agency's new studies and arguments. The 2006 round of the debate introduced new wrinkles, and three new weaknesses, into the analyses:

- The new analyses drastically reduced the estimated annual benefits of AZM and phosmet, to just $18 million for apple growers, and all of $1 million for pear growers.
- In the case of phosmet, the agency claimed that the available data on pesticide risks, created at great effort by EPA itself, should not be believed.

- Although EPA did decide to phase out AZM, it did so with a long, unnecessary delay, based on an inaccurate and undocumented new hypothesis about U.S. export markets.

Second-Round Benefit Estimates Were Sharply Reduced

EPA's economic analysis of AZM and phosmet focused heavily on the benefits to growers, measured as the reduction in growers' net revenues that would result from eliminating the use of the pesticides. As noted above, in the 2001 analyses, the scenario with no AZM or phosmet use reduced apple grower revenues by $114 million annually, and pear grower revenues by $100 million. In the 2006 analyses, EPA introduced new scenarios in which AZM and phosmet were replaced by other pesticides that were not mentioned in the earlier studies: the tongue-twisting names of the new pesticides include thiacloprid, novaluron, and acetamiprid for apples, and acetamiprid and methoxyfenozide for pears.[37] These alternatives cost somewhat more, but work just as well as AZM and phosmet, eliminating the concern about reduced yields. In EPA's new analysis, increased pesticide costs would decrease growers' annual revenues by a total of $18 million in apples, and $1 million in pears.

These new estimates are less than 16 percent of the previous estimate for apples, and a mere 1 percent of the previous estimate for pears. In other words, 84 percent of the benefits of AZM and phosmet for apple growers, and 99 percent of the benefits for pear growers, that had been identified by EPA in 2001 had vanished by 2006. The decline in yield and quality caused by the alternatives, much discussed in the 2001 analysis, had also disappeared.

EPA's more recent analyses could be taken as grounds for optimism about substitution: with minimal cost increases, and no loss of yield or quality, both AZM and phosmet can be replaced in apple and pear orchards. It is difficult to imagine that financial benefits of less than $19 million to apple and pear growers could outweigh substantial risks to people and nature. Moreover, EPA still dismissed the potential of options such as switching to organic production, an alternative that has proven profitable for numerous growers. If former AZM and phosmet users switched to organic production, the financial impact of a phase-out would be even smaller.

EPA Rejects EPA Data

EPA proposed, and ultimately decided, to allow the continued use of phosmet on several crops, including apples and pears, with increases in the restricted entry interval, or length of time when workers should not enter the fields following pesticide application.[38] Yet despite the support for continued use, EPA's newer analysis documented numerous risks of phosmet. The ecological assessment cited numerous cases in which use of phosmet at maximum labeled rates exceeded the level of concern for impacts on fish, aquatic invertebrates, birds, and small mammals. The discussion of these findings largely consisted of pointing out that AZM is even worse.[39] For worker impacts, where an MOE of 100 or more is generally considered safe, the increased restricted entry interval provided MOEs of only 37 for some apple workers, and 11 for some pear workers.[40]

EPA explained its rationale for ignoring these numbers most fully in response to the apple worker MOE of 37: "While this MOE falls short of the target of 100, EPA believes risk is not underestimated because these estimates include worst-case assumptions that may overestimate risk."[41] The document went on to explain that the MOE calculations are based on assuming maximum application rates and thirty days of consecutive work following the end of the restricted entry interval. In addition, EPA suggested that the use of the no-effects level in defining MOEs builds in an additional margin of safety, because it is lower than necessary.

In arguing that the maximum allowable exposure overestimates risk because not all workers are actually exposed to that level of pesticide, EPA was implicitly advocating a radical change to its normal practice: it was calling for analysis based on average, rather than maximum, risk. Consider an analogy: are highway accidents caused by unsafe speed related to the average speed of cars on the road, or to the maximum speed? Following EPA's approach to MOEs, one could claim that basing estimates of highway risk on the fastest vehicles is a worst-case assumption, because most cars are not going that fast. But it is precisely the fastest cars that—like the most heavily exposed farmworkers (i.e., those with the smallest MOEs)—are at greatest risk of harm: they will not receive much protection from the observation that others are driving more slowly, or facing lower pesticide exposures.

To estimate the probable harm resulting from pesticide use, it is entirely appropriate, indeed essential, to consider the effects of maximum allowable exposures. The impact at issue is poisoning from overexposure to pesticides; this depends on maximum individual exposures, not population averages. The industrywide average exposure could be reduced by adding more workers with little or no exposure, without changing the number of workers exposed to high levels of pesticides. Likewise, average highway speed goes down when more slow vehicles show up in the right-hand lane, even if the most recklessly fast drivers maintain their previous speeds. Risks of life in the fast lane, or at maximum exposure, are not changed by misleading reductions in averages.

EPA also objected to the use of the maximum no-effects level of exposure, rather than the minimum level at which adverse effects are detected. In this case, as often happens, the maximum no-effects level falls noticeably below the lowest observable adverse effects level. Continuing the highway analogy, is it better to drive at the maximum speed that is known to be safe, or at the minimum speed that is known to be unsafe? Common sense clearly endorses the standard practice of relying on the former, that is, the maximum safe or no-effects level. EPA's traditional approach to MOEs conforms to this sensible method, unlike the new interpretation suggested in the phosmet decision document.

EPA thus suggested a fundamental redefinition of its own standards and data in the direction of weakening protection against risk in order to justify ignoring the otherwise unacceptable MOE of 37. In effect, EPA invited the reader to believe that its own data should not be relied on, since a different standard could have been used to define harm more loosely.

In summary, EPA acknowledged phosmet's low MOE numbers but argued, in less than lucid language, that its own system of measuring risk routinely results in overestimates:

> EPA recognizes that the worker risk assessment indicates that existing MOEs at current label rates are insufficient to ensure that there is not a concern that workers will be exposed to levels of phosmet that will result in cholinesterase depression—a precursor of adverse neurological effects. . . . Although the mitigation will not result in an MOE of over 100 [i.e., will not reduce exposure to levels traditionally considered safe], the Agency

believes that the MOEs may likely overestimate the risk to reentry workers and EPA is not aware of incident information, monitoring data or other sources of information that numerous worker poisoning incidents are occurring.[42]

Since EPA does not require reports of incident information, monitoring data, or other sources of information on worker poisoning, it is "not aware" of this data by design. EPA's proposal to allow continued uses of phosmet was made possible only by rejection of its own standards and data regarding worker health.

Slow Phase-Out Unwarranted for AZM

EPA's 2006 analysis of AZM recited a long list of ecological and worker health risks associated with AZM, and proposed to phase out all ten remaining uses of the pesticide.[43] For five of the crops, it phased out AZM in 2007. But for five others, including apples and pears, EPA proposed to allow AZM use to continue until 2010.

The need for the extension rested on a new hypothesis about export markets. "In order for U.S. growers to export apples that have pesticide residues, there must be established maximum residue levels (MRL) which are similar to the requirements of U.S. tolerances."[44] EPA suggested that apple growers could face export losses of more than $100 million per year from premature adoption of alternative pesticides, prior to establishment of MRLs overseas.

But was it true that major U.S. export markets had not yet established residue standards for the alternative pesticides that might replace AZM? EPA presented only very partial and inconclusive evidence of the lack of international regulation. With just a quick search of the Internet, I turned up extensive evidence that the process of analysis, testing, and development of regulations for the alternative pesticides is underway. Europe, Japan, and international organizations are well aware of the pesticides that EPA now proposes as replacements for AZM, and are moving rapidly to analyze and set standards for them.[45]

In addition to the export loss hypothesis, EPA also claimed that the benefits outweighed the risks for the AZM extension through 2010 for apples, because it will take growers time to perfect the use of the new alternatives, and because, as with phosmet, EPA does not believe that significant harms are occurring:

> While EPA believes the risk concerns from AZM use are significant, EPA is not aware of incident information, monitoring data or other sources of information that suggest AZM is having immediate large-scale environmental impacts (such as a clear link to species population declines or extirpations) or that severe worker poisoning incidents are occurring. Although incident and monitoring databases are not sufficiently robust to capture the extent of likely adverse effects, EPA believes that if severe adverse human health and environmental effects were occurring on a broad scale, these databases would reflect that fact.[46]

The quoted passage seems to suggest a harsh new standard, namely that regardless of data and standards, chemical risk doesn't matter until it's on the evening news or the front page of the newspaper. But the point of protective regulation is to identify and prevent problems *before* they have "immediate large-scale impacts" that are painfully visible to everyone.

Conclusion

The new analyses of AZM and phosmet released by EPA in 2006 were subjected to a final round of public scrutiny. EPA's final decision on the continued use of AZM, released a few months later, corresponded very closely with the proposal, but allows an even longer phase-out period, stretching out to 2012.[47] The final decision for phosmet likewise corresponds closely to EPA's proposal. The justification for continued use of phosmet relies heavily on the claim that it is a less hazardous substitute for AZM, ignoring the possibility of switching to the even less hazardous options discussed above.

In the 2006 analyses, EPA all but rescinded its previous finding of significant economic benefits to growers from the use of AZM and phosmet. Alternative pesticides, it turns out, can do an equally good job at only modestly greater cost. Meanwhile, no comparable reduction has occurred in the estimated risks to farmworkers, their families and communities, and the natural environment. The only logical conclusion is that the scales should now be tilted far more heavily against the continued use of these pesticides. EPA failed to demonstrate, even with its earlier, much higher benefits estimates, that the benefits outweighed the risks. With the new, minimal benefits figures, less than $18 million per year for apple growers and a mere $1 million for pear growers, this conclusion is even more strongly reinforced.

EPA's decisions for AZM and phosmet are steps in the right direction, but neither one goes far enough. Phosmet was subject to greater restrictions, rather than outright elimination, because EPA no longer believed its own data about the risks of worker exposure. AZM got a six-year reprieve from phase-out in key crops because of EPA's unsubstantiated guess about export markets.

EPA has made the story seem complicated, whereas in fact the bottom line is simple:

- Workers in orchards that use AZM and phosmet face significant health risks.
- Workers' children are also exposed, and may suffer developmental disabilities as a result.
- Both AZM and phosmet greatly exceed the levels of concern for many animal species.
- Nothing remotely persuasive has been said about economic benefits that might outweigh these risks. Rather, EPA's own study has shown that alternative pesticides are equally effective, and impose only minimal cost increases on growers.

The formal methods of cost-benefit analysis contributed nothing to the understanding of these pesticides. The fabled objectivity and transparency of cost-benefit methods were nowhere to be seen. Rather, the discussion of costs and benefits generated long, jargon-filled reports, serving to suggest that something technical was being discussed, beyond the understanding of most readers. This only obscured the otherwise blatant bias of the EPA decision makers in favor of the growers and their freedom to use harmful chemicals, regardless of the effects on workers and nature. No new insights were provided into the value of health and environmental harms, nor even into the economics of growing and exporting apples. Ironically, the only real contribution made by the agency's studies was to demonstrate just how tiny is the economic benefit from the use of these hazardous pesticides.

Chapter 7

Mad Cows and Computer Models

Fears of a bovine spongiform encephalopathy (BSE) or "mad cow disease" epidemic have been kept alive in the United States by the continuing discovery of infected cattle. The eight confirmed North American cases to date (as of 2007) include two found in 2006, including one in the United States. Several were born after the U.S. and Canadian governments banned the use of cattle parts in feed, a policy change that was thought to rule out the most widely suspected transmission route.

There are inherent limits to direct observation of both BSE and the related human disease, variant Creutzfeld-Jakob disease: they have long incubation periods, but are not detectable until the relatively late stages of the disease, and their presence cannot be confirmed, at any stage, except by autopsy. Since the diseases were unknown before the 1980s, and are invariably fatal, it is not surprising that widespread anxiety and dread have surrounded the debate over BSE policy. Modeling the risks correctly, and presenting the results in a transparent manner, is of utmost importance for maintaining public confidence in government policy toward BSE.

Yet just as cost-benefit analysis fails to be objective and transparent in practice, the statistical modeling of BSE also fails to clarify the issues and provide a neutral basis for public policy. Opaque technicalities hide the critical value judgments from view, just as in the economic analysis of pesticides described in chapter 6. As with the evaluation of pesticides, the

Chapter 7 by Frank Ackerman and Wendy Johnecheck.

BSE analysis relied on by the U.S. Department of Agriculture (USDA) concludes that there is nothing to worry about, only because serious problems have been assumed away to begin with. The difference is that in the case of BSE, very complex statistical modeling is involved in estimating the extent of the underlying problem. The intricacy of that modeling effort means that few people will notice if it rests on arbitrary and biased assumptions, and therefore fails to make its case that BSE is unlikely to spread. And as with cost-benefit analysis, the failure of the statistical modeling effort leaves us in a state of deep uncertainty about an important risk, a situation that calls for alternative, precautionary approaches to public policy.

In many respects, U.S. policy toward BSE follows the pattern established in other countries. However, compared to several other countries where BSE has been detected, the United States tests a much smaller proportion of the cattle slaughtered each year. As a result, U.S. policy is unusually dependent on statistical models that estimate the prevalence and potential spread of the disease on the basis of limited observational data. As interpreted by USDA (and discussed below), those models conclude that there is little or nothing to worry about: they find that BSE is extremely rare at present, and is very unlikely to spread to larger numbers of cattle.

This chapter examines the models relied on by USDA to analyze the risks of BSE. We find, in brief, that the models of both the current prevalence and the potential spread of BSE contain a number of unsupported assumptions; these assumptions undermine confidence in the model results. Our argument is not that we know a BSE epidemic *is* likely; rather, we make the more limited, negative claim that the models we describe have failed to disprove the likelihood of an epidemic.

In the next section, we present background on BSE, policy responses, and testing in the United States and other countries. Thereafter, we discuss modeling of the current prevalence of BSE, followed by the more complex model of the potential spread of the disease. We conclude with implications for BSE policy.

Background: BSE and Public Policy

Both BSE and variant Creutzfeld-Jakob disease are relatively new diseases, first recognized in the United Kingdom in the mid-1980s and mid-

1990s, respectively. The original source of BSE remains unclear, but it is generally thought that the early, rapid spread of BSE was due to supplementing cattle feed with protein-rich meat and bone meal (MBM) derived from infected cattle.

The practice of feeding MBM, a byproduct of the rendering industry, to cattle was introduced in the 1970s. Since then BSE cases have appeared in at least twenty-three other countries, most plausibly linked to the importation of cattle and feed products from infected countries.[1] Following the first and worst outbreak of BSE in Britain, and smaller but similar problems elsewhere, many countries have banned beef imports from countries where BSE has been detected, adopted a wide range of safety and sanitary standards, and dramatically increased testing of slaughtered cattle for BSE.

Prior to 2004, U.S. policy toward BSE had three principal components, optimistically labeled as "firewalls": restrictions on imports of animals and meat from countries where BSE was known to exist; a ban on MBM and most (not all) other mammalian protein in cattle feed; and a surveillance program testing a few thousand at-risk cattle each year.[2] In 2004, in response to the discovery of a BSE case in Washington State, the level of surveillance was increased, and two more "firewalls" were added: a ban on the use of "downer" (nonambulatory) cattle in human food, and prohibitions on the use of "specified risk material" (certain tissues known to be at risk for containing BSE) in human food. However, a detailed policy review by Thomas McGarity demonstrated that the firewalls contain numerous loopholes and exemptions; with inadequate enforcement resources, the United States in practice relies heavily on self-policing and self-reporting of sanitary problems by meatpacking firms.[3]

Although some regulatory practices may be unintended consequences of budget cuts and other policies, one of the unique features of the U.S. system is intentional: the low level, by international standards, of testing for BSE. Japan tests every slaughtered animal for BSE. Europe tests every animal above thirty months of age (since the disease has a long incubation period, and is not always detectable in younger animals), as well as every high-risk case. In 2004, 22.9 million adult cattle were slaughtered in the EU.[4] In that year, 1.5 million at-risk animals were tested (finding 520 positives), as well as 9.6 million apparently healthy animals (finding 166 positives).[5] That is, 11.1 million, or more than 48 percent of all slaughtered cattle, were tested. The prevalence of BSE was much greater among at-risk animals (347 per million tests) than among healthy ones (17 per million tests), but about a quarter of all detected cases of BSE were found by testing apparently healthy cattle.

In the United States, 32.9 million adult cattle were slaughtered in 2004, or 44 percent more than in the EU.[6] Despite these large numbers, U.S. testing for BSE has remained far below the European level. Before mid-2004, testing had never exceeded a rate of about 20,000 animals per year, representing only a small fraction of the high-risk groups. Following the detection of two North American BSE cases in 2003, USDA introduced a new testing procedure in June 2004. A new, rapid screening test was adopted and the pace of testing increased, reaching about 24,000 per month in the second half of 2004, and 30,000 per month (360,000 per year) in 2005 and early 2006. Yet even this record level of testing represents just over 1 percent of the cattle slaughtered annually in the United States, compared to 48 percent in Europe and 100 percent in Japan. In mid-2006, USDA announced a reduction in the level of BSE testing to 40,000 per year, just a little more than 10 percent of the 2005 level, on the grounds that so few cases had been found.[7]

Even in countries with high levels of testing, statistical modeling is essential to understand the dynamics of BSE, because the disease cannot be detected in live animals of any age, or in autopsies of most young animals. The role of modeling is all the greater in the United States, where 99 percent of slaughtered cattle remain untested.

U.S. policy relies heavily on the results of two models. First, prevalence models estimate that there are low numbers of existing cases; these models are discussed in the next section. Second, an intricate model estimates the expected spread of the disease, given the existence of a few infected cattle. This model, produced for USDA in 2001 by the Harvard Center for Risk Analysis (HCRA) and revised in 2003, is often cited by U.S. officials as proving that there is essentially no risk of an epidemic.[8] It is the subject of the subsequent section.

Prevalence of BSE in the United States

How many cases of BSE exist in the United States today? If applied to a random sample of the millions of U.S. cattle, the 360,000 tests conducted annually in 2005–2006 could reliably detect BSE only if the prevalence was as high as one in 120,000.[9] Likewise, the 40,000 tests conducted annually after mid-2006 could reliably detect only one in about 13,000. The USDA believes, however, that the wealth of data accumulated through European testing can be applied to improve the efficiency of the U.S. testing effort.

USDA's approach starts with the observation that BSE is much more common among at-risk cattle than among apparently healthy cattle. The limited U.S. testing effort is concentrated on at-risk cattle. Then heroic assumptions about the applicability of European data allow an estimate of the number of cases of BSE in the much larger number of apparently healthy animals.

To explain the calculations, it will be helpful to define a new term, the "at-risk relative prevalence ratio" as

$$\text{at-risk relative prevalence} = \frac{\text{BSE prevalence among at-risk cattle}}{\text{BSE prevalence among apparently healthy cattle}}$$

If this ratio is 20, that means the rate of BSE is 20 times as high among at-risk cattle as among apparently healthy ones. USDA assumes that the value of this ratio found by European testing is applicable in the U.S. as well—and that U.S. testing can determine the rate of BSE among at-risk cattle. Then simple arithmetic leads to an estimate of the number of cases of BSE among the entire cattle population. Two similar but not identical models, using this logic, produce central estimates of 4 and 7 cases of BSE in the United States as of 2006.[10] In the "best guesses" from these models and a handful of related sensitivity analyses, the 95 percent confidence intervals around the estimates of existing BSE cases range from 1 to 30. Even the upper limit of 30 cases implies a prevalence of less than one in a million, a summary statistic that has often been quoted in the press.

However, the uncertainty in the prevalence of BSE may be greater than these confidence intervals suggest. The prevalence models rely on two key assumptions: first, the high-risk group as identified in the United States corresponds to the same group in Europe; and second, the at-risk relative prevalence ratio is the same in both cases.

Regarding the first assumption, USDA estimates that there are fewer than 500,000 at-risk cases per year, or about one-third the number identified in Europe in 2004, despite a much larger inventory of cattle, and larger annual slaughter, in the United States. This contrast between the U.S. and the EU might represent differences in definitions of at-risk animals, differences in animal management, or limitations on U.S. data collection.

Because downer cattle are no longer accepted at commercial slaughterhouses in the United States, their final disposal is handled by rendering establishments, veterinarians, and the producers themselves; USDA data collection depends on voluntary reporting by these groups. Yet cattle owners and other voluntary reporters have financial incentives to avoid reporting the most likely BSE cases.[11] Submitting a specimen that tests positive for BSE can lead to substantial losses, since the guilty establishment may be shut down for some time. This suggests that USDA may not receive a random sample of at-risk cattle to test, but instead could find its data biased, to an unknown extent, against discovering cases of BSE. Similar biases are less likely to exist in Europe or Japan, where every animal in a specified age or risk category is tested, creating fewer opportunities for cattle owners' decisions to influence data collection.

Regarding the second assumption, the at-risk relative prevalence ratio does not appear to be a reliable international constant. Documents on the USDA Web site report European values of this ratio ranging from 8 to 28[12]; the 2004 European data cited above imply a ratio of 347/17, or about 20. A higher value of that ratio implies a lower estimated prevalence: for example, a ratio of 28 means that the (unmeasured) prevalence of BSE among healthy cattle is estimated to be 1/28 of the (partially measured) prevalence among at-risk animals.

In short, the attempt to generate a U.S. prevalence estimate from very limited testing, using patterns established in Europe, faces crucial uncertainties because the at-risk group may be defined differently, measured differently, or underreported in the United States—and because the at-risk relative prevalence ratio may vary from one country to another.

The HCRA Model: Will BSE Spread in the United States?

Uncertainty about the current prevalence of BSE in the U.S. would be of limited importance if the disease were expected to die out quickly, rather than spreading. The HCRA model reached exactly this encouraging conclusion. It assumed the presence of ten initial cases, and then modeled the expected path of the disease over twenty years. The HCRA analysis found, with a high level of confidence, that BSE is expected to die out rapidly in all the scenarios it discussed.

The critical measure of the spread of the disease is the basic reproduction number, R_0, defined as the lifetime total number of new cases of BSE caused, on average, by one existing case. If $R_0 < 1$, the disease dies out naturally; if $R_0 > 1$, the disease tends to spread. Retrospective analysis on the British BSE epidemic suggests that prior to the 1988 ban on feeding MBM to cattle, R_0 may have been as large as 10–12; after the ban, it appears to have fallen well below 1.[13] The central result of the HCRA model is that in the majority of its scenarios for BSE in the United States, there was a 95 percent probability that $R_0 < 1$. However, the report adequately addressed only one of the relevant forms of uncertainty. It identified, but barely discussed, several assumptions and circumstances under which a major BSE epidemic has at least a 25 percent chance of occurrence.

At least three varieties of uncertainty could affect the model. Uncertainty could surround the model's equations, which describe the pathways through which BSE could spread; or the numerical parameters used in the equations; or the specific outcomes that will occur (since the model only predicts probabilities of events). By analogy to a game played with dice, one could be uncertain about the rules of the game, about the weighting of the dice, or about what will happen the next time the dice are rolled. The statistical analysis that occupies much of the HCRA report addresses only the third category of uncertainty. For each scenario, the analysts ran 5,000 separate simulations, using the computer to "roll the dice" each time and decide which of the more or less probable outcomes occurred. (This statistical technique, somewhat reminiscent of casino games, is called "Monte Carlo analysis.") Thus, within each scenario there was ample information about the uncertainties that result from rolling the dice.

There is much less information about the first two types of uncertainty. In the first category, the narrative description of the relationships assumed in the model is detailed, but almost entirely verbal rather than mathematical. The equations that represent these relationships are not provided anywhere in the report or appendices. The problems are, if anything, greater in the second category of uncertainty, involving the estimates of parameters and the choice of scenarios that were analyzed. How, exactly, has nature weighted the dice that are rolled to determine the spread of BSE?

The HCRA model requires at least 49 numerical parameters.[14] The authors focused on 17 of these parameters, divided into three groups: 3 involve cattle population dynamics, 8 describe aspects of the slaughter process, and 6 refer to feed production and feeding practices.[15] For each of the key parameters, they presented the base case, which they consider most likely, and a worst case (the value most likely to spread BSE). There is limited documentation for the selection of the base-case values, and almost none for the worst-case values. Thus the model relies heavily on the incompletely documented professional judgments of the authors, regarding the choice of parameter values as well as the equations.

Even if all the judgments about equations, base-case, and worst-case parameter values are appropriate, a deeper problem remains: how many worst-case parameter values should be considered in a scenario? For no explicitly stated reason, the study's answer was only one. The report almost entirely ignored the uncertainty resulting from the interaction between worst-case values, which, as we will see, can be substantial.

Most of the HCRA analysis consisted of introducing worst-case values, one at a time, for individual parameters, running the model, and studying the results. There are 17 such "single-worst-case" scenarios, each of which has a worst-case value for one parameter and base-case values for the other 16 parameters. The HCRA report's main finding was that in the base case and 14 of the single-worst-case scenarios, $R_0 < 1$ in 95 percent of the 5,000 simulations. In the other three single-worst-case scenarios, $R_0 < 1$ in at least 75 percent but fewer than 95 percent of the simulations.

Changing one parameter at a time could be a useful first step in exploring uncertainty in the model, but other sensitivity analyses should be relevant as well. The peer reviewers of the original report criticized its failure to consider the effects of multiple-worst-case values[16]; the revised report added six scenarios assuming worst-case values for groups of parameters. Three scenarios assumed worst-case values for all the parameters in a single group—cattle demographics, the slaughter process, and feed procedures—and three more assumed worst-case values for each pair of groups. $R_0 < 1$ with 95 percent probability in only one of the six multiple-worst-case scenarios; $R_0 < 1$ with 75 percent probability in only three of the six. That is, three scenarios found at least a 25 percent probability that $R_0 > 1$. One of the scenarios implied at least a 25 percent chance of a raging epidemic, with more than a million infected cattle.

Each scenario assumed the initial presence of ten infected animals in the United States, and then calculated, among other results, the total number of cattle that would be infected over the next twenty years. The typical infection cycle in the model, from infection of one animal to the resulting infection of another, was just under 5 years in length. So if $R_0 = 1$, the critical threshold value, then the original 10 infected cases should each result in four more over the twenty-year simulation period, for a total of 50.[17] More than 50 cases would imply $R_0 > 1$, while fewer than 50 would imply $R_0 < 1$.

Table 7.1 presents selected results, for the base case, the three single-worst-case scenarios with the greatest potential for BSE, and all the multiple-worst-case scenarios. At the 75th percentile, all the scenarios involving the worst-case values for the feed procedures parameters group, alone or in combination with other groups, had well over 50 infected cases (and one scenario had more than a million cases). So there is at least a 25 percent chance that BSE will not die out in these scenarios. At the 95th percentile, all but one of the scenarios shown in table 7.1 (other than the base case) had totals of more than 50 infected cases, implying $R_0 > 1$; so there is at least a 5 percent chance of a self-perpetuating problem in all these scenarios.

Yet the multiple-worst-case scenarios, projecting substantial risks of an epidemic, barely registered in the HCRA report's discussion of the model; they were not mentioned in either the executive summary or the chapter on policy implications.[18] Much more attention was paid to the (much less alarming) results of the three single-worst-case scenarios that implied a 5 percent chance that $R_0 > 1$. This unbalanced emphasis would be justified only if the base-case estimates were known to be correct for at least 16 of the 17 parameters, and the remaining uncertainty concerned merely which single-worst-case might be occurring. No argument for that singular pattern of uncertainty was provided.

TABLE 7.1   Scenario totals of infected cattle.

	Percentile		
	50	75	90
Worst-case parameter values	*Number of cases*		
None (base case)	10	11	26
Single-worst-case scenarios			
Render reduction factor	10	11	**83**
Feed mislabeling	11	14	**160**
Misfeeding of correctly labeled feed	11	26	**430**
Multiple-worst-case scenarios			
All demographic parameters	10	11	**58**
All slaughter process parameters	11	12	**43**
All feed procedures parameters	12	**170**	**1,600**
Demographic and slaughter parameters	11	12	**110**
Demographic and feed parameters	23	**1,300,000**	**4,500,000**
Feed and slaughter parameters	16	**1,400**	**6,200**

Numbers are the total number of cases of infection resulting over twenty years following the introduction of ten infected cattle; fifty corresponds to $R_0 = 1$. Numbers in bold imply $R_0 > 1$ (see text).

Percentiles refer to the distribution of simulation results from the Monte Carlo analysis of each scenario.

   Source: Cohen et al. 2003, Appendix 3D, Table 1, pp. 29, 38, 47.

A later revision to the model in 2005 modified some parameter estimates and made a number of small changes in the model structure; its conclusions were qualitatively unchanged from the 2003 report.[19] The 2005 revision offered a more abbreviated model description and listing of outputs, and did not revisit the multiple-worst-case scenarios. It reran some of the scenarios from the earlier report, including the "misfeeding" scenario, testing the effect of a higher probability of misfeeding correctly labeled, prohibited material to cattle (the third of the single-worst-case scenarios in table 7.1). Commenting on the probability of misfeeding, the revised report said, "the range of plausible values for this parameter remains very uncertain"[20]; the scenario using the worst-case value for misfeeding raised the mean estimate of R_0 to 0.89, compared to 0.24 in the base case. It is all too easy to imagine that a slightly greater value for this "very uncertain" parameter, and/or synergy with slightly worse than base-case values for other parameters, could push R_0 above 1.0, implying that the disease, once started, would be expected to spread.

BSE Policy Making: The High-Stakes Gamble

By now there is an academic literature on the policy problems and public fears, as well as risk analysis, surrounding BSE. For example, it has been shown that the perceived risk of "mad cow disease" relates to worry about environmental risks in general, even more than to knowledge about BSE risks in particular.[21] In a cautionary tale for other countries, the British government's over-reliance on reassuring statements from scientific authorities backfired as the crisis worsened, undermining public trust.[22] The Japanese government also assured its citizens that there was no risk from BSE, only to be embarrassed when cases were later discovered. Drawing on this and other international experience, it has been argued that the United States should adopt additional precautionary measures to reduce economic risks to the beef industry, which would suffer badly from any additional loss of confidence.[23]

The effort expended by the U.S. government to avoid the levels of testing adopted in other countries might suggest that large costs are involved. Yet testing reportedly costs between $30 and $50 per head; the cost of moving the United States up to the European level of testing has been estimated at $210–$450 million per year.[24] With total U.S. beef production of around 25 billion pounds annually,[25] this is a cost of $0.01–$0.02 per pound of beef. The more demanding Japanese approach, testing every slaughtered animal, would cost $1.0–$1.6 billion,[26] or $0.04–$0.07 per pound of beef. These testing costs can be compared to the loss of $2 billion of beef exports in 2004,[27] that is, the twelve months following the discovery of a U.S. BSE case in December 2003. Regardless of one's beliefs about the necessity or utility of European or Japanese testing regimes for the United States, it could have been a smart business move to perform enough tests to keep international customers happy.

It seems safe to guess that most decision makers and members of the public who come into contact with U.S. policy will never explore the details of the models on which it rests. The models do, however, provide impressively credentialed documentation for the claim that there is nothing to worry about. This is a high-stakes gamble: if nothing goes wrong, and BSE never becomes much more common in the United States than it is today, reliance on the reassuring studies will retrospectively appear to have been a success. On the other hand, the models, as we have seen, do not provide solid proof that "it can't happen here." All we actually know is that it hasn't happened here yet.

Statistical modeling, at the level of abstraction and uncertainty that characterizes the HCRA model, generally cannot ensure that public health is adequately protected against the threat of epidemics such as BSE. Once the impact of multiple, interacting uncertainties is recognized—even to the limited extent of two or more of HCRA's "worst-case" parameter values occurring at once—such a model can quickly become indeterminate, unable to offer a firm prediction that we are either above or below the threshold at which the disease tends to spread. We are back to the realm of uncertainty that calls for precautionary policy, as described in chapter 4.

Faced with fundamental uncertainty, there is a clear case for precautionary policies to protect public health against true worst-case outcomes, such as a large-scale epidemic. More protective BSE policies adopted in other countries provide a model that the United States could easily follow. One can of course hope that the optimism of the BSE models, and of USDA statements built upon them, will prove justified in retrospect, and at the same time favor a more cautious and rigorous approach to preventing the spread of BSE, just in case.

Chapter 8

Costs of Preventable Childhood Illness

Exposures to toxic chemicals can make children sick. They can cause lasting disabilities that impair children's ability to grow, learn, and play, and eventually to become productive working adults and parents themselves. These illnesses and disabilities can force children to stay at home, visit doctors, or lie in a hospital bed when they should be in school or at play. They cause parents to miss workdays or even give up their jobs. They require special equipment and services. And no matter what resources are devoted to mitigating these problems, the lives of affected children are never the same as they would be in the absence of the illness or disability.

The most profound effects of children's illnesses cannot be described or understood in monetary terms. It is meaningless to talk about a monetary value associated with lost opportunities to play, learn, and make friends. There is no dollar value that captures the pain to a mother or father of sitting helplessly by a sick child's hospital bed. None of the calculations in this chapter incorporate such effects. The human impact of children's illnesses is, as explained in chapter 1, priceless; an attempt to invent surrogate prices for the emotional dimensions of childhood illness would distort and cheapen these serious experiences. The cost of illness, as we interpret it here, is a narrower and better-defined concept, including only that subset of the consequences of disease that do have meaningful price tags attached.

Chapter 8 by Rachel Massey and Frank Ackerman.

But when policy makers talk about ways to protect children's health, financial considerations often come to dominate the discussion. It is not uncommon to hear arguments to the effect that measures to protect public health and the environment are a luxury we can ill afford. Such arguments are doubly misleading. The costs of protective regulation are routinely exaggerated, as shown in chapter 3; at the same time, the *absence* of public health protection is expensive, imposing the substantial costs of preventable, environmentally induced illness on society. This chapter reports on a case study of the latter point: an attempt to calculate the costs of Massachusetts children's illnesses attributable to environmental causes. The calculations encompass four major categories of disease: childhood cancer, asthma, neurobehavioral disorders, and lead poisoning.

The issues addressed here are national in scope, and a number of the key data sources are more readily available at the national than the state level. Why, then, do this analysis for a single state? Our study was done in response to a request from the Alliance for a Healthy Tomorrow, a coalition of Massachusetts groups that has been effective in raising issues of toxic chemicals, public health, and precautionary policies throughout the state. For their outreach to other Massachusetts groups and individuals, it is valuable to address impacts as locally as possible. Readers outside of Massachusetts may be able to extrapolate from this analysis, and envision a comparable, locally based treatment of children's health in other locales.[1]

Environmental Hazards and Childhood Diseases

Diseases can have multiple, often interacting causes; they can be inherited, caused by infections, and/or caused by chemicals and other factors in the environment in which a child develops or lives. Families can take important steps on their own to keep their children healthy, including decisions about diet, exercise habits, and exposure to alcohol, tobacco, and drugs, but such steps are not enough: exposure to many chemical hazards is involuntary and cannot be controlled by individuals and households. The decision whether or not to protect children from these hazards is inescapably collective.

A growing body of evidence implicates environmental factors as causes of chronic illnesses affecting children.[2] For diseases such as lead poisoning, there is no natural "background rate" of illness; every case of lead poisoning results from environmental factors under human control. In contrast, there are complex interactions among genetic and environmental factors that are responsible for diseases such as cancer, asthma, and neurobehavioral disorders. A portion of these illnesses and disabilities could be avoided by preventing toxic exposures.

In general, children are more vulnerable to environmental hazards than adults. Infants and children breathe, eat, and drink more than adults per unit of body weight. Their organ systems change and develop rapidly, making them vulnerable to small exposures at crucial windows of development. Children's immune systems are underdeveloped, making them more susceptible than adults to injury from toxic exposures. Children are disproportionately exposed to some hazards because they engage in normal childhood behaviors such as playing on the ground and putting objects in their mouths.[3]

A wide variety of preventable exposures to toxic substances affect children's health. Pesticides used in homes, lawns, gardens, and schools can cause cancer as well as neurological and other damage. Drinking water contaminated with organic solvents can cause leukemia and other cancers. Exhaust from buses and cars can cause birth defects when exposure occurs during pregnancy, and can cause or exacerbate asthma in exposed children. Children are exposed to lead in chipping leaded paint and in soil that was contaminated by use of leaded gasoline in the past. Contaminants found in food can damage the developing brain.[4] Poor indoor air quality in schools and at home can contribute to asthma and other disorders. Problems at schools include mold, use of toxic cleaning materials, and exposure to contaminated soil and chemicals from nearby toxic waste sites.[5]

Childhood Cancer

Childhood cancer is linked to environmental factors including exposure to solvents, pesticides, and air pollution. Parental and childhood exposures to pesticides and solvents are consistently linked to some cancers; prenatal exposures can be linked to childhood cancers; and there is particularly strong evidence of a connection between toxic exposures and leukemia, brain, and central nervous system cancers, which account for about half of children's cancers.[6]

Asthma

Asthma is a leading cause of illness in children. It accounts for about a third of all missed school days and is the most common cause of children's hospitalization.[7]

A distinction can be made between the initial development of asthma and the triggers that produce symptoms in asthmatic individuals. Environmental factors contribute to both stages. Exposure to irritants and toxins during fetal and infant development may increase a child's likelihood of developing asthma. Some scientists have postulated a link between the initial development of asthma and exposure to certain pesticides.[8] An individual who already has asthma may suffer symptoms or attacks triggered by natural allergens such as house dust mites, cockroaches, mold, and animal dander, as well as by pollutants such as ozone, sulfur dioxide, particulate matter, and second-hand tobacco smoke. Studies have found that asthma hospitalizations increase during episodes of severe air pollution.[9]

Neurobehavioral Disorders

The broad category of neurobehavioral disorders includes a range of problems, such as attention deficit hyperactivity disorder, autism and related disorders, and a variety of learning disabilities. Evidence both from the laboratory and from epidemiological studies shows links between toxic chemicals and a range of developmental disabilities. Developmental neurotoxicants to which children may be exposed include lead, mercury, cadmium, manganese, nicotine, pesticides such as organophosphates, dioxin, PCBs, and solvents.[10]

For example, prenatal exposures to mercury can produce adverse effects on fetuses even at low doses that do not produce visible effects in the mother. Mercury exposure is associated with problems with fine motor function, attention, language, visual-spatial abilities such as drawing, and verbal memory, among other health effects. In 1999–2000, around 8 percent of U.S. women of child-bearing age had at least 5.8 parts per billion of mercury in their blood; according to EPA, blood mercury above this level can produce adverse effects in fetuses.[11] The threshold above which mercury exposure is considered harmful has declined steadily over time, as researchers have investigated mercury's effects at increasingly low doses.[12]

Lead exposure also causes neurobehavioral disabilities. We treat it as a separate category here because of the extensive data and analysis that are available on the health effects and monetary costs of lead exposure.

Lead Poisoning

Lead, a heavy metal, is toxic to the developing nervous system. In adults, high blood lead levels can produce high blood pressure and other health problems. Lead exposure in babies and children, especially during the first five years of life, causes permanent damage to the developing brain. Lead levels in children are declining, rather than rising, thanks to policy changes that have reduced lead exposure. However, the level at which lead is known to be harmful has also been reduced. It was once assumed that lead was dangerous only at high levels, but evidence has accumulated steadily on the adverse effects of low exposures.

Children are exposed to lead from a variety of sources. Lead-based paint can poison children when it flakes off walls or produces lead-contaminated dust. Although its use has been illegal for many years, lead paint applied in the past remains in many older homes. Another major source of lead exposure is from contaminated soil. Policy measures have led to a steady reduction in lead poisoning rates, but many children continue to be exposed.

Environmental Justice

Environmental threats to children's health affect everyone. Living in a wealthy neighborhood, going to a private school, and getting the best possible medical treatment will not protect a child from all the health hazards of toxic environmental exposures. Not even the wealthiest communities are free from toxic pollution from military and industrial sources, as well as from everyday household products.

Poor and minority neighborhoods, however, bear a disproportionate environmental burden. In Massachusetts, communities of color and working-class communities are home to significantly more hazardous sites and facilities than wealthier and whiter communities.[13] Low-income and minority populations are also more likely to live in areas with risks of high lead exposure, due either to soil contamination or to lead paint.

This disproportionate burden of toxic exposures is mirrored by disproportionately high rates of some illnesses in minority and low-income communities.[14]

The effects of toxic exposures can also be compounded by other aspects of poverty. For example, poor nutrition can exacerbate the effects of lead exposure.[15] Limited income also means fewer choices in housing and nutrition; low-income families are often forced to live in poorly maintained housing and choose food that is cheaper, but less nutritious.

Calculating the Costs of Illness

To calculate the costs of childhood illness due to environmental factors, three types of data are needed:

- the number of children affected by each disease;
- the costs per affected child; and
- the fraction of each disease attributable to environmental causes.

This section provides an overview of all three types of data.

Growing Numbers for Some Childhood Diseases

In the past two to three decades, there have been substantial increases in both incidence (new cases reported each year) and prevalence (total number of children affected in a given year) of some children's illnesses. From 1975 to 2000, cancer incidence increased 32 percent nationwide in children under the age of fifteen.[16]

Autism rates have also risen dramatically. A 1999 report by the California Department of Developmental Services recorded a 273 percent increase in that state's autism rates between 1987 and 1998.[17] A follow-up report concluded that the observed increase in autism rates was real, and was not simply an artifact of changing diagnostic practices.[18] The number of California children with full-spectrum autism (a severe and comparatively easily diagnosed form of autism) rose from 2,778 in 1987 to 18,460 in 2002.[19]

Nationwide, according to EPA, "the self-reported prevalence of asthma increased 75% from 1980 to 1994 to 13.7 million people." This trend was evident "among all races, sexes, and age groups." The most dramatic increase was a 160 percent increase in asthma prevalence among children under five, from twenty-two children per 1,000 to fifty-eight per 1,000. A review of state asthma data found that Massachusetts had the highest self-reported asthma rate among adults nationwide in 2001.[20]

Multiple Categories of Costs

There are numerous categories of costs of illness. Some are relatively easy for researchers to agree upon, while others are controversial or impossible to monetize.

Treatment Costs
The category of treatment costs can include costs of medications, doctor and emergency room visits, therapy sessions, special equipment such as braces or crutches, and costs of hospitalization.

Lost School and Parental Work Time
Sick children miss days of school. This often implies lost workdays for parents. In addition, extensive lost school time can translate into educational deficits, which have implications for income and productivity in adulthood.

Special Education
Increasing numbers of children receive special education services, often paid for by the state. Special education requires high teacher-to-student ratios and costs substantially more per child than regular schooling. Some of those children need special education because they have suffered preventable toxic exposures that impaired their ability to learn.

Home and Institutional Care
Children with illnesses and developmental disabilities often require special care outside school hours, either at home or at an institution. Care at home may be provided by a paid caretaker or by a parent or other family member; in the latter case, the time spent at home may result in foregone earnings. Having a sick or disabled child may make it necessary for one parent to stay at home full time, in a family where both parents would otherwise work outside the home.

Costs of Related Illnesses in Adulthood

Some childhood exposures are associated with illnesses in adulthood. For example, elevated blood lead levels can lead to high blood pressure later in life. Children who suffer from asthma may experience additional lung disorders in adulthood. In addition, some illnesses, including many cancers, have long latency periods, so exposures during childhood do not produce disease until years or decades later.

Loss of Projected Future Earnings

Childhood illnesses and disabilities can translate into decreased productivity and lost income in adulthood. For example, lead exposure in childhood decreases IQ, and radiation therapy for childhood brain cancer can produce serious learning disabilities. These effects predictably lead to reductions in future earnings. In estimates of the societal costs of lead exposure, as shown below, the loss of future earnings due to impaired intelligence is much greater than the cost of medical treatment for lead-poisoned children.

Costs of Suffering and Death

Direct medical costs and lost earnings convey only part of the human cost of disease. Some economic analyses include estimates of the value of pain and suffering, and even estimates of the monetary value of death. These values are either inferred from observation of indirectly related market decisions, or based on surveys that ask people about what economists call "willingness to pay" for things that are not actually for sale (see chapter 1).

Such calculations are conjectural, dependent on indirect hypotheses about how to put a price on priceless human experience. Suffering and death are not exchanged in markets. You cannot buy or sell a unit of pain; you cannot offer to die in exchange for a sum of money, or go to a store and purchase extra years of life. It seems more useful and logical, therefore, to exclude such hypothetical valuations, while noting that the resulting numbers are only part of the human meaning of illness.[21]

Environmentally Attributable Fractions of Illness

The recent increases in a number of childhood illnesses, and the decline in lead poisoning, are occurring much too fast to be attributed to genetic factors; an entire human population's genes simply cannot change, within a few decades, in a way that causes noticeable changes in rates of disease. There are only two possible explanations. On the one hand, the data could be misleading; for instance, definitions of disease might have changed, or the reported increase might reflect more careful and complete screening. On the other hand, if an increase or decrease in disease is real, it must be due at least in part to environmental factors, broadly defined. This is only logical: our genes have been essentially constant over the few generations since the rise of modern industry, while the environment has been changing rapidly. However, it is difficult to identify the precise fraction of disease attributable to environmental causes. (Depending on the context, the term "environment" may be used to refer to all factors that are not genetic, including smoking and other personal choices; or it may be used in a more restricted sense to refer to the physical environment that surrounds us and, in particular, to exposures that are not determined by individual choices or behavior patterns.)

The concept of the "environmentally attributable fraction" (EAF) of illness first appeared in a 1981 report by the Institute of Medicine, and has been used in a number of studies over the past twenty-five years.[22] Although it is still subject to debate, the field continues to evolve.[23] The World Health Organization (WHO) recently produced a report that attempts to quantify the EAF for a wide range of diseases and disabilities.[24] WHO defined "environment" as "all the physical, chemical, and biological factors external to the human host, and all the related behaviors, but excluding those natural environments that cannot reasonably be modified." In particular, WHO excluded smoking and diet from its working definition of environmental factors. Using this definition, WHO estimated that environmental factors were responsible for about 19 percent of cancers worldwide (range: 12–29 percent), or 1.3 million deaths each year. WHO also estimated that environmental factors were responsible for 44 percent of the total disease burden from asthma (range: 26–53 percent), 5 percent of birth defects (range: 2–10 percent), and 13 percent of neuropsychiatric disorders (range: 10–16 percent).

Building on this approach, a path-breaking study set out specifically to estimate the monetary costs of environmentally induced illnesses in children. A team of researchers headed by physician Philip Landrigan of the Mount Sinai School of Medicine looked at estimated costs and environmental contributions to four categories of illness: cancer, asthma, neurobehavioral disorders, and lead poisoning.[25] For each illness, they examined costs of treatment, parents' income lost when taking time off work to care for sick children, children's future earnings lost when their ability to learn was impaired by illness, and an estimate, when applicable, of the value of lives lost.

For the EAF for each category of disease, the Landrigan team relied on estimates developed by groups of experts reviewing the existing data. For the purposes of this study, the EAF was defined to refer *only* to "chemical pollutants in the ambient environment." The researchers "chose deliberately not to consider outcomes that are the consequence at least in part of personal or familial choice," such as tobacco, alcohol, or drug abuse.[26]

The researchers set the EAF for lead exposure at 100 percent, because all lead exposure is caused by human activity (and much of it is beyond personal or family choice). They estimated the EAF for asthma to fall between 10 and 35 percent, with a best guess of 30 percent. Based on a study by the National Academy of Sciences, they used an estimated EAF for neurobehavioral disorders between 5 and 20 percent, with a best guess of 10 percent. For cancer, the expert consensus was that "insufficient evidence exists to assign a best estimate of the fraction of childhood cancer specifically attributable to toxic chemicals in the environment. The panel agreed that the correct EAF would prove to be at least 5–10% and less than 80–90%, but could not further refine that broad range."[27]

Using these EAFs, the Landrigan team calculated an annual cost, in 2002 dollars, of $54–71 billion nationwide for the environmentally attributable fraction of the four categories of childhood illness.[28] In our Massachusetts study, we set out to produce state-specific numbers for the same types of illnesses. While relying on the Landrigan cost calculations in several areas, we excluded their estimate of the monetary value of deaths, on the grounds that it represents a controversial hypothesis about valuation rather than a "hard" monetary cost of illness.

Costs in Massachusetts

Our study looked at the costs of childhood illness in Massachusetts attributable to avoidable environmental exposures. For cancer and autism we were able to find appropriate Massachusetts data. For neurobehavioral illnesses and lead poisoning, we used 2 percent of the Landrigan team's national totals, because Massachusetts represents 2 percent of the national population.[29]

Unless otherwise specified, all monetary costs have been converted to 2002 dollars using the consumer price index.

Childhood Cancer

Incidence in Massachusetts

In 1999, 271 Massachusetts children were diagnosed with invasive cancer; more than half were aged nine or younger. This includes only new diagnoses (i.e., annual incidence); the number of children suffering from cancer in any given year (prevalence) is higher. Among young children, leukemia and cancers of the brain and central nervous system accounted for a substantial number of cases. In 1998, a year for which complete records are available on children's mortality, thirty-four Massachusetts children died of cancer.[30]

Costs of Cancer

Landrigan et al. estimated national costs of children's cancer by looking at costs of medical treatment for children with cancer, costs faced by parents who missed workdays to care for their sick children, and a "cost per life" for each child who dies. According to their calculations, the average cost, per child with newly diagnosed cancer, for physician services, inpatient services, and outpatient services was $271,400. Adding in the cost of laboratory services brought the cost of treatment up to $562,800. Accounting for lost parental wages, based on five lost wage days per seven child hospital days, added another $14,900 to the total cost.

The present value of a child's lost future earnings due to reduced IQ from radiation treatment for brain cancer added another $66,800. Individuals who survive childhood cancer have an increased likelihood of developing a second primary cancer later in life. Landrigan et al. assumed that the cost of treating this second cancer would be the same as the cost of the first. With discounting to account for the time lag, this brought the cumulative total cost for a new case (excluding only the value of death) up to $688,000.

These estimated costs per child imply a national total present value of lifetime cancer-related costs of $5.3 billion for each year's new childhood cancer cases.[31]

Environmentally Attributable Costs in Massachusetts

Based on the Landrigan et al. cost per case, the lifetime cost of children's cancers newly diagnosed in Massachusetts in 1999 was $186 million (again excluding the estimated value of deaths). Using the wide range of plausible EAFs for cancer, from 5 to 90 percent, the annual cost of Massachusetts childhood cancers attributable to environmental factors was between $9 million and $168 million.

Asthma

Massachusetts Prevalence

Most states in the United States lack a systematic tracking system to assess asthma prevalence. Massachusetts is no exception: at the state level, data are collected on asthma-related hospitalizations, but little information is available on the number of children who suffer from, are medicated for, and miss school because of this chronic disease. For Massachusetts children of ages nineteen and under, there were 2,655 asthma hospitalizations in 1999 and 2,410 in 2,000; in both years, two-thirds of the hospitalizations involved children nine or under.[32]

A variety of estimates of total asthma prevalence among Massachusetts children is available; all are based on incomplete information. The American Lung Association estimated the number of children suffering from asthma in Massachusetts at 77,300.[33] A study commissioned by the Asthma and Allergy Foundation of America estimated that 105,900 Massachusetts children age seventeen and under had asthma in 1998. This included 15,100 asthmatic children ages four to five, and 90,800 ages six to seventeen.[34]

Costs of Asthma

The EPA has developed detailed estimates of direct medical costs associated with asthma in its *Cost of Illness Handbook*. EPA provided estimates of the average annual medical costs for asthma treatment, broken down by age group. For four- and five-year-old children, the combination of office visits, drug therapy, emergency room use, and hospitalization added up to an average cost of $822. For children from six to seventeen, the corresponding figure was $977.[35]

EPA noted that several important factors were left out of its calculations, making them a low estimate of direct costs associated with asthma. For example, drugs used to treat asthma can cause other diseases and disorders. Asthma can also exacerbate other existing health problems, and can cause permanent damage to the lungs.[36] None of these additional problems were factored into EPA's cost estimates.

Environmentally Attributable Costs in Massachusetts

We used the number of asthmatic children from the Asthma and Allergy Foundation study, EPA's costs of treatment, and the Landrigan EAFs of 10–35 percent. The result was that the medical costs for environmentally induced asthma cases range from $10.1 million to $35.4 million per year in Massachusetts.[37]

Asthma and Environmental Justice

Increases in asthma rates have affected all sectors of society, but the burden of asthma is not evenly distributed. In general, poorer families have higher rates of asthma. Research from other states demonstrates that asthma prevalence is greatest in low income and minority areas.

In Massachusetts, a study looked at prevalence of asthma among preschool children enrolled in a Head Start program in Lowell.[38] These were children from low income families; most or all were below the federal poverty level. The study found an asthma prevalence of 35 percent among the Lowell Head Start pupils. A total of 510 children were enrolled in the program; 316 participated in the study. Of these, 112 were categorized as having asthma or asthmalike symptoms. (It is possible that the study sample was not random; parents whose children have asthma may have been more likely to participate. However, even if *none* of the nonparticipants had asthma, the prevalence of asthma among Lowell Head Start pupils as a whole would still be 22 percent.)

On average, the 112 asthmatic children suffered from wheezing, coughing, or shortness of breath more than twice a week. The disease required limitations on physical activity for more than half of the children. Most of them were taking medications to control their asthma; some were on more than one medication.

Seventy-four percent of the Head Start children with asthma had been taken to the emergency room for an asthma attack at least once, and forty-one percent had been hospitalized for asthma treatment at least once. Six had been in intensive care. About a fifth of the children had missed at least ten days of school within six months due to asthma, and a fifth of the parents said they had missed five or more days of work within six months because of their child's asthma.

Only 18 of the 112 children with asthma had ever been referred to an allergist or lung specialist. The researchers noted that children at increased risk of asthma are more likely to have inadequate access to health care. In addition to affecting health outcomes, this also means that health care databases may not reflect true prevalence rates in these populations.[39]

If the asthma rate of 35 percent found in this study applies to all children in Massachusetts Head Start programs, then more than 4,500 low-income preschoolers in the state suffer from this disease; the costs of asthma are disproportionately borne by families that have very limited resources to cope with such a problem.

Neurobehavioral Disorders

Prevalence in Massachusetts
The frequency of neurobehavioral disorders is difficult to measure, because Massachusetts, like other states, lacks a systematic means of tracking many of these disorders. In 2001–2002, just over 150,000 Massachusetts children ages three through twenty-one were enrolled in special education programs. The largest category of disability, "specific learning disability," accounted for 81,000 children. Other large categories were developmental delay (10,000), emotional (12,000), communication (17,000), and intellectual (11,000). In smaller but significant categories, 2,900 children had neurological disabilities; almost 3,500 had autism; 5,000 had multiple disabilities; and 4,000 fell into the categories of "physical" and "health" disabilities. The 150,000 children in special education accounted for more than 8 percent of the total population in this age group.[40]

The number of children in special education can be used as an approximation for the number of Massachusetts children with neurobehavioral disorders, although these two categories are not identical. On the one hand, some children receive special education as a result of disabilities that are distinct from neurobehavioral disorders. On the other hand, many children with true neurobehavioral disabilities are not tested or offered special education.[41] Thus the number of children in special education is not an exact measurement, but may be a reasonable proxy, for the number of children suffering from neurobehavioral disorders.

Cost per Child

Massachusetts expenditures for special education were $10,249 per pupil in 1999, compared with $5,487 per pupil for regular education.[42] The incremental cost of special education is the difference between these two figures, or $4,762 (equivalent to $5,143 in 2002 dollars). Thus the annual additional costs for 150,000 special education pupils amounted to $771.4 million, in 2002 dollars. However, this figure does not include any of the medical costs or other costs associated with neurobehavioral disorders.

Environmentally Attributable Fraction

Landrigan et al. estimated the EAF for neurobehavioral disorders at between 5 and 20 percent. Applying this range of EAFs to the additional costs for special education in Massachusetts, the estimated costs ranged from $38.6 million to $154.3 million for special education alone.

Landrigan et al. presented a more complete calculation of the costs of just three neurobehavioral disorders: mental retardation, autism, and cerebral palsy.[43] The cost categories in their analysis included physician visits, prescription drugs, hospitalization, auxiliary devices, therapy and rehabilitation, long-term care, home and auto modification, special education services, and home care. In addition to these sources of direct costs, Landrigan et al. built in estimates of productivity losses in adulthood. Their estimate of the total national cost came to $103 billion per year.

On the basis of population, the Massachusetts share of this national cost estimate would be $2 billion. Applying the range of EAFs described above, the estimated Massachusetts costs attributable to environmental exposures ranged from $103 million to $412 million for care and education plus foregone future earnings. These figures refer only to the three categories of neurobehavioral disorders considered by Landrigan et al.

Lead Poisoning

There are two distinct types of costs associated with lead poisoning: medical treatment costs, for the most severely affected children; and the loss of future incomes associated with reductions in IQ due to lead. The latter costs turn out, in practice, to be the dominant effect in dollar terms.

Blood Lead Levels

In 1994, 12,479 Massachusetts children between the ages of six months and six years were identified as having blood lead levels of 10 microgram per deciliter (μg/dL) or more. There has been a steady decline in the numbers since that year, indicating that efforts to reduce lead exposure have been effective, although significant numbers of children are still exposed. In 2002, there were still 2,940 children in the state with blood lead levels of 10 μg/dL or more.[44]

In 2000–2001, the Childhood Lead Poisoning Prevention Program screened slightly more than half of the state's total population of children between the ages of six months and six years. The results showed that 426 children had "moderately elevated" blood lead levels of 15–19 μg/dL; 159 had "elevated levels" of 20–24 μg/dL; and 159 qualified as "lead poisoned," at 25 μg/dL or higher.

Costs of Lead Exposure

A substantial literature exists on the costs associated with lead poisoning. In this case, unlike cancer and asthma, treatment costs are relatively low compared with the costs of care and education of lead-injured children, and particularly the reduction in future earnings of children whose lifetime productivity is impaired. (Other studies have considered the costs of an even wider range of social costs associated with childhood lead poisoning, including increased costs in the juvenile justice system.[45] We did not include these broader cost categories.) Medical treatment costs are limited in part because much of the damage that lead inflicts on the developing brain is irreversible.

The EPA *Cost of Illness Handbook* explored the direct medical costs of screening and treating children for lead exposure.[46] This includes only the costs of treatment aimed at reducing blood lead levels; it does not include the costs of treating health effects that may result from the exposure.

EPA categorized children into six "risk levels," each associated with a set of costs. Costs for children in the lower risk categories consisted primarily of screenings and family education about lead hazards. Costs for those in the higher risk categories included the cost of chelation therapy, a medical technique used to lower blood lead levels. (Recall from chapter 1 that regulatory critic Randall Lutter thought the costs of chelation should provide the sole measure of the costs of lead exposure.) EPA's costs were estimated for a five-year period beginning with the year of initial screening. The estimates ranged from $825 per child in the level of lowest concern to $8,200 per child for those requiring the most aggressive treatment and follow-up, in 2002 dollars.[47] Elements of the estimates included costs of initial screening; chelation; costs of additional tests, such as checking for iron deficiency; a neuropsychological evaluation; family education; and follow-up tests.[48]

These costs, applied to the number of severely affected children in Massachusetts, amounted to a relatively small part of the total cost of lead exposure. We concentrated instead on the much larger portion of the costs: the estimate of future income losses attributable to childhood lead exposure.

Future Income Losses

Calculation of future income losses attributable to lead exposure requires three numbers:

- Average blood lead levels in children
- Average loss of IQ points per unit of lead exposure
- Average change in lifetime income per IQ point

For blood lead levels, two different survey methods estimated the average among Massachusetts children at 2.5 and 3.6 µg/dL in 2002. This is roughly comparable to Landrigan et al, who found a nationwide average of 2.7 µg/dL among five-year olds in 1997.

On the effects of lead on IQ, Landrigan et al. estimated that each µg/dL of lead in a child's blood corresponds to a reduction in intelligence of 0.25 IQ points. Another recent study estimated that an increase of 10 µg/dL in blood lead level corresponds to a 4.6-point decrease in IQ, implying that each µg/dL of lead lowers IQ by 0.46 points, almost twice the Landrigan estimate. For those children whose blood lead levels never exceeded 10 µg/dL, the study found an effect on IQ even greater than 0.46 points per µg/dL of lead.[49]

For the effect of IQ on earnings, Landrigan et al. cited another researcher's estimate that a single IQ point loss would reduce lifetime earnings by 2.39 percent, or $16,800.[50] This is quite a bit higher than EPA estimates of the same effect. One of EPA's latest and largest figures, updated to 2002 dollars, amounted to a future income loss of $8,700 per IQ point.

The Landrigan estimate of future income losses attributable to lead exposure was made by applying these numbers to the 3.83 million U.S. children who were five years old at the time, that is, multiplying

2.7 µg/dL * 0.25 IQ points/(µg/dL) * $16,800/IQ point * 3.83 million children,

which equaled $43.4 billion nationwide in 1997, or $48.7 billion in 2002 dollars.[51]

Because estimated blood lead levels for Massachusetts children are similar to the national average, it seems reasonable to use 2 percent of the national cost, or $972 million in 2002 dollars, as the comparable cost for the state.

Other Diseases

The loss of future income due to childhood exposure to lead accounts for most of our calculation of the costs of illness for Massachusetts, and most of the Landrigan estimate for the United States as a whole. This is in part because it is the only one of the diseases analyzed here that affects the entire age group; even the low average levels of lead that are still detected in today's children have measurable effects on their future productivity and earnings.

But the apparently dominant role of lead impacts also reflects the incompleteness of the analysis to date. There are other childhood illnesses with environmental causes for which the necessary data are not available to create comparable estimates. To mention just one example, there is a growing literature linking some environmental exposures to birth defects, but there is no authoritative estimate of the EAF of birth defects. Thus the costs in this area are not included in our analysis.

How important could the costs of birth defects be? The first comprehensive report on birth defects in Massachusetts was published in 2001, covering births in 1999. In that year there were 80,866 live births in the state; of these, 875, or 1.1 percent, had one or more birth defects diagnosed at the time of birth. Since some birth defects are not diagnosed until later, this is likely an underestimate of the true rate. Because there were some births with multiple defects, the 875 children had a total of 1,136 diagnosed birth defects.

A California study estimated the costs of eighteen types of birth defects.[52] The authors included direct costs of medical treatment, indirect costs of special education, and estimates of lost future income. Of the Massachusetts birth defects reported in 2001, there were 400, or just over one-third of the year's total, that fell in the categories covered by the California study. For those 400 birth defects, the California cost estimates, updated to 2002 dollars, imply a cumulative Massachusetts cost of $37.1 million. Of that total, $17.1 million was the cost for the 65 Down syndrome babies born in Massachusetts that year.

On the one hand, there is no estimate of the EAF of these costs, so the appropriate costs would likely be lower. On the other hand, these costs cover only about one-third of the reported birth defects; the costs for the other two-thirds would increase the totals. And there may well be other diseases induced by exposure to toxic chemicals; the calculations presented here are constrained by the limited research that is available on this vital and disturbing topic.

Conclusion

A significant number of children in Massachusetts are affected by cancer, asthma, neurobehavioral disorders, lead exposure, and birth defects. The exact fraction of some of these disorders attributable to environmental causes will never be known precisely. However, the weight of the evidence suggests that a subset of the cases in each category (including all the cases,

Table 8.1
Annual costs of childhood illnesses attributable to environmental factors—
Massachusetts, 1997–1999. (costs in millions of 2002 dollars)

	Low EAF		High EAF	
	EAF	Costs	EAF	Costs
Cancer	0.05	9.3	0.90	167.8
Asthma	0.10	14.3	0.35	50.0
Neurobehavioral	0.05	103.0	0.20	412.2
Lead exposure	1.00	972.0	1.00	972.0
Total			1,098.4	1,598.0

for lead) is linked to environmental factors. Whether it is 5 percent or 90 percent, some fraction of the children who have cancer became ill due to avoidable toxic exposures. Whether it is 10 percent or 35 percent, many of the children who have been hospitalized for asthma became ill because of preventable exposures to contaminants.

The financial costs alone of children's environmentally induced illnesses are significant. Society spends hundreds of thousands of dollars per child with cancer; society loses millions of dollars in decreased productivity due to loss of IQ points among children exposed to lead, mercury, and other toxins that affect brain development. The quantifiable dollar costs, of course, are only a tiny portion of the true cost that communities, families, and the children themselves will bear as a result of these illnesses.

Table 8.1 summarizes the costs of the environmentally attributable fraction of these disorders. Using the low end of the range of estimated EAFs, the total costs are $1.1 billion per year. At the high end of the range of EAFs, the costs rise to $1.6 billion per year.

Environmentally induced illnesses are expensive. Treatment is costly, and when permanent impairment results, both society and the affected family and individual are impoverished for decades to come. The costs of environmentally induced illnesses in one state, Massachusetts, are $1.1–$1.6 billion every year. Replacement of toxic chemicals with safer alternatives, and strict regulation of any toxic emissions that cannot be eliminated, will have the added benefit of eliminating the unconscionable harm to our children and the resulting costs that we all bear.

Chapter 9

Phasing Out a Problem Plastic

On May 11, 1996, shortly after taking off from Miami, ValuJet Flight 592 caught on fire and crashed into the Everglades, killing all 110 people on board. The investigation of the accident by the National Transportation Safety Board attributed the crash to the plane's cargo, which included improperly stored oxygen generators, and to the lack of appropriate fire suppression equipment on board.[1]

But there are, inevitably, questions that were ignored in the official account, and it's not just the usual handfuls of conspiracy theorists who have asked them. There is no way to prove that the ValuJet accident was caused by faulty wiring. However, as a leading trade publication, *Aviation Today,* said in a special report on this and another accident,

> The ValuJet Flight 592 accident aircraft was rigged with a type of wire insulation, PVC, that will not pass the FAA's [Federal Aviation Administration's] current flame test. .... Among PVC wire's unacceptable properties, its burning insulation creates copious amounts of smoke, and the insulation can turn to hydrochloric acid when exposed to moisture. It is found on all DC-9s built through 1975. [The accident aircraft was a DC-9 built in 1969.] In addition, the vast majority of 727s ... were built with PVC wire. According to an anonymous telephone call to investigators from a self-described company maintenance technician three days after the

ValuJet crash, the accident aircraft "was continually having electrical problems . . . circuit breakers and wiring were shorting out.[2]

Although it is no longer allowed for wire insulation in airplanes, polyvinyl chloride, also known as PVC or "vinyl," often appears to be used for everything else that could possibly be made from plastic. From its origins as a little-known material with a few specialized uses, such as waterproofing on Navy ships in World War II, it has grown to become one of the most widely used plastics today.[3] Thanks to low prices and aggressive marketing, PVC has become ubiquitous in our homes and communities. We encounter it on a daily basis in products ranging from children's toys, packaging, and lawn furniture to water and sewer pipes, medical equipment, and building materials.

Unfortunately, PVC poses hazards to human health over the course of its life cycle. It is the only common plastic that includes chlorine, a source of many health hazards.[4] Many chlorinated organic compounds are carcinogenic; as discussed in chapter 2, vinyl chloride, the building block from which PVC is made, is classified as a known human carcinogen by U.S. and international agencies, and is known to cause several types of cancer.[5] One of these cancers, angiosarcoma of the liver, is rarely seen except in people exposed to vinyl chloride.

The risks associated with PVC present a challenging case for the economics of environmental protection. Getting rid of vinyl-related health hazards is not a matter of simply replacing one pesticide with another, or rearranging an industrial process to use a different solvent. Rather, PVC is used throughout the economy in countless products, and it is generally inexpensive, often competing successfully with more costly alternatives. What would it cost to replace PVC? Does the dismissal of the tradeoff between environmental protection and economic prosperity, discussed in chapter 3, still apply in this case? If PVC is indeed harmful, are we being poisoned, this time not for pennies but for quite a few dollars? These questions are the subject of this chapter.

The answer, in brief, is that the best available estimate is that PVC could be replaced at a moderate cost, and that there are good reasons to expect the true cost to be lower. Some jobs would change, and some workers would need assistance with the transition, but there is no reason to expect an overall loss of industrial employment from a phase-out of PVC.

The health hazards of the PVC life cycle are most harmful to workers in the industry; they would enjoy a significant reduction in health risks from a transition to alternative materials.

Questions about the economics of phasing out PVC are important, because there are many hazards associated with the vinyl life cycle. I first became aware of the extent of the risks connected with PVC while conducting a life-cycle analysis of more than a dozen packaging materials at Tellus Institute in the early 1990s. Our study focused heavily on the toxicity of the air and water emissions associated with production of the materials. Our initial guesses about what we would find turned out to be inaccurate; to our complete surprise, the result of the study was that PVC was by far the worst of the materials we studied. It generated more toxic emissions per ton of material, or per package, than any of the other materials we examined, including the other plastics. (For a description of the study, see chapter 5 of my earlier book, *Why Do We Recycle?*[6])

The Good, the Bad, and the Plastic

The toxicity of PVC in particular should not be confused with the negative reputation of plastics in general. The material has an unmistakably bad image: dictionary definitions of "plastic" include "artificial or insincere; synthetic; phony."[7] Plastics are not used solely to make tasteless, unnecessary, or low-quality items, but that negative image has stuck to them. (One could equally well place the blame on an economic system that makes it profitable to produce and sell tasteless, unnecessary, or low-quality items of any material.) The stereotypical character of plastics might contribute to cultural alienation, but that is not the same as causing cancer.

When specific plastics are associated with cancer, it's often not the plastic itself, but rather its building blocks, that are the culprits. Most common plastics are polymers (from the Greek word meaning "having many parts"); the simple molecules that are linked to form a polymer are "monomers," having only one part. Polymers are long chemical chains made up of many linked copies of the same monomer. From the perspective of a human cell, polymers are huge molecules. Monomers are much smaller, of a more dangerously convenient size for entering or otherwise damaging a cell.

Not all plastics are carcinogens. The most widely used plastic is polyethylene; the monomer from which it is made is ethylene. Despite decades of industrial production and use of enormous quantities of ethylene, there is no evidence that it causes cancer. Indeed, ethylene is a naturally occurring plant hormone that regulates fruit ripening. Although ethylene is currently produced from fossil fuels, it would be possible to produce moderate quantities of it in a sustainable manner. Factories that make ethylene and polyethylene certainly give rise to other kinds of pollution, but their main chemical products are not carcinogens.

Add just one chlorine atom to an ethylene molecule and the result is vinyl chloride, the monomer of PVC. Vinyl chloride was first synthesized by chemists in the nineteenth century; it does not occur in nature, and could not be produced sustainably. And vinyl chloride is known to be carcinogenic.

The production of PVC inevitably exposes workers and nearby communities to the monomer. Some workers are exposed because they are producing vinyl chloride itself, or turning vinyl chloride into PVC; they therefore face an elevated risk of cancer.[8] There are many more workers in other factories who convert PVC resin into vinyl siding, pipes, packaging, and countless other products; they also experience some (though lower) vinyl chloride exposure from so much contact with PVC, and they also face an elevated risk for developing angiosarcoma of the liver and other cancers.[9]

The hazards of the PVC life cycle extend well beyond vinyl chloride exposure during production. Pure PVC is brittle and hard to use; for most applications, PVC resins are mixed with additives such as stabilizers, to protect against light or heat damage, or plasticizers, to make them more pliable. Phthalates, which are used as plasticizers, may pose hazards to development and reproduction, and have been implicated in the development of respiratory problems in children.[10] Stabilizers used in PVC products include lead and other heavy metals. These additives can leach out of, or volatilize from, a PVC product during the product's useful life.

When vinyl building materials catch fire—or even smolder, before igniting—they release acutely toxic hydrochloric acid fumes.[11] This can make fires unexpectedly dangerous, as, perhaps, in the case of the ValuJet 592 accident. When discarded at the end of their life, items made from PVC can release toxic substances into the environment if they are burned in an incinerator or rural trash barrel, and can leach toxic stabilizers and plasticizers if they are buried in a landfill. When PVC is burned, either intentionally or accidentally, the combustion process can create dioxin, a substance that threatens human health at extraordinarily low concentrations (see chapter 4).[12]

In response to these and related concerns, vinyl advocates argue that the material offers not only low prices but also amazing convenience. PVC promises to provide "maintenance-free" building exteriors, easily installed pipes and plumbing, low-cost coverings for floors and walls, and all manner of molded or flexible plastic objects. It is widely believed that giving up PVC would impose a painful burden on the economy. While researching PVC, I asked a generally knowledgeable Home Depot sales representative about the costs of alternative materials. He assured me that the home he had just built for himself would have tripled in cost if built without PVC. Although, as we will see, he was wildly inaccurate on this point, he is not alone in suspecting that life as we know it, at a price we can afford, depends on vinyl.

The most extravagant claims about the economic benefits of vinyl are simply wrong: PVC does *not* offer enormous advantages over all other materials. Alternatives providing equal or better performance are available for almost every use of PVC. In some cases, the costs of the alternative materials are already comparable to PVC when costs are measured over the useful life of the product. In other cases, the alternatives are slightly more expensive at present, but are likely to come down in cost as their market share expands. The continued use of PVC offers short-term gains in some areas, and none at all in others—in either case at an unacceptable price in terms of environmental and occupational health.

Markets for Vinyl

Sales of PVC grew rapidly in the 1990s, reaching 14.4 billion pounds in the United States and Canada in 2002, or an average of forty-six pounds per person per year. PVC sales are much lower in other industrial countries: thirty-one pounds per person in Western Europe, and twenty-five pounds per person in Japan. Worldwide production was 59 billion pounds (or almost 27 million metric tons) in 2002, an average of nine

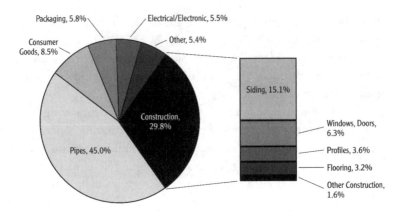

FIGURE 9.1. Uses of PVC, 2002
Source: Linak and Yagi, 2003

pounds per person. With 5 percent of the world's population, the United States and Canada consume 24 percent of the world's PVC.[13]

The uses of PVC in the United States and Canada for 2002 are shown in figure 9.1. The principal uses of PVC, in order of importance, are pipes, construction materials, consumer goods, packaging, and electrical products such as wire and cable. Pipes, siding, windows, doors, and profiles (gutters, fences, decks, etc.) together account for more than two-thirds of PVC use, and are among the fastest growing categories.

In the 1990s, three detailed studies estimated the cost of eliminating PVC. An Environment Canada report, the most recent of the three, examined fourteen product categories that accounted for about 90 percent of PVC use in Canada.[14] In most categories, the study compared costs for PVC products, a common lower-priced alternative, and a common higher-priced alternative, not necessarily the highest or lowest prices on the market. Published in 1997, the study was based on prices and conditions in Canada and construction costs for the Toronto area in 1993. Nine of the fourteen product categories were in the areas of pipes and construction materials, as shown in table 9.1. (Note that in table 9.1 and throughout the discussion of the Environment Canada study, the "cost" of an alternative refers to the increase or decrease in costs, relative to the cost of PVC, not the purchase price of the alternative.)

For pipes, the low-cost alternative to PVC was in each case another plastic, usually high-density polyethylene (HDPE). Traditional pipe ma-

TABLE 9.1.   **Alternatives to PVC in pipes and construction**

End use	Alternative materials		Cost per pound of PVC replaced (US$)	
	Low cost	*High cost*	*Low cost*	*High cost*
Municipal water pipe	HDPE	Ductile iron		
Municipal sewer pipe	HDPE	Concrete	$0.26	$0.38
Drainage pipe, culverts	HDPE	Concrete		
Drain/waste/vent plumbing	ABS	ABS /Copper	($0.05)	$0.25
Industrial pipe, conduits	----------	HDPE ----------		
Siding	Aluminum	Clay brick	$0.38	$6.02
Windows	Wood	Aluminum	($0.82)	$0.38
Flooring	Polyolefin	Ceramic tile/carpet	$13.54	$17.07
Wire and cable	--- Polyethylenes, other plastics ---		$3.00	$3.00

Source: Environment Canada, 1997.

terials such as iron, concrete, and copper provided slightly higher cost alternatives. However, as shown in table 9.1, the increased price per pound of PVC replaced was small for all pipe applications and was actually negative (meaning the alternatives cost less than PVC) for low-cost drain and industrial applications.

The story is more complex for construction materials, where the available options are more diverse and are changing more rapidly than with pipes. For example, Environment Canada's low-cost siding alternative, aluminum siding, has all but disappeared from the market today, while a promising newer option has emerged. Flooring, the area with by far the highest cost, represented only 3 percent of PVC use but accounted for over half of the cost of the entire low-cost PVC replacement scenario. New flooring products have continued to appear, and some of the best alternatives today were not available at the time of the study. Overall, the added costs of non-vinyl construction materials were modest: according to Environment Canada, the use of non-PVC alternatives for all four applications—siding, windows, flooring, and wire and cable—would have increased the cost of new residential construction by 0.4 percent in the low case, or 2.4 percent in the high case.

If these estimates still applied, what would they imply for the costs of phasing out PVC? The Environment Canada low-cost case suggests a weighted average cost increase of $0.55 per pound from switching to alternatives (measured in 2002 U.S. dollars).[15] Applying this cost increase to the 2002 figures of 46 pounds per person and 14.4 billion pounds of total consumption, the cost for substituting alternatives for all PVC sales would be about $25 per person per year, or $8 billion a year for the United States and Canada as a whole.

Thus a decision to replace PVC with alternatives would have noticeable, though not prohibitive, costs. Is the estimate of $8 billion simply the price that must be paid for avoiding the health and environmental damages caused by PVC? Or are there other factors that might reduce or outweigh the higher initial cost of alternatives? This chapter argues for the latter perspective, identifying reasons why the costs of phasing out PVC could be even lower than the Environment Canada estimate.

There are at least four factors that favor phasing out PVC, despite its apparent economic advantage:

- Alternatives that have higher initial costs than PVC may actually be cheaper on a life-cycle cost basis, including maintenance, repair, disposal, and replacement costs as well as purchase and installation.
- The advantages of mass production, including economies of scale and learning by doing, currently favor PVC, but could lower costs of alternatives in the future.
- The health and environmental problems associated with PVC may interfere with product performance in some markets.
- The costs of environmental protection are routinely overestimated in advance (see chapter 3); the usual interpretation of cost estimates exaggerates the economic impacts of environmental improvement.

These themes are explored in the next four sections, and illustrated with examples of PVC applications and alternatives.

Life-Cycle Costs Often Favor Alternatives

Some of the alternatives have higher initial purchase prices than PVC products, but are actually less expensive over the useful life of the product. The Environment Canada study compared purchase prices, or in some cases installed costs, of PVC and alternatives. Such comparisons may give a misleading impression about the total cost of owning, using, and caring for the products in question.

The total cost over a product's life cycle is the cost that ultimately matters to the user. For example, paper plates are much cheaper than ceramic dinner plates, but households, restaurants, and institutional food services often conclude that it is cheaper in the long run to buy, wash, and reuse ceramic plates, rather than continually buying and discarding paper plates.

The concept of life-cycle costs is no more complicated than this commonplace example. Rather than focusing on initial costs alone, a decision should be based on the full costs, over a period of time, of buying, installing, using, maintaining, and ultimately disposing of alternative products. To make the story simple, suppose that a ceramic plate is used daily and is expected to last for 1,000 days, or almost three years. Then the relevant comparison would be the cost of one purchase, 1,000 washings, and one disposal of a ceramic plate, versus the cost of purchase and disposal for 1,000 paper plates. The more expensive initial purchase may be cheaper in the long run if the recurring costs are lower: in this case, washing a ceramic plate presumably costs less than buying and discarding another paper plate every day.

Flooring

A similar contrast between initial and life-cycle costs exists in the market for flooring materials, where vinyl, in sheets or tile, is a popular, seemingly low-cost option. In 2002, U.S. sales of vinyl flooring reached 3.6 billion square feet, worth $1.84 billion.[16] Vinyl is advertised as a uniquely affordable, durable, and easily maintained floor covering. However, while vinyl generally minimizes initial costs of purchase and installation, it may not be the longest-lasting choice, nor the easiest or cheapest to maintain. These factors can actually make it more expensive on a life-cycle basis than environmentally preferable flooring.

Vinyl flooring has largely replaced linoleum, a classic of decades past. Natural linoleum flooring is made largely from renewable materials: linseed oil, pine rosin, ground cork dust, wood flour, mineral fillers, and pigments, often over a burlap or canvas backing. Linoleum was once manufactured widely in the United States, but started to decline in the 1950s; it was all but eliminated from the North American market by the 1970s. A revival began in the 1990s, as customers seeking environmentally friendly materials imported linoleum from Europe. Today it is again produced, although in modest quantities, in the United States and Canada. The reputation of linoleum remains strong, but in building supply stores such as Home Depot, "linoleum" now often refers to a different product, namely vinyl floor coverings designed to look like old-fashioned linoleum.

Linoleum is not the only environmentally attractive alternative to vinyl. Stratica, a composite, chlorine-free flooring material, is manufactured by Amtico, a British company that also produces vinyl flooring. Stratica is the floor covering most similar to vinyl in appearance, with a high-gloss yet low-maintenance surface. The top layer of Stratica is made from Surlyn, a material originally developed by DuPont as an outer surface for golf balls. The Surlyn surface is responsible for Stratica's durability.

Introduced into the U.S. market in 1997, Stratica initially appealed to two categories of customers: health care institutions, which wanted to avoid volatile organic compound emissions from vinyl flooring, and the U.S. Navy.[17] From 1998 to 2000, the Navy Food Service conducted extensive studies on ways to modernize and reduce costs in food preparation and service. Among many other experiments, the Navy tested three floor coverings for food preparation and serving areas: vinyl tiles, Stratica, and a type of ceramic tiles (PRC, or plastic red clay). Some 37,800 square feet of Stratica were installed on ten ships during the test period.

According to Commander Frank Lindell, director of the Navy Food Service at the time, Stratica minimized "total ownership cost" (i.e., life-cycle cost) because it required so much less maintenance:

> Deck maintenance—sweeping, swabbing, stripping, and waxing—is one of the most significant workload drivers afloat. . . . Studies have demonstrated installation of low-maintenance decking such as Stratica provides significant labor savings, increases life expectancy of decking material, and reduces total ownership costs. Swabbing, stripping, waxing, and periodic resealing (required for PRC decking) are eliminated. Life expectancy for Stratica is 10 years, five years for vinyl, and 10 years for PRC (with resealing every six months). Total ownership cost of Stratica decking is 66 percent less than vinyl decking and eight percent less than PRC, over its life span.[18]

Since that time, the Navy has rapidly expanded its purchases of Stratica, even though the initial purchase and installation cost remains lower for vinyl decking.

Siding

A hint of a similar pattern can be glimpsed in the area of siding. Wood siding or shingles still offer the preferred look for housing; wood can be purchased finished or left natural, and it is impact resistant, even in cold temperatures. Wood siding, however, can warp, twist, or be damaged by water if not properly maintained. It is also vulnerable to insect damage and burns readily. A house with a wood exterior requires repeated painting or staining and regular maintenance.

Vinyl siding, now a very popular exterior for low- and moderate-cost housing, is available in a variety of colors, thicknesses, and qualities. Installation is easy, and vendors tout vinyl as "maintenance free." Vinyl is known for its ability to mimic the appearance of other materials, such as wood. It is often said to be resistant to water damage; it is also impervious to insects.

Unfortunately, vinyl siding can warp if it gets too hot. It is also sensitive to cold temperatures, which can cause it to chip or crack and become brittle, and it expands and contracts with temperature changes. Many home improvement sources contest the common claim that vinyl is not damaged by water. Vinyl generally fades with time; once the color has faded, it may need to be painted every four to ten years. In case of fire, vinyl presents the additional problem that it can release dangerous emissions when burning or smoldering, thus threatening the health and safety of people in or near a burning house, as well as of firefighters.

Competition from vinyl has all but eliminated the once-common option of aluminum siding, but other alternatives are available. As with flooring, a new synthetic material offers a promising alternative to vinyl siding. Fiber cement is made primarily from a combination of cement, sand, and cellulose fibers. It is available in planks or shingles, like its counterpart in wood, and can be purchased already primed and painted. It can be cut and installed much like wood, although there is a potential occupational health issue that must be addressed.[19] The look created by fiber cement can vary from rough sawn cedar to stucco, depending on its embossing. It does not warp or twist, is impact resistant, and is impervious to insects. Unlike vinyl siding, it does not expand and contract, nor does it burn or smolder in a fire. Fiber cement does need to be painted, but less often than wood.

A survey by *Consumer Reports* magazine[20] compared the leading alternatives for siding, including prices and estimated lifetimes, for low-cost and high-cost versions of each material. The low-cost vinyl option was indeed the cheapest alternative, at $0.45 per square foot; low-cost fiber cement was almost twice as expensive at $0.84 per square foot. The estimated lifetimes for these options were twenty-five years for vinyl and fifty years for fiber cement.

The resulting purchase cost *per year* for fiber cement, $1.68 per 100 square feet per year, was lower than the comparable cost for vinyl, $1.80. This comparison is far from being a complete life-cycle analysis; it omits the important categories of maintenance, repair and repainting, and disposal costs. Fiber cement might remain more expensive than vinyl siding once these categories are taken into account. However, the *Consumer Reports* data imply that vinyl has a higher purchase price *per year of useful life* than a leading new alternative.

Thus, for both flooring and siding, comparing initial cost does not tell the whole story. When all the costs associated with a product over time are considered, PVC's apparent advantage disappears for flooring, and is sharply reduced for siding.

Mass Production Reduces Costs

Mass production makes everything cost less. Many PVC products have been produced in huge volumes, making them cheap today; the production of PVC alternatives could just as easily grow in volume in the future, making them less expensive and more competitive than they are at present. Two related effects are involved, known as "economies of scale" and "learning by doing" (the latter is also described in terms of "learning curves").

Economies of scale refer to the fact that production costs per unit are often lower when goods are produced in larger batches. Some processes are physically more efficient when performed on a larger scale; a bigger boiler or furnace simply costs less to operate, per unit of heat output, than a small one. In general, a larger scale of production means that more machinery, automation, and standardized procedures can be applied. A company that sells a few hundred plastic objects of a particular shape each year may have workers make them almost by hand, using only basic tools and equipment. A company that sells a few million a year will invest in mold-ing and stamping machines, assembly lines, and so on, allowing much faster, labor-saving production with lower costs per unit.

Learning by doing describes the common pattern in which costs decline over time as an industry gains experience with a production process. This is often combined with economies of scale—as industry gains experience, factories also tend to get bigger—but learning by doing is possible even if factory sizes do not change. Whenever a new process is introduced, it takes a while to debug it—hence the common, informal advice to avoid version 1.0 of any new software package. Much the same is true for manufacturing. Over time, the bugs are worked out, shortcuts and process improvements are developed, and maintenance procedures and schedules are improved. As a result, costs go down. This phenomenon was first documented in the aircraft industry in the 1930s and has been observed in industries ranging from shipbuilding to wind turbines and photovoltaic cells.[21] A common estimate is that when an industry's cumulative production (the total from the beginning of the industry to the present) doubles, the cost per unit drops by 10–30 percent. In one classic example, a study found that the Ford Model T dropped in price by 15 percent for every doubling of cumulative production from 1909 to 1923.[22]

The combined effects of economies of scale and learning by doing can be seen in the evolution of many consumer electronics products. Cell phones, CD players, DVD players, digital cameras, flat-screen computer monitors, and numerous other products started out as expensive and esoteric luxuries and then dropped rapidly in price as the market expanded.

At a certain point, the fact that some people are using a new product means that other people will begin to use it too. If many people have begun to use a new computer program, other people will adopt it to have software compatible with their colleagues. (Back when there was a meaningful choice, I much preferred WordPerfect. But this book, like everything I've written for quite a while, was written in Word.) For a new technology, the fact that people have already adopted it eventually becomes a strong argument for further adoptions. This creates a snowball effect that lowers prices and tends to "lock in" the advantage of the leading product on the market.[23]

Thus, when a product sells for a low price and has a large market share, it may not mean simply that it is widely used because it is cheap. Rather, it may be cheap because it is widely used.

PVC has benefited from mass production in many markets. PVC products have been used for decades, have achieved large sales volume, and thus are mass-produced at low cost. The learning by doing effect appears to have been particularly steep for PVC, with every doubling of production associated with a 30–40 percent drop in price in the 1950s and 1960s.[24] A history of the industry describes a steady stream of process innovations and improvements in production technology in these early years, along with rapid increases in the size of the newest and most efficient plants; these factors undoubtedly drove the price downward.[25]

Alternatives to PVC, which are not currently produced in comparably large volume, could benefit from the economics of mass production in the future. The alternatives might initially be more expensive, but would tend to come down in price over time.

Medical Gloves

A potential example is the case of disposable medical gloves. The market for such gloves grew rapidly in the late 1980s and 1990s, driven in part by concern about HIV/AIDS and other blood-borne diseases. Latex, the preferred material for medical gloves for many years, has become less attractive because large numbers of health care workers and patients have developed allergies to it. The leading alternatives to latex for this use are vinyl and nitrile. Nitrile refers to a family of organic compounds; nitrile gloves are made from acrylonitrile butadiene rubber, a form of synthetic rubber that does not trigger latex allergies, and does not contain chlorine.

Nitrile gloves are almost twice as expensive as vinyl ones, when bought in small quantities. However, there are noticeable quality differences between the two products; nitrile gloves are much more durable.

A study compared the barrier integrity of latex, nitrile, and PVC gloves, meaning, in practice, testing them for water leaks.[26] The researchers looked at each glove type both under "static" conditions, in which the glove was simply removed from the box and tested, and under conditions of activity, in which the glove was manipulated to simulate actual use in health care. For nitrile and latex gloves, failure rates averaged 2–3 percent, both out of the box and in simulated actual use; none of the individual brands tested had failure rates above 5 percent. For vinyl gloves, on the other hand, the failure rate averaged 5 percent out of the box, and

30 percent under simulated use conditions; the worst brands had failure rates of 12 percent out of the box, and 61 percent under simulated use.[27]

The study noted that PVC has relatively poor barrier qualities because of its molecular structure; even when plasticizers are added, "vinyl still lacks the ability to stretch when stressed or snagged, and readily fractures, tears, or separates at the molecular level resulting in barrier loss."[28] At best, if tears or failures in gloves are detected, the result will be the use of additional replacement gloves, thus raising the cost of vinyl glove use. At worst, if a failure is not detected, the medical worker faces the risk of exposure to blood-borne disease.

A 1999 analysis by Kaiser Permanente, the nation's largest not-for-profit health care organization, found that on a "total utilization cost" basis (comparable to the life-cycle costs discussed above), nitrile gloves were cost competitive with the alternatives, owing to their greater durability.[29] On the basis of this analysis, Kaiser Permanente decided to switch to nitrile, purchasing 43 million nitrile gloves.[30] A one-time purchase of this size would strain the suppliers of nitrile gloves in the short run. But recurring purchases of this magnitude would be expected to launch the process of achieving economies of mass production in nitrile gloves, eventually bringing down the cost of this alternative.

PVC Pipes

Similar issues arise in the biggest single category of PVC products. Pipes and pipe fittings account for almost half of PVC use. PVC pipes have been in use for more than thirty years and have become standard in some applications, such as the "drain/waste/vent" tubing that carries wastewater away from kitchens and bathrooms. They have also gained a large share of the market for small-diameter municipal water and sewer pipes. Some observers claim that installation of PVC water and sewer pipes minimizes municipal labor and equipment costs and also minimizes the length of time that streets are blocked for pipe installation. According to industry estimates, PVC accounts for more than 70 percent of all water and sewer pipes now being installed in the United States.[31] PVC has also been adopted for other low-pressure, low-temperature-stress applications such as irrigation pipes, culverts, drain pipes, electrical conduits, and some industrial pipes.

PVC pipes are competing both with traditional pipe materials—copper, iron, concrete, and vitrified clay—and with relatively newer, plastic alternatives, above all polyethylene (PE) pipes. The various pipe materials have contrasting strengths and weaknesses.[32]

- The traditional materials are heavier and, for large-diameter pipes, may be more difficult to install and repair. However, they are strong under extremes of pressure and temperature. Copper plumbing remains the standard for hot and cold water in most buildings.
- PVC is lightweight, lower priced than most alternatives, and requires less skill to install and repair. However, PVC is weaker under high pressure and becomes brittle at below-freezing temperatures.
- PE pipes offer a lightweight alternative with greater strength under pressure, as well as stronger, more leak-proof joints and the ability to withstand temperatures well below freezing.

PE is the only other leading material to approach PVC's light weight and ease of installation.[33] Although some equipment is needed to install PE pipes, small-scale pipe-welding machines are becoming available for homeowner or small contractor use. PE has made inroads in water and sewer pipes for northern areas where the ground often freezes, and in high-pressure applications such as gas pipelines, where PVC cannot be used. Sales of PE pipe in the United States and Canada have grown rapidly, reaching 1.0 billion pounds in 2001, compared to 6.5 billion pounds of PVC pipe sales.[34]

PE pipe is newer to the market and hence less familiar than PVC and traditional pipe materials to plumbers, contractors, and municipal public works departments. The American Water Works Association first gave its approval for the use of small-diameter PE water pipes in 1978, and for larger diameters only in 1990.

Reluctance to embrace new materials such as PE results in part from memories of the failure of an earlier "new" pipe material, polybutylene (PB). Introduced in the late 1970s, PB pipe quickly gained a reputation for frequent leaks. However, it continued to be sold through the 1980s and early 1990s because its ease of installation allowed an up-front savings of hundreds of dollars per home. A class-action lawsuit against Shell, the largest manufacturer of PB pipe, was settled in 1995 for $950 million.[35] A decade later, numerous companies were still offering PB pipe removal services.

Not everyone, however, has been reluctant to adopt PE water pipes. Performance issues, rather than cost, appear to drive the decision. The Indianapolis Water Company has switched to PE because it reduces leaks at the joints and bends in the pipes and because a new installation technique (one that works only with PE) minimizes excavation and disruption.[36] The Los Angeles Department of Water and Power has used PE pipes to replace old water mains after major breaks, because it is the material that minimizes leaks.

Over time, will PE pipes continue to benefit from the economies of mass production, coming to rival PVC pipes in cost as well as performance? The same progression toward larger volume and lower costs for alternatives could occur in other markets as well. The price of PVC fell rapidly in the past, as its volume of production expanded; today it competes, in many different markets, against other materials and products that are sold in much smaller quantities. The problem, for the makers of the alternatives, is to launch the process that leads to economies of scale. A few massive purchases, along the lines of 43 million alternative gloves, could help to jump-start the cycle of increasing volume and decreasing prices. But in general, it seems likely that a campaign to win acceptance for an alternative, such as non-PVC pipes, will be necessary. Proponents of the alternatives have one clear advantage: PVC no longer has much opportunity to benefit from additional economies of scale; in contrast, as the markets for its rivals start to grow, their prices have nowhere to go but down.

PVC Products Can Be Dangerous to Users

Often the harmful impacts of PVC occur after the item has been produced and put into use. For example, flexible PVC products used in health care, such as intravenous bags and tubes, contain phthalates—plasticizers that can leach out of the products during use, potentially posing hazards to patients. Phthalates are also used in some flexible PVC toys, including toys that young children are likely to put in their mouths. In 1999, the European Commission adopted a ban on certain phthalate-containing PVC toys and other products, such as teething rings, intended for children to put in their mouths. Some U.S. manufacturers have voluntarily stopped production of PVC toys containing phthalates.[37]

However, the U.S. Consumer Product Safety Commission has denied petitions to ban PVC in toys for young children or to issue an advisory about hazards associated with these toys.[38]

Another safety problem arises when PVC is exposed, intentionally or otherwise, to heat. PVC is often advertised as "fire resistant," meaning that a fairly high temperature is required to start it burning. However, PVC starts to smolder and release toxic fumes such as hydrochloric acid at a lower temperature, long before it ignites. If PVC is gradually warmed, more than half of its weight can be given off as fumes before it gets hot enough to burst into flames.[39] The hydrochloric acid released by burning PVC is potentially lethal to people caught in a burning building; other products of PVC combustion, such as dioxin, exert their health effects more slowly and are spread across a larger population.

For this reason, some firefighter associations support policies to reduce PVC use. The International Association of Fire Fighters points out that 165 people died in the Beverly Hills Supper Club fire of 1977, and 85 people in the MGM Grand Hotel fire in Las Vegas in 1980, almost all of whom, according to the firefighters, were killed by inhalation of toxic fumes and gases, not by heat, flames, or carbon dioxide. A likely culprit was the hydrochloric acid created by the decomposition of PVC used in wiring and other building materials.[40] Medical researchers have found elevated levels of long-term respiratory and other health problems in firefighters who put out fires involving large quantities of PVC and have identified hydrochloric acid—acting alone or in combination with carbon monoxide and soot—as the probable cause of the damages.[41]

Concerns regarding fire hazards have led some areas, such as New York State and the city of Chicago, to adopt building codes excluding all plastic piping, including both PVC and PE, from commercial and high-rise residential buildings. Industry critics attack such measures as makework regulations that needlessly drive up construction costs in order to protect union jobs. Unions defend them as safety measures, citing the health hazards of PVC fires.[42]

Environmental Protection Costs Less than Anticipated

The costs of environmental protection are often overestimated in advance, as discussed in chapter 3. One of the classic examples of this trend actually occurred in PVC production (as described more fully in chapter 2). A strict standard for workplace exposure to vinyl chloride was established in 1974 by the Occupational Safety and Health Administration (OSHA). Consultants to OSHA estimated the costs of reducing vinyl chloride exposure at around $1 billion; industry estimates were even higher. Actual costs turned out to be around a quarter of OSHA's estimate, because industry quickly developed new, cost-effective technologies to comply with the regulation.[43]

Similar patterns have been found for many environmental standards. A review of this literature for Environment Canada and an Ontario provincial agency, focusing specifically on the costs of controlling chlorinated substances, confirmed that overestimation of regulatory costs is more common than underestimation. Among the cases where the review found serious overestimation of U.S. regulatory costs were the advance predictions of compliance costs for the Montreal Protocol on ozone-depleting substances and the bans on the toxic pesticides DDT and chlordane/heptachlor.[44]

The greatest concern about costs involves the impacts on jobs. Would a transition to safer alternatives throw thousands of PVC workers out of work? Although a phase-out of PVC would inevitably cause changes in the labor market, fears of widespread unemployment are groundless.

Replacing PVC with safer alternatives would change some jobs: from fabricating PVC products to fabricating the same products out of other materials, often other plastics; or from making vinyl chloride monomer (VCM) and PVC resin to making safer substitutes (again, often other plastics). In many cases, the same workers who currently make PVC products could be employed making similar products from PVC alternatives. Moreover, workers who make and use VCM and PVC every day face the greatest health risks from these materials at present; alternative jobs making and using safer materials would provide a substantial risk reduction for those who are now employed in the industry.

In general, the money that is now spent on PVC products, the uses of those products, and the jobs created by production and use of PVC would not disappear from the economy in the transition to alternative materials. The skills that are needed to make many products out of PVC would still be needed to make the same products out of something else; there is no evidence that the substitutes would require less labor or that resources spent on clean alternatives create fewer jobs than resources spent on PVC.

Would Workers Lose Jobs from a PVC Phase-Out?

Government data sources do not report the total number of workers who are employed in making PVC and PVC products. Industry sources report that there are 126,000 workers in PVC fabrication plants; in addition, there are apparently no more than 9,000 workers making VCM and PVC resin.[45]

The workers who make VCM and PVC resin would not necessarily be out of work if PVC were phased out: in many cases PVC would be replaced by other petrochemical products, such as nonchlorinated plastics or synthetic rubber, which might be made by the same companies or in the same communities that now make VCM and PVC. Thus there would be new jobs to be filled making the alternative materials, which current VCM and PVC workers could well perform.

When it comes to the larger number of workers making PVC products, many companies produce or use a diversified set of plastics; ceasing sales of PVC products would often lead to a shift within the company, not putting the company out of business. The PVC Container Company manufactures plastic bottles from both PVC and polyethylene terephthalate (PET), using different equipment, but in the same facility.[46] J-M Manufacturing, the leading producer of PVC pipe, has diversified to make PE pipe as well. Westlake Chemical Corporation is a vertically integrated company that produces both VCM and PVC as well as alternatives, including PE. Westlake's fabricated products include both PVC and PE pipe, among other products.[47] CertainTeed Corporation produces a variety of PVC products, but also produces fiber cement siding, one of the promising alternatives to vinyl siding.[48] Although the employment practices of such companies vary from case to case, corporate diversification creates the possibility of retaining and reassigning workers if PVC were phased out.

The changes that would result from a PVC phase-out are not large relative to the ongoing turnover of employment in the U.S. economy. Jobs are constantly being eliminated, and other jobs created, in enormous numbers. In the twelve-month period from August 2002 through July 2003, when total U.S. employment had a net decrease of 170,000 jobs, there were actually 48,150,000 new hires and 48,320,000 separations (quits, retirements, layoffs, and firings).[49] In manufacturing alone, which was particularly hard hit in the same period, losing just over a million jobs, there were 4,000,000 new hires and 5,020,000 separations. That is, in addition to the net loss of a million manufacturing jobs, there was turnover of another four million jobs—an average turnover of 11,000 manufacturing jobs per day, every day of the year. If every one of the 9,000 jobs in VCM and PVC resin production were replaced by a different job producing substitute materials in a different plant, this would amount to less than one day's average turnover of U.S. manufacturing employment.

Nonetheless, the replacement of jobs in VCM and PVC production with jobs in other industries could impose a real burden on the affected workers, just as employment turnover of all sorts frequently does. Even when the old jobs are replaced with new ones, the labor market does not automatically move the displaced workers into the new positions. Providing protection and support for workers who lose their jobs is an essential responsibility of public policy, both for the small numbers who may be affected by health and environmental policies such as a PVC phase-out and for the much larger numbers who are laid off for other reasons. Proactive labor policies will be of far greater benefit to workers than a doomed attempt to prevent change in the labor market by thwarting environmental protection. Moreover, the transition to a new job will reduce health risks for former PVC workers, a benefit that should not be forgotten.

Conclusion

PVC is ubiquitous today, offering a broad range of low-cost products and a troubling list of health and environmental impacts. These impacts are largely unique to PVC, not characteristics of plastics in general. Fortunately, our prosperity and way of life do not depend on the continued use of PVC, despite claims to that effect. Alternatives are available throughout the range of PVC applications; some are cost-competitive today, while others cost slightly more than vinyl. A detailed but somewhat dated estimate implies a per capita cost of $25 per year, or $8 billion total for the United States and Canada, for replacement of all PVC production.

There are several reasons to suspect that the actual cost could turn out to be lower: life-cycle cost calculations favor some of the alternatives; the economies of mass production will lower costs as the alternatives are more widely used; the hazards of PVC affect its users in some cases; and environmental protection routinely costs less than projected in advance. Employment impacts of a transition would be limited, because similar jobs would have to be done in the same or closely related industries that would produce the alternatives; nonetheless, any workers who are unemployed by the transition deserve assistance and support.

This is one of the most difficult cases for the economics of safer alternatives, because there would, at least in the short run, be some increased costs to eliminating a toxic hazard. But the costs should not be exaggerated; there is a considerable difference between an estimate of $25 per person per year, and the fears about the cost of losing vinyl, such as the (fortunately quite unfounded) threat of tripling the cost of new housing. And the costs, moderate as they are, should go down over time. If this is one of the worst cases, then the transition to safer alternatives in general appears to be an experience we can afford.

The airline industry no longer uses planes with PVC wiring, but it is still flying; indeed, it is flying more safely now that a significant source of risk has been removed. The rest of the economy will be equally able to operate more safely without vinyl.

Chapter 10

The Costs of REACH

Regulations come in different sizes; REACH, the European Union's new chemical policy, is the big one. Its name is an acronym for Registration, Evaluation, and Authorization of CHemicals. Beginning in 2007, REACH requires manufacturers and importers to register, and test for safety, an estimated 30,000 chemicals—any substance with EU sales volume of at least one ton per year. Few regulations have imposed such sweeping new requirements across a major industry in any country. In the United States, regulations with such ambitious scope have not been adopted or even seriously proposed for many years.

The debate about REACH in advance of its adoption was also unusually extensive, stretching from the original proposal in 2001 through to the final vote in 2006. The first round of opposition involved industry-sponsored studies attributing enormous costs and dire economic consequences to REACH. In response, a number of government and academic studies, including our study for the Nordic Council of Ministers, which is described in this chapter, found that the costs of REACH would be quite modest and entirely affordable. (The Nordic Council of Ministers is the forum for cooperation among the governments of the Scandinavian countries.)

The debate came into sharp focus for me in 2004, when I presented that study at a hearing at the European Parliament in Brussels. The issues emerged not only in the gratifyingly well-attended and well-reported hearing itself, but also in the rival presentation by industry lobbyists on

Chapter 10 by Frank Ackerman and Rachel Massey.

the same day. CEFIC, the European chemical industry trade association, was holding a press conference at the European Parliament, to dramatize the damage that would be done by REACH. Their featured speaker was a woman who ran a small cosmetics company. Her firm imported small quantities of many unfamiliar, natural ingredients for use in its unique new products. The message was that the cost of testing each of these ingredients for safety would be impossible for her company to bear. REACH, however well-intentioned, might put this energetic entrepreneur out of business.

Even taken at face value, the industry argument was debatable: should an entrepreneur have the right to invent and sell cosmetics with untested, new chemical ingredients? Or should her customers have the right to know that the substances they put on their faces have passed some basic safety tests? If economic growth is slightly slowed by only allowing the sale of those cosmetics that are known to be safe, will that make Europe better or worse off? As our research showed, the effect of REACH on economic growth will be extremely slight, if, indeed, it is detectable at all.

More fundamentally, the choice of a small importer of chemicals to reflect the effects of REACH was misleading; most chemicals subject to REACH are produced by very large European companies. Big business often hides its agenda behind the more sympathetic face of struggling small business, creating the impression that virtually any new regulation is more than these hardworking but marginally profitable enterprises can bear. The impacts on industry as a whole tell a different story, for regulation in general (as seen in chapter 3) and for REACH in particular.

What Is REACH?

REACH is intended to revamp chemicals regulation in the EU, replacing a complicated set of more than forty interlocking regulations with a single piece of legislation. It lays out a series of requirements for collecting, systematizing, and using information about the health and environmental effects of industrial chemicals.

REACH has several components. Under the *registration* provision, chemical manufacturers and importers are required to carry out health and environmental safety tests on their products; the testing protocols depend on the volume of sales in the EU, with the highest volume chemicals subject to the most stringent testing requirements. In the *evaluation* phase, EU member states evaluate the information provided in the registration phase and assess the hazards associated with each chemical. Substances of particularly high concern are subject to *authorization,* meaning that they can be used only with special permission for specific uses. This includes chemicals that cause cancer, genetic mutations, or birth defects, as well as substances that are persistent and bioaccumulative. Finally, REACH also allows for *restriction* of substances that pose unacceptable risks to health or the environment, including, where necessary, partial or complete bans on chemicals.[1]

Under the EU policy that prevailed prior to REACH, chemicals that were on the market in 1981 were not routinely subject to testing requirements. Chemicals that entered the market after 1981 were subject to extensive safety testing, but the vast majority of the chemicals used in industry are still the pre-1981 ones. Before REACH, the burden of proof was on government agencies to demonstrate that a pre-1981 chemical was harmful. Under REACH, the burden of proof is reversed: companies that produce or import chemicals are responsible for providing the data to support a claim of safety.

The original (2001) version of REACH proposed roughly the same level of testing for *all* chemicals as was previously required for new chemicals. Subsequent compromises, incorporated in the final version of REACH, have reduced the requirements, particularly for chemicals sold in volumes of less than 100 tons per year. Therefore, REACH actually reduces the former regulatory burden on low-volume new chemicals; this could be seen as stimulating innovation in the chemical industry and its customers.

By contrast, the pre-1981 chemicals now face stiffer requirements than they did in the past, as REACH sets up a schedule for completing the testing of all chemicals on the market.

Direct and Indirect Costs

The debate about the economic effects of REACH was not primarily about the direct costs of registration and testing required by REACH. At least thirty-six studies of the costs of REACH were conducted, reaching a near-consensus that registration and testing of chemicals will cost €2–€4

185

billion over eleven years. The European Commission estimated the costs of the original version of REACH at €3.7 billion,[2] and a later, amended version at €2.3 billion. Examining that later version, our study for the Nordic Council of Ministers used slightly different technical assumptions and estimated the costs at €3.5 billion. There are well-defined testing requirements, and a set of standard estimates of the costs of performing such tests in European laboratories; thus, the approximate convergence of cost estimates is no surprise. Even the most critical industry studies usually estimated the direct costs at only about twice the level of other studies. For example, CEFIC thought the direct costs of the original version would be €7 billion.[3]

The meaning of estimates of this size deserves a moment's thought. How large is our estimate of €3.5 billion? (At the time of the original study, the euro was worth only a bit more than the U.S. dollar; by the time this book went to press, one euro was worth almost $1.50, so that €3.5 billion was roughly equal to $5 billion. As seen in chapter 3, a penny per person per day, for the United States, is slightly over $1 billion per year.) Numbers this big require some standard of comparison, some method of visualization.

A natural first reaction is that, if €3.5 billion were on a table in front of you, it would be a very large pile of money. But of course, it is not piled on a table. It is spread across the entire European chemical industry, over a period of eleven years. The annual cost is just over €300 million, or less than one euro per person per year for the population of the EU. It is difficult to interpret this as a crippling burden. The costs for the EU of cleaning up a single category of hazardous chemicals, polychlorinated biphenyls (PCBs), will be many times this large.[4] If REACH prevents just one such problem in the future, it will more than pay for itself.

The annual costs of registration and testing, just over €300 million, should be compared to the chemical industry's annual sales, which totaled €556 billion for the EU in 2003.[5] From this perspective, the direct costs of REACH amount to 0.0006 of the sales revenues of the European chemical industry, or 1/16 of 1 percent (0.06 percent). So if the costs are fully passed on to the industry's customers, REACH will raise the average price of chemicals by 1/16 of 1 percent.

How disruptive is it for industry to experience cost increases of this magnitude? From 1997 through 2003, a period of relative calm in oil markets, the weekly change in the world spot price for crude oil exceeded 0.06 percent more than 98 percent of the time (fifty-one weeks per year).[6] From 1999 through 2003, the EU price index for all intermediate manufactured goods (products of one industry used by another industry), an index averaging many price changes in many industries across many countries, had a month-to-month change greater than 0.06 percent in 85 percent of the cases (ten months per year).[7]

Some of these changes in input prices turn out to be temporary, and are soon reversed; other changes are much more long-lasting. However, businesses frequently can not tell in advance which price changes will last, and which will not. Unexpected changes in price, often of much more than 0.06 percent, are part of normal life in the marketplace; successful businesses manage to thrive despite this uncertainty. By contrast, the cost of REACH can be anticipated, years in advance, and is small compared to normal changes in input prices.

The direct cost burden is minute enough that there is considerable room for disagreement about the details, without challenging the general conclusion that the costs look small. CEFIC has claimed that the direct costs will be twice as great as our estimate, and also that 25 percent of the industry will bear 80 percent of the costs of REACH. If both of these claims are correct, the direct costs of REACH would still amount to less than 0.5 percent of the revenues of the most affected 25 percent of the chemical industry; their prices would rise by less than 0.5 percent if they passed on the full costs to their customers. In general, the cost burden of registration and testing will be lowest, as a percentage of sales, for companies with a few large-volume products, and highest for companies with many low-volume products. A small cosmetics company with a diverse product line is an extreme worst case in this respect. But the average cost is what matters for overall impacts, and the average is very low.

The real debate is about the indirect costs that result from these direct costs—the ripple effects that will be felt throughout the economy. But how large a ripple can a very tiny stone create? Government and NGO (nongovernmental organization) studies estimated the indirect costs of REACH, for the European economy as a whole, at one to six times the direct costs. In contrast, the most widely quoted industry study, performed by Arthur D. Little (ADL) for a German industry federation, implied that the indirect costs are 650 times the direct costs.[8]

Is the ratio of indirect costs to direct registration and testing costs less than 6, or is it more like 650? The higher number is hard to believe, a priori: there is no evidence that modern industrial economies are hypersensitive to regulations, experiencing indirect damages of hundreds of times the direct regulatory costs. The ADL study, discussed below and in appendix C, turns out to involve a ludicrous series of mistaken and exaggerated calculations, combined with misunderstandings of basic economics. Standard methods of economic analysis, on the other hand, suggest a very low ratio of indirect to direct costs, as seen in the next section.

Price Impacts of REACH

What are the predictable economic impacts of the increased cost for registration and testing of chemicals under REACH? Most obviously, prices of chemicals will increase and as a result, sales of chemicals will presumably decrease. This section examines the expected economic effects of a small price increase. The following section discusses other pathways that have been suggested whereby REACH might also cause economic harm, beyond the ordinary effects of price changes.

New regulations such as REACH often mean that industry's costs are increased for any given quantity of output. Standard economic models represent this as an upward shift in the industry supply curve. The interaction of supply and demand then usually leads to a reduction in sales. Meanwhile, prices paid by the industry's customers, or downstream users, are increased. (In the jargon of the REACH debate, customers of the chemical industry were almost always referred to as "downstream users.")

How large are the short-run price effects in the case of REACH? Two analyses of the price impact, based on somewhat simplified models of the chemical industry's structure, both imply that the indirect impact of price changes will be very small.

Monopolistic Competition

One analysis, done by Joan Canton and Charles Allen for the Directorate General for Enterprise and Industry (a division of the European Commission that could be described, in American terms, as the EU's Commerce Department), applied a model of monopolistic competition to the chemical industry.[9] Monopolistic competition is a market structure based on product differentiation, in which many small firms sell similar, but not identical, products. Canton and Allen applied a standard model from economic theory, which assumes that the industry consists of numerous identical-sized firms whose products are close but not perfect substitutes for each other. Much of the expansion or contraction of output in response to regulation and price changes occurs through firms entering or leaving the industry.

In this model, as costs rise, a few firms leave the industry and a few chemical products cease to be available. Downstream users face increased costs and must use substitutes, often other chemicals. Under any of Canton and Allen's scenarios, REACH caused changes of less than 0.5 percent in the number of chemical firms, prices, output per firm, and output of the chemical industry. Based on their assumption of direct costs of €2.3 billion, they found that the cumulative costs to downstream users, including both the registration and testing costs that are passed on through higher prices on chemicals and the costs of substituting higher priced alternatives, ranged from €2.8 to €5.2 billion, or from 1.2 to 2.3 times the direct costs.[10]

In summary, the Canton-Allen model, focused on product differentiation, found only modest cost impacts, not much more than twice the direct costs in their most "expensive" variant.

Single-Market Model

An alternative approach is to apply the standard economic analysis of an increase in regulatory costs on a single market, as shown in figure 10.1. In contrast to the previous analysis, which assumed a high degree of differentiation among chemicals, the single-market model in effect assumes that all chemicals are perfect substitutes for each other. Before REACH, the market equilibrium is at price P_0 and quantity Q_0. REACH increases industry costs, shifting the supply curve upward; the new equilibrium is at a higher price, P_1, and lower output, Q_1.

It is a straightforward matter of algebra to develop the formulas and numerical estimates for the effects of REACH in this model.[11] The decisive factor shaping these estimates is that the direct costs imposed by REACH are a very small fraction of chemical industry annual revenues:

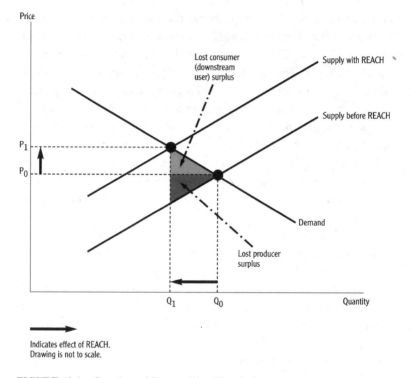

FIGURE 10.1. Supply and Demand for Chemicals

just under 0.0006, or 0.06 percent, as explained above. In the single-market model, REACH would increase prices by almost 0.03 percent, and decrease output by almost 0.06 percent.[12] The industry's total sales revenue would decline by almost 0.03 percent; the net received by the industry (after subtracting the costs of REACH) would decline by 0.085 percent. Standard economic measures of the loss to society resulting from these changes are inconsequentially small.[13]

From some perspectives, it is difficult to visualize cost impacts this small. Figure 10.1, like many economics diagrams, intentionally exaggerates the size of the expected effect to allow clarity of explanation. In fact, the figure as drawn shows roughly a 25 percent change in quantity and a 20 percent change in price—hundreds of times greater than the actual effects of REACH. An attempt to produce a similar diagram, with the shift in the supply curve drawn to scale, fails because the shift is too small to be seen; the supply curves before and after REACH are, to the naked eye, identical.

To show the effects of REACH to scale, it is necessary to "zoom in" on the area around the intersection of the supply and demand curves. Figure 10.2 represents such a graph, with the area around the intersection of the curves greatly enlarged. In figure 10.2, the equilibrium price and quantity prevailing in the market before REACH are represented as 1; the other numbers on the axes can be interpreted as ratios or fractions of the pre-REACH price and quantity. The dotted supply curve, representing the effects of REACH, is shifted up by 0.0006 above the original supply curve, to reflect the direct costs of REACH. As this figure illustrates, REACH will move the market in the expected direction—toward lower output and higher price—but by a *very* small amount.

In this example, the loss of net revenue to suppliers, plus the increased costs to customers, add up to twice the direct costs of REACH. In that sense, one could say that the total costs appear to be twice the direct costs.[14]

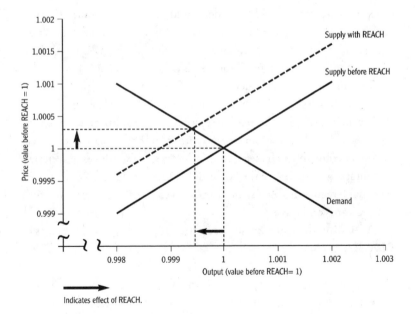

FIGURE 10.2.　Effects of REACH, drawn to scale

Economic Impacts: The Industry View

Neither of the two formal economic models, monopolistic competition or the single-market model, provides any support for the notion of huge indirect costs of regulation. But, as mentioned earlier, both models are oversimplifications of a complex reality; perhaps they have omitted the crucial features of REACH that make it so costly in the eyes of industry.

The ADL study, the first and most influential of the industry-sponsored studies, employed a strange new methodology that seems designed to find large, harmful impacts. Along the way, it also proposed several causal pathways that are said to lead to enormous costs. Although the study raised important issues, it ultimately failed to make the case that immense economic damage will result from REACH.

ADL modeled the impacts of individual cost categories as percentage reductions in output; it then multiplied these reductions, allowing them to generate a cumulative worsening of each other's effects. For example, if one cost category was thought to reduce output by 10 percent, and another by 20 percent, the ADL model would show that the output surviving after the imposition of both costs was 90 percent * 80 percent = 72 percent of the original amount, or a 28 percent reduction. A detailed critique of the ADL model methodology is presented in appendix C.

This unusual model structure rests on an implausible picture of industry as the helpless victim of a hostile world. When regulations impose change in the ADL model, no one responds by innovating and substituting new chemicals for old (or even by hiring lobbyists to talk about small cosmetics companies). Instead, each industry simply reduces output by a percentage appropriate to the last assault, and waits for the next one. After enough regulatory blows, the last person still working may as well turn out the lights and leave.

ADL discussed three major categories of potential indirect costs of REACH:

- Costs to downstream users due to loss of essential chemical inputs
- Losses due to disclosure of confidential business information
- Loss of competitive advantage due to delays in bringing new products to market

For different reasons, it turns out that each of these imposes little or no new costs on industry.

Costs to Downstream Users Due to Loss of Chemical Inputs

If a chemical is subject to authorization or restriction, or if it is withdrawn from the market altogether in response to REACH, then downstream users who lose access to that chemical could potentially experience economic harms. There are two reasons why downstream users might lose access to chemicals under REACH, with very different implications. A chemical could vanish from the marketplace for economic reasons: producers and importers could decide that a chemical's sales volume and profits are too small to justify the registration and testing costs. Or the chemical could be restricted or denied authorization under REACH because it is found to be a health or environmental hazard.

Withdrawal Caused by Loss of Profitability

As we have seen, the average cost burden of REACH will be very small. Generally, it will be far more profitable for industry to pay for registration and testing in order to continue production, rather than to shut down to avoid the modest regulatory costs. But conceivably, this might not be the case for an individual, low-value chemical: the costs of REACH could tip the balance against continuing production.

If a chemical is withdrawn for economic reasons, one has to assume it is of very limited economic value; otherwise, its volume and profits would justify the costs of registration and testing. If a chemical is threatened with withdrawal because it is unprofitable to keep producing it, but its loss is of great importance to downstream users, the price could be adjusted to reflect the chemical's importance; the downstream users would realize that it is in their interest to pay more to maintain access to this essential substance. With a higher price, more accurately reflecting its economic importance, the producer of the chemical would be able to pay for registration and testing. A market economy continually "solves" problems of this sort by adjusting prices, and there is no reason why it should fail to do so in the context of REACH.

If the higher price required to pay for registration and testing makes the chemical unaffordable to its customers, or drives them to use substitutes, then the chemical can be replaced, implying that it was not so important after all. In the absolutely worst case—back to the small cosmetics company with its unique and diverse product line—could a chemical be crucial to one or a few companies, but with a total market size too small to support the cost of REACH compliance? Although this appears possible in the abstract, there are two objections to consider. First, the chemical, and the companies that use it, must represent extremely small fractions of the vast European market; these can only be the exceptions, definitely not the rule. Second, if the chemical is profitable for one small company to use, is it equally profitable for all of that company's competitors? If yes, then the potential market for the chemical is not so small; if no, then the competitors have evidently found a workable substitute.

Limitations on Health or Environmental Grounds

The more difficult case concerns chemicals that are restricted or denied authorization because they are found to be hazardous, or are voluntarily withdrawn because they are suspected to be hazardous. On the one hand, this is a success in protecting health and the environment; identification and control of hazardous chemicals is the goal of REACH. On the other hand, it could potentially impose costs on downstream users, if the hazardous chemical is economically important and there are no viable substitutes. The critical question is: are there chemicals that will be found to be hazardous under REACH, which are economically important to downstream users, and for which there are no close substitutes?

There is no way to estimate the frequency of this problem in advance; indeed, there is not even any solid information on the fraction of all chemicals on the market that are so hazardous that they will be subject to authorization. (Estimates have ranged from 1 to 5 percent, but appear to be purely speculative.) The number of genuine problem cases will be smaller, because good substitutes will exist for some hazardous substances, and authorized uses will be allowed for others.

However, it remains theoretically possible that authorization could be denied for important uses of a chemical. It is also possible that an essential chemical would simply be withdrawn from the market, because the producer does not want to deal with the higher level of regulatory requirements for authorized substances.

Concerns about such impacts on downstream users have been widely discussed, and were addressed in the process of modifying and amending REACH. Some of the original advocates of REACH, in fact, have complained that the regulation as amended protects business more than the environment.[15] The provisions of REACH governing authorization allow a showing of economic benefits from using a substance to outweigh the finding of risks. The same is true in the provisions for restriction of the most hazardous substances, where a decision based on chemical risks can be delayed to allow time for evaluation of socioeconomic impacts.

In short, REACH does not ignore economic considerations. Concerns for possible economic harms due to restriction or denial of authorization, and mechanisms for addressing those harms, are built into the new regulatory apparatus. The greater risk may be in the opposite direction: the provisions for pleading economic necessity may make it possible to overturn too many regulatory decisions with allegations of immense downstream impacts.

Losses Due to Disclosure of Confidential Business Information

The fear of disclosure of confidential information, much discussed by business commentators, is based on a misreading of the regulations. The ADL study asked business representatives, early in the REACH debate, how great they believed the dangers of excessive disclosure would be, and reported their alarming answers as if they were hard data.[16] In fact, REACH contains substantial protection for confidential business information that is shared with regulators. Moreover, the public sector already collects substantial amounts of information in the regulation of new chemicals, without any great losses due to unauthorized disclosure.

Fears of such disclosures may be exaggerated in general. In the United States, the state of Massachusetts has a Toxics Use Reduction Act, adopted in 1989, which requires disclosure of more information about industry's chemical use than REACH.[17] A state agency uses the information to help enterprises develop strategies for reducing their use of toxic chemicals, a program that has won wide acceptance and praise in the state's business community.

Losses Due to Delays in Bringing New Products to Market

The ADL study inappropriately assumed that REACH will cause a large delay in bringing all products to market (six to twelve months for every product, depending on scenario), then applied an arbitrary and unsubstantiated model that translates such delays into huge economic losses. Delays in coming to market, if they occurred, would be important for innovation and development of new chemicals. Yet since REACH, in fact, lightens the regulatory burden on new chemicals, it should be seen as helping, not hindering, in this respect. If anything, it should be credited with speeding the introduction of new chemicals and boosting the competitive position of innovative European producers. On the other hand, chemicals already in use when REACH was adopted will remain on the market pending the completion of testing; thus, there is no new delay created for existing uses of pre-existing chemicals.

However, even the most streamlined new regulations inevitably have an impact on chemical use. That impact should not be thought of as uniformly delaying all innovation; rather, it appropriately favors safer options. REACH creates incentives to use those chemicals that can most quickly be tested and approved, in place of those that will require a lengthy testing process. There is likewise an incentive to accelerate the development of safer alternatives to chemicals that might be hazardous. Any delays experienced today will be offset by the avoidance of future costs, liabilities, and delays associated with innovations that later prove to be hazardous.

Conclusion: Is REACH Worth the Price?

For reasons explained in other chapters, it is impossible to come up with a meaningful monetary value for the complete benefits of REACH. However, a number of studies have offered comparisons to selected, easily monetized benefits. They have routinely found that a very partial accounting of benefits outweighs the costs of REACH:

- Cleanup of PCBs, a category of hazardous chemicals widely used in the past, will cost Europe much more than REACH as a whole;

if REACH prevents one new hazard of the magnitude of PCBs, it
will more than pay for itself.[18]

- If REACH eliminates 1 percent of noncancer occupational diseases
in Europe, because of reduced workplace exposure to toxic chemicals, the savings in medical costs will roughly equal the costs of
REACH.[19]

- An estimate of several categories of benefits by the European Commission found a total of €50 billion, more than ten times the direct
costs of REACH.[20]

- Estimates of health care savings, by British economists David Pearce
and Phoebe Koundouri, also amounted to many times the costs of
REACH.[21]

Of course, it is a gamble; the outcome of the testing called for under
REACH is unknown. If no important new chemical hazards are detected,
then the costs of REACH will have bought nothing more than peace of
mind. But if even a handful of serious hazards are discovered and
promptly controlled, the savings in avoided health care costs and toxic
waste cleanup are likely to be much larger than the modest costs of
REACH.

Even when a regulation is on balance clearly beneficial to society, it
may be possible to find a worst case, a company for whom the change is
a burden. As the chemical industry has pointed out, to a small company
that sells myriad new cosmetics with unfamiliar ingredients, REACH
may feel like an imposition of expensive, bureaucratic controls. But Eu-
ropeans will doubtless still succeed in looking attractive, even when they
are forced to make do with only the abundant varieties of cosmetics that
meet with approval under REACH. Innovative small cosmetics companies should be able, perhaps with some initial help, to adopt the extensive palette of REACH-approved ingredients when designing their future product lines.

And remember that this is a worst case, not the norm. Small cosmetics firms do not produce most of Europe's chemicals. There is not even a
hint, in the industry critiques, of a compelling story about the need for
larger companies to continue producing and using harmful chemicals.
If feeding and housing the poor somehow absolutely required use of a

substance that polluted the rivers and harmed the fish, if providing medical care to all somehow depended on a substance that gave rise to a rare form of cancer, there would be challenging ethical dilemmas involving complex tradeoffs. No such claims have been made; no such dilemmas and tradeoffs have been posed, except as abstract rhetoric. As shown in earlier chapters, that rhetoric rings hollow for lack of factual content. The needs of the small cosmetics firm hardly rise to the challenge: is the right to put untested chemical substances directly on your skin a freedom worth fighting for? It would be far better, for all concerned, to help any struggling small companies find new products that meet the highest standards of health and safety. Bigger businesses, which dominate the production and use of chemicals, can easily afford to clean up their act on their own.

Chapter 11

Impacts of REACH on Developing Countries

Will REACH harm the economies of developing countries? This was one of the last major questions to be raised in the long debate that led to the adoption of REACH; attention was focused, in particular, on the group of African, Caribbean, and Pacific (ACP) countries that historically have been connected to Europe.[1] In 2005, the European Parliament commissioned a research project to assess the potential economic impacts of REACH on the ACP states. This chapter summarizes that research effort.[2] After documenting ACP concerns about REACH and reviewing previous research on environmental standards and development, we focus on the ACP economies, their exports subject to REACH, and the enterprises responsible for those exports. We then consider the overall costs and benefits of REACH for ACP. Ultimately the question is, does environmental regulation in developed countries, such as REACH, help or harm the developing world?

ACP Concerns about REACH

The ACP Group of States consists of seventy-nine developing countries that have a long-standing special relationship to Europe. Many of them are ex-colonies that have traditionally received preferential access to European markets. ACP includes all forty-eight countries of sub-Saharan Africa, plus sixteen countries in the Caribbean and fifteen in the Pacific.

Chapter 11 by Frank Ackerman, Elizabeth Stanton, Brian Roach, and Anne-Sofie Andersson.

In 2005, the ACP Council of Ministers adopted a resolution supporting the general goals of REACH, but expressing "deep concern" about the "potential negative impact of REACH on exports, particularly in commodities such as minerals and metals, from ACP to the EU." The Ministers also stated that they were "convinced" both "that REACH will be expensive to implement," and that REACH would have a negative effect on small, medium-sized, and microenterprises, especially "emerging small-scale miners." They expressed concern that the costs imposed by REACH might "lead to disinvestment from ACP States," potentially resulting in loss of employment for millions of people.[3]

Addressing these concerns, the ACP Ministers asked the EU to exempt ores, minerals, and alloys from registration and authorization requirements; to exempt bulk metals from authorization requirements; and to reduce bureaucratic requirements and attendant costs for ACP countries.

Minerals and ores have since been exempted from registration requirements, but even after that exemption, industry groups such as the Chamber of Mines of South Africa continued to express concerns about REACH authorization requirements for ores.[4] They anticipated that many ores would require authorization, because they contain impurities that are known to be hazardous, such as arsenic in copper ore. Since the proportion of impurities varies widely, even among different batches of ore from the same mine, industry worried that every batch of ore might require a separate authorization. (Asked about this concern, European Commission staff members insisted that a separate authorization for every batch of ore has never been contemplated or proposed. Rather, they anticipate a single authorization for each harmful substance, such as arsenic in copper ore, valid over a range of concentrations.[5])

Standards, Exports, and Development

As a number of researchers have noted, environmental standards set by Europe and other developed countries have the potential either to harm or to help developing countries.[6] Rich-country standards can function as barriers to poor-country exports, thus impeding development[7]; in some cases, food safety standards may end up playing this role.[8] On the other hand, standards set in export markets may serve as a spur to social and environmental progress for developing-country exporters. European retailers have played a crucial role in transmitting information and incentives to their overseas suppliers, as shown in studies of the cut-flower industry,[9] fruit production in Brazil,[10] and the leather industry in India, Pakistan, and elsewhere.[11]

Agricultural exporters and industries, such as leather, which process local agricultural products, play a large part in the economies of developing countries; as a result, most of the case studies have focused on these areas. In these sectors, it is common to find small-scale producers with limited information about export markets and foreign standards, and limited resources for responding to a changing international context.

This chapter explores different sectors of developing economies, focusing on their production of metals, minerals, and chemicals. Almost none of the exports affected by REACH are based in agriculture; the one agricultural example that we examine, essential oils, is the area where we find issues of limited information to be most critical and the need for assistance to be most imperative. As we document below, most of the affected exports from ACP countries come from multinational corporations or large national companies. Although there may be genuine obstacles to exporting faced by the leather industry in Pakistan, or the essential oils producers in Madagascar, these do not apply to major British, American, and Australian mining companies that happen to own mines located in very poor countries. Nor do they apply to South African companies with annual turnover in the billions of euros, international operations of their own, and listings on foreign stock exchanges, which bear more resemblance to multinational corporations than to small rural enterprises.

There has been some concern that strict regulations in the EU would lead polluting industries to locate in countries with more relaxed standards. This "pollution haven" theory was discussed at length in chapter 3: as noted there, empirical evidence has provided little support for this hypothesis. A common conclusion is that the pollution haven effect is minor at best, and that the costs of compliance with environmental regulations are usually too small to determine plant location. Other factors such as natural resource availability, labor costs, and adequacy of infrastructure are more likely to be decisive. For most of the ACP export discussed here, the location of production is determined by the location of valuable ores and minerals; thus the pollution haven questions may not apply.

The pollution haven discussion assumes, as does much of the literature on environmental standards, that regulation is on balance a cost to business. The contrary view is expressed by the Porter hypothesis (see chapter 3), suggesting that regulation may actually stimulate innovation and benefit the businesses that are quickest to respond.[12] In particular, it has been argued that REACH is better for innovation than the patchwork of regulations that it replaced.[13] We discuss the benefits as well as the costs of REACH for ACP later in this chapter.

REACH and ACP Economies

ACP includes many of the world's poorest countries, as well as South Africa and some smaller countries that are at a middle-income level by global standards. As of 2003, ACP's population of 743 million people represented 12 percent of the world population, while its total gross domestic product (GDP) of €434 billion was only 1.3 percent of world output. South Africa, by far the largest and most industrialized economy in ACP, accounts for about one-third of the group's total GDP, and two-thirds of the group's exports that are subject to REACH.

ACP countries depend heavily on trade, and have historically strong connections to Europe. Nonetheless, more than two-thirds of ACP exports go to non-European markets, such as North America and East Asia. Exports to all regions amounted to one-third of ACP's GDP, while exports to the EU were €45 billion, or just over 10 percent of GDP, in 2003.

We began our research on the impacts of REACH by collecting data on the affected ACP exports. Eurostat, the EU's statistical information service, lists exports from each ACP country to the EU. We reviewed the list of export categories,[14] identifying all categories that are potentially affected by REACH. Our goal was to err on the side of inclusiveness: when in doubt, we included any borderline or ambiguous cases, excluding only those that we were certain would *not* be subject to registration under REACH. We identified 235 categories of "REACH exports"—that is, exports to the EU that are potentially subject to regulation under REACH, including all uncertain categories. For each of these 235 trade categories, Eurostat reports the value in euros, and the volume in tons, of exports to the EU from each ACP nation (data were incomplete for a few of the smallest island nations). To reduce the effects of short-term fluctuations in trade data, we calculated the annual average of exports over the years 2002–2004.

For ACP as a whole, exports to the EU that would be subject to REACH averaged 1.4 percent of GDP in 2002–2004. There is, however, wide variation within ACP in terms of exposure to REACH. Only twenty-four of the seventy-nine ACP countries have significant REACH exports, by any of three standards:

- REACH exports are at least 1 percent of GDP; or,
- the annual value of all REACH exports is at least €10 million; or,
- for at least one category of REACH exports, the annual volume of shipments exceeds 1,000 tons.

As shown in table 11.1, these twenty-four countries account for more than 99 percent of the value of all REACH exports from ACP. There are several reasons why other ACP countries are so little affected by REACH. Some are primarily agricultural exporters; some island nations have service-based, often tourist-oriented, economies; and some countries depend on exports of products such as fuels that are exempt from REACH. Although in some cases we examine ACP totals, our analysis focuses largely on the twenty-four countries that meet one or more of the three criteria.

For the group of twenty-four nations, REACH exports averaged 6.3 percent of global exports in 2002–2004; exports to countries outside the EU, and exports to the EU of commodities not covered by REACH, still account for the bulk of exports. In comparison to the size of the national economy, REACH exports were more than 1 percent of GDP in eleven ACP countries, and more than 10 percent of GDP only in Mozambique and Suriname.

And just as ACP has other markets, Europe has other sources of metals, minerals, and chemicals. ACP countries are not the only source of imports to the EU that are subject to REACH; in fact, they represent less than one-tenth of the global total. Other developing nations account for four times as much as ACP, while the United States and other developed countries account for even more.

TABLE 11.1   REACH exports for selected ACP countries (2002–2004 average).

	Value (€ million)	% of GDP	Leading REACH exports
Cameroon	75	0.6	aluminum
Comoros	3	1.0	essential oils
Congo	7	0.2	copper, cobalt
Congo, Dem. Rep.	35	0.7	cobalt, copper
Côte d'Ivoire	18	0.2	essential oils, gold
Cuba	37	0.1	nickel, iron
Dominican Republic	91	0.6	ferroalloys
Equatorial Guinea	46	1.9	acyclic alcohol
Ghana	189	2.8	aluminum, gold
Guinea	54	1.7	aluminum, gold
Jamaica	273	3.7	aluminum
Liberia	1	0.4	ferrous products, gold
Madagascar	16	0.4	essential oils, gold
Mozambique	561	12.4	aluminum
Namibia	10	0.3	zinc, copper
Papua New Guinea	1	< 0.1	monocarboxylic acids
South Africa	4,238	3.0	gold, platinum
Sudan	48	0.3	gold
Suriname	104	11.4	aluminum, gold
Tanzania	257	2.8	gold
Trinidad and Tobago	190	2.0	acyclic alcohol, ammonia
Uganda	13	0.2	gold
Zambia	64	1.6	cobalt, copper
Zimbabwe	100	1.3	ferroalloys, nickel
55 other ACP countries	41	< 0.1	
ACP total	**6,472**	**1.4**	

Leading Export Commodities

To a remarkable extent, ACP's REACH exports are concentrated in just a few commodities. Tables 11.2 and 11.3 show the principal categories of REACH exports, separately for South Africa and for the seventy-eight other ACP countries. Some €5.9 billion, more than 90 percent of the total, consists of mining products, as shown in table 11.2. Both in South Africa and in the rest of ACP, a handful of products account for almost all REACH exports: gold, iron and steel, aluminum, platinum, cobalt,

TABLE 11.2   REACH mining exports (2002–2004 average).

	Value (€ million)	Percent of all REACH mining exports
South Africa		
Gold	1,993	51
Iron, steel, ferroalloys	1,005	26
Platinum group metals	682	17
Aluminum, aluminum oxide	59	2
Copper	35	1
Manganese, manganese oxides	33	1
All other	122	3
All REACH mining exports (South Africa)	**3,929**	**100**
All other ACP countries		
Aluminum, aluminum oxide	1,041	53
Gold	538	27
Iron, steel, ferroalloys	175	9
"Chapter 81" (unspecified metals)[a]	50	3
Cobalt	48	2
Nickel	26	1
All other	90	5
All REACH mining exports (other ACP)	**1,969**	**100**
ACP total: REACH mining exports	**5,898**	

[a]Primarily cobalt and manganese; primarily exported from Zambia and Democratic Republic of Congo.

copper, manganese, and nickel together account for the overwhelming majority of REACH exports from ACP.

Chemical exports amount to €0.6 billion, about half from South Africa, as shown in table 11.3. South Africa has a diverse range of chemical exports; in contrast, chemical exports from other ACP countries are concentrated in just a few categories. Almost half of the non–South African chemical exports consist of acyclic alcohols, for example, methanol and ethanol.

REACH regulates chemicals and mineral products based on the volume of sales in Europe, with stricter regulation for higher volumes. Most ACP countries have very few REACH exports in the top volume tiers,

TABLE 11.3   REACH chemical exports (2002–2004 average).

	Value (€ million)	Percent of all REACH chemical exports
South Africa		
Acyclic hydrocarbons	29	9
Reaction initiators	22	7
Prepared binders	18	6
Hydrazine, hydroxylamine, and their inorganic salts	18	6
Salts of oxometallic or peroxometallic acids	15	5
Organic composite solvents	15	5
All other	192	62
All REACH chemical exports (South Africa)	**310**	**100**
All other ACP countries		
Acyclic alcohols	122	46
"Chapter 29" (unspecified organic chemicals)[a]	61	23
Ammonia	20	8
Essential oils	20	7
Heterocyclic compounds	12	4
Coloring matter	4	1
All other	27	10
All REACH chemical exports (other ACP)	**265**	**100**
ACP total: REACH chemical exports	**575**	

[a] Exported almost exclusively from Trinidad and Tobago and Equatorial Guinea; probably oil industry by-products.

for which REACH registration and testing requirements are the most demanding. The only countries with more than two export categories in the top tier, above 1,000 tons per year, are South Africa, Cuba, Trinidad and Tobago, Zambia, and Zimbabwe. The only countries with more than twenty export categories above REACH's one ton minimum threshold for regulation are South Africa, Cuba, Côte d'Ivoire, and Trinidad and Tobago. All of the twenty-four countries have a very small number of major REACH export categories: the one or two top categories, shown in table 11.1, account for at least 63 percent of each country's REACH exports, and at least 90 percent for sixteen of the countries.

Mineral and metal products are the dominant REACH exports for eighteen countries, including South Africa. In Equatorial Guinea and Trinidad and Tobago, acyclic alcohols and ammonia, byproducts of the oil industry, are the top REACH exports. (In both countries, petroleum, which is not covered by REACH, is the largest export to Europe.) The principal REACH exports from four countries include plant-based products: essential oils from Comoros, Côte d'Ivoire, and Madagascar, and monocarboxylic fatty acids, derived from palm oil, from Papua New Guinea.

South Africa

ACP's largest economy, South Africa, is the source of nearly two-thirds of all ACP REACH exports. South Africa is a special case in several respects: it has reached a higher level of industrial development than many ACP countries, and it possesses an extraordinary amount and diversity of mineral wealth. But the South African economy includes many sectors that are untouched by REACH. Only one-quarter of South Africa's exports to the EU falls under REACH. Coal and diamonds, the country's top exports to Europe, and many manufactured and agricultural exports are not affected. In REACH export sectors, South Africa is the fourth largest supplier of iron and steel to the EU, has a diversified, growing chemical industry, and has the largest mining sector in ACP. We identified more than 200 REACH export categories in South Africa, far more than in any other ACP country.

Most of South Africa's REACH exports consist of metals, particularly gold, platinum group metals, and iron and steel products. The country is the world's largest producer of both gold and platinum. In gold, South Africa has 40 percent of world reserves and produced 14 percent of world output in 2004. In platinum, South Africa is even more dominant, with 88 percent of world reserves and 58 percent of world output in 2004. In iron and steel, South Africa produced 40 million tons of iron ore in 2005 (3 percent of world output), of which 25 million tons were exported as ore and 15 million tons were used locally to produce steel or ferroalloys. South Africa is the nineteenth largest producer and the eighth largest net exporter of steel in the world.

The largest REACH export from South Africa's iron and steel industry is ferroalloys, an intermediate product consisting of iron alloyed with elements such as chromium, manganese, and silicon that add desirable properties for steelmaking. In 2004, South Africa produced 4.3 million tons of ferroalloys, almost one-fifth of world production, and second only to China in volume. Exports amounted to at least 3.4 million tons in 2004, or about 80 percent of production. Under REACH, alloys are treated as mixtures: when alloys are imported into Europe, each of the substances in the alloys must be registered. There are, however, only a limited number of substances used in ferroalloys. Ferrochromium makes up 72 percent of South Africa's ferroalloy production, and ferromanganese and silicomanganese another 23 percent.

South Africa's chemical industry employs 200,000 people, accounting for €7 billion of value added, more than 4 percent of GDP.[15] Its growth has been driven by the demand for explosives in the mining industry, the abundance of cheap coal, and the political environment of the apartheid era (before 1994), which put a premium on national self-sufficiency. However, most of South Africa's chemical production is in product lines that are exempt from REACH: liquid fuels, plastics, rubber, and pharmaceuticals account for 64 percent of the industry.

South Africa is a net importer of chemicals, largely owing to its imports of pharmaceuticals and fine chemicals. At the same time, it is a significant exporter of other chemical products. Most of South Africa's chemical exports to Europe are basic industrial chemicals, with a smaller quantity of finished products such as cosmetics and inks. No single product or small group of products dominates the list, as seen in table 11.3; rather, there are exports of moderate quantities of a variety of industrial chemicals. Only 21 percent of South Africa's chemical exports go to the EU; markets in Africa, Asia, and North America are more important to the industry.

Multinationals versus Local Producers

The great majority of ACP REACH exports are exported in large quantities by large companies. These firms should have no more trouble than European companies in complying with REACH; indeed, in some cases, they *are* European companies.

In South Africa, the largest producers of gold, platinum, and iron ore are subsidiaries of the British mining giant Anglo American, as is one of the major steel companies. Other mineral exporters include large South African companies that have become multinational firms with overseas operations of their own. In the chemical industry there are three dominant firms, one a subsidiary of Dow Chemical. The other two are South African firms that are large by world standards; one of them has annual turnover of €9 billion and is listed on the New York Stock Exchange. A handful of smaller producers are also active in niches in the chemical industry, including subsidiaries of other multinationals as well as local companies.

The role of foreign multinationals in REACH exports is also paramount in the rest of ACP. For example, in aluminum production, Mozambique's exports come from a joint venture led by the Australian mining company BHP Billiton, in partnership with Mitsubishi and government agencies of South Africa and Mozambique. Alcan, the Canadian multinational aluminum producer, is active in Cameroon, jointly with the government. Alcoa, the U.S. firm, produces aluminum in Jamaica and Suriname, in some cases jointly with government agencies and/or BHP Billiton. We did not encounter any evidence of small aluminum producers or exporters.

Small-Scale Gold Mining

A similar picture can be seen throughout ACP's other metal and mineral exports, with one exception. In several gold-producing countries, small-scale or artisanal gold mining exists alongside major commercial mines. Large numbers of people are engaged in searching for gold with only rudimentary tools, under "gold rush" conditions in which most participants earn very little. This style of mining apparently does not occur on a large scale in South Africa, or in mining for anything other than gold.

Artisanal gold mining raises serious issues of poverty, economic development, and environmental health. Yet the existence of these impoverished freelance miners does not imply that gold (or any other mineral) is exported to Europe by ACP microenterprises. Small-scale gold miners sell their gold either on the black market, or to national government agencies that export gold to Europe. In Tanzania, the country best known for artisanal gold mining, three-fourths of the nation's gold output comes from subsidiaries of Anglo American and other multinationals, and one-fourth from hundreds of thousands of artisanal miners. The national government is obligated to buy the gold produced by the small-scale miners, and is building a government-owned gold refinery to handle their output. Thus, it is the government of Tanzania, not the individual miners, that exports the country's artisanal gold to Europe. Although it is difficult to imagine individual artisanal miners complying with REACH, it is easy to envision a Tanzanian government agency carrying out that role.

Small Exporters and Essential Oils

In one area, however, namely the essential oils industry, the producers, exporters, and even European importers are often small- and medium-sized enterprises. Essential oils are products of plants giving the fragrances and tastes characteristic of the particular plant, such as cinnamon and lavender. Plants for essential oils are often grown by small-scale farmers, who sell their products to companies with distillation and packaging facilities.[16] Six ACP countries averaged more than fifty tons of essential oil exports to the EU in 2002–2004. We looked in detail at the industry in Madagascar and Comoros; in both cases, the sector appears to consist entirely of small- to medium-sized farmers and manufacturers.

Madagascar is the largest essential oils exporter to the EU after South Africa, sending an annual average of €6 million of essential oils to Europe in 2002–2004. Vanilla is one of Madagascar's most important exports, but essential oils from many other plants are also being established as export products, including ylang ylang (a main ingredient in many perfumes), clove, palmarosa, geranium, niaouli, and helichryse. Growing consumer interest in essential oils has spurred production. Currently 80–90 percent of the oils are produced for export, and are exported "raw" because of the lack of manufacturing infrastructure.[17] International aid agencies have been active in Madagascar for more than a decade, with several major aid projects aimed at developing the industry. A program sponsored by the U.S. Agency for International Development lists about twenty small- to medium-sized companies that produce essential oils or related substances.[18]

In Comoros, sometimes called the Perfume Isles, essential oils account for 98 percent of REACH exports. Comoros exports 80 percent of the world's supply of ylang ylang essence. The essential oil of vanilla is another important export. Distilleries use their own crops but also buy from smaller farmers, because producing for the export market requires quality controls of the distilled products and registration processes that most small farmers cannot afford on their own.[19]

The importers and suppliers to the EU will bear the costs of meeting REACH requirements for essential oils imports.[20] The European Federation of Essential Oils, which represents importers to the EU and producers in the EU, has emphasized that their 150 members are mainly small- and medium-sized enterprises and would have difficulty complying with REACH. They advocated, unsuccessfully, for exempting essential oils from REACH.[21]

However, the overall costs of REACH compliance for the essential oils industry will be low; there are only a limited number of essential oils exported from ACP to the EU in quantities affected by REACH. According to one estimate, there are 300 essential oils sold in the EU, of which 170 are exempt from REACH because they are produced in amounts less than one ton per year. Another 120 essential oils are below 100 tons per year, and exporters, therefore, face relatively limited testing. Only ten essential oils fall in the higher volume range requiring more extensive testing.[22]

Costs and Benefits of REACH for ACP

REACH has both costs and benefits for ACP. The costs are principally those of registration and testing for exports that are subject to REACH, plus any economic disruption or losses caused by the regulation. The direct costs are small enough, and the producing and exporting enterprises are in most cases large enough, that we expect little or no economic losses in the ACP countries as a result of compliance with REACH. The benefits include increased knowledge of chemical hazards and safety, improved protection of workers' health and the natural environment, and potentially reduced liability for future damages.

Costs of REACH for ACP Exporters

Numerous studies have been conducted on the costs of implementing REACH. A summary of thirty-six early studies, published in 2004, found that the estimated total cost of REACH is between €2.4 billion and €3.9 billion over an eleven-year implementation period.[23] Later changes in REACH were predominantly in the direction of lowering requirements and costs, implying that early studies of costs may now represent overestimates. One of the most recent detailed studies was done by the consulting firm KPMG, jointly commissioned by the chemical industry and the European Commission. KPMG estimated registration and testing costs per substance, ranging from €15,000 for the lowest volume tier, up to €323,000 in the top volume tier, or less (per company) if two or more companies share the cost.[24] Use of available published information on chemicals will often lower costs still further, making the true costs of compliance even lower than the KPMG estimates.

We estimated the costs of REACH for the top twenty-four ACP exporters by applying the KPMG costs per substance to the REACH export data. The results of our calculation are shown in table 11.4. The estimated total cost is about €50 million, or €4.6 million per year over the eleven-year phase-in period.[25] South Africa's exports would bear more than half of this cost, about €2.8 million per year. The next largest costs, more than €200,000 per year, would fall on Cuba and Trinidad and Tobago. In all other countries, the costs would be less than €120,000 per year.

The annual costs estimated in table 11.4 amount to less than 0.1 percent of the value of REACH exports for the twenty-four countries as a whole. The costs exceed 1 percent of the value of REACH exports only in the Congo, Liberia, and Papua New Guinea.

In Liberia, the only country where estimated REACH compliance costs appear to exceed two percent of the value of REACH exports, the data may be particularly unreliable. Liberia, best known in world trade for exports of rubber and timber, and for low-cost ship registrations, was engulfed in civil war during much of 2002–2004, the period covered by our data. Thus it appears to be particularly unlikely to be a significant exporter of metals or chemicals. Reports of small quantities of several dif-

TABLE 11.4 Estimated cost of REACH for ACP

	11-year total compliance cost (€1,000)	Annual compliance cost (€1,000)	Annual cost as a percentage of REACH exports
Cameroon	941	86	0.10
Comoros	106	10	0.40
Congo	811	74	1.10
Congo, Dem. Rep.	1,010	92	0.30
Côte d'Ivoire	1,180	107	0.60
Cuba	2,783	253	0.70
Dominican Republic	1,203	109	0.10
Equatorial Guinea	400	36	0.01
Ghana	1,035	94	0.05
Guinea	751	68	0.10
Jamaica	626	57	0.02
Liberia	335	30	4.60
Madagascar	473	43	0.30
Mozambique	806	73	0.01
Namibia	659	60	0.60
Papua New Guinea	186	17	1.90
South Africa	30,629	2,784	0.10
Sudan	15	1	0.00
Suriname	688	63	0.10
Tanzania	1,102	100	0.04
Trinidad and Tobago	2,396	218	0.10
Uganda	226	21	0.20
Zambia	1,248	113	0.20
Zimbabwe	1,010	92	0.10
TOTAL	**50,616**	**4,601**	**0.07**

ferent REACH exports from Liberia, varying widely from year to year, may represent either re-export of goods produced elsewhere, or simply data errors. The data as reported, however, create an image of a country exporting a diversity of REACH products in small quantities, the worst case for REACH compliance costs.[26]

Even in the sector with the broadest range of REACH exports, South Africa's chemical industry, REACH compliance is unlikely to pose a major challenge. The South African government's 2005 industrial strategy, analyzing in some detail the prospects for expansion of the chemical industry, did not list European regulation as one of the important obstacles. It did, however, express South Africa's commitment to meeting developed country environmental standards as its chemical industry grows.[27]

The central quantitative finding here is the small size of REACH compliance costs, with average annual costs on the order of 0.1 percent of the value of REACH exports. Businesses routinely experience and cope with cost changes of much more than 0.1 percent. No sensible enterprise changes its plans about where to locate its facilities, or decides to abandon a market as large as the EU, in response to the tiny percentage changes in costs that will result from REACH. Prices of energy, materials, and equipment, and the availability of infrastructure and skilled labor, are much larger influences on production and investment decisions. In the case of ACP's REACH exports, of course, the existence of ores and mineral deposits is often the deciding factor for the location of production.

The industries that are affected by REACH, in Europe and in South Africa, expressed grave concern in advance, claiming that costs might be enormous. However, after years of research and debate, there are no credible, published estimates of REACH compliance costs that are large enough to justify those concerns.

Benefits of REACH for ACP

There are benefits as well as costs of REACH, both in the EU and in ACP countries. Regulation of hazardous chemicals should not be viewed as a rich country's luxury imposed on low-income exporters. Some of the greatest beneficiaries of REACH could be businesses and workers in developing countries.

Businesses will gain access to crucial information about the effects of their products and the materials and substances they use; this will help them to identify and adopt safer alternatives, when needed, and to avoid future liability for damages. Public health will be improved by better information and appropriate limits on chemical exposures. A World Bank report reviewed the scientific literature on the subject, and concluded that toxic chemicals are a significant and growing threat to health among the poor in developing countries. Resulting in part from toxic exposures, chronic diseases are emerging as an increasingly important source of illness in developing countries, and could exceed the burden from infectious disease by 2020.[28]

Workers in particular will benefit because many chemicals pose greater hazards to the employees who handle them on a daily basis than to the consumers of finished products. This could be important both in the chemical industry itself and in industries that use chemicals in production. Some of these industries, such as textiles, are increasingly concentrated in developing countries. If REACH generates important health and environmental safety information about chemicals used in textile production, developing countries will be better able to adopt occupational exposure standards that ensure worker safety and reduce the rate of occupational illness.

Conclusions

Are developing-country exporters placed at a disadvantage by European regulations? Is there a need to provide information and assistance to overcome that disadvantage? These understandable concerns emerge from studies of one common market structure: industries in which small local firms in developing countries are producing or processing agricultural products for export. There are a few cases where this market structure applies to ACP exports affected by REACH, most notably in essential oils. In those rare cases in which small- and medium-sized firms are exporting products affected by REACH, assistance from the EU or from national or nongovernmental agencies may be necessary for a smooth transition to REACH compliance. The cost of such assistance will be limited because there are so few export sectors where small enterprises are involved.

Most of the ACP exports affected by REACH, however, follow a different pattern: huge multinational companies are exporting metals and minerals from mines that are located in developing countries. The great majority of exports affected by REACH, both in South Africa and in ACP as a whole, consist of a small number of metals: gold, iron and steel, aluminum, platinum, cobalt, copper, manganese, and nickel. Costs to register this short list of well-known major products will have minimal effects on the large-scale industries that produce and export them. In ownership, financial resources, technical capability, and access to information, multinational exporters of metals and minerals do not resemble a developing country's small local enterprises. In some cases, the same firms also export the same products from North America, Australia, and other locations.

REACH was modified in response to developing-country concerns, as expressed by ACP and others in the long debates before adoption. There is no need for further modifications to REACH to preserve developing countries' interests. While it is often important to provide developing countries with special protections in international trade, it is equally important to ensure that developing countries benefit from the information about chemicals that will be generated under REACH. Overall, compliance with environmental regulations like REACH poses little or no risk to the economies of developing countries, and may in the long run provide significant health and safety benefits not only to Europe, but also to its trading partners.

How Should the United States Respond to REACH?

In the previous two chapters, we have considered the cost of REACH both to European chemical manufacturers and to some of the European Union's trading partners in developing countries. In this chapter, we look at the cost of compliance with REACH to U.S. producers. Are U.S. firms better off paying these costs and retaining access to European markets, or ignoring REACH and going it alone?

U.S. exporters have faced similar dilemmas in the past, with genetically modified crops, and with beef following mad cow disease scares. Unfortunately, those experiences have shown that it is possible to lose foreign markets quite rapidly by ignoring foreign regulations and concerns about health, safety, and the environment.

What is at stake for the United States is substantial: we estimate that chemical exports to Europe that are subject to REACH amount to $13.7 billion per year, and are directly or indirectly responsible for 54,000 jobs. Revenues and employment of this magnitude dwarf the costs of compliance with REACH, which will amount to no more than a few *million* dollars per year. Even if industry remains convinced that REACH is a needless mistake, it will be far more profitable to pay the modest compliance costs than to lose access to the enormous European market.

Chapter 12 by Frank Ackerman, Elizabeth Stanton, and Rachel Massey.

The Industry Argument

In the United States, both the federal government and the chemical industry have actively engaged in efforts to influence the implementation of REACH. U.S. government involvement has included high-level communications from State Department officials, distribution of policy papers, and formal statements on possible implications of REACH for global trade. In parallel, U.S. industry associations, notably the American Chemistry Council (ACC), have engaged in direct and indirect lobbying of EU officials, and have expressed grave concerns about the potentially dire effects of REACH. In some cases ACC went so far as to argue that European business would lose competitive advantage in relation to the United States as a result of REACH—an odd concern for the trade association of an industry that competes with Europe.[1]

The Bush administration's stance on REACH has prompted a series of protests from U.S. health and environmental advocacy networks, and from members of Congress. Critics argue that the U.S. government has used industry analyses wholesale, without interpretation, corrections, or independent analysis, and has overstepped the bounds of normal diplomatic communication and meddled inappropriately in the EU's internal process of policy development.

Some U.S. government responses to REACH have been overt, while others were clandestine at the time that they occurred. Thanks to Freedom of Information Act requests by the Environmental Health Fund and by the office of Congressman Henry Waxman, there is clear documentation of communications by U.S. government officials regarding REACH.

As summarized in a report by Representative Waxman's office, Bush administration officials met repeatedly with representatives of the U.S. chemicals industry to develop a position on REACH. Goals identified in consultation with industry included the possibility of "educating" other countries so that they could join the United States in raising concerns about REACH. In 2002, Secretary of State Colin Powell cabled U.S. diplomatic posts with instructions to "raise the EU chemicals policy with relevant government officials" and to object to REACH as "costly, burdensome, and complex." The Assistant U.S. Trade Representative for Europe and the Mediterranean invited U.S. chemical companies to develop "themes" for the U.S. government to cite in its communications with EU officials regarding REACH. Secretary Powell used these themes—including calls for more in-depth cost/benefit analyses, as well as concerns about REACH's potential to harm small- and medium-sized businesses and to stifle innovation—in a second cable to diplomatic posts in Europe, again urging them to express concern about REACH.[2]

U.S. government officials also actively worked to generate opposition to REACH within Europe. Their efforts included, for example, visits by Environmental Protection Agency officials (together with ACC representatives) to European government and business representatives. Formal comments filed by the United States with the European Commission in 2003 expressed the usual set of concerns, including the possibility of high implementation costs and decreased innovation.[3] In addition, U.S. agencies circulated a chemical industry estimate of $8.8 billion in lost exports—an estimate based on the false assumption that U.S. computer sales to the EU would be cut off by REACH.[4]

Although similar criticisms of REACH were also advocated by some European stakeholders, the efforts of the Bush administration and the ACC may have helped to shift the balance of European discourse. The revised REACH proposal published in October 2003 reflected many of the specific changes that the United States had advocated, including exclusion of polymers, reduced regulation of intermediates, and looser requirements regarding chemicals found in products.[5]

However, these changes did not mollify critics of REACH in Washington. In 2006, the U.S. Diplomatic Mission to the EU organized a joint statement of the missions of Australia, Brazil, Chile, India, Israel, Japan, South Korea, Malaysia, Mexico, Singapore, South Africa, and Thailand, asking the European Parliament to reconsider the implementation of REACH. The joint statement argued that REACH regulation and implementation procedures are opaque, that REACH has the potential to disrupt international trade, and that developing countries in particular will be harmed by REACH.[6] As demonstrated in the next two sections, the U.S. government's keen interest in quashing REACH seems particularly incongruous when the modest implementation costs for U.S. chemicals manufacturers are compared to the much larger value of exports subject to REACH.

U.S. Exports Subject to REACH

Estimates of billions of dollars of U.S. exports that will necessarily be lost as a result of REACH are surely mistaken. If U.S. companies comply with REACH, there is no need for any loss of exports, beyond the presumably small number of substances found to be truly hazardous. It is true, however, that billions of dollars of U.S. exports will be subject to REACH, and that exporters will be required to comply with its regulations.

How much is at stake, in terms of sales revenue and employment? The categories of chemicals subject to REACH do not correspond exactly to the data on exports and imports; there is no official figure available. We have developed an estimate, based on U.S. trade and employment data, and our reading of REACH. Our national estimate, in brief, is that U.S. chemical exports subject to REACH amounted to $13.7 billion in 2004, and were directly or indirectly responsible for 54,000 jobs.[7] (Our estimate includes U.S. exports of chemicals subject to REACH, but not the export of articles that contain these chemicals; the REACH standards for chemicals in articles are generally weaker, and will likely have only minor effects on U.S. exports.)

We include only forty-three states because data are incomplete for Alaska, Hawaii, Idaho, Montana, North Dakota, South Dakota, and Vermont (all states with very limited chemical production). In addition, Puerto Rico is not included because its large chemicals industry consists almost entirely of pharmaceuticals production, which is not regulated under REACH.

The steps that lead to our estimate are as follows (for a more detailed description of our methodology and state-by-state results for each of these calculations, see appendix D):

A. Only about half of chemical industry output consists of substances regulated by REACH. Pharmaceuticals and agricultural chemicals are covered by other European regulations, and plastics are exempt. U.S. production of "REACH chemicals"—that is, chemicals that fall under REACH—in the forty-three states amounted to $234 billion in 2004.

B. For the chemical industry as a whole, data are available on the share of each state's output that is exported to the EU; the national average is that 6 percent of all U.S. chemical production goes to the EU. What we would like to know is the percentage of *REACH chemicals* exported to the EU, but there are no published data directly measuring that. Therefore, we calculated the percentage of each state's chemical production as a whole that is exported to the EU, and assumed that the same export percentage applies to the state's production of REACH chemicals.

C. To calculate the number of jobs, we started with the 848,000 employees in the chemical industry in the forty-three states as of 2004. Based on the information and assumptions in steps A and B, we estimated that about half of them produce REACH chemicals, and that on average, 6 percent of those employees are producing REACH chemicals for export to the EU (the actual percentages vary from state to state). That yields our estimate of the direct employment in each state producing exports that are subject to REACH.

D. An input-output study of U.S. exports, from the U.S. Census Bureau, estimates the total (direct plus indirect) employment related to chemical exports, by state; for the country as a whole, total chemical export–related employment is 1.85 times direct employment. We applied the analogous state-level ratios derived from the input-output study to the direct employment estimates from step C, to obtain each state's total employment dependent on exports subject to REACH.

Although these exports of REACH chemicals to the EU are not a large fraction of the U.S. economy, or even of the nation's total exports, they have been growing at an impressive rate. And the importance of export markets will only grow in the future, as the massive U.S. trade deficit becomes increasingly difficult for economic policy makers to ignore.

The impact of REACH on the U.S. chemical industry is by no means equally distributed across the country. Table 12.1 lists the states where exports of REACH chemicals to the EU are most important, ranked by share of state employment and share of gross state product (GSP), a common measure of economic output.[8] Massachusetts, Kentucky, and South Carolina lead in terms of the share of employment, while Massachusetts, Louisiana, and West Virginia lead in terms of the share of GSP.

TABLE 12.1 States where REACH exports to EU are most important (2004).

	Direct and indirect jobs as % of total employment		Value of shipments as % of gross state product
Massachusetts	0.29	Massachusetts	0.50
Kentucky	0.11	Louisiana	0.43
South Carolina	0.10	West Virginia	0.41
Rhode Island	0.08	Kentucky	0.35
West Virginia	0.08	Texas	0.27
Tennessee	0.07	Mississippi	0.21
New Jersey	0.06	South Carolina	0.19
Minnesota	0.06	Indiana	0.18
Mississippi	0.05	New Jersey	0.17
Texas	0.05	Georgia	0.17
Michigan	0.05	Illinois	0.16
Illinois	0.05	Wyoming	0.16
Ohio	0.05	Tennessee	0.16
Georgia	0.05	Missouri	0.15
Louisiana	0.05	Ohio	0.13

Source: Author's calculations; see appendix D for data sources.

Compliance Costs versus Loss of Export Markets

The expected costs of implementing REACH have been debated extensively in Europe (see chapter 10), and a number of studies have estimated the likely costs to industry of testing and registering chemicals. Some studies look only at the "direct" costs: the actual outlay of funds required to complete the tests, analyze the results, and submit the registration documents. Other studies also attempt to estimate "indirect" costs: the broader effects of a possible increase in the cost of chemicals.

There is broad, order-of-magnitude agreement on the size of the direct costs of registering and testing chemicals, and that cost turns out to be several orders of magnitude smaller than the value of the jobs and sales revenues that are at stake. As seen in chapter 10, compliance costs in Europe will total a few billion euros spread over eleven years, amounting to less than 0.1 percent of chemical industry sales revenue per year.

The same requirements apply to U.S. and European chemical producers selling chemicals in the EU; therefore, we assume that the cost of complying with REACH is the same percentage of sales in the United States as it is in the EU. For the U.S. chemical industry, a cost increase of 0.1 percent of the value of REACH exports would impose additional costs of $13.7 million annually, or $255 per affected job per year. It would cost Massachusetts industries, for example, $2.3 million per year to retain the state's 9,000 chemical industry jobs.

Many states' budgets include hundreds of dollars in workforce development per existing job in that state; these funds are earmarked for attracting new jobs, retaining old ones, and training workers for new careers. For example, the total budget of Massachusetts' Department of Workforce Development was $2 billion for 2007, including both job placement and workforce training programs; that amounted to $625 for every existing job in Massachusetts.[9] Similarly, California spends $760 on workforce development per existing job.[10] This suggests that REACH compliance costs are a bargain at $255 per affected job, amounting to only 30–40 percent of what states are spending, per job, on workforce development.

The chemical testing required by REACH also has potential occupational safety and health benefits. Although no estimate of these benefits exists for the United States, several studies have tried to project the benefits of REACH in the EU. As explained in chapter 10, even very partial calculations of the expected benefits have identified savings worth many times the costs of REACH.

The High Price of Ignoring Foreign Standards

As a number of studies have documented, compliance with REACH is not expensive in relation to total sales of the products it regulates. But compliance will be essential to retain European chemical sales. Recent experience has shown that it is all too possible for the United States to lose access to export markets, based on failure to meet environmental standards and to respond to concerns in the countries that buy American goods.

One cautionary tale is provided by genetically modified corn. Bt corn, a variety of genetically modified corn that was developed in the 1980s, won its first U.S. regulatory approvals in 1992 and burst onto the market in the mid-1990s. (The Bt gene is added to corn in order to repel insect pests.) From 1.4 percent of U.S. planted area in 1996, Bt corn rose rapidly to 32 percent in 2004.[11] U.S. growers, distributors, and exporters are not reliably able to separate conventional from genetically modified corn, so this meant that the whole U.S. corn crop had to be treated as genetically modified. Since European consumers have rejected genetically modified food of any variety, this was a death blow to exports: U.S. corn exports to the EU were above $100 million per year in the early 1990s but essentially vanished within a year or two after the large-scale introduction of genetically modified corn, falling to $8 million or less per year from 1999 to the present.[12]

In chapter 7, we examined a similar but larger loss in meatpacking, when U.S. producers failed to respond appropriately to foreign consumers' fears of bovine spongiform encephalopathy (BSE), or mad cow disease. In most countries that have faced BSE problems, the response has involved a high level of testing for the disease, to ensure that the food supply is safe; in contrast, U.S. regulators have insisted on testing only a small fraction of slaughtered cattle.

Additional testing, which could have reassured foreign markets, was rejected by the United States, even when private parties wanted to perform and pay for the tests. In 2004, Creekstone Farms, a Kansas beef producer, negotiated an agreement with the Japanese government to resume sales in Japan if Creekstone voluntarily adopted Japanese BSE testing standards. However, the Department of Agriculture (USDA) invoked old food safety laws to prohibit any American producer from exceeding U.S. government BSE testing standards! More than $2 billion of annual exports were lost for at least two years, in order to maintain the principle that U.S. industry does not need to meet other countries' safety standards.[13] While U.S. beef exports have now edged back up, some export markets may have been permanently lost to other beef-producing nations such as Australia.

A smarter and happier ending occurred in the wheat industry, one of the most export-dependent sectors of U.S. agriculture. Roughly half of the U.S. wheat crop is exported, with exports of wheat and wheat products to the EU often around $200 million per year.[14] Monsanto, a leading supplier of seeds and agricultural chemicals, applied for permission to grow genetically modified "Roundup Ready" wheat in the United

States and Canada in 2002. Recognizing the threat to foreign markets, advocacy groups throughout wheat-growing areas organized an effective campaign against genetically modified wheat. The campaign quickly gained support from the Montana Legislature, the Canadian Wheat Board, and other major organizations in the region. In 2004, Monsanto announced the withdrawal of its application to grow genetically modified wheat.[15]

The high price of failing to meet other countries' health and safety regulations is painfully clear in the recent histories of the U.S. corn and beef industries: Genetically modified crops mean a loss of access to foreign markets, and the prohibition on internationally accepted levels of testing for mad cow disease has crippled the industry, including meatpackers that wanted to meet those testing levels at their own expense.

Wheat growers, in contrast, understood the importance of foreign markets and rejected a dubious innovation that would have jeopardized their export sales. As the United States faces the dilemma of a huge and mounting trade deficit, the conclusion must be that the wheat growers got it right, making the choices that maintained market access, while the corn and beef industries (and USDA) got it wrong, stubbornly losing foreign buyers who wanted a product that could meet higher and different standards.

Conclusion

The costs to the U.S. chemicals industry for REACH registration and testing will be a very small fraction of sales. Compliance with REACH also has added benefits to public health and occupational safety, especially for workers in the chemical industry. Failing to comply with REACH, on the other hand, would expose an important and growing sector of the U.S. economy to the total loss of its European trade—a lesson that should have been learned from the experience of U.S. corn growers and meatpackers. Annual compliance costs are an estimated $14 *million*; noncompliance would risk the loss of $14 *billion* in exports. The comparison, and the choice, should not be difficult.

The relative impact of REACH is far greater on some states than on the nation's chemical industry as a whole. Massachusetts would risk losing 9,000 jobs and the nation's highest percentage of state output if industry fails to comply with REACH. Texas and California would risk the loss of 6,000 and 5,000 jobs, respectively, while Louisiana, West Virginia, and Kentucky are among the states with the most to lose as a percentage of their total production. No state can afford to lose thousands of jobs, especially when regulatory costs equal to just a few hundred dollars per job could prevent it.

Even if REACH somehow turns out to be a mistake, it is a relatively inexpensive one. And if, on the other hand, REACH has the result of creating an efficient process for regulating dangerous substances and protecting public health, the EU's new regulations could pave the way for similar legislation in the United States and around the world. Far from posing a threat to American industry, REACH could end up providing health and environmental benefits for the United States at a very affordable price.

Conclusion
Economics and Precautionary Policies

The world looks different to economists and environmentalists, because they view reality through rival frames. The economic vision is gradualist: markets are well suited for making marginal adjustments, creating price incentives for small changes, expressing tradeoffs between multiple, incrementally achievable goals, and allowing fine-tuning (optimization) of things that are already being done moderately well. The environmental vision is catastrophist: thresholds for abrupt and irreversible damages are near at hand, ecological limits impose absolute constraints on sustainable human activity, and big changes are needed to avoid serious harm to ourselves and our environment. It is no small challenge to integrate these clashing worldviews, to explain what economic analysis offers to environmental policy.

Cost-benefit analysis offers one attempt at reconciling these opposite perspectives, by forcing all environmental effects and human health impacts into a monetized, market-based framework. This attempt fails on multiple grounds. The things of greatest value, such as human life or the existence of species and ecosystems, are not measured in dollars; no useful insights are gained from contrived methods of pricing the priceless. Uncertainty about the extent of harm stymies the search for precise quantitative measures of damages, whether the uncertainty arises from unresolved debate and differences of expert opinion, as with dioxin or atrazine, or from the complexity of the underlying problem, as with the possible spread of bovine spongiform encephalopathy (BSE). The imagined objectivity and

227

transparency of the economic paradigm is nowhere to be seen when dense technicalities cloak partisan judgments, as with EPA's analysis of the organophosphate pesticides or the business studies of the costs of REACH. Retrospective analysis shows that contemporary cost-benefit techniques could have gotten the wrong answer on a range of past decisions where the right answer is no longer in doubt.

The premise of the case for cost-benefit analysis is the great expense that is thought to be at stake, implying a need to economize on scarce resources when making regulatory decisions. This is a perfectly logical possibility, spoiled by the mere facts of extremely modest costs of regulatory options, as seen throughout this book. Not only are the costs of prevention small and affordable, there are also monetary, as well as health and environmental, costs of inaction, as seen in chapter 8. The most expensive measure considered here, the substitution of alternatives for all PVC production throughout the U.S. economy, has an estimated annual cost of $25 per capita or less. That is less than 0.1 percent of per capita income, a cost that would hardly be the end of affluence as we know it.

How, then, should policy decisions be made? One could conclude from the studies described here that the expenses of environmental protection are small enough to be ignored. This might suggest a return to a 1970s style of environmental policy, with ambitious new measures based on the scientific understanding of the problems, and standards based primarily on technical feasibility. The U.S. economy would not be bankrupted by this "back to the future" policy regime, any more than it was destroyed by 1970s environmentalism the first time around.

But this is an unsatisfying approach, and one that could undermine its own success over time. Eventually, the costs of environmental protection could mount up to a significant amount, especially in the case of climate change policy (an important topic that is beyond the scope of this book). What is needed is a way to integrate the useful information produced by economic analysis of costs and markets into the very different environmental understanding of priceless values, binding ecological constraints, and uncertain thresholds for crisis and irreversible loss.

One straightforward approach is applicable to cases where uncertainty is not involved. Suppose that a proposed policy has monetary costs and nonmonetary health and environmental benefits, all of which are known with certainty. Then, rather than disaggregating and monetizing the benefits, as cost-benefit analysts would conventionally do, it is possible to evaluate the package as a whole: for this many dollars, society can save that many lives (or acres of forest, or endangered species, or a combination of benefits); do we want to buy the package or not? This is what Lisa Heinzerling and I, in the conclusion to *Priceless*, referred to as "holistic cost-benefit analysis."[1] Holistic evaluation of a policy uses almost all of the information collected in a standard cost-benefit analysis. It avoids the distortions that result from reducing a "package" of benefits, occurring in their complex real-world context, to simple, acontextual components, and it escapes the paradoxes of monetization of priceless benefits. Because the costs and benefits of health and environmental policies are normally expressed in incompatible units, such as dollars and deaths, there is no formula that calculates the right answer; holistic evaluation is an inherently deliberative process. Similar-sounding benefits occurring in different contexts may have very different social meanings. As suggested in chapter 1, the similarity of death rates in construction work and downhill skiing does not imply an obligation to spend equal amounts per avoided death in these two activities.

The decision-making problem is more challenging when there is uncertainty about the costs or, more often, benefits of a proposed policy. Waiting for complete certainty is an unreasonable approach, guaranteeing decades of delay in addressing serious hazards. The precautionary principle urges action based on credible warnings of harm, prior to the achievement of scientific consensus. Both dioxin and atrazine provide good examples, where most, but not yet all, scientific opinion suggests that there are important health hazards to address. If probabilities could be attached to the conflicting opinions, then a weighted average or "expected value" of harm could be calculated, but there is no objective way to attach precise probabilities to the two sides of an argument before it is settled.

A theory of decision making under uncertainty was sketched in chapter 4. Suppose that the range of credible forecasts, or the membership of the expert panel qualified to make forecasts, is known, but nothing is known about the probability that any one forecast is correct. Under these assumptions, all that is needed is to look at the best and worst credible forecasts. Risk-averse decision makers, a category that includes most of us, need only look at the credible worst case—a succinct statement of the precautionary principle. This is consistent with the way that people make many ordinary decisions, from buying life insurance and fire insurance to deciding how much time to allow for getting to the airport. When you get to the airport, you will of course spend a bit more time with security procedures that are purely responses to worst-case scenarios.

The precautionary principle calls for applying the same mode of thinking to health and environmental hazards. In contrast, EPA's proposed reinterpretation of its own data, in the analysis of organophosphate pesticides described in chapter 6, would have shifted from worst-case to average exposures as a basis for assessing farmworker health hazards. On that basis, no one would buy insurance and no airport security screening would ever occur, because the average risk in each case is very close to zero.

The hypothesis of extreme uncertainty is an unsatisfying, though possibly realistic, description of the policy problem. Although admitting to uncertainty about which view is correct, it requires a prior decision about the range of views that are credible. The impossible problem of resolving an ongoing scientific debate to everyone's satisfaction is replaced by the very difficult problem of credentialing the participants in the debate. Uncertainty is not a permanent condition; indeed, scientific progress can be interpreted as narrowing the range of credible views that must be considered. At some point, those who maintained that tobacco does not cause lung cancer, or that anthropogenic global warming is a myth, lost their seats on the credible expert panels whose opinions have to be considered. At what point might the dioxin and atrazine skeptics experience a similar loss of status?

As long as extreme uncertainty prevails, the process of precautionary decision making will often follow the general pattern seen in chapters 4 and 5. One option involves strong protective action; the worst-case outcome for this option is that a certain amount of money will be spent unnecessarily, if the potential hazard turns out to be harmless. The alternative option is typically inaction, maintaining the status quo; the worst-case outcome on this side is a certain level of health and environmental damages, if the worst credible warnings about the hazard turn out to be valid. Weighing the two worst cases against each other, as in the discussion of holistic evaluation, is an inherently deliberative process: typically, it involves comparison of potential monetary and nonmonetary losses that occur in complex, varying social contexts. Note that, contrary to some criticisms of the precautionary principle, there is no obligation to spend enormous sums to avoid every health or environmental risk, no matter how small. Nor is there a formula that can replace democratic deliberation and tell us exactly what to do. Good public policy decisions are not a matter of mathematical algorithms.

One further dimension of the policy-making problem is suggested by the last two chapters, examining the effects of REACH on developing countries and on the United States. In an increasingly global economy, environmental standards have implications that stretch beyond the borders of their home countries. Fears of the high cost of regulation have international parallels in the "pollution haven hypothesis," speculating that industry will move to countries with lower environmental standards, and the concern that ambitious regulations such as REACH might act as barriers to trade for developing countries. Although a thorough review of these questions is beyond the scope of this book, it is encouraging to see that REACH does not in fact impede exports from developing countries; it is worth remembering that such exports are often produced by multinational companies with ample resources for environmental compliance.

Finally, it must be a shock, for many Americans, to find the United States on the outside looking in at the world's latest advances in environmental protection. On REACH, on BSE testing, and on genetically modified food, the U.S. government has argued for standards well below those adopted in other industrial countries. Beyond the details of these disputes, there is an important change going on in the position of the United States, both in relation to global markets and in setting environmental standards. A few decades ago the United States thought of itself, with good reason, as both the leading international economic power and a leader in environmental protection. But with chronically high and rising trade deficits, the United States will have to find a way, sometime soon, to export much more than it does now. After years of U.S. foot dragging, or worse, on environmental protection, there will be more situations in the future where foreign standards, not regulatory decisions in Washington, dictate the levels of health and environmental protection that U.S. industry has to adopt to succeed in the global marketplace.

In *Fast Food Nation*, journalist Eric Schlosser described a conversation with workers at an Iowa Beef Processors (IBP) plant. The workers told him that "they always liked days when their plant was processing beef for shipment to the European Union, which imposes tough standards on imported meat. They said IBP slowed down the line so that work could be performed more carefully. The IBP workers liked EU days because the pace was less frantic and there were fewer injuries."[2] It is a national shame, and an international reality, that it now takes foreign pressure to bring the United States up to higher standards of worker safety and environmental protection. Are we so resigned to being poisoned for pennies that we can only hope for "EU days" to save us from obvious risks to health and the environment? Or can we regain the momentum and the will to take precautionary action that will protect ourselves, our children, and our surroundings?

Appendix A
Outline of the Arrow-Hurwicz Analysis

Suppose that an action, such as a public policy decision, has to be taken; its outcome will depend on information about the state of nature, which is unknown at the time when the action is taken. What can be said about the criteria for optimal decision making under these circumstances? Kenneth Arrow and Leonid Hurwicz presented a brief, provocative treatment of this question, although cloaked in the dense language of mathematical logic. Translated into English, it provides a strong argument for precautionary approaches to decision making under uncertainty. This appendix is a simplified, semitechnical summary of their analysis.

Formally, suppose there is a known set of possible states of nature; they will be represented by x in this account. In the dioxin policy problem, x_1 might be "dioxin turns out to be a powerful cause of cancer in humans," x_2 could be "dioxin is moderately carcinogenic," and x_3 could be "dioxin is not carcinogenic at all." One, and only one, of these states of nature will occur, but nothing is known about the probability of any particular state—a condition of extreme uncertainty that Arrow and Hurwicz referred to as "ignorance." In the Woodward and Bishop (see chapter 4) formulation of the "expert panel problem," the states of nature are replaced by individual experts' forecasts; ignorance still prevails about which expert to believe.

An action is a function that assigns a real number $a(x)$ to each state of nature; bigger numbers mean better outcomes. The action "do everything possible to reduce exposure to dioxin" has a high value in the state of nature x_1, where dioxin is highly carcinogenic, and a lower value in the state of nature x_3, where dioxin is not carcinogenic. The action "do nothing about dioxin exposure" has an opposite pattern of outcomes, with a higher value if dioxin is not carcinogenic. Assume that every action has a minimum value and a maximum value; this is guaranteed to occur if there are only a finite number of states of nature.

Suppose that there is a definition of optimality, that is, a set of actions that are known to be optimal. Arrow and Hurwicz demonstrated that, if the definition of optimality obeys a number of simple logical properties, then it depends only on the minimum and maximum values taken on by each action. These properties include the assumptions that the definition of optimality is not affected by removal of suboptimal actions, or by removal of "repetitious states of nature." Two states of nature—call them x_1 and x_2—are repetitious if $a(x_1) = a(x_2)$ for every action a; in the expert panel version of the story, repetitious experts are ones who always make the same forecast as each other. Because literally nothing is known about the probability that one or another state of nature is more likely to occur, no information is gained by considering repetitions. This is the strong assumption about uncertainty that drives the Arrow-Hurwicz result. Alternatively, if all states of nature (or expert forecasts) were equally likely, then the average would be the optimal prediction; removal of repetitious values would not be allowed, since it would normally change the average.

The proof begins by showing that for two actions a_1 and a_2 that always take on one of the same two numerical values, such as m and M, for any possible state of nature, either both are optimal actions or neither is (assuming that both actions take on both values).

Next, starting with any action a, which has a minimum m and a maximum M, Arrow and Hurwicz constructed two other actions, serving as a lower bound and an upper bound for the original action a. For the lower bound, let $a_1(x') = M$ for some x', where $a(x') = M$, and $a_1(x) = m$ for all other x. That is, except for its one point matching the maximum, a_1 is always equal to the minimum of a. The upper bound is virtually the mirror image: let $a_2(x'') = m$ for some x'', where $a(x'') = m$, and $a_2(x) = M$ for all other x. Except for its one minimum point, a_2 is always equal to the maximum of a.

Because a_1 and a_2 take on only the same two values, either both are optimal actions or neither is. But it is clear from the definitions that for every x, $a_1(x) \le a(x) \le a_2(x)$. Thus a cannot be worse than a_1 or better than a_2. As a result, a is optimal if and only if a_1 and a_2 are optimal. Similar logic shows that any action with the same minimum m and maximum

M is optimal if and only if a, a_1, and a_2 are optimal; thus all that matters for determining optimality are the minimum and maximum values taken on by the action.

It is just a short step from this point to the final result of the Arrow-Hurwicz analysis, which shows that, under their handful of simple assumptions, any definition of optimality must be based on a ranking scheme that depends only on an action's minimum and maximum values.

Appendix B
The Fawcett Report on Atrazine Research

Richard Fawcett's report, "Two Decades of Atrazine Yield Benefits Research," is described as a North Central Weed Science Society Research Report, prepared for the Triazine Network (an industry group that advocates continued use of atrazine and similar herbicides). It updates a similar 1996 study by Fawcett; both were prepared as part of the Triazine Network's submissions to EPA in regulatory hearings on triazine herbicides. Fawcett's earlier study was a key source for the EPA analysis discussed in chapter 5, and his later study was likewise one of the bases for the Coursey analysis discussed there. Therefore, an examination of Fawcett's data and analysis is important to the evaluation of some of the leading studies of the economics of atrazine.

In brief, Fawcett's massive database is incompletely documented and contains numerous repetitions of similar-sounding work by the same investigators. Moreover, averages based on his work are strongly influenced by a handful of extreme outliers: 5 of his 236 observations show enormous benefits of atrazine. With those outliers removed, the remaining observations in his database imply a mean yield loss from withdrawal of atrazine of 3.2 percent, and a median loss of 2.3 percent.

Fawcett's 2006 report lists 236 studies performed in the North Central region from 1986 through 2005, each of which contains information on corn yields with and without atrazine. Most of the studies are from Iowa, Illinois, Minnesota, Nebraska, and Wisconsin; a handful come from Indiana, Kansas, and South Dakota. Fawcett's principal data tables list the studies by number and state, and provide yield data, in bushels per acre, with and without atrazine. A list of the 148 studies for 1996–2005 gives the study number, title, principal investigator's name, and academic institution. The 88 studies from the first decade were listed in Fawcett's earlier report. There are no citations to publications or Web sites; there is no description of research methods used to identify the studies or ensure completeness of coverage. (According to a personal communication from Dr. Fawcett, received as this book was going to press, the studies he included all appeared in the *North Central Weed Science Society Research Report*. No citations to volume numbers or page numbers within that publication are included in Fawcett's main report and database tables, although they might appear in his extensive appendix, which is not available online.)

The titles of the 148 studies include strong hints of repetitiveness; by many standards, these would not be counted as 148 distinct pieces of research. In one case, each year of a four-year research project was reported as a separate study. More than a quarter of the studies (39) were performed by a few investigators at three test sites maintained by the University of Minnesota. The titles of many of the studies suggest repetition: "Herbicide performance in corn at Waseca, MN in 1996" was followed by separate studies with the same title (except for the year) in 1998, 1999, and 2000. For 2001–2005, there were two to four Waseca studies each year, separately examining herbicide performance in corn at Waseca's common cocklebur site, tall waterhemp site, common ragweed site, and giant ragweed site. All twenty of the "Herbicide performance in corn at Waseca" studies were conducted by the same principal investigator. Indeed, the list of 148 studies includes only thirty-four different principal investigators.

Fawcett's discussion of the yield data focuses on absolute differences between atrazine and nonatrazine yields, measured in bushels per acre: average yields per acre were higher with atrazine by 6.3 bushels in 1986–1995, 5.4 bushels in 1996–2005, and 5.7 bushels for the twenty-year period as a whole. However, these data span a period in which U.S. average corn yields changed significantly. Thus it may be more appropriate to examine the percentage change in yields due to atrazine in each study. The percentages reported here are the absolute difference divided by the yield with atrazine, that is, the percentage of yield that would be lost by giving up atrazine.

For the 236 studies as a whole, the mean percentage is 4.0 percent, and the median is 2.4 percent. As the large difference between mean and

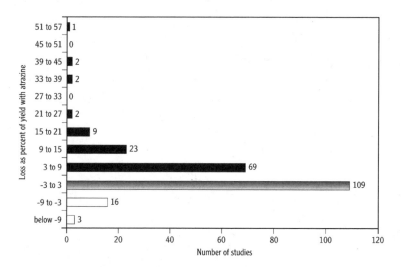

FIGURE B.1. Fawcett Data on Yield Loss without Atrazine

median suggests, the distribution of yield data is skewed to the right. All but five of the observations fall between −11 percent and +23 percent; in contrast, the five outliers imply yield losses of 33–52 percent. The distribution of the data is shown in figure B.1; in the graph, white bars (the bottom two and part of the third) represent studies where yields were higher without atrazine.

If the five outliers are excluded, the mean yield effect of losing atrazine shrinks to 3.2 percent, while the median becomes 2.3 percent.

There is no significant time trend in the percentage yield data, with or without the outliers. Four of the five outliers are in Illinois, implying a significantly higher effect of atrazine in that state. This could have influenced the work of Coursey, whose analysis focused specifically on the effects of atrazine in Illinois. With the outliers removed, there are no significant differences in the mean effects by state. None of the outliers occurred in 2005, the year of Fawcett's calculations reported in the text.

To rely on estimates from Fawcett's extensive data tabulation, it would be necessary to understand his selection criteria in greater detail, to consolidate many of the repetitive entries in his table, and to carefully examine the validity of the few outliers that have such a substantial impact on the mean.

Appendix C
How Not to Analyze REACH:
the Arthur D. Little Model

At 205 pages, the 2002 study from Arthur D. Little (ADL) was by far the most extensive industry-oriented critique of REACH, and offered the most detailed case for huge cost estimates. Sponsored by a German industry federation, the study purported to show ruinous effects of REACH on the German economy as a whole. Industry lobbyists soon backed off from defending it in detail, as critiques began to appear. Yet the damage had already been done: the ADL study, together with a similar but less detailed French study, created the widespread belief that someone had shown that there might be unbearably large costs to REACH. ADL's work was a masterful success, if judged purely as quantitative rhetoric.

As a rigorous analysis, on the other hand, it was a complete failure. The discussion here focuses on the intermediate or "Storm" scenario (the others were "Clouds" and "Hurricane"), the most widely quoted results from the ADL model. The model turns out to provide an object lesson in how *not* to analyze economic impacts—unless, of course, you are trying to exaggerate.

The model concentrates most of its effort on representing losses of manufacturing output. It then assumes that losses in nonmanufacturing sectors are proportional to their sales to manufacturing. The result is that gross domestic product (GDP) loss, in percentage terms, is just under one-third of manufacturing losses: the Storm scenario found 7.7 percent loss of manufacturing output, and 2.4 percent loss in GDP, as a result of REACH.

ADL examined textiles, automobiles, and electronics in depth, and the rest of German industry in more summary fashion. Data were provided on thirty-five industries: twenty narrow subcategories within textiles, automobiles, and electronics, and fifteen broader categories representing the rest of German industry.

The model contains sixteen equations. It calculates percentage losses of output for many individual factors, then multiplies to estimate the combined loss. For example, if one problem caused a 10 percent loss of output, and another caused a 20 percent loss, the model would multiply the surviving percentages, 90% * 80%, finding that only 72 percent of output survived both; it then would report a 28 percent loss for the combined problems. This unusual methodology creates a strong slant toward "discovering" large losses.

The model calculates percentage losses of output separately for what it calls Phase 1 (registering and testing 30,000 "existing," or pre-1981, chemicals) and Phase 2 (addressing new chemicals only). The reported figures for losses include both—that is, the percentages of output surviving Phase 1 and Phase 2 are multiplied to find the percentage surviving both.

Industry Factor

Most cost components related to registration and authorization, in both Phase 1 and Phase 2, are multiplied by an "industry factor" that ranges from 0 to 12, supposedly reflecting the competitiveness or monopoly power of the industry. Cost increases are multiplied by the industry factor to estimate production losses; a more competitive industry has a bigger industry factor and therefore loses more for the same level of cost increases.

At one extreme, ADL claimed that a perfect monopoly can pass on all cost increases to customers with no losses in production, implying an industry factor of 0. At the other extreme, a perfectly competitive industry was said to be unable to pass on any cost increases to customers. The profit margin for German industry averages about 8 percent; so if it were impossible to pass on any cost increases in higher prices, an 8 percent cost increase would wipe out all profits, forcing the industry to shut down— a loss of output equal to about twelve times the underlying cost increase, or an industry factor of 12 in ADL's terms.

Neither extreme of this analysis is correct, according to economic theory. A monopolist facing a cost increase will, in general, sell somewhat less; as in elementary textbook diagrams, the cost increase shifts the supply curve upward, increasing the equilibrium price and decreasing the quantity sold. That is, the industry factor for a monopoly should be greater than zero; the exact value depends on the price elasticities, or the slopes of the supply and demand curves.

On the other hand, in a perfectly competitive industry, if every producer faces a cost increase, the industry supply curve also shifts upward, causing an increase in price. A firm in a competitive industry is unable to pass on cost increases only in the special case where no other producer experiences the increase, so that no one else's price rises. This is clearly not the case for cost increases due to REACH, which affect all producers. As a result, a hypothetical 8 percent cost increase (which is far above any credible estimate of REACH costs) would not all come out of profits, and the industry would not shut down, meaning that the industry factor should be less than 12. Again, the exact value depends on price elasticities of supply and demand.

Nonetheless, ADL accepted 0 for perfect monopoly and 12 for perfect competition as the potential extremes of the industry. The study reported industry factors for thirty-five industries with a median value of 9, apparently based on a complex, ad hoc process of interviews and judgments. In effect, ADL assumed that German industry was three-fourths of the way from monopoly power toward small, powerless firms in competitive markets, which is not necessarily an accurate portrait of Europe's leading industrial nation. For the purposes of the model, the result of this controversial judgment is that all costs of registration and evaluation are multiplied by an industry factor, averaging 9.

Phase 1 Loss Estimates

The industry factor is not the only source of exaggeration in the ADL model. Production losses due to registration costs are calculated as a product of many factors, a method that amplifies any errors, uncertainties, or overestimates. Judgment errors that inflate individual factors are multiplied by other factors, allowing a cascading process of overstatement to begin from small errors.

For Phase 1, the one-time costs of registering 30,000 existing chemicals are spread over only seven years, rather than the full eleven-year phase-in period. With this assumption, ADL effectively multiplied annual Phase 1 costs by another unwarranted factor of 11/7.

The underlying cost per registration is also scaled up to reflect the number of uses, assuming that only five uses are covered by the basic registration. The Storm scenario assumes two additional, or seven total, uses per chemical, with costs varying by size class; it appears that incorporating two additional registrations increases the cost per registration by at least 25 percent of the basic, five-use cost.

The other relevant factor is the cost of registering intermediate products. In the Storm scenario there are three intermediate products per chemical, each requiring an additional one-third of the registration cost of the chemical itself. In other words, intermediate product registration doubles the reported cost of registration.

In sum, ADL multiplied its Storm scenario Phase 1 registration costs by factors of

- 9, on average, for the industry factor;
- 11/7 (i.e., 1.57) for the unduly shortened time horizon;
- 1.25 for additional use registrations; and
- 2 for intermediate product registration.

The combined result (product of the four factors above) is a factor of 35. That is, given an underlying estimate of registration and testing costs, the ADL Storm scenario multiplies those costs by 35 in calculating Phase 1 losses on existing chemicals.

Phase 2 Loss Estimates

ADL estimated that there will be 1,000 new chemicals per year, about three times the number reported in recent years by the European Chemicals Bureau. Because REACH eases the regulatory requirements on new chemicals, one might expect ADL's methodology to project an increase in output; yet in their model, Phase 2 also causes substantial losses.

Phase 2 losses are calculated as the product of losses due to registration cost, time delay, and transparency requirements. Registration costs are calculated, and exaggerated, much as in Phase 1. New approaches are introduced for both of the other components.

Costs of Delay

ADL assumed that there are potentially enormous losses associated with delays in bringing new products to market. This delay is compared to the assumed length of the product life cycle in each industry. Letting R = the ratio of delay to product life cycle, the model assumes that the percentage loss in production due to delay is equal to an unusual, ad hoc formula:

Delay loss percentage = $(1 - [1 - R]^{2R}) * k$

where k is the "inverse cannibalization factor." The only description of the cannibalization factor says that it describes how quickly an existing product can be replaced by an innovation. A factor of 1 means that new products immediately replace old ones; a lower factor means that old ones can coexist with new ones for a while, so that losses in introduction of new products are less than expected. In ADL's data the cannibalization factor is usually 0.5 or 0.2, although a few industries with short life cycles have factors of 0.8.

REACH is assumed to delay all new products by nine months. For the thirty-five industries covered in the study, the median length of the life cycle is 60 months, so R = 9/60 = 15 percent of the product life cycle. With k = 0.5 and R = 0.15, the equation shown above yields 0.024—a relatively modest reduction of 2.4 percent of production in the median industry. However, as R becomes larger (i.e., product life cycle becomes shorter), the estimated losses grow much more than proportionally. (This was true by design; ADL consciously sought a functional form with that property, according to the one vague discussion of the equation.) A quarter of the industries have product life cycles of 30 months or less; at 30 months, R = 9/30 = 0.3, and, retaining the assumption that k = 0.5, the equation yields 0.096—nearly a 10 percent loss.

Three industries have product lifecycles of 12 months (implying that R = 9/12 = 75 percent), and two of these have k = 0.8. For these, the model estimates a loss of production due to time delay of 0.7—that is, two industries experience an incredible 70 percent loss of production due solely to the time delay attributed to REACH.

Disclosure/Transparency Loss

Finally, the projected loss due to disclosure or transparency was simply based on reporting what industry believed the losses will be. The equation for this factor (equation 16, p. 201) shows that there is no equation: at the end of a list of intricately detailed equations on other topics, equation 16 says that the losses due to disclosure "=f(scenario)," without further elaboration. The discussion of this part of the model merely says: "Operationalisation was carried out as follows: the production loss was estimated by industry experts as being the know-how affected."[1]

According to the industry experts, nineteen of the thirty-five industries expected production losses of 5 percent or less, but a handful reported much higher losses. Five industry branches, all in textiles, estimated that production losses of 30 percent or more would result from disclosure of information required under REACH.

There is no simple way to summarize the average exaggeration factor for Phase 2, comparable to the factor of 35 for Phase 1. However, the Phase 1 losses, and the individual components of Phase 2 losses, are estimated separately and then multiplied, hence engaging in mutual cross-exaggeration. Since Phase 2 (new chemicals) involves no net increase in regulation under REACH, all estimates for Phase 2 are effectively exaggerations.

Appendix D
U.S. Impacts of REACH: Methodology and Data

This appendix documents the data sources and methodology used in the calculations reported in chapter 12.

Data Definitions and Sources:

Total Chemicals Employment (TCE): Total Chemicals Employment (TCE_{2002}) for 2002 is the number of paid employees reported in the 2002 U.S. Economic Census, Industry Statistics Sampler, North American Industry Classification System (NAICS) 325, column 7.

Indirect Employment Multiplier (IEM): The Indirect Employment Multiplier (IEM_{2001}) is the ratio of the total (direct and indirect) chemicals manufacturing employment to direct chemicals manufacturing employment. Chemicals manufacturing, here and throughout, is defined as that portion of the U.S. manufacturing sector classified as category 325 under the NAICS. Total and direct employment are for 2001 and are taken from a July 2004 U.S. Census Bureau report, "Exports from Manufacturing Establishments: 2001," table 4, columns 6 and 9 (for 325 only), which uses input-output calculations to derive indirect exports. According to this report, indirect employment is any employment associated with the intermediate goods and services necessary to manufacture exported goods.

Share of 325 Production Exported to the EU-25, 2002 and 2004 (SEU): The share of 325 production exported to the EU-25 ($SEU_{2002/2002}$ and $SEU_{2004/2002}$) is the ratio of the value of all 325 exports to the EU-25 to total 325 value of shipments. The value of 325 exports to the EU-25, for 2002 and 2004, is taken from "TradeStats Express: State Export Data" from the Office of Trade and Industry Information, Manufacturing and Services, International Trade Administration, U.S. Department of Commerce. The total value of 325 shipments is available for 2002 only, and is taken from the 2002 U.S. Economic Census, Industry Statistics Sampler, NAICS 325, column 4.

Share of Production that is REACH-affected (SR): The share of production that is REACH-affected (SR_{2002}) is the ratio of the value of shipments for 2002 in the four-digit NAICS categories assumed to fall under REACH regulation (3251, 3255, 3256, and 3259) to the total 325 value of shipments. The value of 325, 3251, 3255, 3256, and 3259 shipments is for 2002, and is taken from the 2002 U.S. Economic Census, Industry Statistics Sampler, NAICS 325, column 4.

Value of REACH-affected Shipments (VRS): The value of REACH-affected shipments (VRS_{2002}) is the sum of the value of shipments for 2002 in the four-digit NAICS categories assumed to fall under REACH regulation (3251, 3255, 3256, and 3259), and is taken from the 2002 U.S. Economic Census, Industry Statistics Sampler, NAICS 325, column 4.

Total Employment, 2002 and 2004 (TE): Total Employment (TE_{2002} and TE_{2004}) for 2002 and 2004 is the number of nonfarm employees and is taken from the Bureau of Labor Statistics, State and Area Employment, Hours, and Earnings.

Gross State Product, 2002 and 2004 (GSP): Gross state product (GSP_{2002} and GSP_{2004}) for 2002 and 2004 is taken from the Bureau of Economic Analysis, Regional Economic Accounts.

Calculations

Direct and Indirect Employment Related to REACH Exports, 2002 and 2004 (DIE)

Direct and indirect employment related to REACH-exports for 2002 (DIE) is the product of total 325 employment (TCE), the indirect employment multiplier (IEM), the share of 325 production exported to the EU-25 (SEU), and the share of production that is REACH-affected (SR).

(1) $DIE_{2002} = TCE_{2002} * IEM_{2001} * SEU_{2002/2002} * SR_{2002}$

(2) $DIE_{2004} = TCE_{2002} * IEM_{2001} * SEU_{2004/2002} * SR_{2002}$

Direct and Indirect Employment Related to REACH Exports as a Percentage of Total Employment, 2002 and 2004 (%DIE)

Direct and indirect employment related to REACH exports as a percentage of total employment for 2002 (%DIE) is direct and indirect employment related to REACH exports (DIE) divided by total employment (TE).

(3) $\%DIE_{2002} = DIE_{2002} / TE_{2002}$

(4) $\%DIE_{2004} = DIE_{2004} / TE_{2004}$

Value of REACH Exports, 2002 and 2004 (VRE)

The value of REACH exports for 2002 (VRE) is the product of the value of REACH-affected shipments (VRS) and the share of 325 production exported to the EU-25 (SEU).

(5) $VRE_{2002} = VRS_{2002} * SEU_{2002/2002}$

(6) $VRE_{2004} = VRS_{2002} * SEU_{2004/2002}$

Value of REACH Exports as a Percentage of Gross State Product, 2002 and 2004 (%VRE)

The value of REACH exports as a percentage of gross state product for 2002 (%VRE) is the value of REACH exports (VRE) divided by gross state product (GSP).

(7) $\%VRE_{2002} = VRE_{2002} / GSP_{2002}$

(8) $\%VRE_{2004} = VRE_{2004} / GSP_{2004}$

State Data

TABLE D.1 **Employment and value of shipments related to REACH exports to the EU-25 (2002).**

	Employment related to REACH exports	as percentage of total employment	Value of shipments of REACH exports (millions of $)	as percentage of gross state product
Alabama	710	0.038	164	0.133
Arizona	130	0.006	11	0.006
Arkansas	320	0.028	59	0.083
California	5,140	0.036	788	0.058
Colorado	420	0.019	51	0.028
Connecticut	230	0.014	59	0.036
Delaware	140	0.034	77	0.164
Florida	270	0.004	92	0.018
Georgia	1,810	0.047	568	0.185
Illinois	1,800	0.031	540	0.111
Indiana	620	0.021	233	0.114
Iowa	10	0.001	9	0.009
Kansas	290	0.021	70	0.078
Kentucky	1,530	0.085	374	0.307
Louisiana	700	0.037	517	0.385
Maine	70	0.012	9	0.022
Maryland	720	0.029	161	0.080
Massachusetts	3,440	0.106	598	0.208
Michigan	2,290	0.051	369	0.106
Minnesota	740	0.028	92	0.046
Mississippi	480	0.043	127	0.185
Missouri	590	0.022	179	0.096
Nebraska	90	0.010	21	0.035
Nevada	20	0.002	6	0.007
New Hampshire	160	0.026	10	0.022
New Jersey	2,260	0.057	651	0.172
New Mexico	0	0.001	1	0.002
New York	1,520	0.018	639	0.080
North Carolina	510	0.013	139	0.046
Ohio	1,840	0.034	386	0.100
Oklahoma	60	0.004	20	0.021
Oregon	480	0.030	75	0.065

TABLE D.1 (continued).

	Employment related to REACH exports	as percentage of total employment	Value of shipments of REACH exports (millions of $)	as percentage of gross state product
Pennsylvania	390	0.007	144	0.034
Rhode Island	550	0.115	39	0.104
South Carolina	1,800	0.100	242	0.198
Tennessee	1,470	0.055	276	0.144
Texas	3,610	0.038	1,792	0.231
Utah	110	0.010	23	0.031
Virginia	590	0.017	192	0.067
Washington	330	0.012	47	0.020
West Virginia	410	0.056	142	0.313
Wisconsin	590	0.021	157	0.083
Wyoming	30	0.013	22	0.107
43 states	**39,280**	**0.031**	**10,169**	**0.100**

Source: Authors' calculations; see appendix text for data sources.

TABLE D.2 Employment and value of shipments related to REACH exports to the EU-25 (2004).

	Employment related to REACH exports	as percentage of total employment	Value of shipments of REACH exports (millions of $)	as percentage of gross state product
Alabama	690	0.036	159	0.114
Arizona	210	0.009	18	0.009
Arkansas	450	0.039	82	0.101
California	6,330	0.044	971	0.063
Colorado	510	0.023	62	0.031
Connecticut	290	0.017	75	0.040
Delaware	130	0.030	69	0.128
Florida	300	0.004	102	0.017
Georgia	1,830	0.047	575	0.168
Illinois	2,860	0.049	856	0.164
Indiana	1,080	0.037	405	0.178
Iowa	10	0.001	9	0.008

TABLE D.2 (continued).

	Employment related to REACH exports	as percentage of total employment	Value of shipments of REACH exports (millions of $)	as percentage of gross state product
Kansas	230	0.018	57	0.057
Kentucky	1,950	0.108	477	0.349
Louisiana	880	0.046	651	0.425
Maine	40	0.007	5	0.012
Maryland	790	0.032	179	0.079
Massachusetts	9,110	0.286	1,581	0.497
Michigan	2,200	0.050	355	0.095
Minnesota	1,640	0.061	204	0.091
Mississippi	610	0.054	159	0.209
Missouri	1,020	0.038	313	0.154
Nebraska	100	0.011	24	0.035
Nevada	10	0.001	4	0.004
New Hampshire	110	0.018	7	0.014
New Jersey	2,470	0.062	714	0.172
New Mexico	30	0.003	7	0.011
New York	1,690	0.020	710	0.079
North Carolina	970	0.025	263	0.078
Ohio	2,610	0.048	547	0.130
Oklahoma	60	0.004	19	0.018
Oregon	470	0.029	73	0.057
Pennsylvania	520	0.009	191	0.041
Rhode Island	410	0.084	29	0.069
South Carolina	1,880	0.103	253	0.186
Tennessee	1,850	0.068	347	0.159
Texas	4,870	0.051	2,418	0.274
Utah	170	0.016	37	0.045
Virginia	840	0.024	274	0.083
Washington	320	0.012	46	0.018
West Virginia	580	0.079	201	0.407
Wisconsin	550	0.020	148	0.070
Wyoming	60	0.022	39	0.164
43 states	**53,780**	**0.042**	**13,716**	**0.118**

Source: Author's calculations; see appendix text for data sources.

Notes

Chapter 1

1. W. K. Viscusi, *Cigarette Taxation and the Social Consequences of Smoking,* Working Paper No. 4891 (National Bureau of Economic Research, 1994), p. 33.

2. *Public Finance Balance of Smoking in the Czech Republic,* as of December 2007, available at http://tobaccofreekids.org/reports/philipmorris/pmczcchstudy.pdf.

3. R. Lutter, *Valuing Children's Health: A Reassessment of the Benefits of Lower Lead Levels,* Working Paper 00-02 (Washington, D.C.: AEI-Brookings Joint Center for Regulatory Studies, 2000).

4. P. S. Carlin and R. Sandy, "Estimating the Implicit Value of a Young Child's Life," *Southern Economic Journal,* Vol. 58 (1991), p. 186.

5. J. B. Loomis and D. S. White, "Economic Benefits of Rare and Endangered Species: Summary and Meta-analysis," *Ecological Economics,* Vol. 18 (1996), pp. 197, 199, table 1 (figures converted to year 2000 dollars using the consumer price index).

6. The original calculation, based on research by W. Kip Viscusi, can be found in U.S. Environmental Protection Agency (EPA), *The Benefits and Costs of the Clean Air Act, 1970 to 1990,* (1997), Appendix I. For an example of a subsequent analysis citing the Clean Air Act analysis and adjusting only for inflation, see EPA, "Arsenic in Drinking Water Rule: Economic Analysis," (2000). The arsenic study used $6.1 million in 1999 dollars, which is equivalent to $6.3 million in 2000 dollars.

7. See, for example, J. F. Morrall III, "A Review of the Record," *Regulation,* Vol. X (1986), at 25, 30 table 4, relied upon in, among others, S. Breyer, *Breaking the Vicious Circle: Toward Effective Risk Regulation* (Cambridge, MA: Harvard University Press, 1993); W. K. Viscusi, *Fatal Tradeoffs: Public and Private Responsibilities for Risk* (New York: Oxford University Press, 1992); K. J. Arrow et al., "Is There a Role for Benefit-Cost Analysis in Environmental, Health, and Safety Regulation?," *Science,* Vol. 272 (1996), p. 221.

8. T. O. Tengs et al., "Five-Hundred Life-Saving Interventions and Their Cost-Effectiveness," *Risk Analysis,* Vol. 15 (1995), p. 369. For a critique of this study, see L. Heinzerling and F. Ackerman, "The Humbugs of the Anti-Regulatory Movement," *Cornell Law Review,* Vol. 87 (2002), p. 648.

9. T. O. Tengs and J. D. Graham, "The Opportunity Costs of Haphazard Social Investments in Life-Saving," in R. W. Hahn, ed., *Risks, Costs, and Lives Saved: Getting Better Results from Regulation* (Oxford: Oxford University Press, 1996).

10. J. D. Graham, "Risk Assessment and Cost-benefit Analysis: Hearings Before the Committee on Science, U.S. House of Representatives," (104th U.S. Congress, 1st Session 1124, 1995).

11. J. Broome, "Trying to Value a Life," *Journal of Public Economics,* Vol. 9 (1978), pp. 91–92.

12. For further elaboration, see L. Heinzerling, "The Rights of Statistical People," *Harvard Environmental Law Review,* Vol. 24 (2000), pp. 189, 203–6.

13. *Economic Analysis of Federal Regulations under Executive Order 12, 866,* pt. III. B. 5(a) (Report of Interagency Group Chaired by a Member of the Council of Economic Advisors, Jan. 11, 1996).

14. L. Heinzerling, "Discounting Our Future," *Land & Water Law Review,* Vol. 34 (1999), p. 39, 71; L. Heinzerling, "Discounting Life," *Yale Law Journal,* Vol. 108 (1999), pp. 1911, 1913.

15. M. Sagoff, *The Economy of the Earth: Philosophy, Law, and the Environment* (Cambridge, U.K.: Cambridge University Press, 1990).

16. A. Sen, "The Discipline of Cost-Benefit Analysis," *Journal of Legal Studies,* Vol. 29 (2000), p. 931.

17. H. S. Richardson, "The Stupidity of the Cost-Benefit Standard," *Journal of Legal Studies,* Vol. 29 (2000), p. 971. On the importance of allowing preference change in response to deliberation, see also C. R. Sunstein, "Preferences and Politics," *Philosophy & Public Affairs,* Vol. 20 (1991).

18. Survey data from 2000 show that 88 percent of U.S. adults drink water as a beverage, averaging 1.53 liters (52 ounces) per day. At that rate, it takes thirteen days to drink twenty liters of water. B. M. Popkin et al., "Water and Food Consumption Patterns of U.S. Adults from 1999 to 2001," *Obesity Research,* Vol. 13, No. 12 (2005).

19. Skiing: In 1999 there were thirty fatalities and 52.2 million skier/snowboarder visits to ski slopes, for a death rate of 0.57 per million skier-days (National Ski Areas Association, www.nsaa.org).

Construction: In 1997 there were 14.1 fatal injuries per 100,000 full-time construction workers; assuming 250 days per full-time year, the death rate was 0.56 per million days of work. (U.S. Department of Health and Human Services, National Institute for Occupational Safety and Health, *Worker Health Chartbook, 2000,* p. 36).

Arsenic: Male lifetime cancer rates per ppb of arsenic are $2.53 * 10^{-5}$ for bladder cancer and $2.75 * 10^{-5}$ for lung cancer; see EPA, *Arsenic in Drinking Water Rule,* Exhibit B-2, p. B-8. (Female cancer rates are higher.) Death rates are 26 percent for bladder cancer and 88 percent for lung cancer, for a combined male mortality rate of $3.08 * 10^{-5}$ per lifetime ppb of arsenic.

The EPA analysis is based on a person who drinks two liters of water per day. So lifetime consumption over seventy years is $2 * 70 * 365 = 5.11 * 10^{4}$ liters. If risk is proportional to total arsenic consumption, the risk per ppb per liter = $(3.08 * 10^{-5}) / (5.11 * 10^{4}) = 6.03 * 10^{10}$ per ppb per liter, or $3.01 * 10^{-8}$ per liter of 50 ppb water. At that rate, the risk from 19 liters of 50 ppb water equals the risk from a day of skiing.

20. 42 U.S. Code 4331(b)(1).

21. W. J. Baumol, "On the Social Rate of Discount," *American Economic Review,* Vol. 58 (1968), pp. 788, 801.

22. This discussion draws from L. Heinzerling, "Regulatory Costs of Mythic Proportions," *Yale Law Journal,* Vol. 107 (1998), p. 1981; L. Heinzerling, "Five-Hundred Life-Saving Interventions and Their Misuse in the Debate over Regulatory Reform," *Risk,* Vol. 13 (2002); and Heinzerling and Ackerman, "Humbugs."

23. L. Summers, "The Bank Memo," The Whirled Bank Group, www .whirled bank.org/ourwords/summers.html.

24. Ibid.

25. F. Kuchler and E. Golan, *Assigning Values to Life: Comparing Methods for Valuing Health Risks,* Economic Research Service, Agricultural Economic Report No. 784 (U.S. Department of Agriculture, 1999), p. 52.

26. C. R. Sunstein, "The Arithmetic of Arsenic," *Georgetown Law Journal,* Vol. 90 (2002).

27. Given this enormous range of uncertainty, it is difficult to understand Sunstein's belief (expressed in the same article) that cost-benefit analysis is still useful for screening regulatory options. This could be true only if a significant number of serious proposals had costs that were many orders of magnitude greater than their benefits. As we have discussed, this is a widely held, but empirically false, view of environmental regulation.

28. E. Goodstein, "Polluted Data," *American Prospect,* Vol. 8 (1997); H. Hodges, "Falling Prices: Cost of Complying With Environmental Regulations Almost Always Less than Advertised," *Economic Policy Institute,* Briefing Paper #69 (1997). Both publications report on the same study.

29. W. Harrington et al., "On the Accuracy of Regulatory Cost Estimates," *Journal of Policy Analysis and Management,* Vol. 19 (2000), p. 297.

Chapter 2

1. K. Smith, "Choice Cuts," *The American Prospect On-line* (2004), www.prospect .org/web/page.ww ?section=root&name=ViewWeb&articleId=7696.

2. U.S. Environmental Protection Agency (EPA), *The Benefits and Costs of the Clean Air Act 1970–1990* (1997).

3. U.S. Office of Management and Budget, Office of Information and Regulatory Affairs (OIRA), *Informing Regulatory Decisions: 2004 Draft Report to Congress on the Costs and Benefits of Federal Regulations and Unfunded Mandates on State, Local, and Tribal Entities,* table 2 (2004).

4. OIRA, *Informing Regulatory Decisions.*

5. N. Shah, "OMB Official Highlights EPA Problems in Assessing Benefits of Air Rules," *Inside EPA* (2004).

6. R. D. Morgenstern, ed., *Economic Analyses at EPA: Assessing Regulatory Impact* (Washington, DC: Resources for the Future, 1997).

7. G. M. Gray et al., "The Demise of Lead in Gasoline," in J. D. Graham and J. K. Hartwell, eds., *The Greening of Industry: A Risk Management Approach* (Cambridge, MA: Harvard University Press, 1997).

8. R. W. Hahn and C. R. Sunstein, "A New Executive Order for Improving Federal Regulation? Deeper and Wider Cost-Benefit Analysis," *University of Pennsylvania Law Review,* Vol. 150 (2002), pp. 1489, 1523.

9. B. A. Ackerman and R. B. Stewart, "Reforming Environmental Law," *Stanford Law Review,* Vol. 37 (1985), pp. 1333, 1363; R. B. Stewart, "A New Generation of Environmental Regulation?," *Capital University Law Review,* Vol. 29, No. 45 (2001).

10. C. R. Sunstein, "In Praise of Numbers: A Reply," *Georgetown Law Journal,* Vol. 90 (2002), pp. 2379, 2384; C. R. Sunstein, "Cognition and Cost-Benefit Analysis," *Journal of Legal Studies,* Vol. 29 (2000), p. 1059.

11. J. B. Wiener, "Whose Precaution after All?" *Duke Journal of Comparative and International Law,* Vol. 13 (2003), pp. 207, 223.

12. A comprehensive history of the marketing of, scientific research on, and eventual regulation of lead in gasoline is found in G. Markowitz and D. Rosner, *Deceit and Denial: The Deadly Politics of Industrial Pollution* (Berkeley, CA: University of California Press, 2002).

13. 42 U.S. Code §7545(c)(1)(A) (2004). This provision was amended in 1977 to allow the agency to regulate fuel additives whenever they "may reasonably be anticipated to endanger the public health or welfare."

14. H. L. Needleman, "History of Lead Poisoning in the World," (1999), www.leadpoison.net/general/history.htm.

15. Midgley also brought the world another famous compound: chlorofluorocarbons, or CFCs, later implicated in ozone depletion and banned in a global treaty about the same time lead was banned in gasoline in the United States. J. L. Kitman, "The Secret History of Lead," *The Nation,* (March 20, 2000), p. 5.

16. Kitman, "Secret History," p. 6.

17. Ibid., p. 8.

18. Ibid., p. 9.

19. Needleman, "History of Lead Poisoning."

20. Ibid.

21. Kitman, "Secret History," p. 8.

22. J. Lewis, "Lead Poisoning: A Historical Perspective," *U.S. Environmental Protection Agency Journal* (1985), www.epa.gov/history/topics/perspect/lead.htm.

23. Ibid.

24. Kitman, "Secret History," p. 8.

25. C. F. Moore, *Silent Scourge: Children, Pollution, and Why Scientists Disagree* (Oxford: Oxford University Press, 2003).

26. C. Patterson, "Contaminated and Natural Lead Environments of Man," in *Archives of Environmental Health,* Vol. 11 (1965); I. Casanova, "Clair C. Patterson (1922–1995), Discoverer of the Age of the Earth," *International Microbiology,* No. 1 (1998).

27. Kitman, "Secret History," p. 8.

28. 42 U.S. Code §211 (c)(1)(a) (2004), amended by 42 U.S. Code §7545 (c).

29. *A Legislative History of the Clean Air Act Amendments of 1970* (Congressional Research Service, 1974).

30. The Clean Air Act Amendments of 1970 were signed into law by President Nixon on December 31, 1970. Ruckelshaus issued his announcement on January 30, 1971.

31. *Regulation of Fuel Additives,* 36 Federal Register (Jan. 30, 1971), p. 1486.

32. *Lead and Phosphorus Additives in Motor Vehicle Gasoline,* 37 Federal Register (Feb. 23, 1972), p. 3882.

33. 37 Federal Register, p. 3882.

34. Ibid.

35. *Regulation of Fuels and Fuel Additives,* 38 Federal Register, (Jan. 10, 1973), pp. 1258, 1260.

36. 38 Federal Register, p. 1259.

37. Ibid.

38. Ibid.

39. *Regulation of Fuels and Fuel Additives,* 38 Federal Register (Dec. 6, 1973), p. 33,734.

40. In the early 1970s virtually all gasoline was leaded, with an average of 2.4 grams per gallon (gpg). The limit for 1979 at large refineries, and 1982 at small ones, was 0.5 gpg. See A. L. Nichols, "Lead in Gasoline," in R. D. Morgenstern, ed., *Economic Analyses at EPA.*

41. R. V. Percival et al., *Environmental Regulation: Law, Science, and Policy* (New York: Aspen Publishers, 2003).

42. Percival, *Law, Science, and Policy,* p. 362.

43. Ibid.

44. Ethyl Corporation v. EPA, 541 F.2d 1 (D.C. Cir. 1976) (*en banc*).

45. 42 U.S. Code §246 (2004).

46. National Health and Nutrition Examination Study, Centers for Disease Control, www.cdc.gov/nchs/nhanes.htm.

47. H. L. Needleman et al., "Deficits in Psychologic and Classroom Performance of Children with Elevated Dentine Lead Levels," *New England Journal of Medicine,* Vol. 300 (1979), p. 689.

48. D. Davis, *When Smoke Ran Like Water: Tales of Environmental Deception and the Battle against Pollution* (New York: Basic Books, 2002), p. 128. Davis observes: "It was not known then that the work [of Needleman's accusers] was supported by the lead industries."

49. Davis, *When Smoke Ran Like Water,* p. 127.

50. White House Press Statement on the Presidential Task Force on Regulatory Relief (Feb. 17, 1981).

51. E. Olson, "The Quiet Shift of Power: Office of Management and Budget Supervision of Environmental Protection Agency Rulemaking under Executive Order 12291," *Michigan Law Review,* Vol. 80 (1981), p. 193.

52. Davis, *When Smoke Ran Like Water,* p. 130.

53. *Fuel and Fuel Additives; Proposed Suspension of Compliance Date for Small Refineries,* 47 Federal Register (Feb. 22, 1982), p. 7814.

54. *Regulation of Fuel and Fuel Additives,* 47 Federal Register (Feb. 22, 1982), p. 7812.

55. Davis, *When Smoke Ran Like Water,* p. 130.

56. Nichols, "Lead in Gasoline," pp. 50–52.

57. Small Refiners Lead Phasedown Task Force v. EPA, 705 F.2d 506, 531 (D.C. Cir. 1983).

58. Davis, *When Smoke Ran Like Water,* p. 130.

59. Ibid.

60. W. D. Ruckelshaus, "Science, Risk, and Public Policy," *Science,* Vol. 221 (1983), p. 1026.

61. Oral history of Alvin Alm, EPA, www.epa.gov/history/publications/alm/21.htm, www.epa.gov/history/publications/alm/22.htm.

62. Nichols, "Lead in Gasoline," p. 53; personal communication between Lisa Heinzerling and Joel Schwartz (March 4, 2004) (source of specific reference to the ethanol lobbyist).

63. Nichols, "Lead in Gasoline," p. 53.

64. Ibid., pp. 52–53.

65. Ibid., p. 83.

66. E-mail from Robert Percival to Lisa Heinzerling (March 15, 2004) (on file with the authors).

67. A. Alm, "The Multimedia Approach to Pollution Control: An Impossible Dream?" *Multimedia Approaches to Pollution Control: Symposium Proceedings* (Washington, DC: National Research Council, 1987), pp. 114, 115.

68. Under a new method of calculation (described in Nichols, "Lead in Gasoline," pp. 51–52), the lead level allowed under the 1973 rule was now measured as 1.1 gpg (corresponding to 0.5 gpg under the old method, as cited in note 40, above). The 1985 rule required reduction to 0.1 gpg under the new method of calculation.

69. Nichols, "Lead in Gasoline," p. 74, table 3.

70. R. Levin, "Lead in Drinking Water," in R. D. Morgenstern, ed., *Economic Analyses at EPA.*

71. R. Lutter, *Valuing Children's Health: A Reassessment of the Benefits of Lower Lead Levels,* Working Paper 00–02 (Washington, DC: AEI-Brookings Joint Center for Regulatory Studies, 2000).

72. Speech on May 6, 1903, quoted by Theodore Roosevelt Association, www.theodoreroosevelt.org/kidscorner/Grand_Canyon.htm.

73. Videotape: *Grand Canyon, The Price of Power* (The Sierra Club, 1992), quoted in C. L. Riddle, "Protecting the Grand Canyon National Park From Glen Canyon Dam: Environmental Law at its Worst," *Marquette Law Review,* Vol. 77 (1993), p. 115.

74. M. Reisner, *Cadillac Desert: The American West and its Disappearing Water* (New York: Viking-Penguin, 1986). Except as otherwise noted, Reisner is the source for the following account of the Central Arizona Project and related background information.

75. Reisner, *Cadillac Desert,* pp. 267–68.

76. Ibid.

77. The strength of cost-effectiveness analysis is that it avoids the problems of valuation of nonmarketed benefits, such as the existence of the Grand Canyon; it only compares the market costs of alternative means of reaching a single, specified goal. The corresponding limitation is that cost-effectiveness analysis says nothing about the importance of its goal versus other goals. In the case of the Grand Canyon, the relative importance of generating electricity versus preserving the Canyon was the crucial omitted factor that led many people to reject the bureau's analysis.

78. Reisner, *Cadillac Desert,* p. 297.

79. S. M. Cohn, *Too Cheap to Meter: An Economic and Philosophical Analysis of the Nuclear Dream* (Albany, NY: State University of New York Press, 1997), pp. 45–47.

80. Cohn, *Too Cheap to Meter,* p. 127.

81. Ibid., pp. 104–5.

82. A. Carlin, *The Grand Canyon Controversy: Lessons for Federal Cost-Benefit Practices,* (RAND Corporation, 1967), cited the original figures and presented intermediate revisions for Marble Canyon based on more reasonable assumptions about nuclear reactor operations. The final variant charged Hualapai, in particular, for the large water losses caused by evaporation from its reservoir, and made other technical changes, as described in A. Carlin and W. Hoehn, *The Grand Canyon Controversy–1967: Further Economic Comparisons of Nuclear Alternatives* (RAND Corporation, 1967). The Carlin-Hoehn analysis was spelled out in a series of reports, all from RAND, including, in addition to the two just cited, Carlin and Hoehn, *Is the Marble Canyon Project Economically Justified?* (1966); Hoehn, *What the Parsons Study Really Says about Nuclear Power Economics: The Grand Canyon Controversy, Round ?* (1967); Carlin, *The Grand Canyon Controversy or How Reclamation Justifies the Unjustifiable* (1967) (providing a retrospective on the controversy).

83. Interview with David Brower in *Boatman's Quarterly Review,* Vol. 10, No. 3 (1997). www.glencanyon.org/aboutgci/browerinterview.htm.

84. H. Nash, "Other Arguments against Dams in Grand Canyon and Why Grand Canyon Should Not Be Dammed," *Sierra Club Bulletin,* Vol. 51, No. 5 (1966), pp. 5, 9. A mill is one-tenth of a cent. Assuming the quoted costs are in 1966 dollars per kilowatt-hour, and updating them with the consumer price index, the first two are equivalent to 2.3 cents per kilowatt-hour for nuclear power, compared with 3.0 cents for the dams, at 2003 prices. The TVA nuclear cost is equivalent to 1.4 cents per kilowatt-hour at 2003 prices. Nash and other Sierra Club writers, of course, spent much more time and effort on making the environmental case against the dams and describing their impact on the Grand Canyon.

85. Carlin and Hoehn, *The Grand Canyon Controversy—1967,* 15 table 2, line 8, cols. 1 and 3. The number in the text is a weighted average of the cost per kilowatt at each dam, weighted in proportion to their proposed capacities (1,350 MW for Hualapai, 600 MW for Bridge Canyon), converted from 1966 dollars to 2003 dollars using the GDP deflator.

86. Carlin and Hoehn, *The Grand Canyon Controversy—1967,* 15 table 2, notes to line 1, cols. 2 and 4. Weighted average and conversion to 2003 dollars as in the previous note. Although the construction costs were projected to be three times as large for the dams as for the nuclear plants, the benefit/cost ratios are not equally lopsided, both because the dams have lower operating costs, and because the dams would be expected to last longer and therefore their capital costs could be spread out over many more years.

87. Data in figure 2.1, other than the RAND forecast, are from Cohn, *Too Cheap to Meter,* p. 105, table 4.3, converted to 2003 dollars using the GDP deflator as in the previous calculations.

88. See the Central Arizona Project Web site, www.cap-az.com/.

89. Reisner, *Cadillac Desert,* pp. 267–68.

90. The construction cost was reportedly $5.9 billion; capacity is 3,810 MW, implying an average cost of $1,549 per kilowatt. See Wikipedia, "Palo Verde Nuclear Generation Station." Construction began in June 1976 and ended in January 1988; it seems likely that the construction cost is reported in mixed-year historical dollars, with an average vintage of about 1982. In the text, the reported figure has been converted from 1982 to 2003 dollars using the GDP deflator.

91. V. K. Smith and L. L. Osborne, "Do Contingent Valuation Estimates Pass a 'Scope' Test? A Meta-Analysis," *Journal of Environmental Economics & Management,* Vol. 31 (1996).

92. F. Ackerman and L. Heinzerling, *Priceless.*

93. *Exposure to Vinyl Chloride, Occupational Safety and Health Standards,* 39 Federal Register (Oct. 4, 1974), pp. 35890, 35892.

94. D. D. Doniger, "The Law and Policy of Toxic Substances Control" (Resources for the Future, 1978), reprinted in *Ecology Law Quarterly,* Vol. 7, No. 2 (1978).

95. U.S. Department of Health and Human Services, Public Health Service, National Toxicology Program, *Report on Carcinogens* (10th ed., 2002).

96. M. S. Brown, "Setting Occupational Health Standards: The Vinyl Chloride Case," in D. Nelkin, ed., *Controversy: Politics of Technical Decisions* (London: Sage Publications, 1992).

97. 29 U.S. Code §655(b)(5) (2004).

98. Brown, "Occupational Health Standards," p. 134.

99. Ibid., pp. 134–35.

100. Ibid., p. 135.

101. Markowitz and Rosner, *Deceit and Denial,* pp. 176–77.

102. Ibid., pp. 170–71.

103. "OSHA Standards for Vinyl Chloride Plants Upheld," *Environmental Law Report,* Vol. 5 (1975), p. 10042.

104. Doniger, "Toxic Substances Control," p. 45.

105. "OSHA Standards," p. 10042; Brown, "Occupational Health Standards."

106. Doniger, "Toxic Substances Control," p. 31.

107. Brown, "Occupational Health Standards."

108. Markowitz and Rosner, *Deceit and Denial,* p. 181.

109. Ibid., pp. 178–91.

110. Ibid., pp. 178–91.

111. See T. O. McGarity and S. A. Shapiro, *Workers at Risk: The Failed Promise of the Occupational Safety and Health Administration* (Westport, CT: Praeger, 1993), p. 39.

112. *Exposure to Vinyl Chloride, Occupational Safety and Health Standards,* 39 Federal Register (Oct. 4, 1974), pp. 35890–91.

113. Ibid.

114. Ibid.

115. Ibid.

116. 39 Federal Register, pp. 35891–92.

117. 39 Federal Register, p. 35891.

118. P. F. Infante, "Carcinogenic, Mutagenic, and Teratogenic Risks Associated with Vinyl Chloride," *Mutation Research,* Vol. 41 (1976).

119. J. Brady et al., "Angiosarcoma of the Liver: An Epidemiologic Survey," *Journal of the National Cancer Institute,* Vol. 59 (1977), pp. 1383–85.

120. J. K. Wagoner et al., "Toxicity of Vinyl Chloride and Polyvinyl Chloride as Seen through Epidemiologic Observations," *Journal of Toxicology & Environmental Health,* Vol. 6 (1980).

121. W. F. Bi, "Effect of Vinyl Chloride on Testis in Rats," *Ecotoxicology & Environmental Safety,* Vol. 10, (1985). This study exposed rats to 10, 100, and 3,000 ppm vinyl chloride in air, and found that testicular damage increased with increasing exposure levels.

122. R. Pirastu et al., "Mortality from Liver Disease among Italian Vinyl Chloride Monomer/Polyvinyl Chloride Manufacturers," *American Journal of Industrial Medicine,* Vol. 17 (1990).

123. Foster D. Snell, Inc., *Economic Impact Studies of the Effects of Proposed OSHA Standards for Vinyl Chloride* (1974). Study completed for OSHA, U.S. Department of Labor, Contract No. L/A 74–167. Foster D. Snell is a subsidiary of Booz, Allen, and Hamilton, Inc., Florham Park, NJ.

124. This is the sum of $22 million a year in the vinyl chloride monomer industry, to reach a standard of 2–5 ppm, plus $87 million a year to meet a 10–15 ppm standard in the PVC industry. See J. M. Mendeloff, *The Dilemma of Toxic Substance Regulation: How Overregulation Causes Underregulation at OSHA* (Cambridge, MA: MIT Press, 1998), p. 248.

125. Office of Technology Assessment (OTA), *Gauging Control Technology and Regulatory Impacts in Occupational Safety and Health: An Appraisal of OSHA's Analytic Approach,* (Washington, DC: U.S. Government Printing Office, Sept. 1995).

126. The report by OSHA's consultants mentioned, in a footnote, that one of the firms in the industry estimated that the total capital cost for trying to reach the "no detectable" level of vinyl chloride would be $856 million. This number is the only source we have been able to locate for OTA's $1 billion estimate (perhaps rounded off, or with operating costs added, to bring it up to $1 billion). Foster D. Snell, Inc., Exhibit V-15, note 5; also cited in Mendeloff, *Dilemma of Toxic Substance Regulation,* p. 248.

127. The Snell report amortized capital costs over ten years at 12 percent. Applying this rule, the annual carrying cost for a $1 billion investment would be $177 million; for a $856 million investment, the annual carrying cost would be $151 million. Assuming that there are operating costs as well as capital costs for compliance, we obtain a very rough estimate of $200 million per year.

128. Since 2001, the Bush administration has used different methodologies that lead to sharply lower values. See the discussion in Ackerman and Heinzerling, *Priceless.*

129. I. F. H. Purchase et al., "Vinyl Chloride: An Assessment of the Risk of Occupational Exposure," *Food & Chemical Toxicology,* Vol. 25 (1987). A total of 99 cases of angiosarcoma of the liver attributable to vinyl chloride were recorded from 1974 to 1982, or 11 per year. Purchase et al., "Vinyl Chloride," p. 196. Because of the long latency period for developing angiosarcoma, more cases were expected to result from the high rates of exposure before 1974; this study predicts a cumulative total of 150 to 300 more cases.

130. The Pinto was a popular, low-cost, but unfortunately accident-prone car sold in the early 1970s. In response to proposed safety regulations that would have made the Pinto safer, Ford conducted a cost-benefit analysis showing that it was not worth spending an additional $11 per car, or a total of $137 million annually, to avoid 180 deaths in traffic accidents, since a lost life was "worth" only $200,000. Among many other sources, see Ackerman and Heinzerling, *Priceless,* pp. 87–89.

131. E. S. Grush and C. S. Saunby, "Fatalities Associated with Crash-Induced Fuel Leakages and Fires," reprinted in D. Birsch and J. H. Fielder, eds., *The Ford Pinto Case: A Study in Applied Ethics, Business, and Technology* (Albany, NY: State University of New York Press, 1994).

132. Brown, "Occupational Health Standards."

133. The present value of a benefit B, received twenty years from now, at a 3 percent discount rate, is $B/(1.03)^{20}$, which is roughly equal to 0.55B.

134. Mendeloff, *Dilemma of Toxic Substance Regulation,* p. 248.

135. McGarity and Shapiro, *Workers at Risk,* pp. 268–69.

136. OTA, *Gauging Control Technology.*

Chapter 3

1. M. C. Porter and C. van der Linde, "Toward a New Conception of the Environment-Competitiveness Relationship," *Journal of Economic Perspectives,* Vol. 9, No. 4 (1995).

2. Intergovernmental Panel on Climate Change (IPCC), *Climate Change 2001: Mitigation* (Cambridge, UK: Cambridge University Press, 2001).

3. Arthur D. Little, "Economic Effects of the EU Substances Policy," (Wiesbaden: Bundesverband der Deutschen Industrie, 2002). www.adlittle.de/downloads/artikel/EU%20Chemical%20Policy_Basic%20Study_12_2002.pdf.

4. Mercer Management Consulting, "Study of the Impact of the Future Chemicals Policy: Final Report," Union of Chemical Industries (UIC), (2004). www.uic.fr/us/pdf/Final%20Mercerstudy%20%208%204%202004.pdf.

5. This section draws heavily on the work of Eban Goodstein and Kevin Gallagher. E. Goodstein, *The Trade-Off Myth: Fact and Fiction about Jobs and the Environment* (Washington, DC: Island Press, 1999); K. Gallagher, *Free Trade and the Environment: Mexico, NAFTA and Beyond* (Stanford, CA: Stanford University Press, 2004).

6. Goodstein, *The Trade-Off Myth*.

7. Ibid.; F. Ackerman and R. Massey, "Prospering with Precaution" (Global Development and Environment Institute, Tufts University, 2002). www.ase.tufts.edu/gdae/policy_research/PrecautionAHTAug02.pdf.

8. Goodstein, *The Trade-Off Myth*, p. 54.

9. A. B. Jaffe et al., "Environmental Regulation and the Competitiveness of U.S. Manufacturing," *Journal of Economic Literature*, Vol. 33, No. 1 (1995).

10. R. J. Jayadevappa and S. Chhatre, "International Trade and Environmental Quality: A Survey." *Ecological Economics*, Vol. 32, No. 2 (2000).

11. E. Neumayer, *Greening Trade and Investment* (Sterling, VA: Earthscan Publications Ltd., 2001).

12. B. R. Copeland and M. S. Taylor, *Trade and the Environment: Theory and Evidence* (Princeton, NJ: Princeton University Press, 2003).

13. Gallagher, *Free Trade*.

14. M. E. Kahn and Y. Yoshino, "Testing for Pollution Havens Inside and Outside of Regional Trading Blocs," *Advances in Economic Analysis & Policy*, Vol. 4, No. 2 (2004).

15. M. Cole, "U.S. Environmental Load Displacement: Examining Consumption, Regulations and the Role of NAFTA," *Ecological Economics*, Vol. 28 (2004).

16. Cole, "U.S. Environmental Load Displacement," p. 441.

17. L. Heinzerling, "Regulatory Costs of Mythic Proportions," *Yale Law Journal*, Vol. 107, No. 7 (1998); L. Heinzerling and F. Ackerman, "The Humbugs of the Anti-Regulatory Movement," *Cornell Law Review*, Vol. 87, No. 2 (2002).

18. U.S. Congress Office of Technology Assessment, *Gauging Control Technology and Regulatory Impacts in Occupational Safety and Health—An Appraisal of OSHA's Analytic Approach* (Washington, DC: U.S. Government Printing Office, 1995).

19. H. Hodges, "Falling Prices: Cost of Complying with Environmental Regulations Almost Always Less than Advertised," Economic Policy Institute Briefing Paper (1997).

20. W. Harrington et al., "On the Accuracy of Regulatory Cost Estimates," *Journal of Policy Analysis and Management*, Vol. 19, No. 2 (2000).

21. Cheminfo Services, *A Retrospective Evaluation of Control Measures for Chlorinated Substances (Case Studies of Ex-Ante/Ex-Post Socioeconomic Effects)*, Report to Environment Canada and Ontario Ministry of Energy, Science, and Technology (2000).

22. T. O. McGarity and R. Ruttenberg, "Counting the Cost of Health, Safety and Environmental Regulation," *Texas Law Review*, Vol. 80 (2002).

23. U.S. Office of Management and Budget (OMB), *Progress in Regulatory Reform: 2004 Report to Congress on the Costs and Benefits of Federal Regulations and Unfunded Mandates on State, Local, and Tribal Entities* (2004); U.S. Office of Management and Budget, *Validating Regulatory Analysis: 2005 Report to Congress on the Costs and Benefits of Federal Regulations and Unfunded Mandates on State, Local, and Tribal Entities* (2005).

24. OMB, *Progress in Regulatory Reform*, pp. 51–53.

25. M. W. Crain and T. D. Hopkins, "The Impact of Regulatory Costs on Small Firms," U.S. Small Business Administration, Office of Advocacy, (2000). www.sba.gov/advo/research/rs207tot.pdf.

26. H. S. James, "Estimating OSHA Compliance Costs," *Policy Sciences*, Vol. 31 (1998).

27. The polemical nature of this study is suggested by its prominent table of the costs of compliance with OSHA regulations proposed in the late 1970s. Almost all of the costs in the table are for compliance with a generic carcinogen standard—presumably the standard that was rejected in the Supreme Court's 1980 *Benzene* decision. Only in a note many pages later, at the end of the article, does James acknowledge that the generic carcinogen standard was never actually implemented.

28. D. W. Jorgenson and P. J. Wilcoxen, "Environmental Regulations and U.S. Economic Growth," *RAND Journal of Economics*, Vol. 21, No. 2 (1990).

29. Ibid., pp. 314–15.

30. OMB, *Validating Regulatory Analysis*, p. 42.

31. Ibid., p. 48.

32. W. Harrington et al., "On the Accuracy of Regulatory Cost Estimates," *Journal of Policy Analysis and Management*, Vol. 19, No. 2 (2000).

33. S. K. Seong and J. Mendeloff, "Assessing the Accuracy of OSHA's Projections of the Benefits of New Safety Standards," *American Journal of Industrial Medicine*, Vol. 45 (2004).

34. The same discussion applies not just to consumer goods, but to any desirable goods that could be produced with the resources used for regulatory compliance. Likewise, it applies to the resources saved by avoiding new regulation, as well as the resources released by deregulation. For narrative simplicity, this section tells the story purely in terms of deregulation and consumer goods.

35. Goodstein, *The Trade-Off Myth*.

36. F. Ackerman and L. Heinzerling, *Priceless: On Knowing the Price of Everything and the Value of Nothing* (New York: The New Press, 2004), ch. 3.

37. J. A. Tapia Granados, "Increasing Mortality during the Expansions of the U.S. Economy, 1900–1996," *International Journal of Epidemiology,* Vol. 34 (2005).

38. C. J. Ruhm, "Are Recessions Good for Your Health?" *Quarterly Journal of Economics* (2000).

39. S. N. Willich et al., "Weekly Variation of Acute Myocardial Infarction: Increased Monday Risk in the Working Population," *Circulation,* Vol. 90, No. 1 (1994).

40. Ruhm, "Are Recessions Good?"

41. H. M. Brenner, "Commentary: Economic Growth Is the Basis of Mortality Rate Decline in the 20th Century—Experience of the United States 1901–2000," *International Journal of Epidemiology,* Vol. 34 (2005).

42. Ruhm, "Are Recessions Good?"; J. A. Tapia Granados, "Response: On Economic Growth, Business Fluctuations, and Health Progress," *International Journal of Epidemiology,* Vol. 34 (2005).

43. Tapia Granados, "Response: On Economic Growth."

Chapter 4

1. A. Schecter et al., "Dioxins: An Overview," Environmental Research, Vol. 101 (2006).

2. K. Steenland et al., "Dioxin Revisited: Developments Since the 1997 IARC Classification of Dioxin as a Human Carcinogen," *Environmental Health Perspectives,* Vol. 112, No. 13 (Sept. 2004).

3. P. Cole et al., "Dioxin and Cancer: A Critical Review," *Regulatory Toxicology and Pharmacology,* Vol. 38 (2003).

4. European Environment Agency, *Late Lessons from Early Warnings: The Precautionary Principle 1896–2000* (Luxembourg: Office for Official Publications of the European Communities, 2001).

5. D. Gee and M. Greenberg, "Asbestos: From 'Magic' to Malevolent Mineral," in European Environment Agency, *Late Lessons.* This is the source for the remainder of the paragraph as well.

6. S. F. Hansen, "The Precautionary Principle and Unnecessary Precautionary Action," (PhD thesis, Roskilde Unversity, Denmark, 2004).

7. K. Arrow and L. Hurwicz, "An Optimality Criterion for Decision-Making under Ignorance," in *Uncertainty and Expectations in Economics: Essays in Honour of G. L. S. Shackle,* C. F. Carter and J. L. Ford, eds., (Oxford: Basil Blackwell, 1972). According to their footnotes, the analysis was done and circulated informally in the 1950s, but not published at that time.

8. R. T. Woodward and R. C. Bishop, "How to Decide When Experts Disagree: Uncertainty-Based Choice Rules in Environmental Policy," *Land Economics,* Vol. 73 (1997).

9. D. Kelsey, "Choice under Partial Uncertainty," *International Economic Review,* Vol. 34 (1993); I. Gilboa and D. Schmeidler, "Maxmin Expected Utility with Non-Unique Prior," *Journal of Mathematical Economics,* Vol. 18 (1989).

10. U.S. EPA, "Dioxin Reassessment—An SAB Review of the Office of Research and Development's Reassessment of Dioxin," (2001).

11. The word "dioxin" sometimes refers to a family of very similar chemicals, and sometimes just to the most harmful member of that family, whose long chemical name is abbreviated TCDD. Many members of the dioxin family, and members of a closely related chemical family, furans, have similar health impacts, although they vary in strength. To summarize the effects of multiple dioxins and furans, it has become common to express them all in "TCDD equivalents," or TEQ—that is, the quantity of TCDD that would have the same effect as the other dioxins and furans. All the following discussion refers to dioxins and furans as a group, expressed in TEQ terms. The relevant quantities of dioxins and furans are often measured in picograms, or trillionths of a gram, on a TEQ basis. (See box 4.1, "How Big Is a Picogram?") Exposure to dioxin could occur through multiple pathways, but in practice essentially all human exposure comes from eating food that contains tiny amounts of dioxin.

12. H. Becher et al., "Quantitative Cancer Risk Assessment for Dioxins Using an Occupational Cohort," *Environmental Health Perspectives,* Vol. 106, Supplement 2 (1998); K. Steenland et al., "Risk Assessment for 2,3,7,8-Tetrachlorodibenzo-*p*-Dioxin (TCDD) Based on an Epidemiologic Study," *American Journal of Epidemiology,* Vol. 154 (2001); C. Portier, "Risk Ranges for Various Endpoints Following Exposure to 2,3,7,8-TCDD," *Food Additives and Contaminants,* Vol. 17 (2000).

13. See the Draft Dioxin Reassessment, Part I, Vol. 3, Chap. 4, Table 4-34 on p. 4–115. (U.S. EPA, 2000).

14. Strictly speaking, each policy should be evaluated under the conditions where it does worst, and where it does best. However, it is difficult to imagine a dioxin policy for which the best and worst cases occur anywhere except under hypotheses (1) and (2).

15. J. Thornton, *Pandora's Poison: Chlorine, Health, and a New Environmental Strategy* (Cambridge, MA: MIT Press, 2000).

16. "The Resin Review" (2002) (an annual publication of the American Chemistry Council).

17. Chapter 9 discusses a higher cost, $8 billion, because it includes Canada as well as the United States, and uses a higher figure for total PVC consumption in 2002, rather than the 2001 figure used here.

Chapter 5

1. D. Coursey, "Illinois without Atrazine: Who Pays?" (Harris School of Public Policy, University of Chicago, 2007), p. 2.

2. "Weed Killer Deforms Frogs in Sex Organs, Study Finds," *New York Times,* April 17, 2002, p. A19.

3. S. H. Swan et al., "Semen Quality in Relation to Biomarkers of Pesticide Exposure," *Environmental Health Perspectives,* Vol. 111, No. 12 (2003). The study established the correlation between atrazine exposure and low sperm quality (i.e., low sperm counts and motility), but did not assert or prove a causal relationship.

4. T. B. Hayes, "There Is No Denying This: Defusing the Confusion about Atrazine," *BioScience,* Vol. 54, No. 12 (2004); J. B. Sass and A. Colangelo, "European Union Bans Atrazine, While the United States Negotiates Continued Use," *International Journal of Occupational and Environmental Health,* Vol. 12 (2006).

5. M. O. Ribaudo and A. Bouzaher, "Atrazine: Environmental Characteristics and Economics of Management," (USDA Economic Research Service, 1994).

6. P. G. Lakshminarayan et al., "Atrazine and Water Quality: An Evaluation of Alternative Policy Options," *Journal of Environmental Management,* Vol. 48 (1996); M. O. Ribaudo and T. M. Hurley, "Economic and Environmental Effects Associated with Reducing the Use of Atrazine: An Example of Cross-Disciplinary Research," *Journal of Agricultural and Applied Economics,* Vol. 29, No. 1 (1997).

7. The base year for data is never explicitly stated. However, the study refers to "near-term" effects as occurring in 1993–1996, and uses a baseline corn yield of 109 bushels/acre, the U.S. average in 1991.

8. These are the estimates from Lakshminarayan et al., "Atrazine and Water Quality," p. 120, table 6. The USDA report based on the same analysis highlights the sum of (private) producer and consumer impacts, excluding the gains to government support programs, resulting in a larger total loss (see Ribaudo and Bouzaher, "Atrazine: Environmental Characteristics," p. 10, table 7).

9. U.S. EPA, "Assessment of Potential Mitigation Measures for Atrazine," (EPA Biological and Economic Analysis Division, 2003).

10. The Triazine Network's 1996 work is cited in the EPA report on page 20, but does not appear in the list of sources at the end of the report. The reference is presumably to the predecessor to the more recent Triazine Network report, which is discussed below.

11. Detailed studies are available on the expected effects on acreage of small economic changes; see, for instance, W. Lin et al., "Supply Response under the 1996 Farm Act and Implications for the U.S. Field Crops Sector," (Economic Research Service, U.S. Department of Agriculture, 2000).

12. R. S. Fawcett, "Two Decades of Atrazine Yield Benefits Research" (Triazine Network, 2006).

13. For Fawcett's study, and more information on the Triazine Network, see their Web site at www.ksgrains.com/triazine/.

14. Coursey, "Illinois without Atrazine: Who Pays?" www.ilfb.org/uploads/files/Atrazine_Final_Report_02-27-07_13073.pdf.

15. Coursey's note 32, p. 9, included four complete references to journal articles, and one complete title of a government report. Another study was cited to a Web site address that is no longer valid. One citation reads, in its entirety, "Novartis regional models"; another is simply "AGSIM model." All of the studies that have dates are from 1997 or earlier, including a mistaken citation to the Fawcett study discussed above. Coursey's high and low estimates of yield loss are based solely on four of the sixteen studies. Of the four, only the Fawcett study appears to be readily available. (Two e-mails

to Coursey requesting complete citations and copies of his sources received a terse response containing only a location for one of the sources, namely the Fawcett study.)

16. They are described only as "notes on file with author" (notes 52–53, pp. 20–21).

17. Coursey, "Illinois without Atrazine," tables 12 and 13, pp. 22–23.

18. Asked to comment on this problem in his work, Coursey (in the same e-mail mentioned above) said merely, "For the record, there is no double-counting in my analysis."

19. S. M. Swinton et al., "The Effect of Local Triazine Restriction Policies on Recommended Weed Management in Corn," *Review of Agricultural Economics,* Vol. 17 (1995).

20. U.S. EPA Pesticide Fact Sheet: Mesotrione, June 4, 2001.

21. Syngenta Global, Callisto herbicide, www.syngenta.com/en/products_services/callisto_page.aspx.

22. U.S. EPA Pesticide Fact Sheet: Mesotrione, p. 7.

23. G. R. Armel et al., "Mesotrione, Acetochlor, and Atrazine for Weed Management in Corn (*Zea mays*)," *Weed Technology,* Vol. 17 (2003).

24. Ibid., p. 284.

25. Armel et al., "Mesotrione, Acetochlor and Atrazine." Yield data appears in table 3, p. 286. The best non-atrazine treatment was mesotrione plus acetochlor pre-emergence, followed by mesotrione post-emergence. The best treatment with atrazine was atrazine plus acetochlor pre-emergence, followed by mesotrione post-emergence.

26. The same research team also studied the effects of mesotrione on no-till corn cultivation, finding it effective against most weeds; no yield data were presented in that study. G. R. Armel et al., "Mesotrione Combinations in No-Till Corn (*Zea mays*)," *Weed Technology,* Vol. 17 (2003).

27. For Illinois, see B. C. Johnson et al., "Effect of Postemergence Application Rate and Timing of Mesotrione on Corn (*Zea mays*) Response and Weed Control," *Weed Technology,* Vol. 16 (2002). For Arkansas, see D. O. Stephenson IV, et al., "Evaluation of Mesotrione in Mississippi Delta Corn Production," *Weed Technology,* Vol. 18 (2004). Neither study published any comparative numerical data on yields with mesotrione versus atrazine.

28. European Council, "Council Directive 80/778/Eec of 15 July 1980 Relating to the Quality of Water Intended for Human Consumption," *Official Journal of the European Union,* L229 (1980).

29. European Council, "Council Directive 98/83/Ec of 3 November 1998 on the Quality of Water Intended for Human Consumption," *Official Journal of the European Union,* L330 (1998).

30. European Council, "Council Directive of 15 July 1991 Concerning the Placing of Plant Protection Products on the Market, 91/414/EEC," *Official Journal of the European Communities,* L 230 (1991).

31. European Commission, "Opinion of the Scientific Committee on Plants on Specific Questions from the Commission Concerning the Evaluation of Atrazine in the

Context of Council Directive 91/414/EEC," (Brussels: European Commission, Health and Consumer Protection Directorate-General, Scientific Committee on Plants, 2003).

32. European Commission, "Commission Decision of 10 March 2004 Concerning the Non-Inclusion of Atrazine in Annex I to Council Directive 91/414/Eec and the Withdrawal of Authorisations for Plant Protection Products Containing This Active Substance, 2004/248/EC," *Official Journal of the European Union*, L78 (2004).

33. C. Giupponi, "The Substitution of Hazardous Molecules in Production Processes: The Atrazine Case Study in Italian Agriculture," (Milan: Fondazione Eni Enrico Mattei, 2001); J. Tagliabue, "In Rice Fields of Italy, the Waters Are Troubled," *The New York Times*, April 14, 1987.

34. T. Swanson and M. Vighi, eds., *Regulating Chemical Accumulation in the Environment* (Cambridge, UK: Cambridge University Press, 1998).

35. Giupponi, "The Substitution of Hazardous Molecules"; Tagliabue, "In Rice Fields of Italy."

36. Giupponi, "The Substitution of Hazardous Molecules."

37. E. Chynoweth, "Atrazine Gets Reprieve from European Commission," *Chemical Week*, July 22, 1992.

38. Both graphs are based on the FAO's ProdSTAT database. Data for Germany before 1990 are totals for East Germany plus West Germany.

39. More recent data are also available, but starting in 2002 the three-year moving average would include the 2003 data; those data are strongly affected by that year's European heat wave, a factor extraneous to this analysis.

40. For instance, if the cost of corn inputs made up as much as half of the price of a consumer product, a 2 percent increase in the price of corn would be expected to cause a 1 percent increase in the price of the consumer product.

Chapter 6

1. Wikipedia entry for "cholinesterase"; *Law and Order* episode synopsis at www.tv.com/law-and-order-special-victims-unit/loophole/episode/959841/recap.html.

2. See A. S. Felsot, "Adios Azinphos-Methyl, Farewell Phosmet," *Agrichemical and Environmental News*, no. 191 (2002).

3. U.S. EPA, *Azinphos-Methyl Summary* (U.S. Environmental Protection Agency, 2006); U.S. EPA, *Phosmet Summary* (U.S. Environmental Protection Agency, 2006).

4. N. Anderson and T. Kiely, "Apple Benefits Assessment for Azinphos-Methyl and Phosmet," in *Memo to Chemical Review Manager*, Pesticides Office of Prevention, and Toxic Substances (Washington, DC: U.S. Environmental Protection Agency, 2001).

5. Anderson and Kiely, "Apple Benefits."

6. R. Elkins, "Areawide Implementation of Mating Disruption in Pears Using Puffers," in *Pest Management Grants Final Report, Contract No. 98-0265* (Sacramento, CA: California Department of Pesticide Regulation, 2000).

7. C. O. Calkins, "Review of the Codling Moth Areawide Suppression Program in the Western United States," *Journal of Agricultural Entomology*, Vol. 15, No. 4 (1998).

8. R. Earles et al., "Organic and Low-Spray Apple Production," Appropriate Technology Transfer for Rural Areas, *Horticultural Production Guide* (Fayetteville, AR: National Sustainable Agriculture Information Service, 1999).

9. S. L. Swezey et al., "Granny Smith Conversions to Organic Show Early Success," *California Agriculture,* Vol. 48, No. 6 (1994).

10. J. P. Reganold et al., "Sustainability of Three Apple Production Systems," *Nature,* Vol. 410, No. 6831 (2001).

11. U.S. EPA, "Revised Occupational Handler Exposure Assessment and Recommendations for the Reregistration Eligibility Decision Document for Azinphos Methyl," (Washington, DC: U.S. Environmental Protection Agency, 2001).

12. See, for example, California EPA, "Summary of Results from the California Pesticide Illness Surveillance Program, 2002," (Sacramento, CA: Department of Pesticide Regulation, Worker Health and Safety Branch, 2004); and Washington State Department of Health, "2003 Annual Report: Pesticide Incident Reporting and Tracking (PIRT) Review Panel," (Olympia, WA: Washington Department of Health, Office of Environmental Heath Assessments, 2003).

13. Scientific Advisory Committee for Cholinesterase Monitoring, "Cholinesterase Monitoring of Pesticide Handlers in Agriculture: 2004–2006," (Olympia, WA: Washington State Department of Labor and Industries, 2006).

14. S. A. McCurdy et al., "Assessment of Azinphosmethyl Exposure in California Peach Harvest Workers," *Archives of Environmental Health,* Vol. 49, No. 4 (1994).

15. D. K. Y. Chan et al., "Genetic and Environmental Risk Factors and Their Interactions for Parkinson's Disease in a Chinese Population," *Journal of Clinical Neuroscience,* Vol. 10, No. 3 (2003).

16. B. A. J. Veldman et al., "Genetic and Environmental Risk Factors in Parkinson's Disease," *Clinical Neurology and Neurosurgery,* Vol. 100, No. 1 (1998).

17. K. L. Davis et al., "Possible Organophosphate-Induced Parkinsonism," *Journal of Nervous & Mental Disease,* Vol. 166 (1978); A. Seidler et al., "Possible Environmental, Occupational, and Other Etiologic Factors for Parkinson's Disease: A Case-Control Study in Germany," *Neurology,* Vol. 46 (1996). Also see Y. O. Herishanu et al., "A Case-Referent Study of Extrapyramidal Signs (Preparkinsonism) in Rural Communities of Israel," *Canadian Journal of Neurological Sciences,* Vol. 25, No. 2 (1998); and M. H. Bhatt et al., "Acute and Reversible Parkinsonism Due to Organophosphate Pesticide Intoxication: Five Cases," *Neurology,* Vol. 52, No. 7 (1999).

18. M. Moses, "Chronic Neurological Effects of Pesticides: Summary of Selected Studies," in *Human Health Studies* (San Francisco, CA: Pesticide Education Center, 2002).

19. E. P. Savage et al., "Chronic Neurological Sequelae of Acute Organophosphate Pesticide Poisoning," *Archives of Environmental Health,* Vol. 43, No. 1 (1988).

20. K. Steenland et al., "Chronic Neurological Sequelae to Organophosphate Pesticide Poisoning," *American Journal of Public Health,* Vol. 84, No. 5 (1994).

21. C. Loewenherz et al., "Biological Monitoring of Organophosphorus Pesticide Exposure among Children of Agricultural Workers in Central Washington State," *Environmental Health Perspectives,* Vol. 105, No. 12 (1997).

22. 29 U.S. Code §§201–219.

23. P. F. Guerrero, *Pesticides: Improvements Needed to Ensure the Safety of Farmworkers and Their Children,* GAO/RCED-00–40 (Washington, DC: General Accounting Office, 2000).

24. C. L. Curl et al., "Evaluation of Take-Home Organophosphorus Pesticide Exposure among Agricultural Workers and Their Children," *Environmental Health Perspectives,* Vol. 110, No. 12 (2002).

25. R. A. Fenske et al., "Biologically Based Pesticide Dose Estimates for Children in an Agricultural Community," *Environmental Health Perspectives,* Vol. 108, No. 6 (2000).

26. See the discussion in chapter 1, and in F. Ackerman and L. Heinzerling, *Priceless: On Knowing the Price of Everything and the Value of Nothing* (New York: The New Press, 2004).

27. U.S. EPA, "Interim Reregistration Eligibility Decision for Azinphos-Methyl," (Washington, DC: U.S. Environmental Protection Agency, 2001).

28. Ibid.

29. J. C. Ebbert and S. S. Embrey, *Pesticides in Surface Water of the Yakima River Basin, Washington, 1999–2000—Their Occurrence and an Assessment of Factors Affecting Concentrations and Loads,* in Water Resources Investigations Report 01–4211 (Portland, OR: U.S. Geological Survey, 2002).

30. N. M. Dubrovski et al., *Water Quality in the San Joaquin–Tulare Basins, California, 1992–95,* in USGS Circular 1159 (Washington, DC: U.S. Geological Survey, 1998); Ebbert and Embrey, "Pesticides in Surface Water"; D. Wentz et al., *Water Quality in the Willamette Basin, Oregon, 1991–1995,* USGS Circular 1161 (Washington, DC: U.S. Geological Survey, 1998).

31. *Washington Toxics Coalition v. EPA,* C01–132C (W. D. Wash., July 2, 2002).

32. U.S. EPA, *Endangered Species Effects Determinations and Consultations; an Interim Process for Public Input* (2006).

33. See the discussion in chapter 1 and in Ackerman and Heinzerling, *Priceless,* chapter 7.

34. D. Olsen et al., "Existence and Sport Values for Doubling the Size of Columbia River Basin Salmon and Steelhead Runs," *Rivers,* Vol. 2, No. 1 (1991).

35. D. D. Huppert, "Snake River Salmon Recovery: Quantifying the Costs," *Contemporary Economic Policy,* Vol. 17, No. 4 (1999); *River Economics: Evaluating Trade-Offs in Columbia River Basin Fish and Wildlife Programs and Policies* (Portland, OR: Independent Economic Analysis Board of the Northwest Power Planning Council, 1999); K. P. Bell et al., "Willingness to Pay for Local Coho Salmon Enhancement in Coastal Communities," *Marine Resource Economics,* Vol. 18, No. 1 (2003).

36. U.S. EPA, *Fact Sheet—Settlement Agreement Regarding Azinphos-Methyl and Phosmet* (U.S. Environmental Protection Agency, 2006).

37. U.S. EPA, "2005 Grower Impact Assessment for Azinphos-Methyl Use on Pears," (Washington, DC: U.S. Environmental Protection Agency, 2005); U.S. EPA, "2005 Grower Impact Assessment of Azinphos-Methyl Use on Apples," (Washington, DC: U.S. Environmental Protection Agency, 2005).

38. U.S. EPA, "Phosmet Restricted Entry Intervals."

39. Ibid.

40. Ibid.

41. Ibid.

42. U.S. EPA, "Proposed Decisions for the Remaining Uses of Azinphos-Methyl."

43. U.S. EPA, "Phosmet Restricted Entry Intervals."

44. U.S. EPA, "Proposed Decisions for the Remaining Uses of Azinphos-Methyl," p. 9.

45. For acetamiprid, a European Union study found that residues in food have no harmful effect (see European Commission, "Review Report for the Active Substance Acetamiprid," in *Commission Working Document SANCO/1392/2001–Final*, (Brussels: European Commission, Health and Consumer Protection Directorate-General, 2004). MRLs for acetamiprid and thiacloprid were to be voted on by the EU in October 2006 (see U.K. Department of Environment, Food and Rural Affairs [DEFRA], *Potential and Agreed Changes to Maximum Residue Levels [MRLs]* [Department for Environment, Food and Rural Affairs, 2006]). www.pesticides.gov.uk/food_industry.asp?id=546.

An MRL for novaluron was recommended by the Joint Meeting on Pesticide Residues (JMPR, sponsored by the Food and Agriculture Organization [FAO] and the World Health Organization [WHO]) in 2005; see FAO/WHO, "Acceptable Daily Intakes, Acute Reference Doses, Short-Term and Long-Term Dietary Intakes, Recommended Maximum Residue Limits, and Supervised Trials Median Residue Values Recorded by the 2005 Meeting" (paper presented at the Joint FAO/WHO Meeting on Pesticide Residues, Geneva, 20–29 Sept. 2005). Thiacloprid was to be discussed by the JMPR in late 2006; see IPCS. 2006. Pesticides scheduled for evaluation at future meetings, by year. *Chemicals in Food*. Geneva, World Health Organization, International Program on Chemical Safety. Retrieved 11-27-06, from www.who.int/ipcs/en/.

Japan has MRLs for novaluron and for methoxyfenozide; see California Strawberry Commission, "Japan's Final MRL 'Positive List,'" (Watsonville, CA: California Strawberry Commission, 2006), www.calstrawberry.com/fileData/docs/CSC_Green_Sheet_MRL_Chart_FINAL_rev_5.8.06_Japanese_Provisional.pdf; U.S. Department of Agriculture (USDA), *Japan Establishes MRL on Novaluron,* in GAIN Report No. JA3080, USDA Foreign Agricultural Service (Washington, DC: U.S. Department of Agriculture, 2003).

The United Kingdom has a temporary MRL for methoxyfenozide, now under discussion; see DEFRA, *Consolidated Listing of Maximum Residue Level (MRL) Legislation*

(Department for Environment, Food and Rural Affairs, 2006), www.pesticides.gov .uk/food_industry.asp?id=538. An FAO evaluation of methoxyfenozide in 2003 found limited evidence of harm; see FAO/WHO, *Pesticide Residues in Food Report—2003,* FAO Plant Production And Protection Paper 176 (Geneva: Food and Agriculture Organization of the United Nations and World Health Organization, 2004).

46. U.S. EPA, "Proposed Decisions for the Remaining Uses of Azinphos-Methyl," p. 10.

47. U.S. EPA, "Final Decisions for the Remaining Uses of Azinphos-Methyl"; U.S. EPA, "Proposed Decisions for the Remaining Uses of Azinphos-Methyl.," U.S. EPA, "Proposed Decisions on Nine Phosmet Restricted Entry Intervals."

Chapter 7

1. U.S. General Accounting Office "Mad Cow Disease: Improvements in the Animal Feed Ban and Other Regulatory Areas Would Strengthen Other U.S. Prevention Efforts," (Washington, DC, 2002).

2. T. O. McGarity, "Federal Regulation of Mad Cow Disease Risks." *Administrative Law Review,* Vol. 57, No. 2 (2005).

3. Ibid.

4. EU Directorate General for Agriculture and Rural Development, "Agriculture in the European Union: Statistical and Economic Information 2005," http://ec.europa .eu/comm/agriculture/agrista/2005/table_en/index.htm.

5. EU Directorate General for Health and Consumer Protection, "Report on the Monitoring and Testing of Ruminants for the Presence of Transmissible Spongiform Encephalopathy (TSE) in the EU in 2004," http://ec.europa.eu/comm/food/food /biosafety/bse/annual_report_tse2004_en.pdf.

6. U.S. Department of Agriculture (USDA), "Statistical Highlights of U.S. Agriculture 2004 & 2005," 2005.

7. USDA, Animal and Plant Health Inspection Service (APHIS), Factsheet, "USDA's BSE Surveillance Efforts," July 2006.

8. J. Cohen et al., "Evaluation of the Potential for Bovine Spongiform Encephalopathy in the United States: Report to the U.S. Department of Agriculture," (Boston: Harvard Center for Risk Analysis [HCRA]) (original version 2001; revised version 2003). All subsequent references are to the 2003 revision. A USDA Web site presents the original and revised reports, along with peer review comments on the original report from Research Triangle Institute and HCRA responses to the reviewers; see www.aphis.usda .gov/lpa/issues/bse/bse_Harvard.html.

9. If the true prevalence is p > 0 and N independent random tests are conducted, the probability that all N tests will be negative is $(1-p)^N$. Thus 95 percent confidence that at least one of the N tests will be positive requires that $(1-p)^N \leq 0.05$. For small p and large N, this is roughly equivalent to $p \geq 3/N$.

10. APHIS, "An Estimate of the Prevalence of BSE in the United States," (Washington, DC: Animal and Plant Health Inspection Service, USDA, 2006).

11. McGarity, "Mad Cow."

12. The ratio of 28 is an EU average, found in APHIS, "Estimate." The ratio of 8 is for Switzerland, found in J. Cohen and G. Gray, "Comments on USDA Bovine Spongiform Encephalopathy (BSE) Surveillance Plan," (Boston: Harvard Center for Risk Analysis [HCRA], 2004).

13. N. M. Ferguson, "Estimation of the Basic Reproduction Number of BSE: The Intensity of Transmission in British Cattle," *Proceedings of the Royal Society B: Biological Sciences*, Vol. 266, No. 1414 (1999), pp. 23–32.

14. The parameter definitions are presented in Cohen et al., "Potential for BSE," appendix 1, p. 4–8.

15. The list is presented in Cohen et al., "Potential for BSE," table 3-10, p. 80–82.

16. Research Triangle Institute, "Review of the Potential for Bovine Spongiform Encephalopathy in the United States, Conducted by the Harvard Center for Risk Analysis," 2002.

17. Cohen et al., "Potential for BSE."

18. Just slightly more than one page, near the back of the 150-page report, is devoted to the multiple-worst-case results—and a significant part of that page is about the technical difficulties of running the computer model for scenarios with large numbers of infected cattle.

19. Cohen and Gray, "Comments."

20. Cohen and Gray, "Comments," p. 31.

21. M. Setbon et al., "Risk Perception of The 'Mad Cow Disease' in France: Determinants and Consequences," *Risk Analysis*, Vol. 25, No. 4 (2005).

22. M. Jacob and T. Hellstrom, "Policy Understanding of Science, Public Trust and the BSE-CJD Crisis," *Journal of Hazardous Materials*, Vol. 78, No. 1–3 (2000).

23. J. Fox and H. Hanawa Peterson, "Risks and Implications of Bovine Spongiform Encephalopathy for the United States: Insights from Other Countries," *Food Policy*, Vol. 29 (2004).

24. Ibid.

25. U.S. Department of Agriculture Economic Research Service, "Background Statistics: U.S. Beef and Cattle Industry," 2006.

26. Applying testing costs of $30–$50 per animal to the $32.9 million cattle slaughtered in 2004, as cited above.

27. U.S. beef exports were valued at $2.6 billion in 2002, $3.1 billion in 2003, and less than $0.6 billion in 2004.

Chapter 8

1. Since the 2003 publication of the report on which this chapter is based, similar studies have been completed for other states, including Washington and Minnesota. See K. Davies, "Economic Costs of Diseases and Disabilities Attributable to Environmental

Contaminants in Washington State," *EcoHealth Journal*, Vol. 3, No. 2 (June 2006); K. Davies, "How Much Do Environmental Diseases and Disabilities Cost?" *Northwest Public Health* (Fall/Winter 2005); K. Schuler et al., "The Price of Pollution: Cost Estimates of Environment-Related Childhood Disease in Minnesota," Report published by the Minnesota Center for Environmental Advocacy and the Institute for Agriculture and Trade Policy, June 2006.

2. T. Schettler et al., *Generations at Risk: Reproductive Health and the Environment* (Cambridge, MA: MIT Press, 1999); T. Schettler et al., *In Harm's Way: Toxic Threats to Child Development* (Cambridge, MA: Greater Boston Physicians for Social Responsibility, 2000); U.S. EPA, *America's Children and the Environment: Measures of Contaminants, Body Burdens, and Illnesses* (Feb. 2003), pp. 58–59; T. Gouveia-Vigeant and J. Tickner, *Toxic Chemicals and Childhood Cancer: A Review of the Evidence* (Lowell, MA: Lowell Center for Sustainable Production, May 2003).

3. Schettler et al., *Generations at Risk;* Schettler et al., *In Harm's Way.*

4. Schettler et al., *In Harm's Way.*

5. "Sick Schools Affect Health of U.S. Children," 2002. www.webmd.com/baby/news/20021023/is-school-making-your-child-sick.

6. Gouveia-Vigeant and Tickner, *Toxic Chemicals.*

7. U.S. EPA, *The Cost of Illness Handbook (COI).* p. IV. 2-3.

8. B. Eskenazi et al., "Exposures of Children to Organophosphate Pesticides and Their Potential Adverse Health Effects," *Environmental Health Perspectives,* Vol. 107, Supplement 3 (June 1999).

9. U.S. EPA, *COI:* IV. 2-21–IV. 2-23.

10. Schettler et al., *In Harm's Way,* pp. 2–6, 59–94.

11. U.S. EPA, *America's Children,* pp. 58–59.

12. Schettler et al., *In Harm's Way,* p. 15.

13. D. Faber and E. J. Krieg, "Unequal Exposure to Ecological Hazards: Environmental Injustices in the Commonwealth of Massachusetts," *Environmental Health Perspectives,* Vol. 110, No. 2 (April 2002).

14. F. Perera et al., "The Challenge of Preventing Environmentally Related Disease in Young Children: Community-Based Research in New York City," *Environmental Health Perspectives,* Vol. 110, No. 2 (Feb. 2002); S. H. Zahm, "Racial, Ethnic, and Gender Variations in Cancer Risk: Considerations for Future Epidemiologic Research," *Environmental Health Perspectives,* Vol. 103, Supplement 8 (Nov. 1995).

15. U.S. EPA, *COI:* III. 9-3, III. 9-4.

16. National Cancer Institute, Surveillance, Epidemiology and End Results (SEER), Cancer Statistics Review 1975–2000.

17. California Department of Developmental Services, *Changes in the Population of Persons with Autism and Pervasive Developmental Disorders in California's Developmental Services System: 1987 through 1998.* A Report to the Legislature, March 1, 1999. (Sacramento, CA: California Health and Human Services Agency, 1999). Cited and

summarized at www.ourstolenfuture.org/NewScience/behavior/2002/2002-10byrd
.htm#1999califautism.

18. R. S. Byrd, "The Epidemiology of Autism in California: A Comprehensive Pilot Study: Report to the Legislature on the Principal Findings," 2002, cited and summarized at www.ourstolenfuture.org/NewScience/behavior/2002/2002-10byrd.htm #1999califautism.

19. S. Blakeslee, "Increase in Autism Baffles Scientists," *New York Times* (Oct. 18, 2002).

20. Asthma Regional Council. *Asthma in New England, Part I: Adults* (Dorchester, MA: Asthma Regional Council, May 2003).

21. F. Ackerman and L. Heinzerling, *Priceless: On Knowing the Price of Everything and the Value of Nothing* (New York: The New Press, 2004).

22. See Institute of Medicine, "Costs of Environment-Related Health Effects: A Plan for Continuing Study." Washington, DC: National Academy Press, 1981; M. C. Fahs et al., "Health Costs of Occupational Disease in New York State," *American Journal of Industrial Medicine,* Vol. 16 (1989); J. P. Leigh et al., "Costs of Occupational Injuries and Illnesses," *Archives of Internal Medicine,* Vol. 157 (1997).

23. In a recent review of environmental and occupational causes of cancer, a group of scientists argue that the multifactorial nature of cancer causation makes it nearly impossible to develop a meaningful estimate of the percentage of cancers that are caused by toxic exposures. The authors make a convincing case that any effort to define an environmentally attributable fraction for cancer is likely to understate significantly the true role of toxic exposures in causing cancer. R. Clapp et al., "Environmental and Occupational Causes of Cancer: A Review of Recent Scientific Literature," Report published by the Lowell Center for Sustainable Production, 2006.

24. A. Prüss-Üstün and C. Corvalán, *Preventing Disease through Healthy Environments: Towards an Estimate of the Environmental Burden of Disease* (Geneva: World Health Organization, 2006).

25. P. J. Landrigan et al., "Environmental Pollutants and Disease in American Children: Estimates of Morbidity, Mortality, and Costs for Lead Poisoning, Asthma, Cancer, and Developmental Disabilities," *Environmental Health Perspectives,* Vol. 110, No. 7 (July 2002).

26. Landrigan et al., *Environmental Pollutants,* pp. 721–22.

27. Ibid., p. 723. The Landrigan article responded to the uncertainty about the EAF for childhood cancer by using arbitrary values of 2 percent, 5 percent, and 10 percent as low, medium, and high estimates. In contrast, our Massachusetts study follows the findings of the Landrigan team's panel of experts, using a low estimate of 5 percent and a high estimate of 90 percent to span the range of their discussion as reported in the article.

28. The Landrigan study actually reported a range of $49–65 billion; the study suggested that this range was measured in either 1997 or 1998 dollars. The higher figures

reported in this chapter are adjusted from 1998 to 2002 dollars, using the consumer price index.

29. Specifically, in 2002, the Massachusetts population under age eighteen represented 2. 0 percent of the U.S. total population under age eighteen (calculated from U.S. Census Bureau, "State Population Estimates by Selected Age Categories and Sex: July 1, 2002," www.census.gov/popest/archives/2000s/vintage_2002/ST-EST2002-ASRO - 01.html.

30. Massachusetts Community Health Information Profiles (MassCHIP), 2003.

31. The Landrigan calculation of the cost of deaths from primary and secondary cancers adds another $2.0 billion.

32. MassCHIP.

33. Boston Public Health Commission Research Office, *The Health of Boston 2002* (Boston, MA: Boston Public Health Commission, Nov. 2002), p. 55.

34. K. B. Weiss et al., "Trends in the Cost of Illness for Asthma in the United States, 1985–1994," *The Journal of Allergy and Clinical Immunology,* Vol. 106, No. 3 (Sept. 2000).

35. U.S. EPA, *COI:* IV.2-65.

36. U.S. EPA, *COI:* IV.2-21.

37. An alternative approach to estimating costs of asthma in Massachusetts is to take 2 percent of the national costs calculated by Landrigan et al.; this would imply environmentally attributable asthma costs in Massachusetts ranging from $14 million to $50 million.

38. P. Ladebauche et al., "Asthma in Head Start Children: Prevalence, Risk Factors, and Health Care Utilization," *Pediatric Nursing,* Vol. 27, No. 4 (July 2001), p. 396.

39. K. McGill et al., "Asthma in Non-Inner City Head Start Children," *Pediatrics,* Vol. 102 (1998), pp. 77–83.

40. Massachusetts Department of Education Information Services, "Special Education Enrollment by Age/Disability," Dec. 1, 2001.

41. Learning Disabilities Association of Massachusetts, pers. com., August 2003.

42. S. Berman et al., "The Rising Costs of Special Education in Massachusetts: Causes and Effects," in Chester E. Finn Jr. et al., eds., *Rethinking Special Education for a New Century* (Thomas B. Fordham Foundation and the Progressive Policy Institute, May 2001), p. 191.

43. Landrigan et al., *Environmental Pollutants,* p. 725.

44. Massachusetts Department of Public Health, Bureau of Environmental Health Assessment, Childhood Lead Poisoning Prevention Program, Screening and Incidence Statistics, 1994–2002.

45. K. S. Korfmacher, "Long-Term Costs of Lead Poisoning: How Much Can New York Save by Stopping Lead?" University of Rochester, 2003, http://afhh.org/aa/aa _state%20_local_lead_costs_NYrep.pdf ; M. Stefanak et al., "Costs of Child Lead Poisoning to Taxpayers in Mahoning County, Ohio," *Public Health Reports,* Vol. 120 (2005).

46. U.S. EPA, *COI:* III:9.

47. The original data ranged from $522 to $5,200 in 1987 dollars; they were converted to 2002 dollars using the consumer price index.

48. U.S. EPA, *COI:* III.9-9.

49. R. L. Canfield et al., "Intellectual Impairment in Children with Blood Lead Concentrations below 10 μg per Deciliter," *New England Journal of Medicine,* Vol. 348, No. 16 (April 17, 2003).

50. This is the average of the separate numbers for boys and girls presented by Landrigan et al.

51. Using the alternate estimates discussed here, 0.46 IQ points per μg/dL of lead in the blood, and $8,700 of lost lifetime income per IQ point, the result would be similar, $41.4 billion in 2002 dollars.

52. N. J. Waitzman et al., "Economic Costs of Congenital Anomalies," *Morbidity and Mortality Weekly Report,* Vol. 44, No. 37 (Sept. 22, 1995); N. J. Waitzman et al., *The Cost of Birth Defects: Estimates of the Value of Prevention* (Lanham, MD: University Press of America, 1996).

Chapter 9

1. "NTSB blames airline, contractor, and FAA for ValuJet crash," CNN, August 19, 1997, www.cnn.com/US/9708/19/valujet.final/.

2. "Expanded Inspections Needed to Assess Wiring Woes, Experts Say," *Aviation Today* special report (May 25, 1998).

3. For an overview of PVC's history, see P. H. Spitz, *Petrochemicals: The Rise of an Industry* (New York: John Wiley and Sons, 1988).

4. See J. Thornton, *Pandora's Poison: Chlorine, Health, and a New Environmental Strategy* (Cambridge, MA: MIT Press, 2000).

5. U.S. Department of Health and Human Services, Public Health Service, National Toxicology Program, *Report on Carcinogens,* 10th ed. (Dec. 2002), http://ehp .niehs.nih.gov/roc/toc10.html. Also see U.S. Environmental Protection Agency, "Vinyl Chloride Hazard Summary" (2002) and World Health Organization, International Agency for Research on Cancer (IARC), *IARC Monographs on the Evaluation of Carcinogenic Risks to Humans, Supplement 7* (Lyon, France: IARC, 1987), pp. 451–54, http://monographs.iarc.fr/ENG/Monographs/suppl7/suppl7.pdf.

6. F. Ackerman, *Why Do We Recycle? Markets, Values, and Public Policy* (Washington, DC: Island Press, 1997).

7. Dictionary.com Unabridged, http://dictionary.reference.com/browse/plastic.

8. On routes of human exposure to vinyl chloride, see Agency for Toxic Substances and Disease Registry, *Toxicological Profile for Vinyl Chloride* (Sept. 1997, CAS # 75-01-4), p. 153ff.

9. See C. Maltoni, "Two Cases of Liver Angiosarcoma among PVC Extruders of an Italian Factory Producing PVC Bags and Other Containers," *American Journal of*

Industrial Medicine Vol. 5 (1984); J. Kielhorn et al., "Vinyl Chloride: Still a Cause for Concern," *Environmental Health Perspectives,* Vol. 108, No. 7 (2000); and R. H. Wong, "An increased mortality ratio for liver cancer among polyvinyl chloride workers in Taiwan," *Occupational and Environmental Medicine* Vol. 59 (2002).

10. National Toxicology Program and Center for the Evaluation of Risks to Human Reproduction *NTP-CERHR Expert Panel Report on Di(2-ethylhexyl) phthalate* (NTP-CERHR-DEHP-00) (Oct. 2000), http://cerhr.niehs.nih. gov/news/phthalates/ DEHP-final.pdf, viewed Dec. 2003; J. J. K. Jaakkola et al., "Interior Surface Materials in the Home and the Development of Bronchial Obstruction in Young Children in Oslo, Norway," *American Journal of Public Health* Vol. 89, No. 2 (Feb. 1999).

11. R. F. Dyer and V. H. Esch, "Polyvinyl Chloride Toxicity in Fires: Hydrogen Chloride Toxicity in Fire Fighters," *Journal of the American Medical Association* Vol. 235, No. 4 (1976); J. S. Markowitz et al., "Acute Health Effects among Firefighters Exposed to a Polyvinyl Chloride (PVC) Fire," *American Journal of Epidemiology* Vol. 129, No. 5 (1989).

12. See Thornton, *Pandora's Poison* especially pp. 271, 276, and 316–19, and references therein.

13. Government economic data do not usually distinguish between PVC and other plastics; information on PVC sales is largely based on private market research. All figures in this paragraph are calculated from E. Linak with K. Yagi, "Polyvinyl Chloride (PVC) Resins," Chemical Economics Handbook Marketing Research Report (Menlo Park, CA: SRI International, Sept. 2003).

14. Environment Canada, "A Technical and Socio-Economic Comparison of Options to Products Derived from the Chlor-Alkali Industry" (1997).

15. Pipes, where the cost per pound for alternatives was low, represented about half of all PVC use, holding down the average cost. See the original study, F. Ackerman and R. Massey, "The Economics of Phasing Out PVC" (2003), www.ase.tufts.edu/gdae/ Pubs/rp/Economics_of_PVC_revised.pdf for details on the calculation.

16. *Floor Covering Weekly* "Statistical Report 2002."

17. "Amtico: Reinventing Vinyl," interview with then-Amtico CEO Mary Docker, *Floor Focus* (June 2003).

18. F. Lindell, "Navy Food Service: Improving Quality of Life for Sailors," *Navy Supply Corps Newsletter* (March/April 2000), www.seabeecook.com/today/news/ cook0091.htm.

19. A potential hazard arises because fiber cement contains silica (silicon dioxide, or sand). Inhaling silica dust during manufacturing or construction work can cause silicosis, a devastating lung disease. This is a potentially controllable problem, but unless silica dust *is* controlled, fiber cement production and installation could present health hazards to workers who make and install it.

20. "Vinyl Siding: More Uniform Plastic," *Consumer Reports* (August 2003).

21. For details on calculation of learning curve effects, see the "Learning Curve

Calculator," http://cost.jsc.nasa.gov/learn.html. On the economic theory of learning curves, see, for example, A. M. Spence, "Investment Strategy and Growth in a New Market," *The Bell Journal of Economics,* Vol. 10, No. 1 (spring 1979); S. Klepper and E. Graddy, "The Evolution of New Industries and the Determinants of Market Structure," *The RAND Journal of Economics,* Vol. 21, No. 1 (spring 1990); and P. Ghemawat and A. M. Spence, "Learning Curve Spillovers and Market Performance," *Quarterly Journal of Economics,* Vol. 100 Supplement (1985).

22. In that period, cumulative production of the Model T went from less than 20,000 to about 7 million cars, doubling more than eight times. W. J. Abernathy and K. Wayne, "Limits of the Learning Curve," *Harvard Business Review,* Vol. 52, No. 5 (1974).

23. Brian W. Arthur, an economist at the Santa Fe Institute, has argued that many of society's important economic and technological choices are "path dependent." A technology that, perhaps accidentally, gains a slight lead early in its history may be able to solidify that lead by gaining market share and lowering prices, "locking out" other technologies that may be equally or more efficient if adopted on a large scale. The Windows operating system, the standard videocassette format, the dominant nuclear reactor design, and the gasoline-powered automobile engine, for example, all started with only small leads over equally (or more) attractive rival technologies; all have come to be "locked in" and dominate their markets through the path-dependent process that Arthur described. See B. W. Arthur, *Increasing Returns and Path Dependence in the Economy* (Ann Arbor: University of Michigan Press, 1994).

24. This is my calculation from the graph in P. H. Spitz, *Petrochemicals,* p. 415. Spitz presents separate graphs of cumulative production versus price for PVC and copolymers, for value added by polymerizer, and for vinyl chloride monomer. In these three graphs, a doubling of cumulative production is associated with price declines of 34 percent, 31 percent, and 40 percent, respectively.

25. Spitz, *Petrochemicals,* pp. 390–417.

26. A. Rego and L. Roley, "In-Use Barrier Integrity of Gloves: Latex and Nitrile Superior to Vinyl," *American Journal of Infection Control,* Vol. 27, No. 5 (Oct. 1999).

27. The brand with the highest out-of-box failure rate is not the one with the highest failure rate after use. Thus the high average failure rates cannot be attributed to a problem in a single brand.

28. Rego and Roley, "In-Use Barrier Integrity."

29. K. Gerwig, director, Environmental Stewardship and National Environmental Health and Safety, Kaiser Permanente, personal communication (Nov. 2002).

30. Anonymous, "EPP Success Story: Kaiser Permanente," *Environmentally Preferable Purchasing News for Health Care Organizations,* Vol. 2, No. 3 (May 2000).

31. K. Christman, Vinyl Institute, "Vinyl Use in Building and Construction," Vinyl Material Council Newsletter (May 2003), www.aamanet.org/pdf_files/Council_News _pdfs/VMC_Newsletter_May_03.pdf.

32. Qualitative information on pipe materials is drawn from sources including Environment Canada, "A Technical and Socio-Economic Comparison," 1997 and J. Harvie with T. Lent, "PVC-Free Pipe Purchasers' Report," www.healthybuilding.net/pvc/pipes_report.html.

33. This section relies heavily on the Plastics Pipe Institute (PPI) Web site, http://plasticpipe.org, and on personal communication from R. Gottwald, president of PPI, Sept.–Oct. 2002.

34. PPI, "2001 Statistics: North American Shipments of Polyethylene & Crosslinked Polyethylene Pipe, Tube & Conduit."

35. See, for example, USInspect Web site, www.usinspect.com/PBPlumbing/PBBackground.asp.

36. See "Project Profiles: Indianapolis Water Company's Successful Transition to HDPE Pipe Marks Turning Point for Industry," www.isco-pipe.com/isco/project_profiles/indy_water_01.asp.

37. For a survey of toy manufacturers' actions on PVC toys, see the Greenpeace Toy Report Card, www.greenpeace.org/usa/news/2003-toy-report-card.

38. See U.S. Consumer Product Safety Commission, "Re: Petition Requesting Ban of Use of Polyvinyl Chloride (PVC) in Products Intended for Children Five Years of Age and Under," letter to National Environmental Trust and other groups (Feb. 26, 2003), www.cpsc.gov/LIBRARY/FOIA/FOIA03/petition/Ageunder.pdf.

39. Dyer and Esch, "Polyvinyl Chloride Toxicity."

40. "Hazardous Materials: Polyvinyl Chloride," International Association of Fire Fighters, AFL-CIO, CLC (Washington, DC, 1995).

41. Dyer and Esch, "Polyvinyl Chloride Toxicity"; Markowitz et al., "Acute Health Effects."

42. "Safety and Health Activists, Environmentalists and Unions Win Ban on Plastic Pipe in New York State," *NYCOSH Update on Safety and Health* (Jan. 14, 2002). Opposing the union view, J. Zicherman of the consulting firm Fire Cause Analysis concludes, "If proper installation detailing is observed, plastic piping installations present no greater fire risk than other types of piping materials available on the market today." See J. Zicherman, "Plastic Pipe and Fire Safety," *Fire Protection Engineering* spring 2004, www.fpemag.com/archives/article.asp?issue_id=20&i=125.

43. U.S. Congress, Office of Technology Assessment (OTA) *Gauging Control Technology and Regulatory Impacts in Occupational Safety and Health* (Washington, DC: U.S. Government Printing Office, Sept. 1995), p. 89.

44. Cheminfo Services, *A Retrospective Evaluation of Control Measures for Chlorinated Substances (Case Studies of Ex-Ante/Ex-Post Socioeconomic Effects)* Report to Environment Canada and Ontario Ministry of Energy, Science, and Technology (March 2000).

45. For fabrication employment, see www.chlorallies.org/employ.html. For VCM and PVC production, we estimated employment based on plant-level data; see Ackerman and Massey, "The Economics of Phasing Out PVC," for details.

46. PVC Container Company, Eatontown, NJ, interview with sales representative (Oct. 28, 2003).

47. Westlake Chemical Company, www.westlake.com.

48. CertainTeed Corp., www.certainteed.com.

49. Calculated from the Bureau of Labor Statistics, Job Openings and Labor Turnover Survey, tables 4 and 6, www.bls.gov/jlt/.

Chapter 10

1. For a more detailed description of REACH, see the Web site for the European Commission: http://ec.europa.eu/environment/chemicals/reach/reach_intro.htm.

2. Risk and Policy Analysts, Ltd. (RPA) and Statistics Sweden, *Assessment of the Business Impact of New Regulations in the Chemicals Sector*. Prepared for the European Commission Enterprise Directorate-General, June 2002. http://ec.europa.eu/enterprise/reach/docs/whitepaper/bia_report-2002_06.pdf.

3. This is CEFIC's interpretation of an unspecified RPA study, as described in www.cefic.org/Files/Publications/Barometer2002.pdf.

4. J. von Bahr and J. Janson, "Cost of Late Action—the Case of PCB," Copenhagen: Nordic Council of Ministers, 2004, www.norden.org/pub/miljo/miljo/sk/TN2004556.pdf.

5. CEFIC, www.cefic.org/factsandfigures.

6. Calculated from data downloaded from U.S. Energy Information Agency, (www.eia.doe.gov), data series WTOTWORLD ("All Countries Spot Price FOB Weighted by Estimated Export Volume").

7. Author's calculation from data downloaded from Eurostat.

8. In the Arthur D. Little study (described in appendix C), the intermediate or Storm scenario produced the widely quoted estimate that 2.4 percent of German GDP would be lost because of REACH. On the registration and testing costs used in the Storm scenario, see Arthur D. Little, "Economic Effects of the EU Substances Policy," (Bundesverband der Deutschen Industrie, 2002), p. 48. The calculation of indirect costs equal to 650 times direct costs assumed: (a) the eleven-year total cost for registration and testing was €3.7 billion (or €340 million per year), an accepted estimate for the then-current version of REACH; and (b) following the Storm scenario, this cost would cause a loss of 2.4 percent of the EU-15 GDP of €9.2 trillion. The annual loss of GDP would then be €220 billion, or 650 times the annual direct cost.

9. J. Canton and C. Allen, "A Microeconomic Model to Assess the Economic Impacts of the EU's New Chemicals Policy," DG Enterprise, Nov. 2003.

10. Ibid., p. 33.

11. For details, see appendix B of F. Ackerman and R. Massey, (2004), "The True Costs of REACH," www.ase.tufts.edu/gdae/Pubs/rp/TrueCostsREACH.pdf.

12. This calculation follows Canton and Allen in assuming that the price elasticity of demand for chemicals is –2 (based on their reading of a study of price elasticity for British exports), along with the further, arbitrary assumption that the price elastic-

ity of supply is 2. As explained in the original study, the maximum possible impact, occurring when the price elasticity of supply becomes infinite, is twice the impact reported here (holding the demand elasticity constant at −2).

13. Changes in consumer and producer surplus, measures used by economists to depict the effects of changes such as these, are equal to the areas of the shaded triangles in figure 10.1. They would each decline by €45,000 per year, an extremely small amount for the entire European chemical industry.

14. Alternatively, economic theory can be interpreted as suggesting that the loss of consumer plus producer surplus is the correct measure of the impact of regulation on society. These losses amount to an inconsequential fraction of the direct costs, suggesting that there are almost no indirect costs to society.

15. I. Schörling and G. Lind, "REACH—The Only Planet Guide to the Secrets of Chemicals Policy in the EU. What Happened and Why?" Brussels, April 2004.

16. Appendix 6 of the ADL study (pp. 154–55) presents the topics for discussion in the industry interviews. Responses can be found in appendix 8 (pp. 175–80).

17. Under the Toxics Use Reduction Act (TURA), Massachusetts firms that use more than a certain amount of specified toxic chemicals must (a) examine their toxics use and evaluate alternatives, and (b) report the quantities of toxic chemicals used or generated. For an overview, see http://turadata.turi.org/WhatIsTURA/Overview OfTURA.html. Companies' data on toxic chemical use and generation are open to the public, with exceptions for companies that file a special confidentiality request. For data reported under TURA, see http://turadata.turi.org/report.php.

18. J. Von Bahr and J. Jason, "Cost of Late Action—the Case of PCB," (Copenhagen: Nordic Council of Ministers, 2004).

19. S. Pickvance et al., "The Impact of REACH on Occupational Health, with a Focus on Skin and Respiratory Diseases," (University of Sheffield, UK: Report prepared for the European Trade Union Institute for Research, Education, and Health and Safety, 2005).

20. "Extended Impact Assessment of REACH Sec 1171/3," European Commission Directorate General on Enterprise and Industry (2003). For other European Commission studies, see F. Pedersen et al., "The Impact of REACH on the Environment and Human Health," (Report by DHI, Water and Environment for the European Commission, DG Environment, 2005), and RPA, "Assessment of the Impact of the New Chemicals Policy on Occupational Health," (Report prepared for the European Commission, DG Environment, 2003).

21. D. W. Pearce and P. Kondouri, "The Social Cost of Chemicals: The Cost and Benefits of Future Chemicals Policy in the European Union (2003), World Wildlife Fund-UK, http://assets.panda.org/downloads/1654reachcbafindoc.pdf.

Notes to Chapter 11

1. On Europe's longstanding economic and political relationship with the ACP states, see, C. Adelle et al., "Sustainable Development 'Outside' the European Union:

What Role for Impact Assessment?" *European Environment,* Vol. 16 (2006); M. Holland, *The European Union and the Third World* (New York: Palgrave, 2002); N. Robins, "Steering EU Development Co-Operation Towards Sustainability: The Case of the Lomé Convention," *European Environment,* Vol. 6, No. 1 (1998).

2. For the complete research report with detailed methodology, data sources, and results, see F. Ackerman et al., "Implications of REACH for the Developing Countries," in *Policy Department External Policies* (Brussels: European Parliament Directorate-General for External Policies of the Union, 2006), www.ase.tufts.edu/gdae/Pubs/rp/Implications_of_REACH.pdf.

3. ACP Council of Ministers, "Resolutions and Declarations of the 81st Session of the ACP Council of Ministers," June 2005.

4. Republic of South Africa, Chamber of Mines. "The Potential Impact of the European Union's Draft Legislation, REACH, on the Social and Economic Development of Sub-Saharan Africa." Johannesburg: Economic Advisory Unit, Chamber of Mines of South Africa, 2005.

5. Personal communication from Fabio Leone, DG Environment, Brussels, March 2006.

6. K. Nadvi, "The Cost of Compliance: Global Standards for Small-Scale Firms and Workers," *IDS Policy Briefing,* Vol. 18 (May 2003).

7. B. R. Copeland and M. S. Taylor, "Trade, Growth, and the Environment," *Journal of Economic Literature,* Vol. 42, No. 1 (2004).

8. S. Henson and R. Loader, "Barriers to Agricultural Exports from Developing Countries: The Role of Sanitary and Phytosanitary Requirements," *World Development,* Vol. 29, No. 1 (2001).

9. A. Hughes, "Retailers, Knowledges and Changing Commodity Networks: The Case of the Cut Flower Trade," *Geoforum,* Vol. 31 (2000).

10. N. M. Van Der Grijp et al., "European Retailers as Agents of Change towards Sustainability: The Case of Fruit Production in Brazil," *Environmental Sciences,* Vol. 2, No. 4 (2005).

11. M. Tewari and P. Pillari, "Global Standards and the Dynamics of Environmental Compliance in India's Leather Industry," *Oxford Development Studies,* Vol. 33, No. 2 (2005); S. R. Khan, ed. *Trade and Environment: Difficult Policy Choices at the Interface* (London: Zed Books, 2002); R. Jenkins et al., *Environmental Regulation in the New Global Economy: The Impact on Industry and Competitiveness* (Cheltenham, UK: Edward Elgar, 2002).

12. G. Haq et al., "Determining the Costs to Industry of Environmental Regulation," *European Environment,* Vol. 11 (2001).

13. R. Nordbeck and M. Faust, "European Chemicals Regulation and Its Effect on Innovation: An Assessment of the EU's White Paper on the Strategy for a Future Chemicals Policy," *European Environment,* Vol. 13, No. 2 (2003).

14. That is, we examined the four-digit categories of the widely used "Harmonized System" for trade data.

15. An exchange rate of 7.5 rand = 1 euro was used to convert South African data to euros throughout this chapter.

16. United Nations Food and Agriculture Organization (FAO) *World Markets for Organic Fruit and Vegetables—Opportunities for Developing Countries in the Production and Export of Organic Horticultural Products* (Rome: FAO Corporate Document Repository, 2001).

17. FAO, "Opportunities for Developing"; Madagascar Consulate, Essential Oils, in *Madagascar Consulate General* Madagascar Consulate General, www.madagascar consulate.org.za/oils.html.

18. BAMEX, "Now That You Have All Heard of Madagascar, It Is Time to Smell and Taste the Exotic Essence of What Has Been Called the 'Oasis on Earth,'" June 27, 2005, www.madagascarnatural.com/madagascar_press%20.pdf.

19. S. Grainger, "Comoros Seeks Sweet Smell of Success," *BBC* Sept. 14, 2005.

20. A. Jones, "The Potential Impact of REACH on Exports of Biotrade Products to the European Union," Geneva: UNCTAD Biotrade Initiative-Biotrade Facilitation Programme, 2005, p. 20.

21. European Federation of Essential Oils, "Concerning the EU Proposal for a New Regulation on Chemicals (REACH)," in *EFEO Position*. (Hamburg: European Federation of Essential Oils, 2005).

22. Jones, "Potential Impact," p. 19.

23. B. Witmond et al., "The Impact of REACH: Overview of 36 Studies on the Impact of the New EU Chemicals Policy (REACH) on Society and Business," Paper presented at the Workshop REACH Impact Assessment, 25–27 Oct. 2004, The Hague, Netherlands.

24. KPMG, "REACH—Further Work on Impact Assessment, a Case Study Approach, Final Report," (Amsterdam: KPMG Business Advisory Services, 2005), p. 7.

25. This calculation, presented in Ackerman et al., "Implications of REACH for the Developing Countries," assumed that four-digit export categories represent individual substances regulated under REACH, except in the case of South Africa's chemical industries, where we used eight-digit categories to reflect the much greater diversity of exports. While four-digit categories sometimes aggregate multiple REACH substances, the opposite problem arises with eight-digit categories, especially in metals, a single REACH substance may be spread across multiple eight-digit categories. In a subsequent calculation using eight-digit categories for all REACH exports, but consolidating multiple categories representing the same metal, we estimated a total compliance cost of €70 million for the top twenty-four ACP exporting nations.

26. Of the fifty other ACP countries that reported any REACH exports, there were twenty-two with national totals of less than €100,000 per year. If these represented genuine micro-industries exporting products subject to REACH, then REACH compliance could impose a substantial burden in percentage terms; technical and financial assistance to such industries would likely be appropriate, and would be inexpensive due

to the minute scale of the exports. But many of these reported exports are too small to be significant, even in a small national economy.

27. Republic of South Africa, Department of Trade and Industry, "Sector Development Strategy: Chemicals. Version 3.6," 2005.

28. L. Goldman and N. Tran, "Toxics and Poverty: The Impact of Toxic Substances on the Poor in Developing Countries," (Washington DC: World Bank, 2002). In addition, several studies have estimated health and safety benefits of REACH to the EU in the billions of euros per year, as described in chapter 10.

Chapter 12

1. House Committee on Government Reform, "A Special Interest Case Study: The Chemical Industry, the Bush Administration, and European Efforts to Regulate Chemicals; Prepared for Representative Henry Waxman," U.S. House of Representatives Committee on Government Reform Special Investigations Division (2004).

2. Ibid.

3. Ibid.

4. J. DiGangi, "REACH and the Long Arm of the Chemical Industry," *Multinational Monitor,* Vol. 25, No. 9 (2004).

5. House Committee on Government Reform, "A Special Interest Case Study."

6. U.S. Diplomatic Mission to the European Union, "REACH Requires Further Improvements, According to EU Trading Partners," (Brussels: 2006).

7. Because several of the underlying data sets are not released annually, 2004 is the most recent year for which these estimations can be made. For a full discussion of our methodology, see appendix D.

8. Output is measured by gross state product (GSP), the state equivalent of gross domestic product.

9. Massachusetts Governor's Office, *The Governor's Budget Recommendations, Fiscal Year 2007,* 2006.

10. California Department of Finance, *Governor's Budget 2006–2007: Proposed Budget Detail,* 2006.

11. F. Ackerman et al., "Free Trade, Corn, and the Environment: Environmental Impacts of U.S.-Mexico Corn Trade under NAFTA," (Tufts University, Medford, MA: Global Development and Environment Institute, 2003); A. Nadal and T. Wise, "The Environmental Costs of Agriculture Trade Liberalization: Mexico-U.S. Maize Trade under NAFTA," in *GDAE Working Group Discussion Paper* (Tufts University, Medford, MA: Global Development and Environment Institute, 2004). All varieties of genetically modified corn together amounted to 45 percent of the U.S. corn plantings in 2004.

12. U.S. Department of Agriculture, Foreign Agriculture Service (FAS), FASonline: U.S. Trade Internet System (Washington, DC: U.S. Department of Agriculture, Foreign Agriculture Service, 2006).

13. See "U.S. Won't Let Company Test All Its Cattle for Mad Cow," *New York Times,* April 10, 2004.

14. FAS, U.S. Trade.

15. Organic Consumers Association, "Campaign to Stop GM Wheat," 2006, www.organicconsumers.org/.

Conclusion

1. Ackerman and Heinzerling, *Priceless.*

2. E. Schlosser, *Fast Food Nation: The Dark Side of the All-American Meal* (New York: Houghton Mifflin, 2001), p. 264. Schlosser was writing well before the BSE-related curtailment of U.S. beef exports, as described in chapter 7. Even at that time, according to Schlosser, widespread American use of bovine growth hormone meant that most U.S. beef could not be exported to the EU, where the hormone had been banned (p. 142).

Appendix C

1. Arthur D. Little, "Economic Effects of the EU Substances Policy," (Wiesbaden: Bundesverband der Deutschen Industrie, 2002), p. 55.

Bibliography

Anon., *A Legislative History of the Clean Air Act Amendments of 1970*, (Congressional Research Service, 1974).

——, "OSHA Standards for Vinyl Chloride Plants Upheld," *Environmental Law Reporter*, Vol. 5 (1975), p. 10042.

——, *Economic Analysis of Federal Regulations under Executive Order 12,866*, pt. III. B. 5(a) (Report of Interagency Group Chaired by a Member of the Council of Economic Advisors, Jan. 11, 1996).

——, Interview with David Brower in *Boatman's Quarterly Review*, Vol. 10, No. 3, (1997). http://www.gcrg.org/bqr/10-3/brower.html.

——, "EPP Success Story: Kaiser Permanente," *Environmentally Preferable Purchasing News for Health Care Organizations*, Vol. 2, No. 3 (May 2000).

——. "Sick Schools Affect Health of U.S. Children," 2002. www.webmd.com/baby/news/20021023/is-school-making-your-child-sick.

——, "Vinyl Siding: More Uniform Plastic," *Consumer Reports* (August 2003), pp. 23–25.

Abernathy, W. J., and K. Wayne, "Limits of the Learning Curve," *Harvard Business Review*, Vol. 52, No. 5 (1974), pp. 109–19.

Ackerman, B. A., and R. B. Stewart, "Reforming Environmental Law," *Stanford Law Review*, Vol. 37, No. 5 (1985), pp. 1333–65.

Ackerman, F., *Why Do We Recycle? Markets, Values, and Public Policy* (Washington, DC: Island Press, 1997).

Ackerman, F., and L. Heinzerling, *Priceless: On Knowing the Price of Everything and the Value of Nothing* (New York: The New Press, 2004).

Ackerman, F., and R. Massey, "Prospering with Precaution," (Tufts University, Medford, MA: Global Development and Environment Institute, 2002). www.ase.tufts.edu/gdae/policy_research/PrecautionAHTAug02.pdf.

——, "The Economics of Phasing Out PVC" (2003). www.ase.tufts.edu/gdae/Pubs/rp/Economics_of_PVC_revised.pdf.

Ackerman, F., R. Massey, B. Roach, E. Stanton, R. Widenoja, J. Milanesi, W. Parienté, B. Contamin, P. Bond, E. Euripidou, A.-S. Andersson, and P. Rosander, "Implications of REACH for the Developing Countries," (Brussels: European Parliament Directorate-General for External Policies of the Union, 2006).

Ackerman, F., T. A. Wise, K. P. Gallagher, L. Ney, and R. Flores, "Free Trade, Corn, and the Environment: Environmental Impacts of U.S.-Mexico Corn Trade under NAFTA," (Tufts University, Medford, MA: Global Development and Environment Institute, 2003).

ACP Council of Ministers, "Resolutions and Declarations of the 81st Session of the ACP Council of Ministers," June 2005.

Adelle, C., J. Hertin, and A. Jordan., "Sustainable Development 'Outside' the European Union: What Role for Impact Assessment?" *European Environment,* Vol. 16 (2006), pp. 57–62.

Alm, A., "The Multimedia Approach to Pollution Control: An Impossible Dream?" *Multimedia Approaches to Pollution Control: Symposium Proceedings* (National Research Council, 1987).

Anderson, N., and T. Kiely, "Apple Benefits Assessment for Azinphos-Methyl and Phosmet," in *Memo to Chemical Review Manager,* Pesticides Office of Prevention, and Toxic Substances, (Washington, DC: U.S. Environmental Protection Agency, 2001).

Armel, G. R., H. P. Wilson, R. J. Richardson, and T. E. Hines, "Mesotrione, Acetochlor, and Atrazine for Weed Management in Corn (*Zea mays*)," *Weed Technology,* Vol. 17 (2003), pp. 284–90.

———, "Mesotrione Combinations in No-Till Corn (*Zea mays*)," *Weed Technology,* Vol. 17 (2003), pp. 111–16.

Arrow, K. J., M. L. Cropper, G. C. Eads, R. W. Hahn, L. B. Lave, R. G. Noll, P. R. Portney, M. Russell, R. Schmalensee, V. K. Smith, and R. N. Stavins, "Is There a Role for Benefit-Cost Analysis in Environmental, Health, and Safety Regulation?" *Science,* Vol. 272 (1996), pp. 221–22.

Arrow, K., and L. Hurwicz, "An Optimality Criterion for Decision-Making under Ignorance," in *Uncertainty and Expectations in Economics: Essays in Honour of G. L. S. Shackle,* C. F. Carter and J. L. Ford, eds. (Oxford: Basil Blackwell, 1972).

Arthur, B. W., *Increasing Returns and Path Dependence in the Economy* (Ann Arbor: University of Michigan Press, 1994).

Arthur D. Little, "Economic Effects of the EU Substances Policy," (Wiesbaden: Bundesverband der Deutschen Industrie, 2002). www.adlittle.de/downloads/artikel/EU%20Chemical%20Policy_Basic%20Study_12_2002.pdf.

Asthma Regional Council. *Asthma in New England, Part I: Adults* (Dorchester, MA: Asthma Regional Council, May 2003).

Baumol, W. J., "On the Social Rate of Discount," *American Economic Review,* Vol. 58 (1968), pp. 788–802.

Becher, H., K. Steindorf, and D. Flesch-Janys, "Quantitative Cancer Risk Assessment for Dioxins Using an Occupational Cohort," *Environmental Health Perspectives,* Vol. 106, Supplement 2 (1998), pp. 663–70.

Berman, S., P. Davis, A. Koufman-Frederick, and D. Urion, "The Rising Costs of Special Education in Massachusetts: Causes and Effects," in *Rethinking Special Education for a New Century,* Chester E. Finn Jr. et al., eds. (Thomas B. Fordham Foundation and the Progressive Policy Institute, May 2001), pp. 183–211.

Bhatt, M. H., M. A. Elias, and A. K. Mankodi, "Acute and Reversible Parkinsonism Due to Organophosphate Pesticide Intoxication: Five Cases," *Neurology,* Vol. 52, No. 7 (1999), pp. 1467–71.

Bibliography

Bi, W. F., "Effect of Vinyl Chloride on Testis in Rats," *Ecotoxicology & Environmental Safety,* Vol. 10, (1985), pp. 281–89.

Boston Public Health Commission Research Office, *The Health of Boston 2002* (Boston, MA: Boston Public Health Commission, Nov. 2002).

Brady, J., F. Liberatore, P. Harper, P. Greenwald, W. Burnett, J. N. Davies, M. Bishop, A. Polan, and N. Vianna, "Angiosarcoma of the Liver: An Epidemiologic Survey," *Journal of the National Cancer Institute,* Vol. 59 (1977), pp. 1383–85.

Brenner, H. M., "Commentary: Economic Growth Is the Basis of Mortality Rate Decline in the 20th Century—Experience of the United States 1901–2000," *International Journal of Epidemiology,* Vol. 34 (2005), pp. 1214–21.

Breyer, S., *Breaking the Vicious Circle: Toward Effective Risk Regulation* (Cambridge, MA: Harvard University Press, 1993).

Broome, J., "Trying to Value a Life," *Journal of Public Economics,* Vol. 9 (1978), pp. 91–100.

Brown, M. S., "Setting Occupational Health Standards: The Vinyl Chloride Case," in *Controversy: Politics of Technical Decisions,* D. Nelkin, ed. (London: Sage Publications, 1992), pp. 130–46.

Byrd, R. S., "The Epidemiology of Autism in California: A Comprehensive Pilot Study: Report to the Legislature on the Principal Findings," 2002 cited and summarized at www.ourstolenfuture.org/NewScience/behavior/2002/2002-10byrd.htm#1999 califautism.

California Department of Developmental Services, *Changes in the Population of Persons with Autism and Pervasive Developmental Disorders in California's Developmental Services System: 1987 through 1998.* A Report to the Legislature, March 1, 1999. (Sacramento, CA: California Health and Human Services Agency, 1999).

California Department of Finance, *Governor's Budget 2006–2007: Proposed Budget Detail,* 2006.

California EPA, "Summary of Results from the California Pesticide Illness Surveillance Program, 2002," (Sacramento, CA: Department of Pesticide Regulation, Worker Health and Safety Branch, 2004).

Calkins, C. O., "Review of the Codling Moth Areawide Suppression Program in the Western United States," *Journal of Agricultural Entomology,* Vol. 15, No. 4 (1998), pp. 327–33.

Canfield, R. L., C. R. Henderson Jr., D. A. Cory-Slechta, C. Cox, T. A. Jusko, and B. P. Lanphear, "Intellectual Impairment in Children with Blood Lead Concentrations below 10 μg per Deciliter," *New England Journal of Medicine,* Vol. 348, No. 16 (April 17, 2003), pp. 1517–26.

Canton, J., and C. Allen, "A Microeconomic Model to Assess the Economic Impacts of the EU's New Chemicals Policy," Brussels: European Commission DG Enterprise, Nov. 2003.

Carlin, A., *The Grand Canyon Controversy: Lessons for Federal Cost-Benefit Practices* (Santa Monica, CA: RAND Corporation, 1967).

———, *The Grand Canyon Controversy, or How Reclamation Justifies the Unjustifiable* (RAND Corporation, 1967).

Carlin, A., and W. Hoehn, *Is the Marble Canyon Project Economically Justified?* (RAND Corporation, 1966).

———, *The Grand Canyon Controversy—1967: Further Economic Comparisons of Nuclear Alternatives* (RAND Corporation, 1967).

Carlin, P. S., and R. Sandy, "Estimating the Implicit Value of a Young Child's Life," *Southern Economic Journal*, Vol. 58, No. 1 (1991), pp. 186–202.

Casanova, I., "Clair C. Patterson (1922–1995), Discoverer of the Age of the Earth," *International Microbiology*, Vol. 1, No. 3 (1998), pp. 231–32.

Chan, D. K. Y., G. D. Mellick, W. T. Hung, and J. Woo, "Genetic and Environmental Risk Factors and Their Interactions for Parkinson's Disease in a Chinese Population," *Journal of Clinical Neuroscience*, Vol. 10, No. 3 (2003), pp. 313–15.

Cheminfo Services, *A Retrospective Evaluation of Control Measures for Chlorinated Substances (Case Studies of Ex-Ante/Ex-Post Socioeconomic Effects)*, Report to Environment Canada and Ontario Ministry of Energy, Science and Technology (2000).

Christman, K., "Vinyl Use in Building and Construction," Vinyl Material Council Newsletter (May 2003). www.aamanet.org/pdf_files/Council_News_pdfs/VMC_Newsletter_May_03.pdf.

Chynoweth, E., "Atrazine Gets Reprieve from European Commission," *Chemical Week*, July 22, 1992.

Clapp, R., G. Howe, and M. Jacobs Lefevre, "Environmental and Occupational Causes of Cancer: A Review of Recent Scientific Literature," report published by the Lowell Center for Sustainable Production, 2006.

Cohen, J., K. Duggar, G. Gray, and S. Kreindel, "Evaluation of the Potential for Bovine Spongiform Encephalopathy in the United States: Report to the U.S. Department of Agriculture," (Boston: Harvard Center for Risk Analysis [HCRA], original version 2001, revised version 2003).

Cohen, J., and G. Gray, "Comments on USDA Bovine Spongiform Encephalopathy (BSE) Surveillance Plan," (Boston: Harvard Center for Risk Analysis [HCRA], 2004).

Cohn, S. M., *Too Cheap to Meter: An Economic and Philosophical Analysis of the Nuclear Dream* (Albany, NY: State University of New York Press, 1997).

Cole, M., "U.S. Environmental Load Displacement: Examining Consumption, Regulations and the Role of NAFTA," *Ecological Economics*, Vol. 28 (2004), pp. 439–50.

Cole, P., D. Trichopoulos, H. Pastides, T. Starr, and J. S. Mandel, "Dioxin and Cancer: A Critical Review," *Regulatory Toxicology and Pharmacology*, Vol. 38 (2003), pp. 378–88.

Copeland, B. R., and M. S. Taylor, *Trade and the Environment: Theory and Evidence* (Princeton, NJ: Princeton University Press, 2003).

———, "Trade, Growth, and the Environment," *Journal of Economic Literature*, Vol. 42, No. 1 (2004), pp. 7–71.

Bibliography

Coursey, D., "Illinois without Atrazine: Who Pays?" (Harris School of Public Policy, University of Chicago, 2007).

Crain, W. M., and T. D. Hopkins, "The Impact of Regulatory Costs on Small Firms," U.S. Small Business Administration, Office of Advocacy, (2001). www.sba.gov/advo/research/rs207tot.pdf.

Curl, C. L., R. A. Fenske, J. C. Kissel, J. H. Shirai, T. F. Moate, W. Griffith, G. Coronado, and B. Thompson, "Evaluation of Take-Home Organophosphorus Pesticide Exposure among Agricultural Workers and Their Children," *Environmental Health Perspectives,* Vol. 110, No. 12 (2002), pp. A787–A792.

Davies, K., "How Much Do Environmental Diseases and Disabilities Cost?" *Northwest Public Health* (Fall/Winter 2005), pp. 1–3.

———, "Economic Costs of Diseases and Disabilities Attributable to Environmental Contaminants in Washington State," *EcoHealth Journal,* Vol. 3, No. 2 (June 2006), pp. 86–94.

Davis, D., *When Smoke Ran Like Water: Tales of Environmental Deception and the Battle against Pollution* (New York: Basic Books, 2002).

Davis, K. L., J. A. Yesavage, and P. A. Berger, "Possible Organophosphate-Induced Parkinsonism," *Journal of Nervous & Mental Disease,* Vol. 166 (1978), pp. 222–25.

DiGangi, J., "REACH and the Long Arm of the Chemical Industry." *Multinational Monitor,* Vol. 25, No. 9 (2004), pp. 20–25.

Doniger, D. D., "The Law and Policy of Toxic Substances Control" (Resources for the Future, 1978), reprinted in *Ecology Law Quarterly,* Vol. 7, No. 2 (1978), pp. 500–21.

Dyer, R. F., and V. H. Esch, "Polyvinyl Chloride Toxicity in Fires: Hydrogen Chloride Toxicity in Fire Fighters," *Journal of the American Medical Association,* Vol. 235, No. 4 (1976), pp. 393–97.

Earles, R., G. Ames, R. Balasubrahmanyam, and H. Born, "Organic and Low-Spray Apple Production," Appropriate Technology Transfer for Rural Areas, *Horticultural Production Guide* (Fayetteville, AR: National Sustainable Agriculture Information Service, 1999).

Ebbert, J. C., and S. S. Embrey, *Pesticides in Surface Water of the Yakima River Basin, Washington, 1999–2000—Their Occurrence and an Assessment of Factors Affecting Concentrations and Loads,* Water Resources Investigations Report 01-4211 (Portland, OR: U.S. Geological Survey, 2002).

Elkins, R., "Areawide Implementation of Mating Disruption in Pears Using Puffers," in *Pest Management Grants Final Report, Contract No. 98-0265* (Sacramento, CA: California Department of Pesticide Regulation, 2000), pp. 185–98.

Environment Canada, "A Technical and Socio-Economic Comparison of Options to Products Derived from the Chlor-Alkali Industry" (1997).

Eskenazi, B., A. Bradman, and R. Castorina, "Exposures of Children to Organophosphate Pesticides and Their Potential Adverse Health Effects," *Environmental Health Perspectives,* Vol. 107, Supplement 3 (June 1999), pp. 409–19.

European Commission, "Extended Impact Assessment of REACH Sec 1171/3," European Commission Directorate General on Enterprise and Industry (2003).

——, "Opinion of the Scientific Committee on Plants on Specific Questions from the Commission Concerning the Evaluation of Atrazine in the Context of Council Directive 91/414/EEC," (Directorate-General Health and Consumer Protection, Scientific Committee on Plants, 2003).

——, "Commission Decision of 10 March 2004 Concerning the Non-Inclusion of Atrazine in Annex I to Council Directive 91/414/EEC and the Withdrawal of Authorisations for Plant Protection Products Containing This Active Substance, 2004/248/EC," *Official Journal of the European Union* L78 (2004), pp. 53–55.

——, "Review Report for the Active Substance Acetamiprid," in *Commission Working Document SANCO/1392/2001–Final,* Directorate-General Health and Consumer Protection (Brussels: European Commission, 2004).

European Council, "Council Directive 80/778/EEC of 15 July 1980 Relating to the Quality of Water Intended for Human Consumption," *Official Journal of the European Union* L229 (1980), pp. 11–29.

——, "Council Directive of 15 July 1991 Concerning the Placing of Plant Protection Products on the Market, 91/414/EEC," *Official Journal of the European Communities* L 230 (1991).

——, "Council Directive 98/83/EC of 3 November 1998 on the Quality of Water Intended for Human Consumption," *Official Journal of the European Union* L330 (1998), pp. 32–54.

European Commission Directorate General for Agriculture and Rural Development, "Agriculture in the European Union: Statistical and Economic Information 2005," http://ec.europa.eu/comm/agriculture/agrista/2005/table_en/index.htm. 2006.

European Commission Directorate General for Health and Consumer Protection, "Report on the Monitoring and Testing of Ruminants for the Presence of Transmissible Spongiform Encephalopathy (TSE) in the EU in 2004," http://ec.europa.eu/comm/food/food/biosafety/bse/annual_report_tse2004_en.pdf.

European Environment Agency, *Late Lessons from Early Warnings: The Precautionary Principle 1896–2000* (Luxembourg: Office for Official Publications of the European Communities, 2001).

European Federation of Essential Oils, "Concerning the EU Proposal for a New Regulation on Chemicals (REACH)," *EFEO Position Paper* (Hamburg: European Federation of Essential Oils, 2005).

Faber, D., and E. J. Krieg, "Unequal Exposure to Ecological Hazards: Environmental Injustices in the Commonwealth of Massachusetts," *Environmental Health Perspectives,* Vol. 110, No. 2 (April 2002), pp. 277–88.

Fahs, M. C., S. B. Markowitz, E. Fischer, J. Shapiro, and P. J. Landrigan, "Health Costs of Occupational Disease in New York State," *American Journal of Industrial Medicine,* Vol. 16 (1989), pp. 437–49.

Bibliography

FAO/WHO, "Pesticide Residues in Food Report—2003," *FAO Plant Production and Protection Paper 176* (Geneva: Food and Agriculture Organization of the United Nations and World Health Organization, 2004).

———, "Acceptable Daily Intakes, Acute Reference Doses, Short-Term and Long-Term Dietary Intakes, Recommended Maximum Residue Limits and Supervised Trials, Median Residue Values Recorded by the 2005 Meeting" (paper presented at the Joint FAO/WHO Meeting on Pesticide Residues, Geneva, 20–29 Sept. 2005).

Fawcett, R. S., "Two Decades of Atrazine Yield Benefits Research," (Triazine Network, 2006).

Felsot, A. S., "Adios Azinphos-Methyl, Farewell Phosmet," *Agrichemical and Environmental News,* No. 191 (2002), pp. 1–11.

Fenske, R. A., J. C. Kissel, C. Lu, D. A. Kalman, N. J. Simcox, E. H. Allen, and M. C. Keifer, "Biologically Based Pesticide Dose Estimates for Children in an Agricultural Community," *Environmental Health Perspectives,* Vol. 108, No. 6 (2000), pp. 515–20.

Ferguson, N. M., "Estimation of the Basic Reproduction Number of BSE: The Intensity of Transmission in British Cattle," *Proceedings of the Royal Society B: Biological Sciences,* Vol. 266, No. 1414 (1999), pp. 23–32.

Food and Agriculture Organization of the United Nations (FAO), *World Markets for Organic Fruit and Vegetables—Opportunities for Developing Countries in the Production and Export of Organic Horticultural Products* (Rome: FAO Corporate Document Repository, 2001).

Foster D. Snell, Inc., *Economic Impact Studies of the Effects of Proposed OSHA Standards for Vinyl Chloride,* (New York, 1974).

Fox, J., and H. Hanawa Peterson. "Risks and Implications of Bovine Spongiform Encephalopathy for the United States: Insights from Other Countries." *Food Policy,* Vol. 29 (2004), pp. 45–60.

Gallagher, K., *Free Trade and the Environment: Mexico, NAFTA and Beyond* (Stanford, CA: Stanford University Press, 2004).

Gee, D., and M. Greenberg, "Asbestos: From 'Magic' to Malevolent Mineral," in European Environment Agency, *Late Lessons from Early Warnings: The Precautionary Principle 1896–2000* (Luxembourg: Office for Official Publications of the European Communities, 2001), pp. 52–63.

Ghemawat, P., and A. M. Spence, "Learning Curve Spillovers and Market Performance," *Quarterly Journal of Economics,* Vol. 100 Supplement (1985), pp. 839–52.

Gilboa, I., and D. Schmeidler, "Maxmin Expected Utility with Non-Unique Prior," *Journal of Mathematical Economics,* Vol. 18 (1989), pp. 141–53.

Giupponi, C., "The Substitution of Hazardous Molecules in Production Processes: The Atrazine Case Study in Italian Agriculture," (Milan: Fondazione Eni Enrico Mattei, 2001).

Goldman, L., and N. Tran, *Toxics and Poverty: The Impact of Toxic Substances on the Poor in Developing Countries* (Washington, DC: World Bank, 2002).

————, "Polluted Data," *American Prospect* Vol. 8 (November–December 1997).

————, *The Trade-off Myth: Fact and Fiction about Jobs and the Environment,* (Washington, DC: Island Press, 1999).

Gouveia-Vigeant, T., and J. Tickner, *Toxic Chemicals and Childhood Cancer: A Review of the Evidence,* (Lowell, MA: Lowell Center for Sustainable Production, May 2003).

Graham, J. D., "Risk Assessment and Cost-Benefit Analysis: Hearings before the Committee on Science, U.S. House of Representatives," (104th U.S. Congress, 1st Session 1124, 1995).

Gray, G. M., L. Saligman, and J. D. Graham, "The Demise of Lead in Gasoline," in *The Greening of Industry: A Risk Management Approach,* J. D. Graham and J. K. Hartwell, eds. (Cambridge, MA: Harvard University Press, 1997).

Grush, E. S., and C. S. Saunby, "Fatalities Associated with Crash-Induced Fuel Leakages and Fires," Reprinted in *The Ford Pinto Case: A Study in Applied Ethics, Business, and Technology,* D. Birsch and J. H. Fielder, eds. (Albany, NY: State University of New York Press, 1994).

Guerrero, P. F., "Pesticides: Improvements Needed to Ensure the Safety of Farmworkers and Their Children," (Washington, DC: General Accounting Office, 2000).

Hahn, R. W., and C. R. Sunstein, "A New Executive Order for Improving Federal Regulation? Deeper and Wider Cost-Benefit Analysis," *University of Pennsylvania Law Review,* Vol. 150, No. 5 (2002), 1499–1552.

Hamilton, J., D. Huppert, K. Boire, K. Casavant, L. Peters, J. Richards, A. Scott, and P. Sorensen, *River Economics: Evaluating Trade-Offs in Columbia River Basin Fish and Wildlife Programs and Policies,* (Portland, OR: Independent Economic Analysis Board of the Northwest Power Planning Council, 1999).

Hansen, S. F., "The Precautionary Principle and Unnecessary Precautionary Action," (Ph.D. thesis, Roskilde Unversity, Denmark, 2004).

Haq, G., P. D. Bailey, M. J. Chadwick, J. Forrester, J. Kuylenstierna, G. Leach, D. Villagrasa, M. Fergusson, I. Skinne, and S. Oberthur, "Determining the Costs to Industry of Environmental Regulation," *European Environment,* Vol. 11 (2001), pp. 125–39.

Harrington, W., R. D. Morgenstern, and P. Nelson., "On the Accuracy of Regulatory Cost Estimates," *Journal of Policy Analysis and Management,* Vol. 19 (2000), pp. 297–322.

Harvie, J., with T. Lent, "PVC-Free Pipe Purchasers' Report," www.healthybuilding.net/pvc/pipes_report.html.

Hayes, T. B., "There Is No Denying This: Defusing the Confusion about Atrazine," *BioScience,* Vol. 54 No. 12 (2004), pp. 1138–49.

Heinzerling, L., "Regulatory Costs of Mythic Proportions," *Yale Law Journal,* Vol. 107 (1998), pp. 1981–2070.

————, "Discounting Life," *Yale Law Journal,* Vol. 108 (1999), pp. 1911–15.

Bibliography

———, "Discounting Our Future," *Land & Water Law Review,* Vol. 34 (1999).

———, "The Rights of Statistical People," *Harvard Environmental Law Review,* Vol. 24 (2000), pp. 189–207.

———, "Five-Hundred Life-Saving Interventions and Their Misuse in the Debate over Regulatory Reform," *Risk* Vol. 13 (2002).

Heinzerling, L., and F. Ackerman, "The Humbugs of the Anti-Regulatory Movement," *Cornell Law Review,* Vol. 87 (2002), pp. 648–70.

Henson, S., and R. Loader, "Barriers to Agricultural Exports from Developing Countries: The Role of Sanitary and Phytosanitary Requirements," *World Development,* Vol. 29, No. 1 (2001), pp. 85–102.

Herishanu, Y. O., E. Kordysh, and J. R. Goldsmith, "A Case-Referent Study of Extrapyramidal Signs (Preparkinsonism) in Rural Communities of Israel," *Canadian Journal of Neurological Sciences,* Vol. 25, No. 2 (1998), 127–33.

Hodges, H., "Falling Prices: Cost of Complying with Environmental Regulations Almost Always Less than Advertised," *Economic Policy Institute Briefing Paper 69* (1997), pp. 1–15.

Hoehn, W., *What the Parsons Study Really Says about Nuclear Power Economics: The Grand Canyon Controversy, Round?* (Santa Monica, CA: RAND Corporation, 1967).

Holland, M., *The European Union and the Third World* (New York: Palgrave, 2002).

Hughes, A., "Retailers, Knowledges, and Changing Commodity Networks: The Case of the Cut Flower Trade," *Geoforum,* Vol. 31 (2000), pp. 175–90.

Huppert, D. D., "Snake River Salmon Recovery: Quantifying the Costs," *Contemporary Economic Policy,* Vol. 17, No. 4 (1999), pp. 476–91.

Infante, P. F., "Carcinogenic, Mutagenic, and Teratogenic Risks Associated with Vinyl Chloride," *Mutation Research,* Vol. 41 (1976), pp. 131–34.

Institute of Medicine, "Costs of Environment-Related Health Effects: A Plan for Continuing Study," (Washington, DC: National Academy Press, 1981).

Intergovernmental Panel on Climate Change (IPCC), *Climate Change 2001: Mitigation* (Cambridge, U.K.: Cambridge University Press, 2001).

Jaakkola, J. J. K., L. Oie, P. Nafstad, G. Botten, S. O. Samuelsen, and P. Magnus, "Interior Surface Materials in the Home and the Development of Bronchial Obstruction in Young Children in Oslo, Norway," *American Journal of Public Health,* Vol. 89, No. 2 (Feb. 1999), pp. 188–92.

Jacob, M., and T. Hellstrom, "Policy Understanding of Science, Public Trust and the BSE-CJD Crisis," *Journal of Hazardous Materials,* Vol. 78, No. 1–3 (2000), pp. 303–17.

Jaffe, A. B., S. R. Peterson, P. R. Portney, and R. N. Stavins, "Environmental Regulation and the Competitiveness of U.S. Manufacturing," *Journal of Economic Literature,* Vol. 33, No. 1 (1995), pp. 132–63.

James, H. S., "Estimating OSHA Compliance Costs," *Policy Sciences,* Vol. 31 (1998), pp. 321–41.

Jayadevappa, R. J., and S. Chhatre, "International Trade and Environmental Quality: A Survey," *Ecological Economics,* Vol. 32, No. 2 (2000), pp. 175–94.

Jenkins, R., J. Barton, A. Bartzokas, J. Hesselberg, and H. Merete, *Environmental Regulation in the New Global Economy: The Impact on Industry and Competitiveness* (Cheltenham, U.K.: Edward Elgar, 2002).

Johnson, B. C., B. G. Young, and J. L. Matthews, "Effect of Postemergence Application Rate and Timing of Mesotrione on Corn (*Zea mays*) Response and Weed Control," *Weed Technology,* Vol. 16 (2002), pp. 414–20.

Jones, A., *The Potential Impact of REACH on Exports of Biotrade Products to the European Union* (Geneva: UNCTAD Biotrade Initiative-Biotrade Facilitation Programme, 2005).

Jorgenson, D. W., and P. J. Wilcoxen, "Environmental Regulations and U.S. Economic Growth," *RAND Journal of Economics,* Vol. 21, No. 2 (1990), pp. 314–40.

Kahn, M. E., and Y. Yoshino, "Testing for Pollution Havens Inside and Outside of Regional Trading Blocs," *Advances in Economic Analysis & Policy,* Vol. 4, No. 2 (2004).

Khan, S. R., ed., *Trade and Environment: Difficult Policy Choices at the Interface* (London: Zed Books, 2002).

Kelsey, D., "Choice under Partial Uncertainty," *International Economic Review,* Vol. 34 (1993), pp. 297–308.

Kielhorn, J., C. Melber, U. Wahnschaffe, A. Aitio, and I. Mangelsdorf, "Vinyl Chloride: Still a Cause for Concern," *Environmental Health Perspectives,* Vol. 108, No. 7 (2000), pp. 579–88.

Kitman, J. L., "The Secret History of Lead," *The Nation,* March 20, 2000.

Klepper, S., and E. Graddy, "The Evolution of New Industries and the Determinants of Market Structure," *The RAND Journal of Economics,* Vol. 21, No. 1 (spring 1990), pp. 27–44.

Korfmacher, K. S., "Long-Term Costs of Lead Poisoning: How Much Can New York Save by Stopping Lead?" (University of Rochester, Rochester, NY, 2003). http://afhh.org/aa/aa_state%20_local_lead_costs_NYrep.pdf.

KPMG, "REACH—Further Work on Impact Assessment, a Case Study Approach, Final Report" (Amsterdam: KPMG Business Advisory Services, 2005).

Kuchler, F., and E. Golan, *Assigning Values to Life: Comparing Methods for Valuing Health Risks,* Economic Research Service, Agricultural Economic Report No. 784 (U.S. Department of Agriculture, 1999).

Ladebauche, P., R. Nicolosi, S. Reece, K. Saucedo, B. Volicer, and T. Richards, "Asthma in Head Start Children: Prevalence, Risk Factors, and Health Care Utilization," *Pediatric Nursing,* Vol. 27, No. 4 (July 2001), pp. 396–99.

Lakshminarayan, P. G., A. Bouzaher, and J. F. Shogren, "Atrazine and Water Quality: An Evaluation of Alternative Policy Options," *Journal of Environmental Management,* Vol. 48 (1996), pp. 111–26.

Landrigan, P. J., C. B. Schechter, J. M. Lipton, M. C. Fahs, and J. Schwartz, "Environmental Pollutants and Disease in American Children: Estimates of Morbidity,

Bibliography

Mortality, and Costs for Lead Poisoning, Asthma, Cancer, and Developmental Disabilities," *Environmental Health Perspectives,* Vol. 110, No. 7 (July 2002), pp. 721–28.

Leigh, J. P., S. Markowitz, M. Fahs, and P. Landrigan, "Costs of Occupational Injuries and Illnesses," *Archives of Internal Medicine,* Vol. 157 (1997), pp. 1557–68.

Levin, R., "Lead in Drinking Water," in *Economic Analyses at EPA: Assessing Regulatory Impact,* R. D. Morgenstern, ed. (Washington, DC: Resources for the Future, 1997).

Lewis, J., "Lead Poisoning: A Historical Perspective," *EPA Journal* (May 1985).

Lin, W., P. C. Westcott, R. Skinner, S. Sanford, and D. G. De La Torre Ugarte, "Supply Response under the 1996 Farm Act and Implications for the U.S. Field Crops Sector," (Economic Research Service, U.S. Department of Agriculture, 2000).

Linak, E., with K. Yagi, "Polyvinyl Chloride (PVC) Resins," Chemical Economics Handbook Marketing Research Report (Menlo Park, CA: SRI International, Sept. 2003).

Lindell, F., "Navy Food Service: Improving Quality of Life for Sailors," *Navy Supply Corps Newsletter* (March/April 2000). www.seabeecook.com/today/news/cook 0091.htm.

Loewenherz, C., R. A. Fenske, N. J. Simcox, G. Bellamy, and D. Kalman, "Biological Monitoring of Organophosphorus Pesticide Exposure among Children of Agricultural Workers in Central Washington State," *Environmental Health Perspectives,* Vol. 105, No. 12 (1997), pp. 1344–53.

Loomis, J. B., and D. S. White, "Economic Benefits of Rare and Endangered Species: Summary and Meta-Analysis," *Ecological Economics,* Vol. 18 (1996), pp. 197–206.

Lutter, R., *Valuing Children's Health: A Reassessment of the Benefits of Lower Lead Levels,* Working Paper 00-02 (Washington, DC: AEI-Brookings Joint Center for Regulatory Studies, 2000).

Madagascar Consulate, Essential Oils, in *Madagascar Consulate General,* Madagascar Consulate General, www.madagascarconsulate.org.za/oils.html.

Maltoni, C., "Two Cases of Liver Angiosarcoma among PVC Extruders of an Italian Factory Producing PVC Bags and Other Containers," *American Journal of Industrial Medicine,* Vol. 5 (1984), pp. 297–302.

Markowitz, G., and D. Rosner, *Deceit and Denial: The Deadly Politics of Industrial Pollution* (Berkeley, CA: University of California Press, 2002).

Markowitz, J. S., E. M. Gutterman, S. Schwartz, B. Link, and S. M. Gorman, "Acute Health Effects among Firefighters Exposed to a Polyvinyl Chloride (PVC) Fire," *American Journal of Epidemiology,* Vol. 129, No. 5 (1989), pp. 1023–31.

Massachusetts Department of Education, Information Services, "Special Education Enrollment by Age/Disability," Dec. 1, 2001.

Massachusetts Department of Public Health, Massachusetts Community Health Information Profiles (MassCHIP), 2003.

Massachusetts Department of Public Health, Bureau of Environmental Health Assessment, Childhood Lead Poisoning Prevention Program, Screening and Incidence Statistics, 1994–2002.

Massachusetts Governor's Office, *The Governor's Budget Recommendations, Fiscal Year 2007,* (Commonwealth of Massachusetts, 2006).

McCurdy, S. A., M. E. Hansen, C. P. Weisskopf, R. L. Lopez, F. Schneider, J. Spencer, J. R. Sanborn, R. I. Krieger, B. W. Wilson, D. F. Goldsmith, and M. B. Schenker, "Assessment of Azinphosmethyl Exposure in California Peach Harvest Workers," *Archives of Environmental Health,* Vol. 49, No. 4 (1994).

McGarity, T. O., "Federal Regulation of Mad Cow Disease Risks," *Administrative Law Review,* Vol. 57, No. 2 (2005), pp. 289–410.

McGarity, T. O., and R. Ruttenberg, "Counting the Cost of Health, Safety and Environmental Regulation," *Texas Law Review,* Vol. 80 (2002), pp. 1997–2058.

McGarity, T. O., and S. A. Shapiro, *Workers at Risk: The Failed Promise of the Occupational Safety and Health Administration* (Westport, CT: Praeger, 1993).

McGill, K., C. A. Sorkness, C. Ferguson-Page, J. E. Gern, T. C. Havighurst, B. Knipfer, R. F. Lemanske Jr., and W. W. Busse, "Asthma in Non–Inner City Head Start Children," *Pediatrics,* Vol. 102 (1998), pp. 77–83.

Mendeloff, J. M., *The Dilemma of Toxic Substance Regulation: How Overregulation Causes Underregulation at OSHA* (Cambridge, MA: MIT Press, 1998).

Mercer Management Consulting, "Study of the Impact of the Future Chemicals Policy: Final Report, French Union of Chemical Industries (UIC)" (2004). www.uic.fr/us/pdf/Final%20Mercerstudy%20%208%204%202004.pdf.

Moore, C. F., *Silent Scourge: Children, Pollution, and Why Scientists Disagree* (Oxford: Oxford University Press, 2003).

Morgenstern, R. D., ed., *Economic Analyses at EPA: Assessing Regulatory Impact* (Washington, DC: Resources for the Future, 1997).

Morrall, J. F., III, "A Review of the Record," *Regulation,* Vol. 10 (1986).

Moses, M., "Chronic Neurological Effects of Pesticides: Summary of Selected Studies," in *Human Health Studies* (San Francisco, CA: Pesticide Education Center, 2002).

Nadal, A., and T. Wise, "The Environmental Costs of Agriculture Trade Liberalization: Mexico-U.S. Maize Trade under NAFTA," in *GDAE Working Group Discussion Paper* (Tufts University, Medford, MA: Global Development and Environment Institute, 2004).

Nadvi, K., "The Cost of Compliance: Global Standards for Small-Scale Firms and Workers," *IDS Policy Briefing,* Vol. 18 (May 2003), pp. 1–3.

Nash, H., "Other Arguments against Dams in Grand Canyon and Why Grand Canyon Should Not Be Dammed," *Sierra Club Bulletin,* Vol. 51, No. 5 (1966).

National Cancer Institute, Surveillance, Epidemiology and End Results (SEER), Cancer Statistics Review, 1975–2000.

Needleman, H. L., "History of Lead Poisoning in the World," www.leadpoison.net/general/history.htm (1999).

Needleman, H. L., C. Gunnoe, A. Leviton, R. Reed, H. Peresie, C. Maher, and P. Barrett, "Deficits in Psychologic and Classroom Performance of Children with Elevated Dentine Lead Levels," *New England Journal of Medicine,* Vol. 300 (1979).

Bibliography

Neumayer, E., *Greening Trade and Investment* (Sterling, VA: Earthscan Publications Ltd, 2001).

Nichols, A. L., "Lead in Gasoline," in *Economic Analyses at EPA: Assessing Regulatory Impact*, R. D. Morgenstern, ed. (Washington, DC: Resources for the Future, 1997).

Nordbeck, R., and M. Faust, "European Chemicals Regulation and Its Effect on Innovation: An Assessment of the EU's White Paper on the Strategy for a Future Chemicals Policy," *European Environment*, Vol. 13, No. 2 (2003), pp. 79–99.

Olsen, D., J. Richards, and R. D. Scott., "Existence and Sport Values for Doubling the Size of Columbia River Basin Salmon and Steelhead Runs," *Rivers*, Vol. 2, No. 1 (1991), pp. 44–56.

Olson, E., "The Quiet Shift of Power: Office of Management and Budget Supervision of Environmental Protection Agency Rulemaking under Executive Order 12291," *Virginia Journal of Natural Resources Law*, Vol. 4 (1984), pp. 1–80.

Patterson, C., "Contaminated and Natural Lead Environments of Man," in *Archives of Environmental Health* Vol. 11, pp. 344–60 (1965).

Pearce, D. W., and P. Kondouri, "The Social Cost of Chemicals: The Cost and Benefits of Future Chemicals Policy in the European Union (2003), World Wildlife Fund-U.K. http://assets.panda.org/downloads/1654reachcbafindoc.pdf.

Pedersen, F., L. Samsoe-Peterson, K. Gustavson, L. Hoglund, P. Koundouri, and D. Pearce, "The Impact of REACH on the Environment and Human Health," (Report by DHI, Water and Environment for the European Commission, Directorate General Environment, 2005).

Percival, R. V., C. H. Schroeder, A. S. Miller, and J. P. Leape, *Environmental Regulation: Law, Science, and Policy* (New York: Aspen Publishers, 2003).

Perera, F., S. M. Illman, P. L. Kinney, R. M. Whyatt, E. A. Kelvin, P. Shepard, D. Evans, M. Fullilove, J. Ford, R. L. Miller, I. H. Meyer, and V. A. Rauh, "The Challenge of Preventing Environmentally Related Disease in Young Children: Community-Based Research in New York City," *Environmental Health Perspectives*, Vol. 110, No. 2 (Feb. 2002), pp. 197–204.

Pickvance, S., J. Karnon, J. Peters, and K. El-Arifi, "The Impact of REACH on Occupational Health, with a Focus on Skin and Respiratory Diseases" (University of Sheffield, U.K.: Report prepared for the European Trade Union Institute for Research, Education, and Health and Safety, 2005).

Pirastu, R., P. Comba, A. Reggiani, V. Foa, A. Masina, and C. Maltoni, "Mortality from Liver Disease among Italian Vinyl Chloride Monomer/Polyvinyl Chloride Manufacturers," *American Journal of Industrial Medicine*, Vol. 17 (1990), pp. 155–61.

Popkin, B. M., D. V. Barclay, and S. J. Nielsen, "Water and Food Consumption Patterns of U.S. Adults from 1999 to 2001," *Obesity Research*, Vol. 13, No. 12 (2005), pp. 2146–52.

Porter, M. C., and C. van der Linde, "Toward a New Conception of the Environment-Competitiveness Relationship," *Journal of Economic Perspectives*, Vol. 9, No. 4 (1995), pp. 97–118.

Portier, C., "Risk Ranges for Various Endpoints Following Exposure to 2,3,7,8-TCDD," *Food Additives and Contaminants,* Vol. 17 (2000), pp. 335–46.

Prüss-Üstün, A., and C. Corvalán, *Preventing Disease through Healthy Environments: Towards an Estimate of the Environmental Burden of Disease* (Geneva: World Health Organization, 2006).

Purchase, I. F. H., J. Stafford, and G. M. Paddle, "Vinyl Chloride: An Assessment of the Risk of Occupational Exposure," *Food & Chemical Toxicology,* Vol. 25 (1987), pp. 187–202.

Reganold, J. P., J. D. Glover, P. K. Andrews, and H. R. Hinman, "Sustainability of Three Apple Production Systems," *Nature,* Vol. 410, No. 6831 (2001), pp. 926–30.

Rego, A., and L. Roley, "In-Use Barrier Integrity of Gloves: Latex and Nitrile Superior to Vinyl," *American Journal of Infection Control,* Vol. 27, No. 5 (Oct. 1999), pp. 405–10.

Reisner, M., *Cadillac Desert: The American West and Its Disappearing Water* (New York: Viking-Penguin, 1986).

Republic of South Africa, Chamber of Mines, "The Potential Impact of the European Union's Draft Legislation, REACH, on the Social and Economic Development of Sub-Saharan Africa," (Johannesburg: Economic Advisory Unit, Chamber of Mines of South Africa, 2005).

Republic of South Africa, Department of Trade and Industry, "Sector Development Strategy: Chemicals, Version 3.6," 2005.

Research Triangle Institute, "Review of the Potential for Bovine Spongiform Encephalopathy in the United States, Conducted by the Harvard Center for Risk Analysis," 2002.

Ribaudo, M. O., and A. Bouzaher, "Atrazine: Environmental Characteristics and Economics of Management," (Washington DC: USDA Economic Research Service, 1994).

Ribaudo, M. O., and T. M. Hurley, "Economic and Environmental Effects Associated with Reducing the Use of Atrazine: An Example of Cross-Disciplinary Research," *Journal of Agricultural and Applied Economics,* Vol. 29, No. 1 (1997), pp. 87–97.

Richardson, H. S., "The Stupidity of the Cost-Benefit Standard," *Journal of Legal Studies,* Vol. 29 (2000), pp. 971–1003.

Risk & Policy Analysts, Ltd., "Assessment of the Impact of the New Chemicals Policy on Occupational Health," (Report prepared for the European Commission, Directorate-General Environment, 2003).

Risk & Policy Analysts, Ltd. and Statistics Sweden, *Assessment of the Business Impact of New Regulations in the Chemicals Sector,* Prepared for the European Commission, Directorate-General Enterprise, June 2002. http://europa.eu.int/comm/enterprise/chemicals/chempol/bia/bia_report_06-2002.pdf.

Robins, N., "Steering EU Development Co-Operation Towards Sustainability: The Case of the Lomé Convention," *European Environment,* Vol. 6, No. 1 (1998), pp. 1–5.

Bibliography

Ruckelshaus, W. D., "Science, Risk, and Public Policy," *Science,* Vol. 221 (1983), pp. 1026–28.

Ruhm, C. J., "Are Recessions Good for Your Health?" *Quarterly Journal of Economics* (2000), pp. 617–50.

Sagoff, M., *The Economy of the Earth: Philosophy, Law, and the Environment* (Cambridge, U.K.: Cambridge University Press, 1990).

Sass, J. B., and A. Colangelo, "European Union Bans Atrazine, While the United States Negotiates Continued Use," *International Journal of Occupational and Environmental Health,* Vol. 12 (2006), pp. 260–67.

Savage, E. P., T. J. Keefe, L. M. Mounce, R. K. Heaton, J. A. Lewis, and P. J. Burcar, "Chronic Neurological Sequelae of Acute Organophosphate Pesticide Poisoning," *Archives of Environmental Health,* Vol. 43, No. 1 (1988), pp. 38–45.

Schecter, A., L. Birnbaum, J. J. Ryan, and J. D. Constable, "Dioxins: An Overview," Environmental Research, Vol. 101 (2006), pp. 419–28.

Schettler, T., G. Solomon, M. Valenti, and A. Huddle, *Generations at Risk: Reproductive Health and the Environment* (Cambridge, MA: MIT Press, 1999).

Schettler, T., J. Stein, M. Valenti, and D. Wallinga, *In Harm's Way: Toxic Threats to Child Development* (Cambridge, MA: Greater Boston Physicians for Social Responsibility, 2000).

Schlosser, Eric, *Fast Food Nation: The Dark Side of the All-American Meal* (New York: Houghton Mifflin, 2001).

Schörling, I., and G. Lind, "REACH—The Only Planet Guide to the Secrets of Chemicals Policy in the EU, What Happened and Why?" Brussels: The Greens/European Free Alliance in the European Parliament, April 2004.

Schuler, K., S. Nordbye, S. Yamin, and C. Ziebold, "The Price of Pollution: Cost Estimates of Environment-Related Childhood Disease in Minnesota," Report published by the Minnesota Center for Environmental Advocacy and the Institute for Agriculture and Trade Policy, June 2006.

Scientific Advisory Committee for Cholinesterase Monitoring, "Cholinesterase Monitoring of Pesticide Handlers in Agriculture: 2004–2006," (Olympia, WA: Washington State Department of Labor and Industries, 2006).

Seidler, A., W. Hellenbrand, B.-P. Robra, P. Vieregge, P. Nischan, J. Joerg, W. H. Oertel, G. Ulm, and E. Schneider, "Possible Environmental, Occupational, and Other Etiologic Factors for Parkinson's Disease: A Case-Control Study in Germany," *Neurology,* Vol. 46 (1996), pp. 1275–84.

Sen, A., "The Discipline of Cost-Benefit Analysis," *Journal of Legal Studies,* Vol. 29 (2000).

Seong, S. K., and J. Mendeloff, "Assessing the Accuracy of OSHA's Projections of the Benefits of New Safety Standards," *American Journal of Industrial Medicine,* Vol. 45 (2004), pp. 313–28.

Setbon, M., J. Raude, C. Fischler, and A. Flahault, "Risk Perception of The 'Mad Cow

Disease' in France: Determinants and Consequences" *Risk Analysis,* Vol. 25, No. 4 (2005), pp. 813–26.

Shah, N., "OMB Official Highlights EPA Problems in Assessing Benefits of Air Rules," *Inside EPA* (June 18, 2004).

Smith, K., "Choice Cuts," *The American Prospect On-Line* (2004), www.prospect.org/web/page.ww?section=root&name=ViewWeb&articleId=7696.

Smith, V. K., and L. L. Osborne, "Do Contingent Valuation Estimates Pass a 'Scope' Test? A Meta-Analysis," *Journal of Environmental Economics & Management,* Vol. 31 (1996), pp. 287–301.

Spence, A. M., "Investment Strategy and Growth in a New Market," *The Bell Journal of Economics,* Vol. 10, No.1 (Spring 1979), pp. 1–19.

Spitz, P. H., *Petrochemicals: The Rise of an Industry* (New York: John Wiley and Sons, 1988).

Steenland, K., P. Bertazzi, A. Baccarelli, and M. Kogevinas, "Dioxin Revisited: Developments since the 1997 IARC Classification of Dioxin as a Human Carcinogen," *Environmental Health Perspectives,* Vol. 112, No. 13. (Sept. 2004), pp. 1265–68.

Steenland, K., J. Deddens, and L. Piacitelli, "Risk Assessment for 2,3,7,8-Tetrachlorodibenzo-*p*-Dioxin (TCDD) Based on an Epidemiologic Study," *American Journal of Epidemiology,* Vol. 154 (2001), pp. 451–58.

Steenland, K., B. Jenkins, R. G. Ames, M. O'Malley, D. Chrislip, and J. Russo, "Chronic Neurological Sequelae to Organophosphate Pesticide Poisoning," *American Journal of Public Health,* Vol. 84, No. 5 (1994), pp. 731–36.

Stefanak, M., J. Diorio, and L. Frisch, "Costs of Child Lead Poisoning to Taxpayers in Mahoning County, Ohio," *Public Health Reports,* Vol. 120 (2005), pp. 311–15.

Stephenson, D. O., IV, J. A. Bond, E. R. Walker, M. T. Bararpour, and L. R. Oliver, "Evaluation of Mesotrione in Mississippi Delta Corn Production," *Weed Technology,* Vol. 18 (2004), pp. 1111–16.

Stewart, R. B., "A New Generation of Environmental Regulation?" *Capital University Law Review,* Vol. 29, No. 45 (2001), pp. 21–182.

Sunstein, C. R., "Preferences and Politics," *Philosophy & Public Affairs,* Vol. 20, No. 1 (1991), pp. 3–34.

———, "Cognition and Cost-Benefit Analysis," *Journal of Legal Studies,* Vol. 29, No. 2 (2000), pp. 1059–103.

———, "The Arithmetic of Arsenic," *Georgetown Law Journal,* Vol. 90 (2002), pp. 2255–309.

———, "In Praise of Numbers: A Reply," *Georgetown Law Journal,* Vol. 90 (2002), pp. 2379–85.

Swan, S. H., R. L. Kruse, F. Liu, D. B. Barr, E. Z. Drobnis, J. B. Redmon, C. Wang, C. Brazil, J. W. Overstreet, and the Study for Future Families Research Group, "Semen Quality in Relation to Biomarkers of Pesticide Exposure," *Environmental Health Perspectives,* Vol. 111, No. 12 (2003), pp. 1478–84.

Bibliography

Swanson, T., and M. Vighi, eds., *Regulating Chemical Accumulation in the Environment* (Cambridge, U.K.: Cambridge University Press, 1998).

Swezey, S. L., J. Rider, M. R. Werner, M. Buchanan, J. Allison, and S. R. Gliessman, "Granny Smith Conversions to Organic Show Early Success," *California Agriculture,* Vol. 48, No. 6 (1994), pp. 36–44.

Swinton, S. M., D. W. Lybecker, and R. P. King, "The Effect of Local Triazine Restriction Policies on Recommended Weed Management in Corn," *Review of Agricultural Economics,* Vol. 17 (1995), pp. 351–67.

Tapia Granados, J. A., "Increasing Mortality during the Expansions of the U.S. Economy, 1900–1996," *International Journal of Epidemiology,* Vol. 34 (2005), pp. 1194–202.

———, "Response: On Economic Growth, Business Fluctuations, and Health Progress," *International Journal of Epidemiology,* Vol. 34 (2005), pp. 1226–33.

Tengs, T. O., M. E. Adams, J. S. Pliskin, D. Gelb Safran, J. E. Siegel, M. C. Weinstein, and J. D. Graham, "Five-Hundred Life-Saving Interventions and Their Cost-Effectiveness," *Risk Analysis,* Vol. 15 (1995), pp. 369–90.

Tengs, T. O., and J. D. Graham, "The Opportunity Costs of Haphazard Social Investments in LifeSaving," in *Risks, Costs, and Lives Saved: Getting Better Results from Regulation,* R. W. Hahn, ed. (Oxford: Oxford University Press, 1996).

Tewari, M., and P. Pillari, "Global Standards and the Dynamics of Environmental Compliance in India's Leather Industry," *Oxford Development Studies,* Vol. 33, No. 2 (2005), pp. 245–67.

Thornton, J., *Pandora's Poison: Chlorine, Health, and a New Environmental Strategy,* (Cambridge, MA: MIT Press, 2000).

U.K. Department of Environment, Food and Rural Affairs (DEFRA), *Consolidated Listing of Maximum Residue Level (MRL) Legislation,* (2006).

———, *Potential and Agreed Changes to Maximum Residue Levels (MRLs),* (2006), www.pesticides.gov.uk/food_industry.asp?id=546.

U.S. Congress Office of Technology Assessment (OTA), Gauging Control Technology and Regulatory Impacts in Occupational Safety and Health: An Appraisal of OSHA's Analytic Approach (Washington, DC: U.S. Government Printing Office, Sept. 1995).

U.S. Department of Agriculture (USDA), "Japan Establishes MRL on Novaluron," in *GAIN Report No. JA3080,* USDA Foreign Agricultural Service (Washington, DC: U.S. Department of Agriculture, 2003).

———, "Statistical Highlights of U.S. Agriculture 2004 & 2005," www.usda.gov/nass/pubs/stathigh/2005/2005Stat.PDF.

———, Animal and Plant Health Inspection Service (APHIS), Factsheet, "USDA's BSE Surveillance Efforts," (July 2006), www.aphis.usda.gov/publications/animal_health/content/printable_version/fs_BSE_ongoing_vs.pdf.

———, "An Estimate of the Prevalence of BSE in the United States," (Washington, DC: Animal and Plant Health Inspection Service, USDA, 2006).

———, Economic Research Service, "Background Statistics: U.S. Beef and Cattle Industry," (2006), www.ers.usda.gov/news/BSECoverage.htm.

———, Foreign Agriculture Service (FAS), FASonline: U.S. Trade Internet System. Washington, DC, U.S. Department of Agriculture, Foreign Agriculture Service, 2006.

U.S. Department of Health and Human Services, Agency for Toxic Substances and Disease Registry (ATSDR), *Toxicological Profile for Vinyl Chloride* (Sept. 1997), www.atsdr.cdc.gov/toxprofiles/tp20.html.

———, National Institute for Occupational Safety and Health, *Worker Health Chartbook, 2000.*

———, National Toxicology Program and Center for the Evaluation of Risks to Human Reproduction, *NTP-CERHR Expert Panel Report on Di(2-ethylhexyl) phthalate* (Oct. 2000), http://cerhr.niehs.nih.gov/news/phthalates/DEHP -final.pdf.

———, Public Health Service, National Toxicology Program, *Report on Carcinogens,* (10th ed., 2002), http://ehp.niehs.nih.gov/roc/toc10.html.

U.S. Diplomatic Mission to the European Union, "REACH Requires further Improvements, According to EU Trading Partners," (Brussels: 2006).

U.S. Environmental Protection Agency, *The Benefits and Costs of the Clean Air Act, 1970 to 1990,* (Washington, DC: U.S. Environmental Protection Agency, 1997).

———, "Arsenic in Drinking Water Rule: Economic Analysis," (Washington, DC: U.S. Environmental Protection Agency, 2000).

———, "Draft Dioxin Reassessment," Part I, Volume 3, (Washington, DC: U.S. Environmental Protection Agency, 2000).

———, "Dioxin Reassessment—An SAB Review of the Office of Research and Development's Reassessment of Dioxin," (Washington, DC: U.S. Environmental Protection Agency, 2001).

———, "Interim Reregistration Eligibility Decision for Azinphos-Methyl," (Washington, DC: U.S. Environmental Protection Agency, 2001).

———, "Revised Occupational Handler Exposure Assessment and Recommendations for the Reregistration Eligibility Decision Document for Azinphos Methyl," (Washington, DC: U.S. Environmental Protection Agency, 2001).

———, EPA Pesticide Fact Sheet: Mesotrione, (Washington, DC: U.S. Environmental Protection Agency, June 4, 2001).

———, "Assessment of Potential Mitigation Measures for Atrazine," Biological and Economic Analysis Division (Washington, DC: U.S. Environmental Protection Agency, 2002).

———, "Vinyl Chloride Hazard Summary" (Washington, DC: U.S. Environmental Protection Agency, 2002).

———, *America's Children and the Environment: Measures of Contaminants, Body Burdens, and Illnesses* (Washington, DC: U.S. Environmental Protection Agency, Feb. 2003).

Bibliography

———, *The Cost of Illness Handbook (COI)*. www.epa.gov/oppt/coi.

———, "2005 Grower Impact Assessment of Azinphos-Methyl Use on Apples" (Washington, DC: U.S. Environmental Protection Agency, 2005).

———, "2005 Grower Impact Assessment for Azinphos-Methyl Use on Pears" (Washington, DC: U.S. Environmental Protection Agency, 2005).

———, *Azinphos-Methyl Summary* (Washington, DC: U.S. Environmental Protection Agency, 2006).

———, *Endangered Species Effects Determinations and Consultations; an Interim Process for Public Input* (Washington, DC: U.S. Environmental Protection Agency, 2006).

———, *Fact Sheet—Settlement Agreement Regarding Azinphos-Methyl and Phosmet* (Washington, DC: U.S. Environmental Protection Agency, 2006).

———, "Final Decisions for the Remaining Uses of Azinphos-Methyl," Pesticides Office of Prevention, and Toxic Substances (Washington, DC: U.S. Environmental Protection Agency, 2006).

———, *Phosmet Summary* (Washington, DC: U.S. Environmental Protection Agency, 2006).

———, "Proposed Decisions for the Remaining Uses of Azinphos-Methyl," (Washington, DC: U.S. Environmental Protection Agency, 2006).

———, "Proposed Decisions on Nine Phosmet Restricted Entry Intervals," (Washington, DC: U.S. Environmental Protection Agency, 2006).

U.S. General Accounting Office "Mad Cow Disease: Improvements in the Animal Feed Ban and Other Regulatory Areas Would Strengthen Other U.S. Prevention Efforts," (Washington, DC: 2002).

U.S. House of Representatives Committee on Government Reform, "A Special Interest Case Study: The Chemical Industry, the Bush Administration, and European Efforts to Regulate Chemicals; Prepared for Representative Henry Waxman," (2004).

U.S. Office of Management and Budget, Office of Information and Regulatory Affairs (OIRA), *Informing Regulatory Decisions: 2004 Draft Report to Congress on the Costs and Benefits of Federal Regulations and Unfunded Mandates on State, Local, and Tribal Entities* (2004), www.whitehouse.gov/omb/inforeg/regpol-reports_congress .html.

———, *Progress in Regulatory Reform: 2004 Report to Congress on the Costs and Benefits of Federal Regulations and Unfunded Mandates on State, Local, and Tribal Entities* (2004), www.whitehouse.gov/omb/inforeg/2004_cb_final.pdf.

———, *Validating Regulatory Analysis: 2005 Report to Congress on the Costs and Benefits of Federal Regulations and Unfunded Mandates on State, Local, and Tribal Entities* (2005), www.whitehouse.gov/omb/inforeg/2005_cb/final_2005_cb_report .pdf.

Van Der Grijp, N. M., T. Marsden, and J. S. Barbosa Cavalcanti, "European Retailers as Agents of Change towards Sustainability: The Case of Fruit Production in Brazil," *Environmental Sciences,* Vol. 2, No. 4 (2005), pp. 445–60.

Veldman, B. A. J., A. M. Wijn, N. Knoers, P. Praamstra, and M. W. Horstink, "Genetic and Environmental Risk Factors in Parkinson's Disease," *Clinical Neurology and Neurosurgery,* Vol. 100, No. 1 (1998), pp. 15–26.

Viscusi, W. K., *Fatal Tradeoffs: Public and Private Responsibilities for Risk* (New York: Oxford University Press, 1992).

———, *Cigarette Taxation and the Social Consequences of Smoking,* Working Paper No. 4891 (National Bureau of Economic Research, 1994).

von Bahr, J., and J. Janson, "Cost of Late Action—The Case of PCB," (Copenhagen: Nordic Council of Ministers, 2004), www.norden.org/pub/miljo/miljo/sk/TN2004556.pdf.

Wagoner, J. K., P. F. Infante, and R. B. Apfeldorf, "Toxicity of Vinyl Chloride and Polyvinyl Chloride as Seen through Epidemiologic Observations," *Journal of Toxicology & Environmental Health,* Vol. 6 (1980), pp. 1101–7.

Waitzman, N. J., P. S. Romano, R. M. Scheffler, and J. A. Harris. "Economic Costs of Congenital Anomalies," *Morbidity and Mortality Weekly Report,* Vol. 44, No. 37 (Sept. 22, 1995).

———, *The Cost of Birth Defects: Estimates of the Value of Prevention,* (Lanham, MD: University Press of America, 1996).

Washington State Department of Health, "2003 Annual Report: Pesticide Incident Reporting and Tracking (PIRT) Review Panel," (Olympia, WA: Washington Department of Health, Office of Environmental Heath Assessments, 2003).

Weiss, K. B., S. D. Sullivan, and C. S. Lyttle, "Trends in the Cost of Illness for Asthma in the United States, 1985–1994," *The Journal of Allergy and Clinical Immunology,* Vol. 106, No. 3 (Sept. 2000), pp. 493–99.

Wentz, D., B. Bonn, K. Carpenter, S. Hinkle, M. Janet, F. Rinella, M. Uhrich, I. Waite, A. Laenen, and K. Bencala, *Water Quality in the Willamette Basin, Oregon, 1991–1995,* USGS Circular 1161 (Washington, DC: U.S. Geological Survey, 1998).

Wiener, J. B., "Whose Precaution after All?" *Duke Journal of Comparative and International Law,* Vol. 13 (2003), pp. 207–62.

Willich, S. N., H. Lowel, M. Lewis, A. Hormann, H. R. Arntz, and U. Keil, "Weekly Variation of Acute Myocardial Infarction: Increased Monday Risk in the Working Population," *Circulation,* Vol. 90, No. 1 (1994), pp. 87–93.

Witmond, B., S. Groot, W. Groen, and E. Dönszelmann, "The Impact of REACH: Overview of 36 Studies on the Impact of the New EU Chemicals Policy (REACH) on Society and Business," Paper presented at the Workshop REACH Impact Assessment, 25–27 Oct. 2004, The Hague, Netherlands.

Wong, R. H., "An Increased Mortality Ratio for Liver Cancer among Polyvinyl Chloride Workers in Taiwan," *Occupational and Environmental Medicine,* Vol. 59 (2002), pp. 405–9.

Woodward, R. T., and R. C. Bishop., "How to Decide When Experts Disagree: Uncertainty-Based Choice Rules in Environmental Policy," *Land Economics,* Vol. 73 (1997), pp. 492–507.

Bibliography

World Health Organization, International Agency for Research on Cancer (IARC), *IARC Monographs on the Evaluation of Carcinogenic Risks to Humans, Supplement 7,* (Lyon, France: IARC, 1987), pp. 451–54. http://monographs.iarc.fr/ENG/Monographs/suppl7/suppl7.pdf.

World Health Organization, International Program on Chemical Safety, *Pesticides Schedules for Evaluation at Future Meetings, by Year,* (2006). www.who.int/ipcs/en/.

Zahm, S. H., "Racial, Ethnic, and Gender Variations in Cancer Risk: Considerations for Future Epidemiologic Research," *Environmental Health Perspectives,* Vol. 103, Supplement 8 (Nov. 1995), pp. 283–86.

Zicherman, J., "Plastic Pipe and Fire Safety," *Fire Protection Engineering,* spring 2004, www.fpemag.com/archives/article.asp?issue_id=20&i=125.

Index

Note: Page numbers in *italics* refer to figures or tables; those followed by "n" or "nn" indicate an endnote or notes.

Index

Index

315

Index